PREDESTINATION

The American Career
of a Contentious Doctrine

Peter J. Thuesen

OXFORD
UNIVERSITY PRESS

OXFORD
UNIVERSITY PRESS

Oxford University Press, Inc., publishes works that further
Oxford University's objective of excellence
in research, scholarship, and education.

Oxford   New York
Auckland   Cape Town   Dar es Salaam   Hong Kong   Karachi
Kuala Lumpur   Madrid   Melbourne   Mexico City   Nairobi
New Delhi   Shanghai   Taipei   Toronto

With offices in
Argentina   Austria   Brazil   Chile   Czech Republic   France   Greece
Guatemala   Hungary   Italy   Japan   Poland   Portugal   Singapore
South Korea   Switzerland   Thailand   Turkey   Ukraine   Vietnam

Published by Oxford University Press, Inc.
198 Madison Avenue, New York, New York 10016
www.oup.com

First issued as an Oxford University Press paperback, 2011.

Oxford is a registered trademark of Oxford University Press

Library of Congress Cataloging-in-Publication Data
Thuesen, Peter Johannes, 1971–
Predestination : the American career of a contentious doctrine / Peter J. Thuesen.
p.   cm.
Includes bibliographical references and index.
ISBN 978-0-19-517427-4 (hardcover); 978-0-19-983239-2 (paperback)
1. Predestination—History of doctrines. 2. United States—Church history. I. Title.
BT809.T48 2009
234.'9—dc22   2008049919

1   3   5   7   9   8   6   4   2

Printed in the United States of America
on acid-free paper

TO JANE, WHO SEES THE HUMOR

Creeds mathematically precise, and hair-splitting niceties of doctrine, are absolutely necessary for the salvation of some kinds of souls, but surely the charity, the purity, the unselfishness that are in the hearts of men like these would save their souls though they were bankrupt in the true religion— which is ours.
—Mark Twain, *The Innocents Abroad*
(1869)

Acknowledgments

O N MORE THAN one occasion during my work on this project, people asked what would possess me to write a book on predestination. My joking response ("I really go for light topics") belies my real answer: if I am going to lose years of this short life working on a book, I want it to be on a question of enduring consequence. The practical problem with such big questions, of course, is that the potential sources are virtually endless. This project therefore spanned more than a decade and involved a great deal of gathering and winnowing. Along the way, a significant number of people kindly lent a hand. Ken Minkema at Yale listened to an early overview of the whole project and offered helpful suggestions, drawing on his extraordinary historical knowledge. At Tufts, I was blessed not only with generous leave time from Deans Susan Ernst and Kevin Dunn and the Faculty Research Awards Committee, chaired by Andrew McClellan, but also with interest and encouragement from colleagues in the Department of Comparative Religion, including Peggy Hutaff, Elizabeth Lemons, Gary Leupp, Father David O'Leary, Beverley O'Riordan, Joseph Walser, and, though only briefly, Mohamed Mahmoud. Even Tufts president Lawrence Bacow accepted my invitation to visit my class and hear me lecture on the transition from Puritanism to Universalism in Medford. Finally from Tufts, my emeritus predecessor, Howard Hunter, who as a Methodist *and* a Unitarian Universalist knows the difference between prevenient grace and universal salvation, graced me with his lunchtime company and many a well-wrought tale.

Colleagues in Indiana, especially at my home institution, Indiana University–Purdue University Indianapolis, have been no less generous. Philip

Goff, director of the Center for the Study of Religion and American Culture, and Tom Davis, former chair of the Department of Religious Studies, have been wonderfully supportive in so many ways. Likewise, my next-door office neighbor, Rachel Wheeler, has shared her expertise and occasionally her books. Other departmental and school colleagues who have made IUPUI such a great place to do research include Debbie Dale, who keeps Religious Studies running, and Matthew Condon, David Craig, Edward Curtis, Art Farnsley, Johnny Flynn, David Ford, Vicki Hale, Rick Hanson, Kelly Hayes, Bill Jackson, Ted Mullen, Joy Sherrill, Jan Shipps, Uday Sukhatme, Becky Vasko, Rick Ward, Bob White, and Marianne Wokeck. Steve Stein at IU Bloomington has been a faithful friend who hosted a discussion of an early draft of chapter 5. At Notre Dame, Jim Turner kindly invited me to present a portion of chapter 2 to his intellectual history seminar, while Mark Noll has been following my work and freely giving his time since before I finished graduate school. Notre Dame's Cushwa Center for the Study of American Catholicism, administered by Timothy Matovina, Kathleen Sprows Cummings, and Paula Brach, provided a late-stage research travel grant that helped me to find some important additional sources in the archives at Hesburgh Library.

Other critical sources of grant support for this book included the IU New Frontiers in the Arts and Humanities Program, administered in Bloomington by Geoff Conrad; the IU School of Liberal Arts at IUPUI, led by Deans Bob White and now Bill Blomquist; the Louisville Institute, directed by James Lewis; and the National Endowment for the Humanities summer stipend program, overseen by Leon Bramson. Respondents or co-presenters at conferences who gave food for thought along the way included Karen Bruhn, Andrew Finstuen, Scott McGinnis, and the dean of scholars of Puritan predestinarianism, Dewey Wallace. Peter Williams graciously invited me to give a lecture on predestination at Miami University of Ohio, where I met many engaging listeners. Brooks Holifield, through his personal interest and his own scholarship, also helped in considerable ways. Benjamin Friedman read the manuscript at a late stage and offered helpful comments and encouragement. And for support at every step of my academic odyssey, I must always thank John Wilson and my other mentors at Princeton University, Al Raboteau, Leigh Schmidt, and Bob Wuthnow.

As the son of a librarian, I have always had a special place in my heart for stewards of books and manuscripts. Librarians or archivists who helped in various ways include Christopher Barbour, Edward Oberholtzer, and Anne Sauer at Tufts; Christina Baich, Debra Brookhart, Sharon Fish, Joe Harmon, Dolores Hoyt, Karen Janke, David Lewis, Rebecca Mock, Bill Orme, and Tony Stamatoplos at IUPUI; Anne Marie Menta of the Beinecke Rare Book and Manuscript Library at Yale; Mark Loest of the Concordia Historical Institute in St. Louis; Laura Clark Brown, Matthew Turi, and John White of the Southern Historical Collection of the University of North Carolina at Chapel Hill; and Jennifer Capps of the President Benjamin Harrison Home in Indianapolis. I am also grateful to the staff of the Andover-Harvard Theological Library and to Tufts University for funding my borrowing privileges at Harvard.

Brief portions of chapters 4 and 6 appeared in an earlier form as "The 'African Enslavement of Anglo-Saxon Minds': The Beechers as Critics of Augustine," *Church History* 72 (2003): 569–92. I am grateful to the journal's readers and editors, especially Grant Wacker and Elizabeth Clark, for their helpful suggestions. Another editor, Lauren Bryant of IU's *Research and Creative Activity* magazine, not only profiled my project but also alerted me to one of the comic strips that I have used as an illustration in the glossary. Others who deserve mention include Tom Holladay of Saddleback Church, who warmly granted an interview to this somewhat skeptical outsider; and several people in my own parish homes past and present, including Pastor Albert H. Keck, Jr. (who gave me his three-volume set of Muhlenberg's *Journals*); Father Michael Ray and Father Tom Cook (both of whom shared with me extended discussions of matters religious); Dorothy Asch; Adele Travisano and Dennis Hale; Nancy and Jack Brown; and Kathy and Jim Poole. Most recently, the Browns and the Pooles prodded me forward by asking me weekly, "Is the book finished yet?"

Predestination would not have seen print without Cynthia Read, my editor at Oxford University Press, whose extraordinary patience in awaiting the final manuscript was a metaphor for what predestinarians call free grace. Others who helped at various stages in the publication process included Theo Calderara, Woody Gilmartin, Merryl Sloane, Christi Stanforth, and Justin Tackett, as well as Linda Webster, who prepared the index.

I am above all thankful for those whose lives are closely linked with mine. During my final feverish months of writing, two family losses brought home questions of eternal destiny. The death of Serena Brooke Kenyon, infant daughter of Brian and Alicia Kenyon, gave me some sense of what my own parents must have endured after the death of their infant son Erik Daniel Thuesen. Throughout the centuries, cloistered theologians spun theories about the eternal destinies of adults, but when confronted with a baby's death, the dogmaticians almost invariably became less dogmatic. "In the midst of life we are in death"—so begins the committal anthem in the burial rite of the Book of Common Prayer. Were we to remember this at all times, not only when death strikes, compassion would triumph over dogmatism. The second family death occurred while I was finishing the Lutheran portion of this book. My aunt Rebecca Wise Derrick (1927–2008), who with my late uncle Curtis E. Derrick, Jr., spent her whole life in faithful service to the Lutheran Church, passed away in White Rock, South Carolina. I am sorry she did not live to see this book, but I am grateful for the many memories she gave me.

At bedtime during my childhood, my parents would sometimes sing an old Danish folk song that begins, "Evening star up yonder, / Teach me like you to wander / Willing and obediently / The path that God ordained for me!" Perhaps Mary and Ted Thuesen thereby planted the seed of my later academic interest in predestination. If so, they got more than they bargained for, as I have kept them well supplied with chapter drafts even in what they thought was their retirement. The heritage and love they bestowed are precious indeed. Sarah Thuesen (my sister and co-Americanist) and Scott Clarke (our 24/7 family physician) have also given so much of themselves, especially as long-distance confidants. In the other half of the family, my parents-in-law, Janie and Jack Kenyon, have been enormously supportive. Janie is the rare and wonderful individual who actually reads theology for fun, and Jack's genealogical research even unearthed a forebear on his side, Lorenzo Dow Tipton, whose parents must have been fans of that rough-hewn bard of frontier anti-Calvinism, Lorenzo Dow. The Reverend John Allen, on the other hand, helped me to see the Calvinists' perspective and even gave me (among other gifts) his copy of the Puritan Stephen Charnock's *Existence and Attributes of God* after I pulled it off his shelf during one Christmas break in Chattanooga.

How can I thank my wife, Jane Allen Kenyon, and our children, Isaac, Joanna, and Margaret? The completion of any project of this magnitude inevitably comes at the cost of family time. I wrote some of this book during summers while they were a thousand miles away visiting Jane's parents and siblings in Colorado. I hope that my labor was not in vain and that the final product will prove to be of some enduring value. But nothing can completely remove the debt I owe to Jane and the children, nor can words express my gratitude and love for them. Jane's hospice work has been an incomparable lesson in the life-and-death realities that finally frustrate all career pursuits. When I lose sight of this—or fail to see life's humor—Jane reminds me. I cannot imagine a more valuable gift.

Contents

Illustrations   xiii

Introduction: Doctrine of Discord: Predestination in
American Christianity   1

1. The Predestinarian Labyrinth: Historical Background   14
2. The Agony and the Ecstasy: Predestination in New
   England Puritanism   44
3. "Shall the Hellish Doctrine Stand?" Enlightenment
   Doubts and Evangelical Division   73
4. From Methodists to Mormons: Attacking Predestination
   in the Young Republic   100
5. Domesticating a Doctrine: Catholics and Lutherans   136
6. Debating a Doctrine: Presbyterians and Baptists   172
Epilogue: The Purpose-Driven Life? Predestination and the
Decline of Mystery   209

Glossary of Theological Terms   219
Notes   229
Index   289

Illustrations

Makeshift memorial to the eight people killed in a tornado at
Utica, Illinois, on 20 April 2004   3
John Calvin on his deathbed. Anonymous engraving after a
painting by Joseph Hornung   15
Augustine of Hippo, from *Canones Aurelii Augustini* (1490)   21
Chart illustrating God's predestinarian decrees, from
William Perkins, *A Golden Chaine* (1608)   35
Labyrinth (gloss on Psalm 119) from Francis Quarles,
Emblemes (1643)   41
William Twisse by Thomas Trotter (1783), after an unknown artist   50
Samuel Willard by an unknown artist   53
Michael Wigglesworth headstone, Malden, Massachusetts   64
George Whitefield confronted in the pulpit by an opponent
of his revival preaching   93
John Wesley at the London grave of his mother, Susanna   96
Thomas Paine by John Wesley Jarvis (c. 1806–1807)   102
Alexander Metcalf Fisher by Samuel Finley Breese Morse (1822)   131
The Beecher Family by Matthew Brady (c. 1859)   133
Archbishop Francis Patrick Kenrick   146
Tomb of C. F. W. Walther, Concordia Cemetery, St. Louis,
Missouri   165
President Benjamin Harrison by T. C. Steele (1900)   174
John Gill, engraving by George Vertue (1748), after
Joseph Highmore   195

Cushing Biggs Hassell   196

John R. Rice and Billy Graham with an unidentified clergyman
    in Scotland in 1955   203

Church sign in Hickory, North Carolina (2006)   214

Foxtrot by Bill Amend (2003)   222

Frazz by Jef Mallett (2005)   227

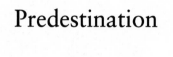

Predestination

Doctrine of Discord

Predestination in American Christianity

This I know, that no one has been able, without falling into error, to argue against this predestination, which we defend according to the holy Scriptures.

—*Augustine*, On the Gift of Perseverance *(429)*

That afternoon I came to understand that one of the deepest purposes of intellectual sophistication is to provide distance between us and our most disturbing personal truths and gnawing fears.

—*Richard Russo*, Straight Man *(1997)*

DESPITE THE CLOUDY and unseasonably chilly weather, I was in good spirits as I drove down Interstate 74 from Indianapolis toward Cincinnati in the early spring of 2006. My three young children and I were on our annual "give-Mom-a-break" trip to see my parents in North Carolina. The early morning had been the usual last-minute frenzy as I packed the Toyota minivan to the hilt and we said goodbye to my wife. Now I was savoring a calm moment in the car as my seven-year-old son sat absorbed in a book and my five-year-old and two-year-old daughters scribbled on notepads with new markers whose novelty had not yet worn off in the 45 minutes we had been on the road.

I was jolted from my reverie by a highway sign flashing "Caution: Tornado Damage Ahead." The previous night, the tornado siren in our Indianapolis neighborhood had sounded, but when the thunderstorm passed without incident, we breathed a sigh of relief and went about our business. Now I wondered if the same thunderstorm had spawned a twister after all. A mile later, the houses beside the interstate told the terrible tale of nature's fury. Where one home stood intact with only light debris littering its roof, the one next door was a pile of rubble. Dozens of people were outside under overcast skies picking through their scattered belongings. The sight left me with a sick feeling, and I reflexively glanced in the rearview mirror to see if my children were also watching. To my relief, all three were still absorbed in books and drawing. Since our move from Massachusetts to Indiana two years earlier, our son had expressed concern about the frequent talk of tornadoes in the Hoosier State. I was glad to escape the burden of explaining this disturbing scene. Yet the arbitrary wrath of tornadoes inevitably haunts adults too with the question of why one person escapes destruction and another does not. Tornadoes, in other words, prompt questions of predestination.[1]

Chicago Tribune writer Julia Keller expressed this eloquently in her Pulitzer Prize–winning series on a deadly tornado that struck the town of Utica in northern Illinois on 20 April 2004, killing eight people. "The survivors," she wrote, "would henceforth be haunted by the oldest, most vexing question of all: whether there is a destiny that shapes our fates or whether it is simply a matter of chance, of luck, of the way the wind blows."[2] Keller described the disaster's cruel ironies, including the story of three friends who, on the storm's approach, fled their mobile home park by car and took refuge in the basement of a solidly built, 117-year-old tavern, only to die there when the funnel cloud hit the building directly. Another tavern only a block away was spared.

For Christians, such tragedies invariably revive the question of predestination in its most general sense, namely, whether God foreordains all things for his purposes. Though this is often called *predestination* in the popular press, it is more properly called *providence*, meaning the divine superintendence of all events toward preordained ends. For many Christians, the Utica deaths, like any deaths, also prompt questions of predestination in its technical sense, meaning the divine foreordination of each person's eternal destiny in either heaven or hell. For persons who perish suddenly, as did the Utica eight, perhaps without having experienced a firm sense of religious conviction or assurance, the question of predestination can torment their loved ones left behind. Does God predestine certain persons for salvation regardless of their actions, or does salvation depend in some sense on a person's cooperation? Either possibility can be unsettling for those unsure

Makeshift memorial to the eight people killed in a tornado at Utica, Illinois, on 20 April 2004. Photograph by Zbigniew Bzdak, *Chicago Tribune*.

of a loved one's (or their own) status. A strict doctrine of absolute predestination can make God's sovereign will seem as arbitrary and cruel as a tornado, whereas a thoroughgoing emphasis on human cooperation can seem to impose an impossible responsibility, especially in the case of a life cut short. Yet for those who find assurance that God has foreordained them to heavenly bliss, absolute predestination can be the sweetest of all doctrines, providing comfort even amid a tragedy like Utica's tornado. And for those who rest their confidence in free cooperation with the divine invitation, life's chaos is held at bay by the assurance that God does not act capriciously but instead saves persons by a logic adapted to human capacities. Predestination is thus an idea that typically elicits strong reactions: either it is the rock of Christian certainty, without which no true hope is possible, or it is the most dangerous of doctrines, one that risks negating the "Come unto me" of Jesus' gospel promise.

This book is about the American career of this contentious doctrine. My primary concern will be predestination in its proper theological sense, referring to the eternal destinies of individuals. Of all traditional Christian doctrines, few, if any, have caused as much controversy as this question of whether a person's fate in either heaven or hell is sealed from the beginning of time. It is not that Christianity lacks other contentious doctrines. In the earliest centuries of the tradition, Christians were consumed by infighting over the divinity of Jesus and the doctrine of the Trinity. But whereas these questions were more or less settled by the early church councils and the ecumenical creeds they hammered out, there has never been a reigning orthodoxy on predestination. This is evident in the division between Eastern and Western Christianity, which arose not only over linguistic and political issues but also over predestination, with the East rejecting Augustine's absolutist view that God elects certain persons apart from any foresight of their conduct. Even within the West, strict Augustinianism has always had critics, and this became uniquely apparent in the United States, where doctrinal disagreements routinely gave rise to new factions and denominations. Indeed, I argue in this book that predestination has been one of the most important but unacknowledged sources of discord in churches across the denominational spectrum.

As an intellectual history of this clash of ideas and parties, this book is written for anyone—academic or not, religious or not—who has ever been curious about predestination and why it has often inspired such vehemence. The existing literature on predestination is mostly Protestant and confessional and rarely deals with the American context.[3] As a historian, I do not seek to advance a particular theological position. Neither will I attempt to catalogue the opinions of every major thinker and denomination; such an exhaustive account would make for tedious reading. I have likewise ruled out any effort to survey the many compelling treatments of predestinarian themes in American literature or politics, tasks undertaken by other scholars.[4] This volume instead paints the big picture of predestination's career in American theology, situating the most notable debates on the broad canvas of Western Christianity since Augustine. To be sure, predestinarian debates are not unknown outside of this Western Christian (Catholic and Protestant) orbit. A broad study remains to be written, for example, of predestinarianism in Islamic theology and its role in the worldviews of Muslims in the United States. But the present volume is intended as a guidebook through the thickets of predestinarian controversies among U.S. Protestants and Catholics.

Predestination as a source of Christian doctrinal conflict must be distinguished from predestination as a subject of debates in classical and contemporary philosophy. Predestination is not the same as what philosophers call *fatalism*, which is usually defined as the absolute and unalterable determination of all things by an impersonal force (personified in Greek mythology by the Fates, or *Moirae*, the fearsome determiners of human destiny). Fatalism suggests that human action is futile, whereas another philosophical term, *determinism*, simply means that all events occur as part of a chain of causation, whether the causes be divine (in the case of the Christian predestination) or some other (including mechanical, genetic, environmental, and psychological). Determinism does not necessarily exclude a measure of human involvement within the complicated chain of causation; indeed, the theory of *compatibilism* (sometimes called soft determinism or reconciliationism) maintains that determinism is not incompatible with human free will, which is defined as the absence of external physical constraints or coercion.

Most Christian predestinarians have been in some sense compatibilists because to define predestination otherwise would imply fatalism. "[W]e are falsely and maliciously charged with this very dogma," complained John Calvin, who cited talk of "fate" as one of the "profane and vain babblings" condemned by the apostle Paul.[5] Yet to maintain, as Calvin and others influenced by Augustine always have, that the unaided human will is "free" (not compelled) *only* to act wickedly, since original sin obliterated humans' innate ability to choose the good, is to raise at the very least certain logical difficulties about how genuine human freedom really is. Compatibilism, as historian Allen Guelzo has memorably put it, "always has an air of unreality to it, of talk that somehow masks the obvious."[6] Contemporary secular philosophers, meanwhile, typically find religious versions of compatibilism unreal for a different reason, namely, their reliance on traditional theistic language about God, sin, and the like. For such philosophers, scientific discoveries in evolutionary biology and quantum physics have permanently altered the terms of discussion about free will and determinism.[7] An ancient theologian such as Augustine looks hopelessly superstitious and irrelevant from a rigorously naturalistic perspective.[8]

I do not intend to tackle compatibilism as a purely philosophical question, nor do I wish to wade into post-Darwinian discussions of determinism and free will. Instead, the American religious debates that concern me here presuppose the deep influence of Augustinian anthropology—the idea that humans are sinful to the core and therefore deserve eternal damnation. Only within contexts where this notion of original sin is taken for granted does predestination become for its most ardent believers a doctrine of mercy. That is, if everyone's default destination is presumed to be hell, then the idea that God grants executive clemency to certain condemned people becomes a singular comfort. If, on the other hand, original sin is denied or at least tempered by the idea that all humans receive an initial gift of grace that enables the damaged will to turn freely to Christ, then the doctrine of God's unilateral choice to save some and to damn others seems arbitrary and even cruel. These are the terms of the debates I trace in this book. I am particularly interested in the question of conditionality, which has dogged Christian predestinarians from the beginning: does God predestine individuals—and even the Fall of humans into original sin—without regard to their foreseen conduct? Few Christian thinkers have denied predestination outright, but instead some have conceived of the issue in this way—whether God elects (and reprobates) people unconditionally or whether the divine decree is somehow conditional upon a human response. As such, the doctrine of predestination is inseparable not only from the problem of original sin but also from other theological questions. Do the church's rites of baptism and the Eucharist have any saving benefit if the elect are already determined? Does purgatory exist as a middle state of purification offering a way out of the all-or-nothing equation of heaven and hell? In the wake of the Enlightenment, still more questions surrounding predestination emerged, including doubts about the existence of a literal hell, the authority of the Bible, and the extent of God's providential involvement in the lives of individuals. Predestination cannot be viewed in isolation but must be seen as part of a package of these interrelated issues. Christian believers who accept the total package necessarily reject or deemphasize certain alternatives.

Yet what precisely does a strong belief in predestination exclude? Predestination is usually regarded as the opposite of free will, and though this dichotomy recurs frequently in the account to follow, I would argue that it misses the more important religious consequence of believing that God preselects the saved and the damned. (The compatibilist position, in any case, is that predestination and free will are not mutually exclusive.) A second major argument of this book, in addition to the claim that predestination is the proverbial elephant in the living room of American denominationalism, is that the most interesting antithesis is not between predestination and free will but between predestinarianism and sacramentalism. In using two words with the suffix -ism, I mean to suggest that these are two larger ways of being religious—two forms of piety, two religious aesthetics—that have existed in tension throughout Christian history. Predestinarianism presupposes the utter transcendence and hiddenness of an all-determining God. It is no coincidence that the strongest predestinarians have often been equally strong iconoclasts—people who, like the New England Puritans, insist that any representation of God in earthly media violates the biblical commandment against idolatrous "graven images." Predestinarian piety entails abject surrender to God's infinite majesty and trust in his divine purpose to save his elect from the mass of fallen humans. Sacramentalism presupposes the real presence of God in the earthly elements of water, bread, and wine. In common with many traditional religions in other cultures, it assumes the efficacy of priestly sacrifice and takes for granted that reception of the consecrated elements opens wide the gate of heaven to all below, to paraphrase one medieval liturgy.[9] In place of predestinarianism's mystical awe before God's electing decree, sacramentalism cultivates mystical wonder before the power of priestly ritual.

These two forms of piety appear to be mutually exclusive. If God chose his elect before the foundation of the world, as the King James Bible phrases it, then no worldly ritual would seem to have genuine saving power. Consequently, it is frequently assumed (particularly by Protestant polemicists) that Catholicism, as the most sacramental of Western traditions, has no use for predestination. Catholics are seen as interested only in doing the right works to get into heaven. By the same token, a strongly predestinarian tradition such as Puritanism appears in Catholic eyes to have thrown the baby out with the bath water, or sacrificed the promise and comfort of the sacraments in an excessive zeal to purge idolatrous confidence in anything but God's electing grace.

The reality is more complicated. Just as Christians in various contexts have attempted to reconcile predestination and free will, both the Catholic and Puritan traditions have produced important thinkers who have attempted to argue for the compatibility of predestinarian and sacramental piety. Yet the latter form of compatibilism has proved no less elusive than the former, and the tension drives some persons to embrace extremes, either a magical view of the sacraments as working automatically like charms (a notion Catholic officialdom has roundly rejected) or a self-described Christian fatalism that views all human efforts (not only churchly sacraments but even missionary preaching) as futile. I will explore these extremes, as well as the more ambiguous options in the spectrum's broad middle, in the pages to follow.

Chapter 1 surveys the long historical background to American debates from the early church to the turn of the seventeenth century. In the first millennium of Western Christianity, in the wake of Augustine's debate with his contemporary Pelagius, predestination's tension with free will preoccupied the theologians. With the rise of medieval eucharistic devotion, however, the sacraments gained increasing prominence in Christian theology. The Protestant reformers' reassertion of Augustine's strong predestinarianism in the sixteenth century was in large measure a reaction to the perceived abuses of the medieval sacramental system. Yet the reformers did not abandon the sacramental economy completely, and their infighting over the efficacy of the church's rites proved to be the greatest obstacle to Protestant unity and further complicated future debates over predestination. So began the great age of confession writing, as the various Protestant factions crafted careful statements of their respective positions. These confessions became the foundation for Protestant scholasticism, which produced the most sophisticated elaborations of predestination since the Catholic scholasticism of Thomas Aquinas and other medieval schoolmen. Out of the Protestant scholastic debates emerged two lasting options—dubbed Calvinist (unconditional predestination) and Arminian (conditional predestination)—that mirrored in certain respects earlier Catholic opinions (not all of them orthodox). Understanding these debates, even at a basic level, requires a high tolerance for technical distinctions, so some readers may wish to bookmark the glossary of theological terms at the back of the book while perusing chapter 1. Because predestinarian disputes have sometimes hinged partly on terminology, I have specified in the glossary how I use certain words in this book.

In the last third of chapter 1 and throughout chapter 2, I focus on the transatlantic Puritan movement, which was the most important conduit of the Protestant scholastic heritage in colonial America. In treating the Puritans as my foundational American case study, I am not suggesting that predestination's American career actually began with them. Symbolically, at least, the doctrine came to what is now the United States in the sixteenth century, with the first forays into Florida by Spanish Dominicans and Jesuits, whose leading theologians would later clash in a major predestinarian controversy, and by an ill-fated group of French Calvinists (Huguenots), who lost their lives and their Florida outpost to the Spanish. English Protestants, meanwhile, brought the Church of England's Book of Common Prayer and predestinarian beliefs to the Roanoke "Lost" colony in 1584 and to Jamestown in 1607. The initial Puritans did not arrive in New England until 1620, when a group of separatists landed at Plymouth. By then, the Dutch had gained a foothold in New Netherland (New York), where the first Dutch Reformed minister in America, Jonas Michaelius, arrived in 1628 and began preaching to his congregation on Calvinist themes.[10] In 1630, more than a century after Ponce de León claimed Florida for the Spanish, we at last come to the founding of the most important Puritan colony, Massachusetts Bay. To the chagrin of its leaders, it was quickly followed by Maryland, the first Catholic-founded colony in British America, where Father Andrew White, an English Jesuit who lost his Louvain professorship because of his conservative Thomism (which tended away from the Jesuit emphasis on free will), celebrated the first Mass in 1634.[11] Thus, by the early 1630s, predestinarian doctrine was already implicitly or explicitly present in America in a variety of "denominational" guises.[12]

Yet compelling reasons remain for paying special attention to the Puritans. As we will see, the New England innovation of requiring would-be church members to make public professions of their conversion experiences put questions of election and reprobation in the foreground of the average Puritan's lived religion. I will consider the doctrine's everyday consequences in the religious experiences of believers and wade into a muddy debate among historians: did predestination engender agony or ecstasy? The answer is far from simple and requires us to plumb the depths of a kind of ecstatic agony—that elusive hybrid of anxiety and assurance—that was the pious goal indoctrinated in the laity by Puritan clergy. From the standpoint of the history of doctrine, Puritanism also affords an especially striking example of the abiding tension in Western Christianity between sacramentalism and predestinarianism. Though Puritans, like most Protestants, were ardently opposed to "popery" and its emphasis on the saving efficacy of the Mass, a persistent sacramental strain in Puritan piety shaped the New England experience of predestination in significant ways. The founding Puritans of the Massachusetts Bay colony were not separatists but dissidents within the Church of England, which was perennially torn between ritualists, who leaned in a Catholic direction, and low-church, zealously committed Protestants such as the Puritans. Although the Puritan movement was dedicated to purifying the English church of all the alleged impurities of Catholicism, Protestant and Catholic elements were not easily separated in the thought of Puritan theologians, who were not averse, as we will see, to invoking Catholic authorities in support of a predestinarian agenda. The Puritan case, in other words, vividly illustrates two foundational premises of this book: predestination was not an exclusively Protestant doctrine, and the sacramental-predestinarian tension cut across the Catholic-Protestant divide.

Chapter 3 examines the emergence of Arminianism and other challenges to absolute predestination in eighteenth-century America. Much of the early opposition to the old Puritan synthesis came from Anglican missionaries bent on bringing their wayward brethren back into the fold of England's established church. Some of these Anglicans were motivated by high-church sacramentalism, and it is often forgotten that this outlook informed the young John Wesley, the Methodist founder and the most famous Arminian in U.S. history. Wesley came to blows with other evangelical revivalists over predestination, and the resulting rift remains starkly apparent in evangelicalism to this day. The eighteenth century was also the Age of Reason, and as such, it bequeathed to American culture an enduring strain of doubt about predestination and the associated doctrines of hell and providence. The Puritan synthesis was thus buffeted from two sides: by Arminian evangelicals who viewed the predestining God of Calvinism as an impediment to spreading the gospel, and by Enlightenment rationalists whose emphasis on reasonability and proof would ultimately infect even many evangelicals with an aversion to mystery in religion.

The American Revolution unleashed yet another indirect but profound threat to absolute predestination—the overthrow of monarchy by republicanism—and set the stage for the religious ferment described in chapter 4. This political context, in which white male Americans became the masters of their own destinies, helped to propel a variety of groups, including not only the ubiquitous Methodists but also the upstart Campbellites, Stoneites, Mormons, and Adventists. What united them, in addition to charismatic founders driven by a back-to-the-Bible mentality, was the burning conviction that scripture testified conclusively against Calvinistic determinism. And though the U.S. Constitution originally denied the power of self-determination to women and African Americans, they too rode the wave of anti-predestinarianism in the young republic. Some achieved new heights of perfectionist zeal, preparing the way for later movements such as Pentecostalism, which would subvert predestination by the most radical means available to Christians—a direct pipeline to the Holy Spirit. Others, such as the women of New England's patrician Beecher clan, turned to writing as a balm for wounds inflicted by their ancestral Calvinism. The product of their labors, though not accepted into the theological canon of their day, would be nothing less than an intellectual reassessment of the entire Augustinian-Puritan heritage.

Yet old-style European confessionalism did not go gently into the night, and in chapter 5 we will see it revived by immigrant Catholics and Lutherans. These seemingly strange bedfellows shared a history of internal strife over predestination (at least among their theologians) and a robust sacramentalism that set them apart from most other Christians in the United States. In different ways, both of these immigrant groups attempted to domesticate the werewolf of predestination—Catholics by entrusting the fate of dead individuals in part to living family members, who sought the masses of the church and the intercession of local saints; Lutherans by an ongoing process of confessional reinterpretation aimed at tempering Martin Luther's harshest predestinarian conclusions. Catholic theologians were no less versed than their Protestant brethren in the theoretical facets of predestination, but in actual practice, Catholicism was distinctive because of its belief in purgatory. Despite popular images of the fire and pain of purgatorial punishment, the underlying assumption of a middle state was optimistic: most persons who died in communion with Rome would attain heavenly bliss after enduring an intermediate trial. Because the length of purification could be shortened by the efforts of the living faithful, however, purgatory appeared to Protestants as a mischievous effort by the church to inflate its own inter-cessory authority, in violation of Protestantism's "grace alone." Purgatory thus became a favorite subject of predestinarian polemics between Catho-lics and Protestants, with Lutherans eagerly joining the melee. Ironically, Lutherans had their own way of blunting predestination's sharp edges by multiplying distinctions and qualifications in a way that would have made a medieval schoolman proud. This effort, begun in the sixteenth century under the conciliatory Philipp Melanchthon, proceeded apace in America until the domesticating zeal of the first wave of immigrants ran up against the back-to-Luther mentality of a new boatload of arrivals. The result was a spectacular predestinarian controversy in the 1880s that ensnared not a few laypeople and has affected Lutheran synodical alignments down to the present day. In 1999, descendants of the domesticating party signed a his-toric ecumenical declaration with Rome that pointed indirectly to broad areas of agreement between Catholics and Lutherans on predestination.

Chapter 6 brings the narrative back to two Anglo-Protestant groups with genetic links to Puritanism: the Presbyterians and the Baptists. Both are well known in U.S. history for the splits they suffered over revivalism, biblical interpretation, and slavery. But predestination always lurked just below the surface, and controversy erupted every time some faction attempted to artic-ulate the definitive Presbyterian or Baptist position. Presbyterians were every bit as confessional as Lutherans—"Westminster" had no less of a talismanic quality than "Augsburg"—so when a movement arose in the late nineteenth century to soften the Westminster Confession's statement on God's eternal decree, traditionalists cried foul. The revisionists eventually won a partial victory, but not before drawing a reluctant former U.S. president into the fray, igniting a firestorm in the denominational press, and contributing to North-South tensions dating from before the Civil War. Baptists, mean-while, were purportedly noncreedal and nonconfessional, but ever since their origins in the seventeenth century, they had disagreed over statements of faith, with predestination usually the major sticking point. In the South-ern Baptist Convention (today, America's largest Protestant denomination), these tensions simmered until the turn of the twenty-first century, when con-servatives who engineered a successful takeover of denominational insti-tutions descended into name calling and recriminations in a family feud over the Calvinistic doctrine of election. This led to the spectacle of a lieu-tenant of fundamentalist stalwart Jerry Falwell denouncing the "Calvinist jihad" waged by fellow Baptist conservatives. The no-holds-barred nature of the dispute was abetted by the freewheeling culture of the Internet, which opened to armchair theologians the opportunity to proclaim, like Martin Luther long ago, "Here I stand!"

The Internet is one of two profound cultural developments in recent American religion; in the book's conclusion, I ponder the other: the Protestant megachurch, pioneered by figures like California pastor Rick Warren. Because megachurches downplay doctrinal and denominational distinctions in order to reach the widest possible audience, they would seem to spell the eventual demise of a dogma as technical and contentious as predestination. (Warren's Saddleback Church is in fact Southern Baptist, an affiliation not apparent to the casual visitor.) Yet though precisely delineated doctrines may be treated like mildewed artifacts from the basement of some declining town-square parish, a vaguer language of foreordination is arguably stronger than ever in the megachurch-driven evangelicalism of today. The bible of this perspective is Warren's runaway bestseller, *The Purpose-Driven Life*, which dances around predestination without actually using the word and which takes as its fundamental premise that nothing in life (or death) is arbitrary. This unreflective blend of predestination and providence, long a characteristic of lived Christianity, is meant to be comforting in times of trial: a loved one's death happens because God has a "higher purpose" in store for that person. The goal of a purpose-driven life is to banish the specter of randomness, the haunting fear that humans are subject only to the way the wind blows. Even a tornado has purpose, though in this life we cannot know why it visits destruction on some persons and not others. Historian Elaine Pagels once speculated that the doctrine of original sin had endured for 1,600 years because "people often would rather feel guilty than helpless."[13] So too with the doctrines of destiny: many people would rather believe that a wise God predetermines everything—even unpleasant things—than contemplate the alternative.

Yet as soon as one probes beneath the general assumption that God is in control, the knottier problem of predestination invariably reemerges. As a university professor, I am always struck by this when I teach the history of Christianity and my students are confronted, often for the first time, with the logic of the Augustinian position. As soon as it hits them that God, by this reasoning, predestines future persons without regard for what they will do, many of my students are indignant. "How can that be fair?" some ask. Others, even some from purportedly Calvinistic traditions, insist that this is not the God in whom *they* believe. Then, I further muddy the waters by interrogating Arminianism. If God predestines for salvation only those people he foresees will have faith, does that mean his sovereign will somehow *depends* on the free choices of his creatures? Then again, if he foresees those choices, are they truly free?

These perennial questions troubled me too as an undergraduate, and it was only years later, in working on this book, that I realized how truly complex predestination really is, like a thick forest of tall trees with branches scaling the mystical heights of heaven and roots planted in many layers of human culture. In plunging as an intellectual historian into this dense woodland—entangling myself in technical theology and inquiring into the cultural contexts that gave rise to such complexity—I also realized how easy it is to miss the forest for the trees. That is, in approaching predestination as purely an academic problem, one can all too quickly lose sight of the simple question underlying it all: where do we go when we die? Intellectualism can become a refuge from the unsettling, even visceral, nature of this question, which haunts nearly all people from time to time. Predestination at its heart is elemental, indeed mystical. I hope this book helps to analyze and contextualize this troublesome doctrine without demystifying it, for when its mystery is lost, so too is its power.

CHAPTER I

The Predestinarian Labyrinth

Historical Background

No one who wishes to be thought religious dares simply deny predestination.

—*John Calvin*, Institutes of the Christian Religion *(1559)*

IN THE 1540s, after the French reformer John Calvin made his permanent home in Geneva and restructured its church government in hopes of making the city a model of Protestant virtue, some of the townspeople chafed under his discipline. Tensions mounted when he excluded several prominent citizens from receiving the Eucharist on grounds of sexual or other immorality. One June day in 1547, Calvin ascended his pulpit in the Church of Saint-Pierre to find a death threat scrawled on a sign: "We've had enough of blaming people. Why the devil have these renegade priests come here to ruin us? Those who have had enough, take their revenge." Beware, the message warned, that you don't meet the fate of Monsieur Werly—a reference to a Fribourg man who had been murdered in a riot 14 years earlier.[1]

The authorities quickly arrested Jacques Gruet, who though descended from a respectable family was something of a village atheist. A search of his house turned up papers accusing Calvin of blatant hypocrisy, blaspheming Christ as a madman and impostor, and condemning the Christian God as a cruel monster who created humans merely for destruction. Some members of the city council also suspected Gruet of being part of an alleged French plot to invade Geneva. Under repeated torture, he confessed to having left the note in the pulpit. He was found guilty of blasphemies against God, offenses against the civil magistrates, and threats to the ministers of God. On 26 July, barely a month after his arrest, he was beheaded.[2]

Gruet's execution hardly quelled all dissent, for a few years later, controversy erupted anew when several Genevans, one of them a prominent theologian, accused Calvin of making God the author of sin with the idea that certain people were predestined to wickedness and thus to eternal destruction. Calvin retorted that in failing to respect the "secret judgments" of God, his "ignorant and malicious" critics were turning a blind eye to the manifest testimony of scripture that God fitted vessels both of mercy and of wrath.[3] The critics nevertheless prompted Calvin to expand his treatment of predestination, a doctrine mentioned only twice in the first edition of his *Institutes of the Christian Religion*. By the end of Calvin's life, the cumulative disputes had left him not a little defensive and embittered. "[Y]ou are a perverse and unhappy nation," he wrote, addressing his countrymen from his deathbed in 1564, "and you will have troubles when God shall have called me away." "I have not falsified a single passage of the Scriptures, nor given it a wrong interpretation to the best of my knowledge."[4]

John Calvin on his deathbed. Anonymous nineteenth-century engraving, after painting by Joseph Hornung. Meeter Center, Calvin College.

Two centuries later, the career of America's Calvin, the New England theologian Jonathan Edwards, mirrored the travails of his Geneva predecessor. After Edwards preached on predestinarian themes with a vengeance in the Connecticut Valley revival of 1734–1735, one restive citizen, the elderly Bernard Bartlett, was sentenced to a whipping—punishments had moderated slightly by then—for calling Edwards "as Great an Instrument as the Devil Had on this Side [of] Hell to bring Souls to Hell."[5] Yet Edwards had more to contend with than an isolated crotchety layman. Among his fellow clergy, the Calvinist doctrine of predestination was under assault by the theological perspective known as Arminianism, drawing Edwards into pamphlet wars and prompting him to seek the help of ministerial associations in policing unorthodoxy. The worst trouble for him personally came when he began restricting the Lord's Supper to persons judged to be truly godly. As we will see in the next chapter, this rigorist stance, informed by predestinarian logic, denied to the laypeople automatic access to what many felt was a Christian birthright: the saving benefit of the sacrament. The result was Edwards's dismissal from his Northampton, Massachusetts, congregation, which left him, like Calvin, defensive and embittered. In a farewell sermon to his parishioners, he warned that they would one day stand with him before the judgment seat of Christ. The hearts of all would then be turned inside out, revealing in a "clear, certain and infallible light" who had been right and who had been wrong. Edwards further admonished them to guard in the interim against the encroachment of the Arminian error, which was "creeping into almost all parts of the land, threatening the utter ruin of the credit of those doctrines, which are the peculiar glory of the gospel."[6]

What were these doctrines, the defense of which plunged Edwards into a self-described "abyss of trouble and sorrow" and caused Calvin to lament that he had lived "amid continual strifes"?[7] Though the conflicts in Geneva and Northampton involved many doctrinal complexities, including issues of human nature and sacramental efficacy, underneath them all was the fundamental, burning question of predestination. If, as Calvin and Edwards taught, God had already chosen a select few for salvation, then this stark reality had profound consequences for other Christian doctrines. "This the Scripture has told us, that there are but few saved," Edwards told his flock in his farewell, "and we have abundant confirmation of it from what we see."[8] It was a hard message, and it drove some laypeople to rebel against their ministers. But for the clergy themselves, the flak they took for predestination, however painful in the short term, confirmed in their own minds the correctness of the doctrine. Such zealous ministers consoled themselves with Christ's own words from the Sermon on the Mount: "Blessed are they which are persecuted for righteousness' sake: for theirs is the kingdom of heaven."

PREDESTINATION'S ORIGINS: FROM PAUL TO AUGUSTINE

In order to understand how predestination became such a contentious doctrine and why it was inseparable from other key issues of belief and practice, we must look back two millennia, long before Calvin or Edwards, to the beginning of Christianity itself. The Christian idea of predestination is rooted in the New Testament, which reflects the Greco-Roman philosophical interest in questions of fate and destiny as well as the Hebrew Bible's central theme of Israel's election. Consequently, the Greek New Testament uses both the verbs *proorizō* (to predestine, to decide beforehand) and *eklegomai* (to choose, to elect).[9] The verb *proorizō* occurs six times in the New Testament. Of these instances, two refer in a general sense to God's prior determination of events (Acts 4:28; 1 Cor. 2:7) and four refer to the predestination of persons (Rom. 8:29, 30; Eph. 1:5, 11). The verb *eklegomai* occurs more frequently, sometimes in the general sense of choosing, as when Jesus refers in John 6:70 to his choice of the 12 disciples, and sometimes in clear reference to the election of persons for ultimate salvation (e.g., Mark 13:20; John 15:16). Other terms that factor into later predestinarian controversies include *proginōskō* (to foreknow), as in Romans 8:29, and *prognōsis* (foreknowledge), as in Acts 2:23. These words, as their appearances suggest, are the roots of the English "prognosticate" and "prognosis." Similarly, the adjective *eklektos*, referring to the elect or chosen, figures prominently in scripture (e.g., Mark 13:20; Rom. 8:33), in reference not only to humans but also to angels (1 Tim. 5:21; cf. Jude 1:6, which refers to angels who fell from grace). Both the ideas of foreknowledge and of the elect are combined in 1 Peter 1:2, which the King James Bible translates as "elect according to the foreknowledge of the Father," a phrase charged with meaning for those who would later maintain that election was only in light of a person's foreseen faith.

Of all the New Testament references to predestination and election, the most sustained discussion, and the most significant for eventual American debates, occurs in Paul's Epistle to the Romans, chapters 9–11. The apostle could not have foreseen the elaborate edifices of Catholic and Protestant theology that would be built upon these three short chapters. In his own time, before the codification of creedal orthodoxies or the birth of powerful church institutions, the issue was rather different: how God's election of Israel could be reconciled with the fact that many Jews had not accepted Christ. The question was particularly troubling for Paul, a Jewish convert to Christianity. His conclusion—"not all Israelites truly belong to Israel" (9:6)—would be spun out by later Americans in manifold ways. Salvation had never been by virtue of physical descent or good works but through God's gracious favor alone. As proof, Paul cited God's preference for Jacob over his brother, Esau (Gen. 25), and quoted the reference to this from the prophet Malachi: "I have loved Jacob, but I have hated Esau" (Mal. 1:2–3; Rom. 9:13). Paul also invoked God's words to Moses: "I will have mercy on whom I will have mercy, and I will have compassion on whom I will have compassion" (Ex. 33:19; Rom. 9:15). As a further illustration of his point, Paul compared humans to clay in the hands of a potter—an image beloved of later Augustinians and Calvinists—and asked: "Has the potter no right over the clay, to make out of the same lump one object for special use and another for ordinary use?" (Rom. 9:21).

Paul's conviction that certain persons were chosen for "special use" stemmed in part from his own conversion experience, which he elsewhere recounted with predestinarian overtones, noting that God had set him apart before he was born and called him through his grace (Gal. 1:15). Yet in his letter to the Romans, he acknowledged the obvious objection to predestinarian logic—that it was unfair. Was God unjust, he asked rhetorically, in choosing certain persons over others? "By no means!" Salvation depended in no way on works but entirely on God's mercy, which he showed to all those, whether Jew or Gentile, who had faith in Christ (9:14–16). "Everyone who calls on the name of the Lord shall be saved" (10:13). Though only a remnant of the Jews had accepted Christ and thus were "chosen by grace" (11:5), this too was part of God's plan of election. A "hardening has come upon part of Israel, until the full number of Gentiles has come in," at which point "all Israel will be saved," in fulfillment of God's promise (11:25–26).

As the infant Christian movement separated from Judaism and canonized a new body of sacred texts, Paul's writings acquired the timeless status of scripture. Romans 9–11 became the great Rorschach test for Christians' opinions—now formed in a variety of new contexts—on the preexisting question of predestination. Absolute predestinarians pointed to the images of Jacob and Esau and of the potter molding the clay as proof that God's grace was utterly gratuitous and that the salvation of sinners was the divine prerogative alone. Defenders of free will interpreted Paul's words as primarily a discourse on Israel's destiny and seized upon the promise to all who call on the name of the Lord as proof that God saves anyone who freely responds to him. Which view held sway often depended on the apologetic needs of the moment and the external forces weighing on the apologist.

In the early church, the emphasis fell on human freedom as the antidote to the perceived fatalism of astrologers, Gnostics, and Stoics.[10] The Stoic teaching that all things happen according to the necessity of fate, complained Justin Martyr (c. 100–165), relieved humans of any responsibility for their actions, rendering true virtue impossible. Justin insisted that God endowed both humans and angels with free will and justly punished the sinful ones with eternal fire.[11] This outlook particularly affected the Eastern churches, which followed figures such as John Chrysostom (c. 347–407), the patriarch of Constantinople, in refusing to read Paul in a deterministic way. Thus, on Romans 9, Chrysostom argued that it "is not on the potter that the honor or dishonor of the vessel depends but rather on those who make use of it. It is the same way with people—it all depends on their own free choice." Chrysostom linked predestination to God's foreknowledge of each individual's freely chosen action: "God does not have to wait, as we do, to see which one will turn out good and which one will turn out bad. He knew this in advance and decided accordingly."[12]

It is sometimes forgotten that the greatest thinker of the early Western church, Augustine of Hippo (354–430), also at first insisted that "God only predestined those whom he knew would believe and follow the call."[13] Augustine drew this conclusion partly from Romans 8:29 ("For those whom he foreknew he also predestined to be conformed to the image of his Son"), upon which he remarked in an unfinished pair of commentaries in 394–395.[14] Yet barely two years later, in his first literary work as bishop of Hippo Regius in North Africa, Augustine turned again to Romans in response to a friend's query and reached a radically different conclusion: God did not choose Jacob (or anyone else) in view of foreseen faith. "In resolving the question," he later recalled, "I really worked for the free choice of the human will, but the grace of God won out."[15] Humans could not choose God; he chose them. Why he chose some and not others was not for fallible creatures to understand. His grace was a free gift that no one deserved. This conviction helped to inspire Augustine soon thereafter to write his most famous work, the *Confessions*, which recounted how God chose him despite his earlier life of sexual immorality and religious skepticism.

Though the *Confessions* would prove timeless as a spiritual autobiography, in Augustine's own day the text helped to spark a major predestinarian controversy. At issue was his famous prayer in book 10, expressing the powerlessness of humans to obey God and to bring about their own election:

"Give what you command, and command what you will."[16] When a bishop in Rome quoted the line approvingly, one listener, the British layperson and ascetic Pelagius, was indignant. Augustine's words seemed to reduce humans to puppets, insulting not only their own integrity but also the goodness of their creator. Pelagius soon wrote a response to Augustine, criticizing him for abandoning his position from an earlier treatise, *On Free Choice of the Will*. So began more than a decade of bitter debate in which Pelagius, set opposite the influential Augustine, became the whipping boy of Western theology after his positions were condemned by a succession of councils, emperors, and popes. Even his corpulent appearance became the subject of ridicule; the celebrated biblical scholar Jerome compared him to a tortoise and elsewhere said he was weighted down with porridge.[17] Yet the real weight of the Pelagian controversy was in the volume of polemical literature produced, including some of Augustine's most unqualified and influential defenses of predestination.

In *On the Predestination of the Saints*, Augustine again insisted that God did not select persons for salvation because of their foreseen faith. He repeatedly appealed to the "unchangeable truth" of John 15:16: "You did not choose me but I chose you."[18] Surely, God did not save or damn people based on their future actions since some lives were cut short, before the individuals had a chance to come to saving faith.[19] Augustine then invoked the case of infants—a move fated to win him no friends among the most ardent American defenders of free will. Those who died in infancy, he went on in *On the Gift of Perseverance* (a companion piece to his predestination treatise), proved that foreseen actions could not be the ground of salvation; otherwise, we would be left with the absurd conclusion that persons are damned or saved for things they *would have done* had they lived. Even the issue of infant baptism revealed God's predestinarian designs in this world and the next. Why, Augustine asked, did the infants of Christian parents sometimes die before they could be baptized, whereas the dying infants of unbelieving parents sometimes lived long enough for a priest to intervene and administer the sacrament? "Clearly this shows that there is no respect of persons with God," Augustine concluded (echoing Matt. 10:29).[20] Just as God determined whom to admit to heaven, God also controlled admission to the hospital of the church's sacraments.[21]

Indeed, in Augustine's mind, predestination ultimately came down to this: all humans are born terminally ill with sin and thus deserve damnation. Birth defects prove the point. If babies suffer defects through no fault of their own, then we are forced to abandon all faith in divine justice. Surely, then, some infants are born disfigured or crippled as punishment for their own inbred sin.[22] The fact that God preserves other equally sinful infants

Augustine of Hippo, from *Canones Aurelii Augustini* (1490). Beinecke Rare Book and Manuscript Library, Yale University.

from harm—and elects only certain persons to ultimate salvation—merely reveals grace for what it is: something completely unmerited. "In giving to some what they did not deserve, clearly [God] willed that his grace be gratuitous and thus truly grace."[23]

Augustine could not foresee the vehemence of some modern objections to the justice of his doctrine of original sin—the idea that Adam and Eve transmitted a sinful nature to their posterity. Like other ancients, he lacked the resources of modern science for explaining the causes of things he observed in the world. It was therefore plausible to him that birth defects were the wages of an inherited sin. It also seemed obvious to him that humanity was a *massa perditionis* (mass of perdition)—a universally fallen multitude. How else could one explain the constant turmoil and sorrow of human existence? In the final days of his life, when Augustine was writing on predestination, the world seemed particularly dark as Vandal invaders closed in and laid siege to Hippo. Predestination in this context, as historian Peter Brown has noted, was "a doctrine of survival, a fierce insistence that God alone could provide men with an irreducible inner core."[24] God's elect saints might endure earthly tribulations, but thanks to God's free gift of grace, they would ultimately persevere in faith and attain heavenly bliss.

Augustine's basic insight on the primacy of God's electing grace was destined to become more or less official in the West, though predestinarian debates hardly ended with his death in 430. One of his contemporaries, John Cassian, a monk in Gaul, had expressed many Christians' difficulty in reconciling strict predestination with the biblical assurance that God "desires everyone to be saved" (1 Tim. 2:4). Cassian's solution, much later misleadingly labeled "semi-Pelagianism," did not go so far as to deny original sin (the Pelagian position, which Cassian abhorred) but did allow for a measure of human cooperation with God. The human will's capacity to choose the good was not obliterated by Adam's sin but merely injured. Humans retain enough God-given natural ability to take the initial step toward Christ, whose additional grace is needed to bring the process of salvation to completion. Those people who fail to exercise their wills in taking the initial step are entirely culpable for their own damnation and are acting against God's own will for all to be saved.[25] Theologians in Augustine's orbit in North Africa, meanwhile, reiterated his strongly predestinarian views, arguing that when Paul wrote in 1 Timothy 2:4 that God desires everyone to be saved, "everyone" means the elect, who are chosen from all classes and conditions of persons.[26]

Ultimately, after a century of debate and convoluted church politics, the Second Council of Orange (529) endorsed Augustinianism, but not without qualification. The beginning of faith in a person is always due to divine grace, the council decreed, dealing a blow to anything resembling a Pelagian confidence in human nature. At the same time, the council strongly warned against emphasizing predestination to such an extent that both salvation and damnation were seen as equally willed by God.[27] Such a doctrine of "double" predestination was an ever-tempting logical conclusion for those who would maximize the sovereignty of God. Three centuries after Orange, what one historian has called a theological free-for-all ensued in Germany and France when the monk Gottschalk (c. 804–869) argued for double predestination, insisting that anything less violated God's complete sovereignty.[28] On this view, any admixture of human free will would make God somehow dependent on the actions of his creatures, somehow subject to change. And "for God to change would be for him to die, to cease to exist," Gottschalk reasoned. Not surprisingly, his absolutist position did not sit well with some members of the church hierarchy, who feared that it would give the laypeople license to neglect the sacraments. Gottschalk's impetuous and tactless personality, moreover, clashed with the equally impatient and autocratic style of Hincmar, archbishop of Reims, who sentenced him to be scourged in front of a fire until he agreed to burn the supporting texts he had collected from scripture and the fathers. Later, when Gottschalk refused to renounce his own views, he was imprisoned until the end of his life and was denied the sacrament, even on his deathbed.[29] Yet Hincmar did not enjoy a lasting victory. The synods convened to deal with the ninth-century controversy, like the Second Council of Orange, left a mixed legacy: Gottschalk's position was condemned by a meeting of bishops in 853, only to be supported by another gathering two years later.[30]

THE RISE OF MEDIEVAL SACRAMENTALISM

The councils of the sixth and ninth centuries, in addition to revealing the bishops' divided opinions over the human and divine wills, left unresolved a question that would prove far more significant for predestination's subsequent career: in what sense is a person saved by the church's sacraments? While the Second Council of Orange had maintained that the grace of baptism enabled Christians "to perform all things that pertain to the soul's salvation," it remained unclear how to square this with the idea that God saves only the elect.[31] One solution was to say that God allows only the elect to be baptized, but this seemed unlikely in the case of people who lapsed into mortal sin after baptism and remained unrepentant at their deaths. To restrict baptismal regeneration to the elect, moreover, seemed to render the church and its rites superfluous. Ever since Augustine, Catholic tradition had defended the objective efficacy of the sacraments against Donatist rigorists who insisted that baptism and the Eucharist had no effect if administered by unworthy priests. Even so, many medieval theologians found Augustine frustratingly vague on how a predestining God saved through water, bread, and wine.[32]

Augustine also bequeathed to the Middle Ages the question of whether living persons could do anything to influence God's judgment on the dead. In his *City of God*, he presupposed that certain people who had completed insufficient penance for their sins would endure a period of purifying punishment after death.[33] That such people were ultimately predestined for salvation was not at issue; the question was whether the prayers of the living could shorten the temporal penalties inflicted on the dead. The Bible suggested as much in 2 Maccabees (part of the Apocrypha, which Protestants later rejected), where the Jewish hero Judas Maccabeus prays for a group of his dead soldiers "that they might be delivered from their sin" (12:45).[34] Similarly, Augustine prayed for his dead mother, Monica, in a fervent concluding section to book 9 of his *Confessions*. In his other writings, however, he stopped short of specifying what sins could be atoned for after death or of naming the place of purification (the term *purgatory* did not emerge until the twelfth century). To describe an actual place in lurid detail would be to stoop to the level of popular religion—something the intellectually aristocratic Augustine was loath to do.[35]

Augustine's aversion to unreflective popular piety resembled the attitude of the medieval scholastic theologians, whose rise paralleled the emergence of universities in Europe. The greatest scholastic was Thomas Aquinas (c. 1225–1274), whose encyclopedic *Summa Theologiae* subjected popular assumptions about the magical efficacy of the sacraments and prayers for the dead to dispassionate analysis. It was not that Aquinas lacked sacramental zeal. According to tradition, Pope Urban IV commissioned him to write the liturgy for Corpus Christi, a feast commemorating the institution of the Eucharist, which involved elaborate processions of the Host (the consecrated wafer) through the streets of many European towns.[36] One part of the liturgy, the hymn "O Salutaris Hostia" (O Saving Victim), expressed Aquinas's fervent hope in the Eucharist's saving power: "O saving Victim,/opening wide the gate of heaven to us below;/our foes press on from every side;/your aid supply, your strength bestow!" At the same time, the liturgy expressed the Catholic belief that although the Blessed Sacrament unfailingly conveys Christ's body to all, the actual reception of grace presupposes the recipient's standing in a right relationship to God: "Good and bad,/they come to greet him;/unto life the former eat him,/and the latter unto death."[37] Aquinas elaborated this idea in his *Summa Theologiae*, where, as theologian Joseph Wawrykow has noted, he consistently rejected "a mechanistic or automatic bestowal of grace through sacramental performance."[38]

Similarly, on the question of whether the predestination of individuals could be influenced by prayers or masses for the dead, Aquinas was careful not to claim too much. Here, he invoked the distinction between primary and secondary causes. God, as primary cause, preordains each person's destiny: this cannot be changed. But the effects of his prior decision play out through secondary causes such as the prayers of the faithful. Predestination can therefore be "helped by creatures, but not blocked."[39] On predestination more broadly, Aquinas's outlook was essentially that of the late Augustine. He dismissed as "mad" the notion that a person's merit, as foreseen by God, could play any role in election; otherwise, grace would lose its gratuitous character. As for the charge that God is unfair in choosing only a select number for salvation, Aquinas insisted that this would be unjust only if God deprived people of something they were owed. But God owes humans nothing; they are all equally sinful and deserving of damnation. Aquinas also quoted Augustine on why God saves certain persons and not others: "Wherefore he draws this one and not that one, seek not to decide if you wish not to err."[40] It was an admonition that Protestant disciples of Augustine could later cite with relish—an apparent reality check on the popular belief that religious rituals or other meritorious actions could somehow win God's favor.

Yet popular religion has a way of reasserting itself, for as the famous sociologist Max Weber once observed, the security provided by a tested and proven "magical" formula can be far more reassuring than the experience of worshipping an omnipotent God who is not subject to magical influence.[41] Popular religion, in Weber's definition, assumes that certain sacrifices, incantations, or other ritual actions can in effect coerce god(s) through an unfailing relationship of cause and effect. This was how many late medieval laypeople came to view the efficacy of the Mass, whether offered for the living or the dead. Ironically, the cool logic of the theologians indirectly contributed to popular enthusiasm about the Mass as performed magic. The decisive idea was transubstantiation, elaborated by Aquinas, which applied the logical categories of Aristotle to explain the miraculous transformation of the "substance" of the eucharistic elements into the body and blood of Christ, even though the "accidents" (or appearances) of bread and wine remained. Popular religion was unconcerned with Aristotelian categories but came to regard the moment of transubstantiation in the Mass—believed to coincide with the words of institution, "Hoc est corpus meum" (This is my body)—with special awe. Once transformed into Christ's body, the Host acquired magical powers. For many laypeople, simply viewing the wafer when the priest elevated it after saying the words of institution became a substitute for actual reception of the Eucharist, which most parishioners did infrequently, often out of fear of unworthiness. The moment of elevation, typically signaled with the ringing of a bell, became the supernatural high point of the Mass for the laity, prompting one thirteenth-century bishop to complain that people ran into the church at the bell's sound.[42] Seeing the Host was thought to bring benefits both in this life (safe childbirth, safe travel, cure for illness) and in the life to come. Many people sought to view the Host at least once a day and complained to church authorities when not enough masses were provided in local parishes.[43] Masses were also popularly viewed as having saving power for the dead, prompting reports of souls who returned from purgatory to haunt their living relatives until the Blessed Sacrament was offered in their memory.[44] And though theologians would always rail against superstitious abuses (for example, people carrying consecrated wafers away from church in their mouths and using them as charms), the consolation afforded by a magical or quasi-magical view of the sacraments was too considerable for church authorities to ignore.[45]

Indeed, the perceived readiness of the church to exploit popular belief in sacramental magic to enhance its own power was a major reason for the Protestant Reformation, especially after another of the church's seven sacraments, penance, was linked to abuse of the system of indulgences. Penance involved confession of one's sins to a priest, who pronounced absolution. Forgiven sins, however, still carried temporal penalties in purgatory, which could be remitted through works of satisfaction in this life. Temporal penalties could also be removed by indulgences, which drew on the church's "treasury of merit"—the storehouse of good works performed by Jesus and the saints—to lessen time in purgatory both for the living and for those already dead.[46] These slips of paper promising relief from purgatorial punishment became controversial in the early sixteenth century when the German church began selling them to pay debts to the pope and to help build a new St. Peter's Basilica in Rome. As the indulgence preacher Johann Tetzel's notorious jingle put it: "As soon as the coin in the coffer rings / The soul from purgatory springs." This was the famous occasion for Martin Luther's Ninety-five Theses (1517), which ignited a firestorm after they were published in both Latin and German. "It is sure that when a coin tinkles greed and avarice are increased," one thesis asserted, "but the intercession of the church is the will of God alone." Another thesis condemned as vain any confidence in salvation because of a letter of indulgence, even if guaranteed by the soul of the pope himself.[47]

Although Pope Pius V ultimately banned all sales of indulgences in 1567, the controversy indelibly colored Protestant perceptions of Catholic piety. Centuries later in America, many Protestants still equated Catholicism with the fraudulent trafficking in what Luther called "cheap grace." They condemned the Mass as "hocus pocus," dismissing it as superstition at best and sorcery at worst. What such views ignored was the profound comfort that many Catholics derived from the sacramental system. Historian Miri Rubin has written eloquently of this in her book on the Eucharist in late medieval culture. Sacramental mediation, she notes, was "this-worldly in emphasizing that channels of regeneration and salvation were available and attainable, renewable and never exhaustible." The Eucharist in particular was a promise "fulfilled here and now, offering powerful and tangible rewards to the living in the present, as well as to their relatives, the dead."[48]

PROTESTANTISM AND PREDESTINARIAN PIETY

Elements of medieval sacramentalism persisted in some forms of Protestantism, despite Protestants' nearly universal hostility toward such doctrines as transubstantiation and purgatory. Luther's own faith in the real presence of Christ in the Eucharist is well known. To those who would explain the bread and wine's significance in purely symbolic terms, he thundered: "Before I would have mere wine with the fanatics, I would rather receive sheer blood with the pope."[49] Even Reformed Protestants such as the Scottish Presbyterians, heirs of the furiously anti-Catholic John Knox, developed a tradition of annual communion occasions—four-day festivals centering on the celebration of the Lord's Supper.[50] Yet in their rebellion against Roman authority and the sacramental abuses of the medieval church, the early Protestants rediscovered the spiritual power of predestination to strip away all intermediaries between the individual and God. Aesthetically, predestination was no less mystical than medieval sacramentalism. The goal of both was an awestruck apprehension of God's grace, but whereas sacramentalism achieved it through ritual, predestination achieved it through contemplation. To surrender oneself to the inscrutable divine will—to accept the doctrine of humans' utter powerlessness to redeem themselves—was to prostrate oneself before God's absolute glory and majesty. Those who embraced this piety regarded it as religion pure and undefiled, monotheism in its most authentic and compelling form. "All things happen by necessity," declared Luther in refuting the humanism of Erasmus.[51] To deny divine control over all things is to deny God himself. The human will, Luther said, borrowing an earlier medieval image, is like a beast of burden that either God or Satan rides. The will is powerless to choose which rider will mount it, "but the riders themselves contend for the possession and control of it."[52]

Here was Christianity in its undiluted biblical essence, or so predestinarians have often claimed. In reality, the "strong wine" of predestination (as Luther called it), like the medieval eucharistic ritual, was mediated by church tradition.[53] The first great mediator was the late Augustine, whose reading of Romans 9 influenced Luther to conclude that the election of Jacob over Esau was not based on any foreknowledge of Jacob's merits but simply on God's inscrutable choice to save him from the mass of sinful humanity.[54] Luther's strong predestinarianism must also be seen as a reaction to the late medieval *via moderna*, or "modern way," of William Ockham (c. 1285–1347) and his follower Gabriel Biel (c. 1420–1495). This school of theology taught, contrary to the earlier view of Thomas Aquinas, that humans retain enough natural ability to initiate their own salvation by "doing their best," which God rewards with an infusion of grace. Confounded by the uncertainty of what counts as one's "best," Luther conjured up Augustine the exegete to do battle against the "new Pelagians."[55] Augustinianism was already in the air thanks to the fourteenth-century theologians Gregory of Rimini and Thomas Bradwardine, archbishop of Canterbury, who, like Gottschalk five centuries before, spoke unflinchingly of both election and reprobation and insisted that God saves people without any regard for their future good conduct.[56] Thus, when Luther made his storied discovery that humans are justified by grace through faith, he was in one sense simply rediscovering Augustine's basic claim that God bestows righteousness on sinners as a pure gift. Where Luther differed from the Neoplatonic Augustine was in his comparatively hostile attitude toward philosophical speculation and human reason.[57] Consequently, Luther always cautioned against speculation about predestination, which he warned was the devil's way of making the passion of Christ and the sacraments of no effect. The sacraments, he insisted, were instituted "to drive such speculations out of your mind."[58]

Luther's confidence in sacramental efficacy, motivated by his antirational trust that Christ meant what he said when he proclaimed "This is my body," helped to make Lutherans a special case among Protestants on the question of predestination, as we will see in chapter 5. Luther's view contrasted sharply with that of his Swiss contemporary Huldrych Zwingli (1484–1531) of Zurich, who insisted that by the "is" in "This is my body," Christ meant "signifies." After the two men failed to reconcile their differences on the Eucharist at the Marburg Colloquy in 1529, Luther wrote to his wife in disgust that God must have blinded the Zwinglians.[59] Luther and Zwingli also differed on the authority of the Bible, on which Zwingli had resolved to preach in its entirety, verse by verse—even the epistle of James, which Luther had rejected because of its emphasis on works. Finally, whereas Luther made justification the linchpin of his theology, Zwingli stressed God's absolute sovereignty in a way that almost seemed to revive the Stoicism of Seneca, whom the Zurich reformer admired. An affinity for Stoic determinism was perhaps not surprising for a man who narrowly escaped death from the plague when it ravaged Zurich in 1519–1520. Believing himself to be God's chosen instrument, Zwingli carried the same sense of destiny to his death in battle against an army of Switzerland's Catholic cantons.[60]

Zwingli foreshadowed the fighting spirit of Reformed Protestant-ism when it became an international movement, but it was the second-generation reformer John Calvin (1509–1564) of Geneva who gave the Reformed tradition its most influential early statements on predestination. Calvin's name is virtually synonymous with the doctrine, a popular associ-ation that Calvin specialists never tire of lamenting. Their complaint is not without merit. Calvin was in one sense no more of a predestinarian than Luther, whom he admired for restoring the purity of the gospel. Calvin was also closer to Luther than to Zwingli on the Eucharist—for Calvin, Christ's presence was spiritual but still "real"—and he waged an unsuc-cessful campaign for more frequent celebrations of the Lord's Supper in Geneva.[61] The sections on predestination in the final edition of Calvin's *Institutes of the Christian Religion* (1559) come well into the work and occupy only around 5,000 words, compared to the 14,000 words devoted to civil government.[62]

Nevertheless, in a crucial respect, predestination loomed larger for Calvin than for Luther. Calvin found the doctrine more *pastorally* useful than Luther did, and the social context in Geneva helps to explain why. After the city-state embraced the evangelical cause in 1536, it became a haven for Protestant exiles fleeing persecution in other parts of Europe. Calvin himself was an exile from Catholic France who hoped throughout his life that his homeland would one day embrace the Reformed religion. As a city of refu-gees, Geneva was hypersensitive to the advancing Catholic military threat. The defeat of the Protestant Schmalkaldic League in Germany in 1547 came as an ominous sign, as did the accession of the Catholic Mary Tudor ("Bloody Mary") in England in 1553, which sent more exiles, including the zealous Scotsman John Knox, fleeing to Geneva. Predestination served in this context, much as it did for Augustine facing the disintegration of the Roman Empire, as a doctrine of consolation and survival. Earthly existence, Calvin taught, was perpetual warfare, and the righteous would always suf-fer the hatred of the sinful majority. Yet persecution and dislocation did not happen without reason. Such adversity was God's providential means of testing his elect, who would be vindicated in the end.[63] Predestination and the broader doctrine of providence therefore served the same purpose of convincing a beleaguered community of Christians that God was firmly in control of their destinies. "We have no other place of refuge than his providence," Calvin wrote. Commenting on this, the late Reformation historian Heiko Oberman argued that outside of the context of persecuted refugees, "Calvin's doctrine of election is not only abhorrent but also ungodly. But within this horizon of experience it is a precious experiential asset."[64]

Not surprisingly, therefore, the discussion of predestination in book 3 of the *Institutes* reads like a practical manual for the believer and, as such, is more systematic than anything Luther wrote on the subject.[65] Calvin admitted that predestination was a "baffling question" for many and conceded that excessive curiosity about God's secret counsels could be spiritually perilous. "If anyone with carefree assurance breaks into this place, he will not succeed in satisfying his curiosity and he will enter a labyrinth from which he can find no exit."[66] Yet he hastened to add that within the limits of what God revealed in scripture, predestination must be preached to the faithful. To avoid the subject for fear of disturbing "weak souls" was to reproach God himself, "as if he had unadvisedly let slip something hurtful to the church."[67] Calvin went on to discuss the facets of the doctrine point by point, insisting with Augustine that the case of Jacob and Esau proved that election was not based on divine foreknowledge of human merits. Why God chose one over the other was simply because it pleased him. Since God's will is by definition righteous, his choice of humans is also just; to question his will is to succumb to the blasphemous error that human standards of judgment are higher than divine wisdom.[68]

In defending the divine prerogative, Calvin did not shy away from the conclusion that God actively wills reprobation just as he wills election.[69] Here, the Geneva reformer departed from the more typically Augustinian way of describing reprobation, that God simply passes over some people, leaving them in the mass of condemned humanity.[70] For Calvin, logical consistency demanded a double decree of election and reprobation. As one theologian has explained Calvin's reasoning, God could not be thought of as doing anything by default.[71] Calvin saw evidence of God's active reprobation of persons in scripture, including Pharaoh's hardened heart (Ex. 4:21), the vessels of wrath fitted for destruction (Rom. 9:22), and even the many parables spoken by Christ, which transmitted his doctrine "wrapped in enigmas" so as to cast the reprobates into "greater stupidity." Calvin quoted Jesus' answer to his disciples on why he spoke in parables: "To you it has been given to know the secrets of the kingdom of heaven, but to them it has not been given" (Matt. 13:11).[72] Such biblical passages in his view clearly precluded any possibility that scripture taught universal salvation. He reverted to the Augustinian method of explaining 1 Timothy 2:4 ("who desires everyone to be saved"): this meant only that the elect are chosen from all stations of society.[73] The stark truth of predestination was that God did not discriminate in fitting either vessels of wrath or vessels of mercy. "The decree is dreadful indeed, I confess," Calvin wrote. But for the elect, predestination is "very sweet fruit" when they realize that the mercy of election is illumined by the justice of reprobation. Both sides of the decree reflect God's glory.[74]

The glory of predestination for Calvin was a bit like a painting that reflects the supreme artifice of its creator. And yet, as with any aesthetic object, its beauty is in the eye of the beholder. Calvin's dig in the *Institutes* at the carping of "stupid men" against predestination reflected the reality that even in the holy commonwealth of Geneva, there were Philistines who failed to perceive the beauty of an unconditional double decree.[75] His substantially expanded discussion of predestination in successive editions of the *Institutes* was partly in response to objections raised by several Genevans to his preaching. During the height of these controversies in the 1550s, he also penned a significant treatise defending predestination.[76] The most famous of the critics was the French physician and former Catholic Jérôme-Hermès Bolsec, who accused Calvin of making God the author of sin. After public disputations that left some of the civil authorities mystified by the technicalities ("The things they talk and dispute about are vast and difficult," one official confessed), Bolsec was banished from the city.[77] Not long after, another Frenchman was hauled before the consistory for cursing Calvin's doctrine of predestination with an expletive. The authorities reproached him for his vulgarity, but he defended himself with the explanation that he came from "a country where they talk that way."[78] The incident hardly stifled all criticism. Soon, several pastors from other Swiss cities weighed in with their own attacks on Calvin's predestinarian doctrines. Meanwhile, in Bern, where opposition to Calvin had coalesced under Bolsec's influence, the authorities banned all polemical exchanges on the issue, hoping to keep the peace.[79] By Calvin's death in 1564, predestination was well on its way to becoming what one scholar has called the "werewolf of Reformed theology."[80]

The controversies of the 1550s proved that even in communities that were the most sociologically predisposed to see themselves as enclaves of elect saints, a doctrine that was comforting to many would never be comforting to all. Similar tensions would emerge in the Calvinist commonwealths of New England, but not before Protestantism experienced its birth pangs in the mother country. In the Reformation's tumultuous course in England, predestination emerged front and center, with Geneva playing an important supporting role as the midwife of a Calvinist movement that would seek to remake the English church in its own image.

THE ENGLISH REFORMATION AND THE RISE OF PURITANISM

The spiritual economy of England on the eve of the Reformation was deeply sacramental, characterized by what historian Diarmaid MacCulloch has called a "gigantic consumer demand of the dead."[81] Masses for the dead were the spiritual good demanded by their living relatives, who took for granted the power of the Blessed Sacrament to lift souls from purgatory and save all those who trusted in the literal communion with Christ's body. Like most of his subjects, King Henry VIII was wedded to this traditional sacramentalism and even issued (with the probable help of a few theologian ghostwriters) a treatise attacking Martin Luther's views, including his repudiation of purgatory and masses for the dead.[82] In gratitude for the book, Pope Leo X bestowed upon Henry the title "Defender of the Faith," not knowing that a later pope would excommunicate the king in the famous dispute over his request for an annulment of his marriage to Catherine of Aragon.[83] For all his lingering sympathies with Catholic doctrine, however, Henry's declaration of himself as supreme head of the Church of England in 1534 set the stage for his reform-minded archbishop of Canterbury, Thomas Cranmer, to begin moving the church in a new direction. The extent of Cranmer's Protestant inclinations became clear in 1547 when Henry died and his nine-year-old son succeeded him as Edward VI. Having received a thoroughly Protestant education—one of his tutors was a correspondent of Calvin—Edward was hailed upon his accession as the new Josiah, the latter-day counterpart to the reforming Judean boy-king of scripture. For Edward's handlers, especially Cranmer, the Tudor Josiah created an incomparable opportunity to fashion a distinctively Protestant English church.

Two months after Edward's coronation, the Catholic emperor Charles V dealt the Protestant cause on the Continent a serious blow by defeating the Schmalkaldic League at Mühlberg, Saxony. Cranmer quickly rolled out the welcome mat for some of the Continent's leading evangelical refugees, including Peter Martyr (Pietro Martire Vermigli) and Martin Bucer, and saw to their appointment as regius professors of divinity. Steeled by a faithful-remnant mentality, Bucer and Peter Martyr were thoroughgoing predestinarians, and Cranmer shared their zeal. Though some modern interpreters have wanted to see the archbishop as "sweetly reasonable and Anglican," notes MacCulloch, "Thomas Cranmer, theologian, without the doctrine of predestination is *Hamlet* without the Prince of Denmark."[84] Likely with help from the continental refugees, Cranmer proceeded to draft a doctrinal statement for the Church of England, the Forty-two Articles. Article 17 asserted that "before the foundacions of the worlde were laied," God decreed by his secret judgment to save those whom he had chosen and to "bring them to euerlasting saualtion by Christ, as vesselles made to honour." In a swipe at the Catholic economy of salvation, the articles also dismissed purgatory as "repugnant to the woorde of God."[85] The question now was whether Cranmer's reformation could win over ordinary people, many of whom were still attached to the idea that salvation for the living and the dead could be procured sacramentally.

The reformation of the "common sort," as the theologians called them, would have to wait. Barely two weeks after Edward VI promulgated the Forty-two Articles, the young king died suddenly and was succeeded by his Catholic half sister Mary, who would execute 282 men and women for heresy, including Cranmer, who went to the stake repudiating the pope as "Christ's enemy and [the] antichrist." Now it was the English Protestants' turn to be refugees, and some 800 fled to the Continent, many to Calvin's Geneva, where they continued to develop predestination and the associated doctrines of grace as bulwarks against the alleged Pelagianism of the Catholic oppressors.[86] One product of the exiles, the Geneva Bible (1560), helped to disseminate a predestinarian theology through its extensive annotations, which were expanded in successive editions. Predictably, the marginal notes on Romans 9, printed in small type, occupied nearly two-thirds of a page in the 1602 edition, which bore the exegetical stamp of Theodore Beza, Calvin's colleague and eventual successor.[87]

Fortunately for the exiles, Mary's reign was even shorter than the sickly Edward's. When she died in 1558, Protestantism again became official under Elizabeth I, who promulgated the Thirty-nine Articles (still printed in modern editions of the Book of Common Prayer), which retained the Forty-two Articles' basic doctrine of predestination. The reiteration came on the heels of a report submitted to Elizabeth by one returned exile, Edwin Sandys, the future archbishop of York, who complained that "some men of late are risen, which do gainsay and oppugn [the] truth" of predestination.[88] Sandys was evidently referring to a group of populist Protestant "free-willers," some of whom had been incarcerated together with their predestinarian opponents during Mary's reign, sparking an unlikely theological debate behind the walls of London's King's Bench Prison.[89] But this populist undercurrent was not the only reason that many Elizabethan clergy sought to reinforce predestinarian doctrine. Increasingly, they saw predestination as a way of inoculating the laity against the scourge of a resurgent Catholic Church, which was then concluding the counterreformation Council of Trent and dispatching missionaries of the new Jesuit order to the New World. Fears of Catholicism were also running high thanks to John Foxe's immensely popular *Actes and Monuments* (1563), which catalogued gruesome stories of the Protestant martyrs. Many clergy feared a Catholic conspiracy to revive "works righteousness" among the laity and suspected that the Protestant free-willers were unwittingly abetting the cause.

So began a major offensive by the Elizabethan "godly" (the nickname of those clergy who later would be denominated as Puritans)[90] to disabuse the laity of what one godly divine, George Gifford, called "common man's pelagianism."[91] In published sermons and popular dialogues, clergy such as Gifford taught a Protestant theology of grace alone. Predestination was the fortress that safeguarded the all-sufficiency of God's grace—no magical sacramental formula or work of penance could alter the divine decree—and was a practical source of comfort for the believer. The comfort derived from the assurance of one's election, which could be obtained by scrutinizing one's life for the signs of holiness that would inevitably arise in persons chosen by God. The suspicious resemblance of such self-scrutiny to the meritorious works of Catholicism was a latent contradiction that radical Puritan "antinomians" would later exploit. But in the Elizabethan years, godly clergy trafficked heavily in practical manuals urging the laity, as Gifford memorably put it, to "beate [their] braine[s] more earnestly about heavenly thinges."[92]

As they were writing how-to manuals for the laity, the godly clergy also were theorizing about predestination in increasingly technical fashion. The most important writer of both technical and practical works was the Cambridge theologian William Perkins (1558–1602).[93] Like the young Augustine, who sowed his wild oats before converting, Perkins was reputedly promiscuous and drunken in college until a profound conversion experience turned him to a pastoral vocation. His early preaching about damnation, according to one chronicler, "left a doleful Echo in his auditours ears a good while after," though in his "older" age (he died at 44 of an apparent gallstone), Perkins "altered his voice, and remitted much of his former rigidnesse, often professing that to preach mercie was that proper office of the Ministers of the Gospell."[94] Ironically, Perkins's powerful sense of God's mercy toward the elect led him to articulate predestination in a way that many later critics regarded as anything but merciful.

Perkins's most famous treatment of predestination was not a treatise but a chart, specifically the table included in his book, *A Golden Chaine*, which appeared in the first of many editions in 1591.[95] The book's title referred to the so-called *armilla aurea* (golden chain), the name used by Reformed theologians for the unbreakable sequence of salvation spelled out by the

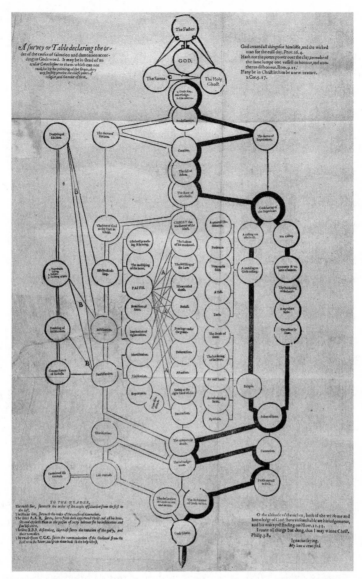

Chart illustrating God's predestinarian decrees, from William
Perkins, *A Golden Chaine* (1591), photographed from the
1608 edition. Beinecke Rare Book and Manuscript Library,
Yale University.

apostle Paul in Romans 8:30 ("Whom he did predestinate, them he also
called: and whom he called, them he also justified: and whom he justified,
them he also glorified"). Based on this biblical foundation and drawing on
a similar chart by Calvin's successor Theodore Beza, Perkins's diagram systematized the *ordo salutis* (order of salvation) in elaborate detail, showing

the main stages (election, effectual calling, justification, sanctification, glorification) and the possible "tentations" (trials, temptations) of the godly. The chart likewise schematized the stages of reprobation, which together with election pointed to "Gods Glorie" and which is manifested when the reprobates receive justice and the elect receive mercy.[96]

The chart's most controversial feature, however, was its attempt to illustrate how predestination fit into the sequence of God's own logic. The top of the diagram depicted the triune God as decreeing election and reprobation *prior* to decreeing the creation of the world and the Fall of Adam. Here, it seemed, was absolute predestination pushed to its logical extreme: God took nothing into account—not even Adam's future sin—in deciding to save some and to damn others. Election and reprobation were utterly gratuitous; they depended on no merit or demerit that God foresaw in individuals. Predestination was God's great primal act and was logically influenced by nothing—not even the pitiable (or, viewed from a different angle, contemptible) sight of the future mass of fallen humanity. The very creation of the world was subordinate to the prior manifestation of God's mercy and justice in the decrees of election and reprobation. Such a stark view came to be known among Reformed theologians as *supralapsarian* (from the Latin *supra lapsum*), meaning that predestination occurred "above" or prior to the Fall in the sequence of God's logic. (The sequence is logical rather than temporal, the dogmaticians stressed, since everything is eternally present in the divine mind.) Supralapsarianism departed from the more typical *infralapsarian* view, classically expressed by Augustine, that predestination occurred "below" or after the Fall, meaning that God first decreed the creation and the Fall and only then decreed to save some and damn (or "pass over") others.[97]

Perkins apparently devised his table as a practical aid for understanding his larger work. The only problem was that some readers looked only at the table.[98] The larger text of *A Golden Chaine*, along with Perkins's later works, such as *A Christian and Plaine Treatise of the Manner and Order of Predestination*, revealed the complex qualifications in his thinking about the decrees. As Richard Muller has shown, Perkins was in some respects actually milder in his views than Calvin, though many later interpreters have assumed the opposite. For Perkins, the decrees of the creation and Fall differed in that God positively willed the former and "permitted" the latter; for Calvin, both were positively willed acts.[99] Perkins also anticipated the objection that supralapsarianism portrayed God's "loving" or "hating" *future* persons, a logical stumbling block for some critics. Perkins's solution to this problem involved a multiplication of distinctions. He subdivided the divine decrees of election and reprobation into "double acts"—the ends and the means. The end of election was God's eternal purpose to manifest his mercy in saving certain persons, regardless of their merits. The means of election was the actual saving of chosen persons through the merits of Christ, who as a co-eternal member of the Trinity was both the elect and the electing mediator. Perkins further subdivided the means into five "degrees" involving the ordaining, promising, exhibiting, applying, and accomplishing of Christ's mediating work. As for reprobation, its end was God's eternal purpose to manifest his justice in forsaking certain persons, regardless of their sins. The means of reprobation was the actual ordaining of forsaken persons for destruction, which Perkins further subdivided into two "degrees" involving God's deserting (or denying persons the grace to persevere in goodness) and damning (or punishing persons for the sin they freely willed "in Adam"). God therefore hated and damned actual persons for actual sins; only his *initial* act of reprobating future persons was decreed in the abstract, apart from sin.[100]

The technical heft of Perkins's exposition of the decrees—the preceding summary reveals merely the tip of the iceberg—was typical of the output of the Protestant scholastics who flourished between the late sixteenth and late eighteenth centuries. The Puritan doctrines of predestination must be seen in the context of this international movement of Protestant orthodoxy in which English, Dutch, German, and other nationalities of dogmaticians shared a common language (Latin) and developed a common specialized vocabulary.[101] Predestination was not the controlling principle of their systems, which attempted to elaborate all subtopics of Christian theology. Neither were the doctrines of the decrees intended to violate the unity of God's essence. The scholastics in fact insisted on God's simplicity (again, using a technical term: *simplicitas Dei*), meaning that there were no logical distinctions in the divine mind. Perkins explained that he had divided and subdivided the decrees solely for the sake of human understanding.[102] Yet in giving predestination its most laboriously precise exposition since the scholasticism of the Middle Ages, figures such as Perkins left themselves open to the charge, later leveled against the New England Puritans, of intellectual arrogance. Many critics simply did not believe the scholastics' denial that their systems were intended to penetrate the impenetrable mysteries of God's essence. The ambitious scope of the scholastic project also created many possibilities for technical disagreements among the theologians themselves.

ARMINIANISM VERSUS "FIVE-POINT" CALVINISM

The most spectacular of the Protestant scholastic disputes originated in the work of the Dutch theologian Jacob Arminius (1559–1609), whose teachers had included Theodore Beza. While serving for 15 years as a Reformed pastor at Amsterdam, he wrestled extensively with the predestinarian intricacies of both Catholic and Protestant scholasticism and wrote a refutation of Perkins's *Manner and Order of Predestination*.[103] In 1603, after plague broke out in Leiden and killed two of the university's three theology professors, Arminius was appointed to the faculty. He soon clashed with his colleague Franciscus Gomarus, an ardent supralapsarian, in a protracted controversy that led Arminius to make his famous *Declaration of Sentiments* (1608) just one year before his death.[104]

As the *Declaration* made clear, Arminius opposed both the supra- and infralapsarian versions of the decrees, though he reserved particular scorn for supralapsarianism, which he found utterly at odds with scripture and repugnant to God's wisdom, justice, and goodness. Anticipating later objections to absolute predestination among many American evangelicals, he accused the supralapsarians of extinguishing all zeal for the conversion of sinners. Even prayer in a supralapsarian scheme was rendered futile, he charged, except as a way of worshipping God.[105] As an alternative to supra- and infralapsarian predestination, both of which he felt made God the author of sin, Arminius outlined his own fourfold order of the decrees whereby God (1) appointed Jesus Christ as Savior, (2) determined to save all those who repented of their sins and believed in Christ, (3) provided in a "sufficient and efficacious manner" the means necessary for repentance and faith, and (4) elected to salvation those persons he foresaw would believe and persevere.[106]

The third and fourth decrees in Arminius's fourfold scheme revealed the crux of his disagreement with Calvinism. He believed that through the saving death of Christ, God provided prevenient grace (Latin, *gratia praeveniens*: grace that "comes before") to all persons, not just the elect.[107] This initial infusion of grace preceding conversion enables fallen humans to cooperate with God, if they so choose, by not resisting the Holy Spirit's workings in their souls. As one contemporary theologian has explained it, prevenient grace created not so much a *free* will but a will *freed* to accept or reject Christ. Without this initial gift of grace, humans would remain completely in bondage to sin and unable to turn to God. Indeed, Arminius strenuously denied the accusation that his theology amounted to Pelagianism or semi-Pelagianism, which taught that the Fall did not obliterate all freedom in humans to choose the good. To the charge that his system violated the cardinal Protestant principle of grace alone, Arminius pleaded not guilty.[108] He also insisted that he still believed in predestination. As the fourth decree in his scheme defined it, Arminian predestination was conditional upon humans' freely willed response to God.

Conditional predestination, however, raised the same logical difficulties that had once vexed Augustine. In what sense does an all-knowing, all-determining God leave predestination open to human response? If God knows how each person will respond, does this foreknowledge not amount to foreordination? Arminius insisted that prevenient grace gives humans genuine freedom, but his explanation of the nature of divine foreknowledge of human choices was typically scholastic in its complexity. Occasional references in his writings to "middle knowledge" (*scientia media*) have led some interpreters to conclude that he accepted the theory of Luis de Molina (1535–1600), a Spanish Jesuit, that God knows certain things hypothetically. That is, God foreknows how a free creature will respond, given a particular set of circumstances. Though God creates circumstances based on this foreknowledge and in this way predestines for salvation those people he foresees will accept his grace, humans' future actions remain "free" because they are logically prior to—indeed, they are the ground of—God's electing choice.[109]

Regardless of whether Arminius was influenced by Molinism, the idea that any future human action could be the cause of God's decision was anathema to strict Calvinists, who considered it a grave affront to absolute divine sovereignty.[110] Arminius's death in 1609 hardly put an end to the controversy, for the next year in the Arminian Articles, or *Remonstrance*, his supporters (known as Remonstrants) formally reasserted three anti-Calvinist positions: election is based on divine foresight of faith; the atonement is universal, remitting the sins of all who believe; and grace is resistible. The Remonstrants further provoked their opponents, who tended to be older, more established ministers, by calling for a national synod to reconsider the Calvinism of the Belgic Confession (1561). Soon, a contra-Remonstrant party issued its own statement reasserting a Calvinistic line against the young Turks. The battle lines were drawn, and in an age when preaching still served as a form of popular entertainment, persuasive clergy drew many laypersons into the fray. "People argued about the issues on passenger barges and sang partisan songs in front of the houses of prominent members of the opposite faction," notes social historian Philip Benedict.[111] Nothing less than the future of the Reformation in Holland seemed to be at stake. A national synod was finally convened, but in the end, the contra-Remonstrants outmaneuvered their opponents. Reformed orthodoxy was enshrined in the Canons of Dort (1618–1619), whose predestinarian propositions henceforth were known by an acronym that spelled an appropriately Dutch flower, TULIP: total depravity, unconditional election, limited atonement, irresistible grace, and perseverance of the saints. Though the synod rejected a minority attempt to endorse supralapsarianism, opting instead for the milder infra- position, TULIP was nevertheless a strict rule of faith. All people sin in Adam, and from this mass of condemned sinners, God elects a certain number according to the "good pleasure of his will," without regard to their foreseen faith. Christ's death, though sufficient for the whole world, is effective only for the elect, who cannot fail to receive God's grace and persevere to the end.[112]

The codification of "five-point Calvinism" (another nickname for TULIP) at Dort resembled an earlier attempt by Puritans in England to give predestinarian orthodoxy official creedal status. Historians still debate whether an informal Calvinist theological consensus existed among late Tudor and early Stuart church leaders (even those who were not "hot" Puritans), or whether the hallmark of English Protestantism was by then a distinctively Anglican moderation on contentious doctrinal questions.[113] What is clear is that late in Elizabeth's reign, an anti-Calvinist faction emerged at Cambridge University, prompting the archbishop of Canterbury, John Whitgift, to issue the Lambeth Articles (1595) in hopes of quelling the unrest. Drafted in their initial form by the Cambridge Puritan theologian William Whitaker, the articles anticipated Dort's affirmation of unconditional election and the perseverance of the saints. To the archbishop's embarrassment, however, Queen Elizabeth refused to make the articles officially binding. In a letter to Whitgift, the queen's privy counselor noted that Her Majesty disliked the parading of disputed points of predestination, "a matter tender and dangerous to weak and ignorant minds."[114]

After the Virgin Queen died in 1603 and was succeeded by Scottish monarch James I, he too rebuffed a request, this time by the Puritans, who presented their grievances at the Hampton Court Conference (1604), to incorporate the Lambeth statements into the Thirty-nine Articles in the Book of Common Prayer. Like Elizabeth, the king feared that "stuff[ing] the book" with the arcane conclusions of theologians would confuse and divide the "simple people."[115] James himself was not unsympathetic to the cause of international Calvinism. When the Arminian controversy arose in Holland, he authorized the public burning in England of books by Conrad Vorstius, Arminius's likeminded successor at Leiden. He also urged the Dutch authorities to convene the Synod of Dort and sent an English delegation. In so involving himself in Dutch affairs, the king hoped to prevent Arminianism from "creep[ing] into the bowels of our owne Kingdom."[116] Nevertheless, by the early 1620s, a religious and political crisis was unfolding in Europe, and James began to back away from his public pro-Calvinist rhetoric. The Protestants had just lost Bohemia and the Palatinate to the Catholics in the first phase of the Thirty Years' War, and Spain appeared bent on reconsolidating its former control

I I.

*Oh that my wayes were Directed
to keepe thy Statutes. Ps.119.5.*

w. Simpson Sculp:

Labyrinth (gloss on Psalm 119) from Francis Quarles, *Emblemes*
(1643). Beinecke Rare Book and Manuscript Library, Yale
University.

over the Netherlands. James hoped to negotiate a peace through an ill-fated
Anglo-Spanish marriage alliance for his son Charles. Amid these delicate deal-
ings with a Catholic power, the king rejected a request by English Calvinists
to make the Canons of Dort binding in England.[117]

In the meantime, it was becoming clear that a distinctive English brand of Arminianism (whose proponents nevertheless usually rejected the name) was making significant inroads among the nation's religious intelligentsia. These English Arminians, more sacramental and high church than their Dutch counterparts, cultivated what they called the "beauty of holiness"—a ceremonialism enriched by the very things the Puritans regarded as abominable papist idolatries: vestments, candles, crosses, incense, altars fenced off by rails, and gestures such as genuflecting and making the sign of the cross. To the English Arminians, these high-church features elevated the dignity of the sacraments as actual means of grace, whereas the Puritans' predestinarianism inevitably weakened belief in the sacraments' inherent power. The Puritans' insistence on preaching predestination further undermined sacramentalism by making the sermon, rather than priestly ceremonies, the focal point of religious services. Thus, advocates of a higher ceremonialism, such as the bishop of Winchester, Lancelot Andrewes, urged a respectful agnosticism on predestinarian questions. The rout of the Dutch Arminians at the Synod of Dort only increased the alarm of English Arminians that an aggressive predestinarianism was on the march. By the final years of James's reign, tensions between Arminians and Puritans were running so high that the king banned all clergy below the rank of bishop from preaching on the "deep points of predestination, election, reprobation, or of the universality, efficacy, resistibility, or irresistibility of God's grace."[118]

James died in 1625, and as had been the case ever since Henry VIII's break with Rome, the change in monarch brought religious upheaval as well. A few weeks after the king's death, his son Charles I married Princess Henrietta Maria of France, sparking a new controversy over the reality— finally consummated this time after the failed Spanish marriage scheme—of a Catholic queen at court. Outwardly, Charles remained loyal to England's established Protestantism and adhered to the anti-Catholic policies of his predecessors. (He broke a number of promises made to France, as conditions of his marriage alliance, to improve the legal status of English Catholics.) Charles also was willing to criticize Arminianism when such censures served his political purposes. But while his innermost theological views remained an enigma, temperamentally the new king was cut from the same cloth as the English Arminians, with their hierarchical, ceremonial vision of religion and society. Though the Puritans also accepted many traditional social hierarchies, the implicit egalitarianism of absolute predestination (that God elects without regard to status or merit), combined with the perceived air of moral superiority among the self-proclaimed godly, often set Puritanism at odds with royalist ideology. The Arminians' priestly, high-church style, along with their firm Anglican commitment to ecclesiastical government by bishops, was far better suited for ceremonially reinforcing the king's prerogatives as head of both church and state.[119]

Consequently, when Archbishop of Canterbury George Abbot, a card-carrying Calvinist appointed by King James in 1611, died in 1633, Charles seized the opportunity to elevate the influential Arminian bishop of London, William Laud (1573–1645), to the see of Canterbury. Like the late Lancelot Andrewes, whom he had succeeded for a time as dean of the Chapel Royal, Laud regarded debate over predestination as unseemly and divisive. He had no patience for godly preachers who repeatedly hammered home strict Calvinism, which he believed made God "the most unreasonable tyrant in the world." The focus of his own piety was instead the Eucharist. As he once explained, in terms that would have set Puritan teeth on edge, "the altar is the greatest place of God's residence upon earth, greater than the pulpit; for there 'tis *Hoc est corpus meum*, This is my body; but in the other it is at most but *Hoc est verbum meum*, This is my word."[120] Upon becoming archbishop, Laud wasted no time in implementing this eucharistic vision. He oversaw the refurbishment of altars in many churches and beefed up the enforcement of prescribed prayer book rituals. He hounded outspoken Puritan clergy and disbanded a lay organization that sought to purchase church livings for godly preachers. Charles, meanwhile, reissued his father's Book of Sports, which allowed games and other entertainments on Sundays after religious services, and required all clergy to read the directive from the pulpit—a slap in the face to strict Puritan sabbatarians. All of these developments prompted accusations of popery from beleaguered Puritans, who feared that the Church of England was capitulating to the forces of the Antichrist. The inhospitable climate soon drove some of the most zealous clergy to the woods of America, where they assumed they could preach predestination unmolested by the doctrine's sacramentalist detractors. Little did these exiles know that Old World tensions would all too soon reemerge in New World guises.

CHAPTER 2

The Agony and the Ecstasy

Predestination in New England Puritanism

This doctrine, with all the pathos of its inhumanity, had one principal consequence for the mood of a generation which yielded to its magnificent logic: it engendered, for each individual, a feeling of tremendous inner loneliness....[M]an was obliged to tread his path alone, toward a destiny which had been decreed from all eternity. No one and nothing could help him.

— *Max Weber,* The Protestant Ethic and the Spirit of Capitalism *(1905)*

The beginning and fountaine of all our happinesse and consolation consists in this, that we are the elect of God.

— *William Ames,* An Analyticall Exposition of Both the Epistles of the Apostle Peter *(1641)*

WHEN THE 80-year-old Increase Mather rose to preach to his congregation on a March day in 1720, age had by then slowed his step, contributing to his aura of patriarchal gravity. Never a lighthearted personality, the celebrated minister and former Harvard president, long-nosed and thinner in face than in his youth, had always exuded Puritan seriousness. "When Increase laughed," one historian has noted, "men did not believe their ears."[1] These days, he was telling admirers that he expected every sermon to be his last. Because his own trembling hand prevented him from writing out his sermons in full, a female parishioner adept at shorthand recorded his words for publication. During nearly 60 years as pastor of North Church, he had seen Boston change dramatically from a town of wooden houses, barns, and dirt roads, to a cosmopolitan seaport with cobblestone streets, brick homes, bookstores, and dozens of alehouses. Boston's merchant elite now cultivated British refinement, and even some of the ministers were preaching in a "modish" style that softened the hard edges of their forefathers' Calvinism.[2] In this polite context, Mather, a staunch traditionalist to the end, ascended the pulpit and preached on an old Puritan theme: predestination.

His particular concern was a favorite of predestinarians: how many people were chosen for salvation? His conclusion, dismal by his own admission, was that the greatest part of humanity would perish eternally. Though the New Testament taught that Christ's blood was shed for many, this was true only in absolute terms; in a comparative sense, the elect were a fearfully small percentage of the earth's population. Observe, Mather urged his listeners, how most of the world's people had fulfilled the words of the psalmist in serving graven images and boasting of idols. "Mahometans" surely were lost, as were Catholics, for "a Papist living up to the Principles of his Religion cannot possibly go beyond a Reprobate." Even many Protestants were wicked and profane idolaters. The Lord's chosen were but a "little flock" (Luke 12:32), a "remnant" (Rom. 11:5), and the "fewest of all people" (Deut. 7:7). Persons should therefore "fear and tremble and be concerned" about their salvation before it was too late. Mather ended with a warning to merely nominal Christians: beware, lest you find yourself among those Christ foretold would pretend to follow him, only to miss heaven at the last.[3]

In declaring the elect to be few in number, Mather echoed the first-generation Bay colony minister Thomas Shepard, who nearly a century earlier, before joining the Great Migration to New England, had ominously pronounced to his flock in Essex, "'Tis a thousand to one if ever thou bee one of that small number whom God hath picked out to escape this wrath to come." The Bible, he explained, proved that God saved but a handful in each generation, as in the case of Noah and his family, who alone survived the Flood. Like Mather, Shepard decried the idolatry of the "popish" and non-Christian worlds but also the rampant false Christianity in England's own church. Indeed, it was "a harder matter to convert a man in England than in India" because most of the English assumed themselves to be Christians even though a majority were in fact reprobates.[4]

Shepard's grim thousand-to-one odds belied the popularity of his message, which appeared as *The Sincere Convert* in at least 20 British and

4 colonial American editions between 1640 and 1800.[5] Perhaps New England readers could console themselves that in their "city upon a hill," their likelihood of being elect improved relative to the long odds in the rest of the world. The same faithful-remnant mentality had animated true believers in Calvin's Geneva, which John Knox, fleeing Queen Mary's persecution in the 1550s, once described as "the most perfect school of Christ that ever was in earth since the days of the Apostles."[6] In the 1630s, Shepard and other Puritans fleeing persecution under Archbishop of Canterbury William Laud saw New England as a similarly righteous enclave that was, according to the retrospective of Cotton Mather in 1702, "nothing in Doctrine, little in Discipline, different from that of Geneva."[7]

Yet in the end, every Puritan or other Calvinist knew that election was an individual matter, for as the apostle Paul had warned, "they are not all Israel, which are of Israel." When Shepard and other first-generation New England ministers began requiring all would-be church members to give a formal relation of their faith as evidence of election, this greatly heightened not only the laypeople's introspection and anxiety but also the clergy's output of sermons and treatises analyzing the relationship between conversion and God's eternal decrees.[8] New England was destined to become a perfect laboratory of predestinarian piety in all of its psychological complexity. And though the New Englanders' rigorous spiritual regimen, which pursued an elusive balance of anxiety and assurance, was born of Old World politics and concerns, it would become a uniquely American source of religious conflict and change.

THE DOCTRINES THEY CARRIED

The predestinarian intensity of early New England cannot be understood apart from the political pressures that drove clergy like Thomas Shepard to leave England. In the previous chapter, we saw Archbishop William Laud's efforts to rein in the agitators among the Puritan godly. Shepard, a pastor in Essex, was one of the preachers targeted by Laud even before the archbishop's enthronement at Canterbury. The story of the two men's encounter, preserved in Shepard's own words, appeared in New England lore more than a century later in a chronicle by Thomas Prince. Laud, while still bishop of London in 1630, hauled in Shepard to interrogate him on his activities. The bishop "look'd as tho' Blood would have gush'd out of his Face, and did shake as if he had been haunted with an Ague Fit ... by Reason of his extream Malice and secret Venom." Laud then railed against Shepard: "you prating Coxcomb! Do you think all the Learning is in your Brain?" He forbade Shepard from preaching in the London diocese, warning him: "if you do, and I hear of it, I'll be upon your back and follow you wherever you go, in any Part of the Kingdom, and so everlastingly disenable you."[9]

However much Shepard may have embellished this recollection, Laud's treatment of him confirmed Shepard's suspicion that the English church had fallen into the hands of crypto-papist reprobates. By 1635, Shepard was on his way to Massachusetts Bay, joining more than 20,000 other men, women, and children who would settle in New England in the same decade. The reasons for the Great Migration were many, but for clergy like Shepard, religious motivations predominated. The Puritan movement, which began as an undercurrent of dissatisfaction with the Elizabethan settlement, was now a militant minority under Laudian persecution. New England offered zealous ministers such as Shepard the opportunity to continue their aborted reformation of the church and society according to the alleged purity and simplicity of the primitive biblical model.

Yet a curious thing happened once the refugees arrived in the New England Geneva. Finally out of reach of Archbishop Laud's long arm, the Puritans found themselves deprived of the embattled minority status that had so fueled their predestinarian ardor. The elect remnant was now the establishment, and one without a defining opposition. Shepard, as historian Michael Winship has noted, soon spoke almost nostalgically about the good old days of persecution back in England. "New-Englands peace and plenty of means," Shepard lamented, "breed strange security."[10] Faced with this new reality, the colonial ministers mounted a predestinarian offensive—an effort to distinguish the truly godly by means of the aforementioned conversion relation required of all would-be church members. This prerequisite struck many observers back in old England, which had an umbrella-like territorial church, as rank sectarianism, but for Shepard and other first-generation clergy, it was the only way of separating the sheep from the goats. The singling out of goats, as Winship has astutely observed, also conveniently provided a new common enemy for the godly.[11]

We will return to goats and sheep in due time, but first the shepherds demand greater scrutiny. Exactly what was the predestinarian orthodoxy that men like Shepard brought across the Atlantic? For the earliest migrant ministers, the "five points" of Dort were the closest thing to an official creed on predestination.[12] Essential to this orthodoxy was an anti-Arminian insistence that predestination was absolutely unconditional. As the prominent Puritan theologian William Ames explained, if election depended upon anything in humans, "who are weak and changeable every houre," it would afford no consolation to the believer.[13] The doctrine of perseverance further reinforced the notion that election was an unshakable foundation. God's "plan cannot be changed," the Dort Canons declared. "[H]is promise cannot fail." No evil, whether internal or external, could ultimately deflect the elect from the narrow way leading to salvation. As the apostle Paul wrote: "If God be for us, who can be against us?" Perseverance was a fighting doctrine that called to mind Theodore Beza's image of the elect church as "an anvil that has worn out many hammers." The Huguenots adopted Beza's image for their motto, but it could have applied equally to predestination as espoused by Puritan ministers such as Shepard. As the verse on the old Huguenot coat of arms put it, "Hammer away ye hostile bands/Your hammers break/God's anvil stands."[14]

A decade after the establishment of Massachusetts Bay, a similarly militant sense of election motivated "God's Englishman," Oliver Cromwell, to lead the Puritan overthrow of the monarchy during the English Civil Wars (1641–1651). During this tumultuous period, Parliament convened an assembly of divines to address the Puritans' unfulfilled goal of revising the Thirty-nine Articles. The result was the Westminster Confession (1647), which remained in force in England until the Restoration of the monarchy in 1660. By the confession's publication, Archbishop Laud had been beheaded, and King Charles himself would soon meet the same fate. New Englanders hailed the revolution—a "blessed work of a public Reformation," according to Shepard—and quickly adopted the Westminster Confession as their own doctrinal standard, modifying only its presbyterian model of church government to accommodate the congregational polity of the colonial churches.[15]

Westminster's theology closely resembled Dort's. The five points of TULIP were there, though in different language. Total depravity found expression in the assertion that fallen humans were "dead in sin," having lost "all ability of will to any spiritual good accompanying salvation." Unconditional election appeared in the statement that God elected persons "out of his mere free grace and love, without any foresight of faith or good works...or any other thing in the creature." Limited atonement emerged in the insistence that Christ saved none "but the elect only." Irresistible grace was implied by the section on "effectual calling," which described how the elect were unfailingly drawn to Christ. Perseverance of the saints was clear in the declaration that the elect could "neither totally, nor finally, fall away from the state of grace."[16]

The Dort and Westminster standards would remain the baseline of predestinarian belief in New England long after the Restoration had reinstated the Thirty-nine Articles in the Church of England. (Cotton Mather would later boast that "every one knows" of the New England churches' perfect adherence to this orthodoxy.)[17] The Dort-Westminster consensus nevertheless elided a great deal of internal Puritan disagreement on the finer points of predestinarian doctrine, and two of these merit further consideration: the supralapsarian-infralapsarian debate and the tricky relationship between predestination and the covenant.

SUPRALAPSARIANS VERSUS INFRALAPSARIANS

The supra-infra debate appears more than a little anachronistic in the twenty-first century, when the idea of subscribing to *any* strict confessional position seems as quaint to many Americans as iceboxes in an age of frost-free refrigerators. In hindsight, the supra-infra distinction also looks suspiciously beside the point: if predestination were truly unconditional (as both sides claimed), then it hardly mattered—at least from the perspective of human time—whether election occurred before or after the Fall in the immemorial sequence of God's logic. Yet in the scholasticism that New England ministers inherited from theologians like William Perkins, the supra-infra debate arose precisely from an impulse to defend predestination's unconditional nature. The Arminian alternative of conditional predestination, the Puritans alleged, compromised the free grace of the gospel and went against the weight of church tradition. Perkins had taken pains to point out that even the medieval schoolmen "in the midst of Papacie" had taught the unconditionality of predestination. He appealed especially to Aquinas, who in the *Summa* insisted that why God chose some and rejected others had no reason but the divine will. Perkins seemed to take Aquinas's comments as an implicit endorsement of supralapsarianism, even though the Angelic Doctor wrote the *Summa* long before the Reformed debate about the order of the decrees. To Perkins, the supra sequence of election/reprobation, creation, and Fall ensured that even reprobation (considered from the eternal perspective of God's logic, as we saw earlier) could not have been for sin. Sin was the result, not the cause, of God's "permission and desertion" in the Fall, which he allowed only after he had already decreed election and reprobation.[18]

Perkins's ruminations helped to elevate the order of the decrees as a favorite occult question for later Puritans, including those who convened in the Westminster Assembly. The gathering's prolocutor, or presiding officer, William Twisse (1578–1646), was on record as a defender of Perkins's supralapsarianism. Legendary for his encyclopedic scholastic knowledge, Twisse was old and in poor health by the time of the assembly, during which he sometimes exasperated delegates by allowing speakers to "harangue long and very learnedlie" over abstruse doctrinal matters.[19] Ultimately the assembly's divines, like their counterparts at Dort, opted for infralapsarian language in the Westminster Confession, declaring that after the decree of election, God was "pleased" in his unsearchable wisdom to "pass by" the rest of humans (implying that he left them in an already fallen state). Yet the confession retained enough ambiguity on the decrees—asserting, for example, in double predestinarian fashion that "some men and angels are predestinated unto everlasting life, and others foreordained to everlasting death"—to preclude any merciful foreclosure of the supra-infra debate.[20]

Indeed, Twisse's last book, not published until just before his death in 1646, was an extended refutation of an early predestinarian treatise by the American Puritan John Cotton (1585–1652), a supralapsarian and by all accounts a natural ally.[21] Cotton had circulated his piece in manuscript in the mid-1620s, prior to his emigration to New England, and after reading

William Twisse by Thomas Trotter (1783), after unknown artist. National Portrait Gallery, London.

it, Twisse became convinced that Cotton was soft on reprobation and dangerously close to the Arminian heresy of conditional predestination. Like Perkins, Cotton subdivided the decree of reprobation into a first "negative" act of non-election or desertion and a second "positive" act of damnation for sin. But on the positive side, Cotton inserted a further subdivision prior to damnation—judgment according to works. Cotton was, as historian David Como has explained, "trying to insinuate the Covenant of Works into his schema of predestination."[22] The *covenant of works* was the Puritans' term for the first bargain that God made with humanity—the promise of salvation in exchange for perfect obedience, which Adam violated in the Garden of Eden. To Twisse, Cotton seemed to be inserting an element of conditionality into supralapsarianism, which destroyed the supra part (that God's electing and reprobating were radically prior to all else). Cotton's scheme struck Twisse as a Jesuitical shell game—as insidious as the Molinist account of "middle knowledge," which Twisse had attacked in another treatise. In Twisse's view, Cotton had betrayed himself as one of those weak-kneed Calvinists who could not endure the full arbitrariness of absolute predestination. Similar discomfort had driven some, such as French theologian Moïse Amyraut, to deny the *L* of the TULIP, replacing limited atonement with a "hypothetical universalism" by which God *conditionally* willed to save all who believed and *unconditionally* willed to save particular persons. Amyraut insisted that human logic could not fully reconcile the contradiction.[23]

Twisse's attack on the early Cotton's apparent flirtation with conditional predestination was particularly ironic given Cotton's later theological evolution and his association with the condemned "antinomian" Anne Hutchinson, who so exalted the free grace of unconditional election that she accused ministers such as Thomas Shepard of preaching a covenant of works. Twisse's reproof of Cotton's casuistry also was more than a little hypocritical, given the Westminster prolocutor's own reputation for doctrinal hairsplitting. In the end, however, Twisse conceded that all the "perturbation" about the order of the decrees was in vain because God's decisions were inseparable and simultaneous in his own eternal mind. Twisse admitted that for many years, he had been "carried away with the common error" of ordering the decrees and thus had found himself in an endless "labyrinth."[24]

The international Reformed fraternity did not heed Twisse's warning about the labyrinthine nature of "decretal" theology. Seven years after his death, Twisse's *Riches of Gods Love unto the Vessells of Mercy, Consistent with His Absolute Hatred or Reprobation of the Vessells of Wrath* (1653) appeared in print together with a "vindication of Dr. Twisse" from the criticisms of the English Arminian John Goodwin. A massive folio volume replete with citations of Catholic and Protestant scholastics, Twisse's *Riches* overflowed with enough supra-infra complexities to leave even the most determined student begging for mercy. While supralapsarians in particular continued to read (or at least invoke) Twisse appreciatively, infralapsarians gained an influential ally in the Geneva theologian Francis Turretin. In his systematic theology (1679–1685), he derided Twisse for "mak[ing] himself hoarse" repeating the supralapsarian argument that God's last act in order of execution (the salvation of the elect and the damnation of the reprobate) ought to be his first in order of intention.[25] To Turretin, supralapsarianism, though containing "nothing absolutely repugnant to the foundation of salvation," was nonsensical because it made a "non-entity" (the not-yet-created person) the object of predestination. Infralapsarianism—the "common [view] among the Reformed"—not only prevented this problem but also avoided the appearance of making God's first decree (in reprobation) an arbitrary act of hatred.[26]

Turretin's work became a standard reference for many later New Englanders, including Jonathan Edwards, who reiterated the infralapsarian position that God elected "created" (not merely "creatable") humans.[27] But supralapsarianism also had prominent American defenders, including Boston minister Samuel Willard (1640–1707), whose *Compleat Body of Divinity*, written in the 1690s but published posthumously in 1726, was the first truly systematic theology produced in America. Willard, the acting president of Harvard from 1701 until his death, claimed that infralapsarianism (which he called "sublapsarianism") was mistaken in fixing election upon already fallen humans rather than on "possible beings" whose very creation, fall, and redemption in Christ were all means to God's great end of glorifying his grace. Election and reprobation had no prior causes, Willard insisted. Even Christ was not "the meritorious cause of our Election."[28] Turretin too had affirmed this: he argued that election according to God's "good pleasure" by definition excluded every cause.[29] But Willard insisted that supralapsarianism better expressed the biblical truth of the utter gratuity of God's grace. Willard's God, in his primal act of election, was magnificently solipsistic. Because his last end was to glorify his own grace, he could not "look at any thing out of himself" in decreeing election, for to do otherwise would be to suggest the possibility of an end greater than God's own glory, which was impossible.[30]

The transatlantic conflict between supralapsarians and infralapsarians highlighted the lack of any single Puritan orthodoxy on predestination. The weightiness of argumentation on both sides continually belied the fact that most theologians, when pressed, conceded with Twisse that the decrees were simultaneous in God's own mind. In the end, the Puritan divines tacitly

Samuel Willard by unknown seventeenth- or eighteenth-century artist. Harvard University Art Museums.

accepted both supra and infra as legitimate Reformed positions. This agreement to disagree resembled the inconclusive outcome of the dispute in Spain between Dominican followers of Aquinas and Jesuit followers of Molina over predestination's relationship to foreseen merits. In that case, Pope Paul V finally ruled in 1607 that both orders could teach their respective positions. Puritans had no pope to settle the issue, only the Dort and Westminster standards, which bespoke the fundamental Reformed consensus on predestination's unconditionality. This was the basic principle that Arminianism had violated, thereby smuggling "popery and Pelagianism in by the back door," as Turretin put it.[31] To Reformed theologians, unconditional predestination was the pure gospel thread woven through St. Paul, Augustine, the Protestant reformers, and those Catholic scholastics not corrupted by Molinism and other reputed sophistries. Thus, both supralapsarians and infralapsarians followed the revered Perkins in selectively appealing to the medieval schoolmen to defend unconditionality. Twisse invoked Aquinas on how "mad" it was to think that human merit was the cause of election; Turretin cited Aquinas on how Christ's own merit was no cause or condition of God's initial electing choice.[32]

THE LOGIC OF THE COVENANT

The Puritans did not, however, banish all conditionality from their thinking about predestination. While the supra-infra dispute concerned the inner workings of God's mind (a hard thing to probe at best) and preoccupied mainly the theologians, another issue entangled both clergy and laity in a web of complexity about the human side of the predestinarian equation. The basic question was an old one: how to reconcile Christ's call to repentance and conversion with the doctrine of absolute predestination. Did human response to the gospel play any meaningful role in salvation if God had already decided, apart from any foresight of human merit, who would go to heaven and who would go to hell? The question was particularly urgent for the Puritan laity. On the one hand, the clergy demanded a response from them—a conversion relation testifying to the "work of grace" in their souls. On the other hand, the clergy preached that individuals could "do" nothing to effect their own salvation. Contradictory as this seemed, the laypeople could not simply dismiss their pastors as double dealers. Any Puritan worth his salt knew that the tension between the unconditionality of predestination and the conditionality of the covenant originated in the Bible itself.

Unconditionality was nowhere starker than in God's sovereign pronouncement in Exodus 33:19 and Romans 9:15: "I will have mercy on whom I will have mercy." Puritan divines on both sides of the Atlantic loved to expound this verse. Stephen Charnock, a chaplain in Ireland during the Cromwell regime, asked rhetorically why humans should question God's absolute sovereignty when they took for granted that they could do with their own possessions—their household utensils, their houses, their dogs—as they saw fit, without giving "any other reason than 'tis my own." William Twisse highlighted instead the dissimilarity between God and his creatures, noting that while a human physician might sin if he refused to treat a sick person, the divine physician was bound to none. Samuel Willard declared flatly that it was "a sign of an unconverted man" not to love the doctrine of God's unconditional sovereignty.[33] Yet for every affirmation of unconditionality in the Bible and in Puritan sermons, there was a statement of conditions—a ringing "unless" or "if"—or a reminder of covenantal obligations. Jesus himself repeatedly uttered "unless" ("except" in King James

English): unless you convert (Matt. 18:3), unless you repent (Luke 13:3), unless you are born again (John 3:3), you cannot see the kingdom of God. St. Paul too—for all his unconditional imagery of the potter and the clay, and Jacob and Esau—left a resounding "if" in Romans 4:24: "if we believe on him that raised up Jesus our Lord from the dead," then our belief, like Abraham's faith in God's promise, shall be imputed to us as righteousness. And who could forget the choice posed by God in laying out the terms of the Mosaic covenant? "I have set before you life and death, blessing and cursing: therefore choose life" (Deut. 30:19). How could this choice be reconciled with predestination?

The Westminster Confession gave Puritans a framework for dealing with the problem in the theory known as *double covenant federalism* ("federalism," in this case, from the Latin *foedus*, a covenant or pact). We have already seen the first of these two bargains between God and humans: the covenant of works, demanding perfect obedience to the moral law, which Adam violated in the Garden of Eden. Because Adam was the federal head of humanity, according to Puritan dogmaticians, his posterity inherited the perpetual obligation to abide by the covenant of works. But humans also inherited Adam's sinful tendency, which made perfect adherence to the covenant of works impossible. Thus, God made a second bargain with humans: the covenant of grace, enacted by Christ, the new Adam. Christ fulfilled the old covenant's test of perfect obedience, which humans had failed. God then applied Christ's redemptive work to humanity.[34]

Yet a question remained concerning the application of redemption to humans: was the covenant of grace conditional or absolute? The Westminster Confession employed the language of conditionality in stating that God "freely offereth unto sinners life and salvation by Jesus Christ, requiring of them faith in him." But the same section also referred to God's promise to give the Holy Spirit to "all those that are ordained unto life"—a clear reminder of the absoluteness of predestination. The covenant of grace was therefore paradoxical; it was both conditional and absolute. It epitomized what one historian has called Puritanism's "conscious ambivalence."[35] Without some sense of conditionality and voluntary human response, predestinarian doctrine would devolve into fatalism; yet without an unqualified affirmation of divine sovereignty, the Protestant "grace alone" would be compromised. In this dialectic of human agency and divine sovereignty, the latter clearly took precedence, though Puritan theologians believed that the paradox was not thereby destroyed. As Thomas Hooker, founder of the Connecticut colony, put it, "the Lord indeed requires a condition: no man can be saved but he must beleeve." But "as he makes this condition with the soule, so also he keepeth us in performing the condition."[36] God, in other words, both established the covenant and enabled the elect to accept it. Elsewhere, Puritan clergy spoke of the two wills of God: revealed and hidden. The revealed will consisted of the conditions of salvation laid out in scripture; the hidden will entailed God's sovereign and inscrutable choice of particular persons, whose number could not be known until the Second Coming.[37]

While laypeople rarely theorized about God's will in the same abstract way, they were adept at citing biblical proof texts for both human responsibility and divine sovereignty. One sample of lay conversion relations from Thomas Shepard's congregation at Cambridge, Massachusetts, reveals that the most frequently mentioned New Testament passage was one stressing human initiative: "Come unto me, all ye that labour and are heavy laden, and I will give you rest" (Matt. 11:28). But coming in at a close second was a verse favored by predestinarians: "All that the Father giveth me shall come to me" (John 6:37).[38] That laypeople were able to hold such verses in fruitful tension did not mean that the tension itself never nagged. One woman in Shepard's congregation recalled his assertion that not all who heard the call of the gospel were elect, which prompted her to wonder how she could ever know her own status.[39] Such temptations to doubt or despair (as we will see shortly) always threatened as individuals wrestled with the question of whether they had been engrafted into the covenant.

What is less clear is how often the laity in early New England actually questioned the whole system of covenant theology. Doubts about one's eternal status, or even doubts about the ministers' teachings on self-examination or assurance, were not the same thing as outright skepticism about the Westminster presuppositions. To be sure, there were a few maverick voices in the transatlantic Puritan orbit of the seventeenth century. The great poet John Milton, blind by the 1650s and relying on his remarkable memory of scripture, dictated his *De Doctrina Christiana* as a manifesto of biblical Christianity uncorrupted by the scholastic subtleties of the theologians. Milton found absolute predestination unbiblical and incompatible with human agency and responsibility. He was particularly unpersuaded by the Westminster Confession's argument, formulated earlier by Perkins, that God merely "permitted" the Fall, thus making sinners entirely responsible for their own actions. This was a "common subterfuge," Milton charged, that did not really mitigate the doctrine of absolute reprobation, which he found to be unbiblical.[40]

Milton's incredulity toward Puritan avowals of human agency foreshadowed the skepticism of many modern interpreters of Puritanism, including the sociologist Kai Erikson. To believe in predestination while still maintaining that reprobates sin of their own accord, Erikson quips, "is almost like saying that a man who finds himself falling from a tree will decide on the way down that this is what he really planned to do anyway."[41] The most prolific twentieth-century interpreter of Puritanism was Harvard's Perry Miller, who argued that covenant theology "slyly substituted" a juridical relationship for an absolute divine decree. Miller regarded the "subtle casuistry" of the covenant as a departure from the unflinching predestinarianism of the original Protestant reformers. Thoroughgoing supralapsarians like Twisse were among the few Puritans who "retained the strong theological stomach of the sixteenth century."[42] A chorus of revisionists subsequently upbraided Miller for overplaying the discontinuity between the sixteenth and seventeenth centuries and for neglecting the roots of covenant thought (and the covenant-predestination dialectic) in the Bible itself.[43] Critics also pointed out that Puritan theologians lacked the modern tendency to see predestination and the covenant as blatantly contradictory because of Puritanism's acceptance of medieval theories of multiple causation, which allowed for human agency as a secondary cause within the divinely ordained causal chain.[44] Yet the fact that many later Americans *perceived* a fundamental incompatibility between predestination and human agency—and surely this perception cannot be attributed entirely to modern myopia—would have tremendous consequences in the eventual proliferation of anti-Calvinist religious alternatives. Miller's own words might well have been spoken by Calvinism's discontents in the early American republic: "The Covenant was but a glove upon the hand of iron. Even though it was an agreement, a deed, a legal transaction, yet the ability which enabled any man to take it up was the gift of a fitful and desultory power; God could do what He would with His own and yet do wrong to none."[45]

PREDESTINATION AS EXPERIENCED: AGONY

In the short run, however, the greatest threat to the Puritan experiment in New England was not the logic of the covenant per se but the more practical problem of assurance: how do I know if I am elect? Here we come again to the question that sparked antinomian upheaval in Massachusetts Bay's first decade and that has fueled another great debate among Puritanism's modern interpreters. The problem concerned predestination's experiential consequence: was the doctrine primarily a source of anxiety for the Puritan faithful, or did it bring assurance and comfort? Alternatively (and with apologies to the late novelist Irving Stone), we might speak of the tension between the agony and the ecstasy; the semantic advantages of these terms will be spelled out in the conclusion of this chapter.

The inherited picture of predestination, drawn by the pioneering German sociologist Max Weber (1864–1920), is one of anxiety. In his most famous work, *The Protestant Ethic and the Spirit of Capitalism* (1905), Weber described the "profound inner isolation" of the Puritan confronting the question, "Elect or reprobate?" None of the usual persons, mechanisms, or institutions could help the individual facing this stark uncertainty: not the preacher (for Puritans ultimately afforded him little actual priestly status over an elect layperson), not the sacraments (because Puritans rejected the view that these conveyed grace in any substantial way), not the church (since despite efforts to make it a gathered community of the godly, it was assumed to include both elect and reprobate), and not even God (because Christ died for the elect alone, as Dort and Westminster orthodoxy taught).[46] Puritanism, like Protestantism generally, deprived the individual of the traditional ways of relieving predestinarian anxiety—a "gradual storing up of meritorious achievements" through hearing masses, undertaking pilgrimages, and performing other works of satisfaction. The Protestant watchword of grace alone seemed almost to obliterate merit, at least as far as humans were concerned.

Yet the crux of the Weber thesis was that Puritan anxiety was not ultimately destructive but productive because of the novel means of alleviating it that Puritanism devised. The Puritan sought relief through hard work—tireless labor in her calling and tireless self-examination about the quality of her temporal and spiritual exertions. Productivity became the sure sign—an indirect but reliable proof—of election. Conversely, unwillingness to work was a symptom of a person who was not in a state of grace. Wasting time was the cardinal sin of the Puritan; "every lost hour [meant] one less hour devoted to labor in the service of God's glory." This is the "Protestant ethic" that gave rise to the acquisitive spirit of capitalism. Whereas traditional Catholics "lived to a certain extent 'from hand to mouth,'" Weber claimed, Puritans elevated constant labor in their callings to the level of a system that governed all of life. Thus, it was the Protestant, particularly the Reformed, societies that produced the "tough, upstanding, and active mind of the middle-class capitalist entrepreneur."[47]

The century since the publication of Weber's book has not put an end to the debate. An obvious objection to his thesis is how it played into national and individual stereotypes about the passivity and otherworldliness of Catholicism. Such assumptions typically undergirded the nineteenth-century doctrine of manifest destiny, by which Anglo-Saxon (or "Teutonic") Protestants were providentially chosen to conquer and subdue the American continent. Though Weber was not an American, his Protestant upbringing and sympathies should come as no surprise.[48] Other scholars have seized upon Weber's own concluding caution against "one-sided" spiritual explanations of capitalism's origins and have argued that he failed to emphasize how much the Protestant ethic actually derived from capitalism itself. That is, Puritan covenant theology arose as an idiom uniquely intelligible to a middle class already immersed in the contractual exchanges of the market economy.[49] And then there is the question of anxiety versus assurance. Sociologist Malcolm MacKinnon has strenuously argued that Weber misunderstood covenant theology, which negated absolute predestination and made assurance available to all sincere strivers. Puritans achieved this assurance entirely through introspection and other spiritual means, not through worldly economic activity, which Protestants, no less than traditional Catholics, regarded as religiously indifferent. MacKinnon provoked vigorous rebuttals from other scholars, lending credence to historian Alastair Hamilton's conclusion about the seemingly never-ending debate: "it is just as difficult to demolish Weber's thesis as it is to substantiate it."[50]

Hamilton also correctly put his finger on a problem faced by Weber, Perry Miller, and anyone who has ever tried to write about the psychological effects of a doctrine: to do so requires describing a "singularly evasive object, a mentality."[51] More often than not, we are forced to rely on printed sources, which may, as in the case of doctrinal treatises, bear little resemblance to the lived religion of average persons. Even when manuscript sources such as conversion relations are available, these often exhibit some of the same performative qualities as printed works. Puritan laypeople seeking admission to the church inevitably said some of what the pastor wanted to hear, regardless of whether it always reflected their innermost attitudes.

That said, the paper trail left by the Puritans suggests that the anxiety so emphasized by Weber was not simply a figment of his imagination. Puritanism on both sides of the Atlantic was in many ways a reprise of the culture of anxiety that had often characterized medieval Catholicism. Historian T. Dwight Bozeman has explored this irony with great acumen in his book *The Precisianist Strain*. The earliest Protestant reformers strongly reacted against the "works righteousness" of Catholicism, which they felt left people doubtful and anxious about their salvation. But in the religious ferment of the Elizabethan church, hot-blooded godly ministers "drew moderate Puritanism into its age of anxiety" in their zeal to Protestantize the laity through introspection and associated spiritual disciplines. Elizabethan Puritans thus launched the first great Pietist movement in mainstream Protestantism, preceding the German Pietism of the seventeenth and eighteenth centuries.[52]

For all the Puritans' anti-Catholicism, the parallels between their anxiety and that of late medieval Christians are indeed striking. Several motifs of angst recur in both Puritan and Catholic sources. First was the refrain, which we saw at the beginning of this chapter, that few were chosen by God.

This idea was rooted in scripture and in Augustine, but medieval Catholics, despite their confidence in sacramental efficacy, also repeated sobering estimates of the handful who would attain heaven. Aquinas, who invoked Augustine on how the number of the predestined could neither be increased nor diminished, concluded that "those who are saved are in the minority." Cardinal Robert Bellarmine (1542–1621), a Jesuit sympathetic to the Molinist account of human free will, nevertheless grimly elaborated a metaphor from the prophet Isaiah: "The number of the reprobate will be as the multitude of olives that fall to the earth, when the olive tree is shaken; and the tiny number of the chosen will be as the few olives that, having escaped the hands of the gatherers, remain in the highest branches and are picked separately."[53] Puritans were no less insistent on this theme. William Perkins was perhaps the source of Increase Mather's argument (quoted earlier) that the elect were numerous only if considered by themselves; compared with the rest of humanity, Perkins explained, the elect were a small minority, for scripture taught that "many are called, but few are chosen" (Matt. 22:14). Arthur Dent, whose *Plaine Mans Path-way to Heaven* (1601) was a popular manual of predestinarian teaching, argued that it was a wonder that anyone was saved at all, given that "we have (as they say) the Sun, Moone, & seven Stars against us," namely, the world, the flesh, and the devil. It was plainly evident to Dent, whose book reached a 25th edition by 1640, that a "thousand thousands are carried headlong to destruction," while the numbers of the elect "are very fewe in comparison."[54] Later, in New England, Samuel Willard offered what modern Americans would see as cold comfort. Yes, only a small number constitute the elect, as Matthew 7:14 ("narrow is the way, which leadeth unto life") proved, but Christians should not despair: "If among a thousand capital offenders, it were published that one of them should have a pardon, would not every one hope to be the man?"[55]

It was no wonder, then, that many Puritan clergy and laity admitted to having endured bouts of spiritual discouragement or even despair. In Thomas Shepard's congregation, Nathaniel Eaton, the first head of Harvard College, who had studied briefly with William Ames in the Netherlands, confessed he had once feared that "it was with me as with Esau." Nathaniel Sparrowhawk, a wealthy layman, divulged that "assurance of the Lord's love I have not found." Roger Haynes, son of Connecticut governor John Haynes, worried that he was "another Francis Spira"—a reference to Francesco Spiera (d. 1548), a Venetian lawyer and convert to Protestantism who, after recanting under pressure from Catholic officials, died in extreme despair that he was eternally damned. Spira's story, as David D. Hall has pointed out, was a Puritan bestseller. Massachusetts magistrate Samuel Sewall recorded in his diary that his 15-year-old daughter, Betty, came into his bedroom and reported that she had awakened in terror that she "should go to Hell, [and] was like Spira, not Elected."[56] Hell was, of course, a person's default destination under the Augustinian doctrine of original sin. Tales of terror like Spira's only increased the possibility that overly scrupulous Puritans would despair of being among the small number whom God would rescue from the mass of condemned humanity.[57]

In addition to the theme that few are chosen, a second anxiety-producing motif in Puritan sources, also anticipated in medieval Catholicism, was the fear that partaking unworthily of the Lord's Supper would seal one's fate in hell. "For he that eateth and drinketh unworthily," Paul warned, "eateth and drinketh damnation to himself, not discerning the Lord's body" (1 Cor. 11:29). In the medieval church, stories about the dreadful consequences of receiving the Eucharist in a sinful state were not uncommon. The twelfth-century mystic Hildegard of Bingen had a vision of five categories of communicants ranging from the morally pure to the mortally sinful; the last group approached the altar dripping with blood and smelling of decaying flesh.[58] Catholic scrupulosity stemmed in no small part from the awe with which people regarded the literal eucharistic presence of Christ's body, which the church taught that even the wicked received, if only to their damnation. Puritans emphatically rejected the literal presence of Christ's body and tended to echo William Perkins that sacraments were not "absolutely necessary" but only "confirme[d] the bond mutually before made" in the covenant of grace.[59] Yet as E. Brooks Holifield has argued, the Puritans were "ambidextrous theologians: what the right hand took way, the left hand could retrieve." Thus, they approached the Lord's table with the utmost seriousness, regarding communion as God's pledge of covenantal faithfulness. As the Cambridge divine John Preston, whose preaching helped to convert Thomas Shepard, explained, once God affixed his seal to the covenant in the Lord's Supper, it was "as if he should say, I have promised to forgive you your sins, let the Sacrament witnesse against me, if I performe it not." To be sure, as Holifield has observed, Preston's "rhetoric was more striking than the substance, since the seal obligated God only to save the truly faithful, the elect."[60] But this belief only increased the Puritans' sense of gravity toward communion, which, as Perkins warned, could cause a person to be judged "guilty of high treason" if partaken of unworthily.[61]

Such warnings worked all too well, for many Puritans came to regard the Lord's table as a "zone of danger," to use David Hall's term.[62] Evidence abounds from Massachusetts throughout the colonial period. A female parishioner of Wenham minister John Fiske reported that "[g]oing to the seals she thought to turn back" because she feared eating damnation. The young Michael Wigglesworth, later ordained pastor of Malden, confessed to his diary that the "Lord's Supper being nigh: I am affraid at the thoughts of it" because he sensed that his heart was "so vastly unsutable." The poet Jane Colman Turell, daughter of prominent Boston minister Benjamin Colman and wife of Medford minister Ebenezer Turell, delayed seeking admission to the Lord's Supper because her "[f]ears were great lest 'coming unworthily she should eat and drink Judgement unto her self.'" Turell's apprehension was no surprise, given the determination of many ministers to engender holy fear in their flocks. Jonathan Edwards, preaching to his Northampton congregation in 1731, declared that those who partook unworthily mocked and murdered Christ in the same manner as those who stood by when he was crucified.[63]

A third source of anxiety was the oft-repeated motif of sudden death and judgment. Here too we find a strong continuity with medieval Catholicism. It is a truism that death was ever present for people in premodern times. Epidemics of plague or smallpox could snuff out untold lives with alarming swiftness. Equally fearful for medieval Catholics was any sudden demise that deprived a person of a deathbed "housel and shrift" (the archaic English terms for communion and confession). Persons who suffered a *mors repentina* (sudden death) or *mors improvisa* (unforeseen death) were popularly assumed to be under some divine judgment for sin. The medieval church capitalized on such beliefs to exhort the faithful to repentance before it was too late. For their part, laypeople sought the intercession of one of the saints, such as Barbara or Erasmus (Elmo) of Formiae, who were credited with the power to avert sudden death. Sermons and iconography used imagery of decaying corpses, maggots, and the like to evoke death's horror. Another favorite homiletical theme was the day of doom—the dreaded last judgment—when Christians believed Christ would return, as described in Matthew 25:31–46, and separate the sheep from the goats, pronouncing to the latter, "Depart from me, ye cursed, into everlasting fire."[64]

Puritanism rejected all popular beliefs in the intercession of saints or the efficacy of deathbed sacraments. The earliest New England Puritans, moreover, treated funerals as purely secular and unceremonious affairs, in reaction against medieval masses for the dead.[65] Yet sermonic use of sudden death and judgment continued unabated as ministers sought to "improve," or apply, the motif toward the reformation of the people. In old England, the London plagues of 1603 and 1625 prompted Puritan divines such as Richard Sibbes to exhort the faithful: "What is the plague and other judgements but so many messengers sent to everyone of us to knocke, and our answer must be, Lord I will repent of my evil ways."[66] In New England, the ancient tradition of *memento mori*, a reminder of one's mortality, gradually evolved among the otherwise iconoclastic Puritans into an elaborate tradition of gravestone folk art. Skulls, scythes (representing Time), inscriptions of "fugit hora" (the hour flies) and "memento mori," as well as other carved representations all served a didactic purpose for the living. Preachers, meanwhile, seized upon sudden deaths—especially of the young—for their hortatory value. In 1696, when two Harvard students drowned while skating on a Cambridge pond, Increase Mather urged their grieving classmates to prepare for unexpected death: "nothing is more certain [than] that every man shall Dy, and nothing more uncertain than the Time when."[67]

New England Puritans also fixated on the day of doom, thanks in no small part to the long poem of the same title by Malden pastor Michael Wigglesworth (1631–1705). A tortured individual who as a postgraduate fellow at Harvard had confessed to his diary—in secret code—his "filthy lust" toward his male pupils, Wigglesworth produced in *Day of Doom* (1662) what is arguably the most frightening treatment of predestination in all of American literature. Like the modern-day *Left Behind* novels, which depict the last days, Wigglesworth's poem was a tremendous blockbuster, outselling every other American imprint, save for the Bay Psalm Book, for the next 100 years. (The initial sales made Wigglesworth enough money to pay for a trip to Bermuda to nurse his chronic sore throat!)[68] The poem is essentially an imaginative gloss on Matthew 25, informed by standard Puritan predestinarianism. The last judgment begins when a light breaks forth at midnight, causing sinners to awake "[t]rembling [in] their loyns" and "almost dead with fear." Some "rashly leap into the deep," hoping to escape by drowning themselves. But not even this can save them from the terrible *dies irae* (day of wrath). The quick and the dead, both "renate" (elect) and reprobate, are all brought to the dreadful throne of Christ's judgment. He arrays the sheep on his right and the goats on his left. To the sheep, he speaks with "mild aspect," pronouncing their election and pardon. Then, with ominous implication for the goats, he explains the Augustinian logic of predestination:

> My Grace to one is wrong to none:
> None can Election claim.
> Amongst all those their souls that lose,
> None can Rejection blame.
> He that may chuse, or else refuse,
> all men to save or spill,
> May this man chuse, and that refuse,
> redeeming whom he will.

Christ demands of the reprobate "a strict and straight account" of their sins. They can hide nothing from his all-seeing eye: "All filthy facts, and secret acts, / however closely done, / And long conceal'd, are there reveal'd / before the mid-day Sun." The condemned persons offer various desperate pleas, including the argument that Christ gave them a "pledge" of his love in the bread and wine of the sacrament. Christ retorts with a warning to all who profane these mysteries: "As things divine, they seal and sign / you to perdition." Similarly, those individuals who died sudden deaths protest that they had intended to repent. But Christ replies, "You had a season; what was your Reason / such precious hours to wast[e]?" Finally, Christ pronounces the inevitable sentence to the reprobate multitude—"Depart together from me for ever"—as the "hideous noise of their sad voice / ascendeth to the skies."[69]

Wigglesworth's poem combined all three motifs of predestinarian anxiety—few are chosen, the reprobate eat and drink damnation, and death and judgment can come suddenly—into one exquisitely unnerving portrait. Given the prevalence of the text in New England, it should not surprise us that a few overanxious Puritans were driven to suicidal despair. This was the pathological version of the predestinarian "melancholy" that ministers knew well as an affliction among their flocks. Increase Mather described a perverse wager that he had witnessed in some laypeople, who concluded themselves to be reprobates: "if I destroy my self, I shall have less punishment in Hell,

Michael Wigglesworth headstone, Malden, Mass. Photograph by Peter Thuesen (2004).

than if I lived longer in the World." Mather warned against such logic since persons could never know for sure whether they were reprobate or elect. He pointed to the jailer in Acts 16 who was tempted to kill himself after Paul and Silas escaped amid an earthquake. The jailer's subsequent conversion, Mather explained, indicated that even God's elect are sometimes tempted to suicide. Yet despite the clergy's attempts to show the irrationality of suicide, mini-epidemics of "self-murder" still afflicted New England periodically. "Above four Years ago," Mather admitted, "I saw Occasion to insist on a subject of this Importance, because within the space of but Five Weeks, there had been Five Self-Murders!"[70] Such tales stretched from the founding era to Jonathan Edwards's day. Massachusetts Bay's first governor, John Winthrop, reported in his diary the case of Boston parishioner Anne Hett who, fearing she was probably a reprobate but wracked by the uncertainty of it, "took her little infant and threw it into a well, and then came into the house and said, now she was sure she should be damned, for she had drowned her child." (Miraculously, the child was saved, though Winthrop did not specify how.)[71] During the revivals in Edwards's congregation in 1735, Thomas Stebbins, a man in "great spiritual trouble," unsuccessfully attempted suicide by cutting his throat. (Increase Mather had attributed such cases to the devil, who seemed to be saying: "Stab thyself,—Shoot thyself,—Choak thyself,—& Dy!")[72] A few weeks later, Edwards's uncle, Joseph Hawley, fatally slit his own throat, casting a pall over the revivals. The incident was immortalized by twentieth-century New England poet Robert Lowell, who paraphrased Edwards's own words from his revival account, *A Faithful Narrative* (1737), describing Hawley as one who "durst not entertain much hope of his estate in heaven" and comparing the devil to a peddler who urges, "My friend, Cut your own throat. Cut your own throat. Now! Now!"[73]

CONVERTING AGONY TO ECSTASY

Though today people like Hawley might be diagnosed with clinical depression, that colonial ministers so often connected such cases to anxiety over eternal election suggests the genuine perils of predestinarian psychology. Reformed divines had another name for this affliction—*tentatio praedestinationis* (predestinarian temptation or trial), a term used in the Second Helvetic Confession (1566), which was written by Zwingli's successor at Zurich, Heinrich Bullinger. Conceding that there was "scarcely any other more dangerous" temptation than this, Bullinger assured anxious Christians that it was "beyond doubt that if you believe and are in Christ, you are elected."[74] Indeed, this was the perennial challenge of Puritan piety: how to maintain a healthy anxiety while simultaneously converting it into assurance.[75] In England, Puritan attempts to address this problem spawned an industry of books on "cases of conscience." This publishing boom had the fringe benefit of advancing the careers of a cadre of godly ministers, who became, as Dwight Bozeman has put it, "esteemed consultants in the heavenly science of comfort."[76]

The centerpiece of Puritan casuistry—here used as a technical term for the study of cases of conscience—was the "practical syllogism." Like *a posteriori* proofs of God's existence, which work backward from observable effects, such as the created world, to the existence of a creator, the *syllogismus practicus* sought to prove the election of individuals by appeal to the biblically promised effects in their lives. In its simplest form, the argument was thus: "Whoever believes in Christ is elect.... But I believe.... Therefore I am elect."[77] Belief, or faith, was just one of the promised effects; the others were part of the "golden chain" (based on Rom. 8:30), made famous by William Perkins. As Perkins elaborated the logic, the entire chain of events— election, vocation (calling), faith, adoption, justification, sanctification, and glorification—was like a series of "inseparable companions" that "goe hand in hand." If a person could be assured that she had experienced one of them, then the rest would unfailingly follow.[78] Similarly, experiencing any of the later links in the chain was reliable evidence that a person was already the beneficiary of the first—election. Variations of this *a posteriori* logic appeared throughout the writings of England's Reformed divines. Richard Baxter, in his posthumously published casuistical manual, *The Signs and Causes of Melancholy*, stated a succinct proof: "To repent is the best way to prove that I am elected to repent." Joseph Alleine, whose ominously titled *Alarme to Unconverted Sinners* (1672) appeared in many editions on both sides of the Atlantic, balanced warnings of hellfire with this reassurance: "Whatever the decrees of Heaven be, I am sure, that if I repent and believe, I shall be saved; and that if I repent not, I shall be damn'd. Is not here plain ground for thee?" Alleine appealed to a series of biblical passages promising salvation to those who believed. "Whatever God's purposes be," he concluded, "I am sure his promises be true."[79] Decades earlier, Arthur Dent, in his immensely successful *Plaine Mans Path-way*, had pointed to Paul's comment about the language of "Abba, Father" (Rom. 8:15–16) as similar proof that believing Christians were truly adopted by God: "How can a man in truth call God his Father, when he saith, Our Father which art in heaven: And yet doubt whether [God] be his Father or no? For if God indeed be our Father, & we his children, how can we perish?" Dent insisted that believers must look to Christ's promises, not to themselves, for encouragement. He offered the metaphor of a man bound by secure ropes to the world's highest steeple: when he looks down at the earth far below, he is seized by fear; but when he looks upward and sees himself still securely bound, he is reassured. Similarly, "when we looke downward to ourselves, we have doubts & fears: but when we looke upward to Christ, and the truth of his promises, we feele our selves cock-sure, and cease to doubt any more."[80] Of course, the practical syllogism required looking both downward at oneself and upward at Christ, which meant that the Christian life would always be a mixture of doubt and assurance. But since assurance rested on the promises of Christ himself, even a predestinarian, it seemed, could be "cock-sure."

Puritans on the American side of the Atlantic also rushed to reassure anxious souls with a variety of arguments designed to supplement the practical syllogism. If your parents are elect, Increase Mather counseled, then chances are you are too, for the "vein of election doth run through the loins of godly parents for the most part." Puritan poet Anne Bradstreet found comfort in the opposite argument—that election was individual, not hereditary. What about good parents of bad children, and bad parents of good children? We should be glad that God "takes and chooses when and where and whom he pleases."[81] Increase Mather's son Cotton warned readers never to assume that they were lost. He described the case of a wise physician who once heard a man despair, "If I am Elected, I shall be Saved; If I am not Elected, no care of mine will signify any thing to Save me." When the man later took ill and became the physician's patient, the good doctor told him: "Sir, If it be Decreed, that you shall Recover your Health, you shall do so; but if it be not so Decreed, no Counsels, or Methods of mine will recover you; why should I trouble my self any further about you?" The man immediately saw his error, and a "Double, and therefore, an Happy cure, was wrought upon him!"[82] Benjamin Colman, meanwhile, urged the faithful to take comfort in melancholy. As an affliction brought on by Satan, it proved that the devil hated those persons because they were elect. Earlier, Samuel Willard had insisted that even an unregenerate person still mired in a state of sin should not conclude himself to be a reprobate because it was never too late to realize God's electing grace. (Back in England, William Perkins had taken this idea so seriously that he sometimes accompanied prisoners to the gallows in hopes they would reveal last-minute signs of election.)[83]

In the end, however, the practical syllogism and other casuistry may have provided less assurance than the *P* of the proverbial TULIP. Perseverance— the simple idea that once elect, always elect—gave those who believed it a profound sense of security, as we saw earlier in this chapter. To be sure, a person first had to convince himself that he was elect, but if he could do so, then the doctrine of perseverance was an incomparable source of consolation. As Arthur Dent put it, not even "a thousand infirmities, nay all the sinnes in the world, nor all the divells in hell" could overthrow God's election. Similarly, Cotton Mather urged: "Look Forwards. Will the Lord Repent of His Choice? Never; never. 'Tis unalterable."[84]

Indeed, for all the hellfire and damnation in their sermons, the Puritans were capable of extraordinary ecstasy as they contemplated the unwavering love of Christ. Sometimes, this led to strange juxtapositions, as when Thomas Shepard described Christ as a dominating bridegroom who caused the faithful to tremble even as his breasts offered milk and comfort.[85] The same juxtaposition is still visible in New England graveyards, where alongside headstones adorned with skulls and crossbones, one occasionally runs across stylized images of breasts.[86] Even more obviously erotic imagery was not uncommon in Puritan writings. Puritan minister and poet Edward Taylor wrote that the redeemed would "ly in Christ's bosom, and be ravished with his dearest love, and most intimate embraces." He imagined a "featherbed...with gospel pillows, sheets, and sweet perfumes," where Christ and the believer together would conceive the "babe of grace." Cotton Mather spoke of being "swallowed up with the ecstasies of [Christ's] love." Jonathan Edwards revealed flashes of an almost medieval mysticism—Puritan ecstasy, like Puritan agony, had Catholic parallels—in his frequent references to "sweetness" and "honey" and his rapturous meditations on the elect's consummated union with Christ. "Eat, O friend; yea, drink; yea, be drunken," Edwards imagined Christ saying, echoing the invitation of Canticles 5:1.[87]

THE ECSTATIC AGONY OF PREDESTINATION

What, then, are we to conclude about the mass of scholastic subtleties, contradictory images, and conflicting emotions that made up predestination's Puritan career? In the final analysis, the irrepressibly dialectical Puritans aimed for a dialectic in their everyday piety as well, alternating self-abasement with meditation on heavenly joys—a regimen attested in such Catholic devotional masters as Bernard of Clairvaux, Thomas à Kempis, and Francis de Sales.[88] For the Puritans, this spiritual discipline aimed for what we might call an *ecstatic agony*. Unlike a sudden, acute pain caused by injury or disease, ecstatic agony was the constructive pain of ongoing struggle—the spiritual equivalent of the bodybuilder's motto "no pain, no gain." It is worth noting that the word "agony" comes from the Greek root for contest; similarly, an *agonothete* was the official who presided over the public games in ancient Greece. Agony in this sense was not always distinguishable from ecstasy, especially since the ultimate goal of any contest was to experience the exhilarating rush of victory. In fact, one of the definitions of agony in the *Oxford English Dictionary* is "intensity or paroxysm of pleasure." This might well describe the subjective experience of the Puritan who, after arduous spiritual struggle, finally reached a new high point of predestinarian assurance.

But that sense of assurance would always remain paradoxical. As historian Michael McGiffert has put it, the "central paradox" of a Puritan's piety was thus: "the less assured he felt, the more assurance he actually had." The Puritan divines themselves explained it similarly. For Thomas Shepard, "the greatest part of a Christian's grace lies in mourning for the want of it." Edward Dering, who once dared in a sermon before Queen Elizabeth to chide her personally for the sorry state of the English church, described the paradox of fearing hell: "the nearer we feele it, the further we are from it." William Perkins called it "holy desperation," a state of mind that could only subsist in the elect.[89] This "combination of dis-ease and comfort," to quote historian Peter Kaufman, took on therapeutic, even theatrical qualities. Shakespeare's Hamlet, among other tortured Elizabethan characters, knew it well.[90]

Ecstatic agony was both the strength and the weakness of Puritanism. Its strength was its productivity. Whether or not Weber was right that Puritan angst was a decisive contributor to capitalism, the Puritans produced a corpus of writings whose intellectual depth and devotional power have rarely been equaled in modern U.S. religion. The last great theologian in the American Puritan tradition, Jonathan Edwards, left an immense body of treatises, sermons, letters, biblical commentaries, and miscellaneous reflections that still engage scholars and latter-day Calvinists today.[91] The weakness of ecstatic agony as a subjective goal, however, was twofold. First, it entailed something of a Catch-22. If you were not anxious about your eternal election, you were obviously not elect. But continuous (or at least cyclical) anxiety about election denied you the very comfort that predestination was supposed to bring. Comfort, in other words, could be notoriously elusive in this system. Predestinarian anxiety, as we have seen, all too easily passed from salutary struggle to genuine distress. The second problem of ecstatic agony as a spiritual goal was its sheer intensity—what we might call (with thanks to Dwight Bozeman) the strain of the precisianists. Not everyone was a spiritual marathon runner like Edwards or an accomplished soliloquist like Hamlet. Many Americans, including many Puritan laypeople, were happy simply muddling through. They looked to religion for the sort of automatic and tangible comforts that medieval laypeople once sought in merely watching the Mass. But such a view of the sacrament was the very thing Puritan clerics were bent on dispelling.

By Edwards's day, New Englanders typically regarded the Puritan synthesis in one of four ways, each of which foreshadowed a widespread attitude toward predestination in later American culture. The first was a sacramental attitude that resisted the churches' system of reserving certain benefits for persons judged to be "visible saints" (people whose faith suggested that they were also among the "invisible saints" of the elect, known only to God). The sacramental attitude demanded, if not a return to England's umbrella-like parish system, at the least an easier way for whole families to be incorporated into the local congregation. This was the origin of the famous Half-Way Covenant in New England. As second-generation colonists came of age, many declined to submit to the test of a conversion relation for full church membership. Yet because they had been baptized as infants, they wanted the same benefit for their own children. The Half-Way Covenant, widely adopted after a synod endorsed it in 1662, allowed baptized (half-way) members—those who agreed to "own" the baptismal covenant made by their parents and abide by the church's norms—to present their own children for baptism. One minister, Edwards's grandfather Solomon Stoddard, went even further and opened not only baptism but also the Lord's Supper to all persons not leading openly scandalous lives. He reasoned that the church could never reliably distinguish elect from reprobate and that the sacraments ought to be freely offered in the hope that recipients would ultimately be converted and saved. When Edwards (Stoddard's successor at Northampton) announced in 1749 that he was discontinuing his grandfather's open communion policy, an uproar ensued. The next year, Edwards's congregation fired him. Like the Elizabethan godly ministers, Edwards was a precisianist, and this was his downfall. His parishioners proved themselves to be "strikingly premodern," as Anne Brown and David Hall have argued, in their desire for an automatic, sacramental incorporation of the family unit into the church.[92] This stance would become far more common in American culture in the next century as millions of Catholic immigrants arrived, bringing with them the medieval sacramental system that incorporated family members even beyond the grave, through the ideas of purgatory and prayers for the dead.

While the sacramental attitude denied the necessity (or even the possibility) of discerning the likely elect, the second attitude insisted that saints could be identified not through angst-ridden striving but by using an altogether more radical method. This was the antinomian option, which arose as a backlash against the disciplinary religion of the precisianists.[93] The term *antinomian* (meaning "against the law") was an epithet used by the orthodox, but it contained a grain of truth. This perspective repudiated all legalistic means of assurance and instead looked to the immediate witness of the Spirit as the distinguishing mark of the elect. The Holy Spirit, in other words, communicated directly with the chosen, giving them an unparalleled, indeed supernatural, sense of assurance. In New England, the seeds of this attitude were in the thought of the ever-elusive John Cotton, but his follower Anne Hutchinson (1591–1643) went in a more radical direction, subverting the male clerical hierarchy by claiming to have received the ongoing power of prophecy.[94] For this, Hutchinson was banished from Massachusetts Bay. She later died in an Indian massacre, but her antinomian idea of the immediate witness (or "seal") of the Spirit would live on as a perennial challenge to orthodox predestinarianism. As Douglas Winiarski has shown, manuscript accounts from the Great Awakening reveal a surprising number of laypeople who experienced entranced visions of themselves transported to heaven, where Christ showed them their names written in the Book of Life (Rev. 20:12). Through such visions, laypeople overturned the precisianists' ecstatic agony and replaced it with sheer ecstasy. Enraptured laypeople also denied the orthodox assumption that the Book of Life was sealed until the Second Coming. Ironically, it was the supercharged revival preaching of orthodox figures like Edwards that led some people to such out-of-body ecstasy. Edwards and many of his colleagues soon grew fearful of the disruptive potential of trances and visions, and they excised or discredited references to such phenomena in revival accounts. But the ecstatic laypeople would have the last laugh, for in modern times, Pentecostalism would subvert predestination in much the same way—by claiming a literal Spirit blessing as the infallible mark of the saved.[95]

The third attitude toward the Puritan synthesis was that of Arminians and other advocates of free-will theology in its various forms. The Arminian opponents of unconditional predestination had been the bugbear of Puritans since the Synod of Dort, but by Edwards's day, fears were rising that Arminianism (or, more accurately in many cases, an incipient liberalism) was making inroads even in the orthodox preserve of New England Congregationalism. In 1734, when it appeared that the church at Springfield, Massachusetts, was on the verge of calling a reputed Arminian, Robert Breck, as pastor, Edwards and his allies attempted unsuccessfully to block Breck's settlement by invoking the authority of the local ministerial association, which had recently voted to require clergy to subscribe to the Westminster Confession or a comparably orthodox statement. The controversy quickly turned into a pamphlet war, pitting Edwards and his allies against a group of Boston ministers intent on defending the traditional autonomy of local congregations in choosing ministers. Edwards's readiness to empower a presbyterian-style ministerial association to enforce predestinarian orthodoxy revealed the extent of his suspicion that the Dort-Westminster five-point standard was facing a new threat. His fears were not unfounded. While Breck himself disclaimed any Arminian sympathies, other brands of Christians were arriving in colonial America, from high-church Anglican missionaries to revivalistic Methodist circuit riders, who did not regard "Arminian" as a dirty word. As we will see in the next chapter, these new Arminians were the vanguard of a great tide of anti-Calvinism that would transform American religion in the antebellum period.[96]

Lest we forget, however, the fourth attitude toward the Puritan synthesis was that of the latter-day Edwardseans and sundry other Calvinists, who would remain doggedly determined to defend unconditional predestination as, in their view, the only truly biblical option on the theological spectrum. It was once assumed, thanks to Perry Miller and others, that Puritanism by Edwards's day was already an outworn system that he futilely, though brilliantly, sought to redescribe in terms convincing to the Age of Reason. Miller appreciated Edwards for the same reason the twentieth-century theologian H. Richard Niebuhr did: his uncannily modern sense of tragedy and his almost Freudian apprehension of how humans are governed by obscure passions beyond their control.[97] Yet Edwards's five-point Calvinism was, to Miller, a relic of seventeenth-century scholasticism. What Miller failed to appreciate, or perhaps preferred to ignore, was the perennial appeal of strict, confessional predestinarianism to certain segments of the American religious population. In the late twentieth and early twenty-first centuries, the term *Puritan* is a badge of honor for a minority of conservative Protestants, who have republished classics by Shepard and other ministers and have even adopted "Puritan" as an institutional designation (witness the Puritan Reformed Theological Seminary, founded in 1995 in Grand Rapids, Michigan). Thus, the career of Puritan predestinarianism is not so much a story of declension—though, to be sure, five-point Calvinism lost favor in much of New England by the early nineteenth century—but a story of sporadic resurgence, a tale as winding and fascinating as the logic of Puritanism itself.

CHAPTER 3

"Shall the Hellish Doctrine Stand?"

Enlightenment Doubts and Evangelical Division

All objects are said to appear yellow to the jaundiced eye. Predestination is to the mind what the jaundice is to the body. The whole Bible appears tinctured with a sickly, yellow hue, when the predestinarian looks into it, especially if he be of a morose and vindictive temper, as most commonly is the case.

—*Bishop Samuel Seabury,* Discourses on Several Important Subjects
(published posthumously, 1798)

The doctrine of predestination, as maintained by the rigid Calvinists, is very shocking and ought utterly to be abhorred, because it charges the most holy God with being the author of sin.

—*Susanna Wesley,* letter to her son John *(1725)*

IN THE SUMMER of 1763, Great Britain had just prevailed over France in the Seven Years' War and was the world's dominant colonial power. Such good fortune might be enough to convince any Englishman of God's electing favor, but to the 22-year-old Anglican curate in charge of Blagdon parish in southwest England, Britannia's might was no match for

God's wrath in a thunderstorm. Traveling on foot near his home, the young cleric found himself scrambling for shelter from the lightning and pelting rain that suddenly came down one day as he was passing by the Burrington Combe, a rugged limestone gorge. Finding refuge inside the cave, he caught his breath and discovered on the ground beside him a playing card left by some previous visitor. Using this profane scrap of paper, the curate was inspired to jot down some sacred stanzas exalting God's preserving grace amid the storm:

> Rock of Ages, cleft for me,
> Let me hide myself in thee;
> Let the water and the blood,
> From thy riven side which flowed,
> Be of sin the double cure,
> Cleanse me from its guilt and pow'r.

So began one of the most beloved hymns in the history of evangelical Protestantism, a song that would be sung in countless revival tents on both sides of the Atlantic. The pious young cleric was Augustus Montague Toplady, whose name would become synonymous in evangelical circles with "Rock of Ages."[1]

Less well known, or conveniently ignored by his later admirers, is that Toplady was a militant controversialist and bitter enemy of another evangelical great, John Wesley, founder of the Methodist tradition. In 1778, as Toplady lay dying from tuberculosis, one of his last acts was to dispel a rumor that he desired to reconcile with Wesley. "I most sincerely hope," Toplady wrote, "my last hours will be much better employed, than in conversing with such a man."[2] Toplady's death did not end the dispute, however, which would be carried on by followers of the two men. Even "Rock of Ages," which is sung today no less by Methodists than by other Protestants, would be drawn into the fray as the opposing parties made sly theological redactions to the text. Scholars, meanwhile, would come to doubt the cherished local tradition about the hymn's origin, a story that looks suspiciously more like hagiography than history.[3]

Why did Toplady and Wesley despise each other, and what was so controversial about "Rock of Ages"? The problem, in a word, was predestination. Toplady, a zealous Calvinist, and Wesley, a zealous Arminian, clashed over the time-worn question of whether God elects persons absolutely or conditionally. To Wesley, absolute predestination made God into a fearfully arbitrary tyrant. Surely, a just and loving God would save those persons he knew would cooperate with him in faith. To Toplady, if election depended in any sense on human cooperation, then salvation lost its rock-like certainty. The third stanza of his famous hymn expressed humans' utter inability before God:

> Nothing in my hand I bring,
> Simply to thy Cross I cling;
> Naked, come to thee for dress;
> Helpless, look to thee for grace;
> Foul, I to the fountain fly;
> Wash me, Savior, or I die.

Not a few singers of the hymn over the years have been uncomfortable with its absolutist implications. The Mormons, whom we will meet in the next chapter as heirs of early American anti-Calvinism, omit the third stanza from their hymnal. Another line from the original hymn, "Not the labor of my hands/Can fulfill thy law's demands," appears subtly modified in the Latter-day Saints' hymnal as "Not the labors of my hands/Can fill *all* thy law's demands."[4] Similarly, Methodists have long been familiar with another toned-down version of the hymn, which removes the stark images of humans as naked and helpless.[5]

This chapter will explore how early American evangelicals, particularly those who participated in the transatlantic religious revivals of the eighteenth century, came to blows over predestination. The conflict arose not only from native evangelical personalities and ideas but also from forces outside of the movement, including the Age of Reason, which cast doubt on predestination as well as on the associated doctrines of hell and providence. We will encounter some of the more radical American Enlightenment figures in chapter 4, but in the present chapter we will see their moderate forerunners in the Anglican latitudinarians, whose writings were widely read and discussed in colonial America. A more obvious catalyst of conflict was Anglicanism's high-church wing, which had its own political reasons for opposing predestination and which influenced the eighteenth century's most important anti-predestinarian thinker, John Wesley. This convergence of factors and factions left the infant evangelical movement in Anglo Protestantism permanently divided over the same intractable doctrine that had bedeviled Christians since Augustine.

THAT "FATAL" DOCTRINE: ANGLICANS AGAINST PREDESTINATION

Long before the first high-church Anglicans dared to challenge the New England way, Anglicans in the mother country had perfected the art of predestinarian satire. During the mid-seventeenth century, royalist opponents of Cromwell's regime published anonymous tracts ridiculing the predestinarian views of the Puritan establishment and the commission of Triers, which was charged with examining the Calvinist orthodoxy of all candidates for the ministry. Such an inquest was the subject of a satirical dialogue by Laurence Womock, the future bishop of St. David's, entitled *The Examination of Tilenus before the Triers; in Order to His Intended Settlement in the Office of a Publick Preacher in the Common-wealth of Utopia* (1658). The names of Womock's fictional examiners indicate his own attitude toward predestination: Dr. Absolute, Mr. Fatalitie, Mr. Fri-Babe, Dr. Dam-Man, Mr. Narrow-Grace, Mr. Preterition, and so on. The hapless protagonist, Tilenus, pleads with the Triers to understand that absolute predestination militates against "Conversion of an Infidel, and the correction of the carnall, and the quickning of the careless, and the consolation of the afflicted." He also complains that predestination destroys the efficacy of the sacraments and even of prayer. Ultimately, the Triers cite these opinions, along with Tilenus's failure to study adequately the works of "Mr. Calvin and Mr. Perkins," in rejecting his application for ordination.[6]

In real life, the Triers were disbanded and Puritans put on the defensive at the Restoration in 1660. Two years later, the Act of Uniformity reinstated the Book of Common Prayer for public worship, required all clergy to be ordained by bishops, and excluded nonconformists from political office. Some 2,000 clergy were ejected for failing to conform. Though the Toleration Act (1689) granted dissenters freedom of assembly, they were still barred from holding public office. By the turn of the eighteenth century, outspoken Calvinists were becoming a rare breed within the Church of England.[7] A notable exception was John Edwards (1637–1716), who doggedly defended absolute predestination from the charge that it drove people to despair. Arminians instead should despair, Edwards insisted, because their salvation depended on their own free choice rather than on God's election. "It is certain," he concluded, "that we are safer in God's Hands than in our own." Yet even Edwards (whose works Cotton Mather once recommended as an antidote to "Fashionable Divinity")[8] was sensitive to his fellow Anglicans' accusations that absolute predestination amounted to fatalism. To the dismay of some of his supporters, he once suggested a surprising expedient for reconciling strict predestination with those Arminian-friendly passages of scripture that implied free choice. Perhaps, he speculated, there is a "third sort" of persons who are neither elect nor reprobate but who are "in a state of Probation." God leaves himself the liberty to decide their fate based on their conduct, just as he left the fate of the unrepentant cities in Matthew 11:20–24 open to their repentance.[9]

John Edwards nevertheless maintained his reputation as one of England's stoutest defenders of predestination, and in this role, he became a favorite target of a new breed of anti-predestinarians—the nonjurors, or those clergy who refused to take the oath of allegiance to William of Orange after he overthrew England's last Catholic king, James II, in the Glorious Revolution of 1688. While not seeking to return the English church to Catholicism, the nonjurors nevertheless believed that they had taken a sacred oath to James II and his hereditary successors. They also believed in the divine right of kings, a royalist ideology that easily melded with a high-church, sacramental aesthetic. To many of the nonjurors, the Glorious Revolution looked like a foreign conspiracy—William was a Dutch Calvinist—to revive the five points of Dort and Westminster as the official English creed. Consequently, it was a nonjuror, the Irish Anglican divine Charles Leslie (1650–1722), who produced some of the era's most colorful anti-predestinarian polemics. In his biweekly newspaper, the *Rehearsal* (1704–1709), Leslie railed against John Edwards, whom he accused of enlisting Dutch aid to "bring us all back again to the rigid and most abhorrent Calvinism of predestination" and thus "throw men into despair." Calvinist predestination, declared Leslie, "is more fatal to the souls of men than idolatry itself, or the worst form of popery." The doctrine's effects among the "common presbyterians" were terrible, filling their heads with abstruse notions, only to leave them crying in vain on their deathbeds for assurance of salvation. The doctrine, moreover, illogically attempted to explain God's activity by using a human standard of time. Leslie insisted that Christians should leave the "fore" out of "foreordain" when they spoke of the divine punishment of the wicked, since even "Dr. Edwards" would acknowledge that "there is no fore or after in God."[10]

The nonjuring schism, in which Leslie and some 400 other nonjuring clergy (including Archbishop of Canterbury William Sancroft) were deprived of their livings, did not quell the enthusiasm of New Englanders for William and Mary's revolution, which most regarded as a providential deliverance from the papal Antichrist. Yet in the first decades of the eighteenth century, as word spread of periodic Jacobite plots to install James II's son (and later, his grandson) on the throne, many New Englanders began to fear a high-church, Jacobite fifth column in America.[11] Their fears seemed confirmed when a Boston bookseller, the Anglican John Checkley, reprinted in 1719 a treatise by Charles Leslie arguing that church government by bishops was the only apostolically pure model.[12] In republishing the book, Checkley in effect declared New England's Congregational (and thus non-episcopally ordained) ministers illegitimate. But Checkley did not stop there. A year later, he recycled verbatim whole sections of Leslie's *Rehearsal* in a tract purporting to be a dialogue between an "honest country-man" and his minister. The fictional parson counsels the layman, who is concerned about his eternal destiny, not to be taken in by John Edwards and others who would infect the church with "Dutch Presbyterian Notions concerning Election and Predestination." Repeating Leslie's argument, the minister insists that the *pre-* in predestination is nonsensical since everything is present to God.[13] Clearly an Arminian, the minister explains that while God's grace is necessary for every good work, "something is still left for us to do. We must work with Him, because He works in us both to will, and to do."[14]

Checkley's publishing efforts eventually landed him before the Massachusetts General Court, which fined him £50 for seditious libel. By then, however, other Anglicans were making even bigger waves in New England. In 1716, an Anglican missionary, George Pigot, had begun canvassing southern Connecticut and later met repeatedly with seven local ministers, including Yale College rector Timothy Cutler and former tutor Samuel Johnson. The seven Congregational clergy proved ripe unto harvest, for on commencement day at Yale in September 1722, Cutler signaled their Anglican sympathies by concluding the ceremony with a biblical phrase favored by the high-church set, "And let all the people say, Amen." The ensuing uproar, as historian Henry F. May memorably described it, was akin to what might have happened in the twentieth century if the entire Yale football team had joined the Communist Party.[15] Yale's trustees, convened by Connecticut governor Gurdon Saltonstall, immediately dismissed Cutler and voted to require of future rectors and tutors evidence of "opposition to Armenian [*sic*] & prelatical Corruptions."[16] Meanwhile, the *Boston News-Letter* reported that Yale College, which had been "set up...according to Scripture Rule, Free of Humane Traditions and Impositions...is now become Corrupt." The aging Increase Mather, holding forth at Boston's Old North Church, bewailed the "Connecticut Apostacie," and within a year, the shock of creeping infidelity contributed largely to his death, according to his son Cotton and the poet Edward Taylor, who opined that "Cutler's Cutlary gave th' killing Stob."[17]

Cutler and Johnson subsequently sailed to England, where they were reordained as Anglican priests at St. Martin-in-the-Fields, London, by the bishop of Norwich. Upon their return to America, Cutler became rector of Christ Church (Old North) in Boston, where he lived out the rest of his days as a thorn in the side of the establishment. The more temperate Johnson, meanwhile, served as rector of Christ Church, Stratford, Connecticut, until becoming the founding president of King's College (later, Columbia University) in New York in 1754. He also defended an essentially Arminian theology in printed exchanges with predestinarian opponents.[18] One lively debate ensued when fellow Connecticut minister Samuel Cooke published a sermon on Exodus 33:19 ("I…will be gracious to whom I will be gracious"), arguing that those who denied that salvation was entirely from God's "mere sovereign, arbitrary good Pleasure" incurred "a very black Mark" of divine disfavor.[19] Johnson fired back that the Calvinist doctrine of absolute, unconditional predestination was "manifestly repugnant to the general Drift of the whole Word of God" and that he could no more assent to it than to the proposition "that 2 and 2 are equal to 5." Though God exercised absolute sovereignty in the distribution of "Talents and Favours" to individuals, Johnson argued, it was entirely "out of the Question" that he would distribute future rewards and punishments without regard to a person's response or behavior. God's goodness, in fact, "must be a Law to Him which he cannot vary"; it in effect *compels* him to predestine persons conditionally and to enable them to respond to his offer of salvation. Any "Man of Common Sense" could plainly see that scripture abounds with "exceeding great and precious promises" (2 Pet. 1:4) of redemption to those who would believe ("ask and ye shall receive"; "knock and it shall be opened"; "come unto me…and I will give you rest"). The doctrine of absolute, unconditional predestination ignored the "plain, easy, and obvious" sense of these verses and instead ensnared unwitting Christians in the "empty Cob-webs of Scholastic Metaphysics."[20]

Johnson's statements provoked a response from another future college president, Presbyterian minister Jonathan Dickinson, who was then securing a charter for the College of New Jersey (later, Princeton). To Dickinson, God's absolute and inscrutable sovereignty was empirically verifiable by the fact that most of the world's people were left in a state of "Ignorance, Impiety, and abominable Idolatry." That so many people died unaware of the gospel, while other persons who were no more deserving received the good news of salvation, proved that God was not bound by human standards of fairness. Dickinson hastened to add, however, that God's sovereignty put no one under a "compulsive Necessity" to sin. Though all things happened according to God's eternal counsel, this in no way infringed upon the liberty of human creatures, who acted under no physical duress or compulsion.[21]

The hint of defensiveness in Dickinson's response was a theme that would be replayed increasingly as the century wore on. Neither predestinarians nor their opponents wanted to be accused of denying human liberty. On the surface, of course, predestinarians labored under a greater burden to prove that their doctrine of divine sovereignty was compatible with genuine human free will. Yet it was hardly a foregone conclusion that Anglicans were the greater champions of liberty. Despite their rhetoric about human freedom, Anglicans at their core believed in absolute obedience to God, king, lords, and bishops—a traditional hierarchy they regarded as the only divinely instituted safeguard of social stability. The seventeenth-century Puritan revolution had upset that order and had revived a strong predestinarianism that theoretically transcended all class distinctions. As historian John Woolverton has aptly put it, "anyone could call himself God's chosen vessel and persevere in endless and stubborn independence." From an Anglican perspective, an overemphasis on predestination threatened to undermine the laity's patriotic allegiance to the royal heads of state and church. "Anglicans," Woolverton explains, "simply did not trust the common herd to behave patriotically of their own accord."[22]

The same royalist inclinations that led Anglicans, paradoxically, to trumpet liberty against the tyranny of the Calvinist God also led them to push for a resident bishop in America, provoking sometimes hysterical opposition from other colonists.[23] By the time the first bishop, Samuel Seabury of Connecticut, was finally consecrated in 1784, the American Revolution had occurred and the Church of England in America had become the Protestant Episcopal Church. Seabury shared his predecessors' distaste for absolute predestination. A high churchman sympathetic to the nonjuror tradition, he was consecrated in Scotland by nonjuring bishops to avoid taking the oath to the English Crown, which his U.S. citizenship prohibited. Against some of his less high-church Anglican brethren in New England, he advocated weekly communion and spoke highly of sacramental efficacy: "when we worthily receive baptism, we obtain through Christ remission of all past sins, so when we worthily communicate at God's altar, we obtain remission of all sins committed since baptism."[24] Such a view led him away from any version of predestination that would render the sacraments merely "seals" of a condition (election or reprobation) that already existed. He wanted to leave the door ajar for genuine human cooperation with God—a tacitly Arminian position that put him at odds with New England Calvinists. Seabury's Anglican colleague Thomas Bradbury Chandler, in fact, once urged him to compose a refutation of Jonathan Edwards's *Freedom of the Will* (1754), which Chandler derided as the "Connecticut Alcoran" because of its alleged resemblance to the reputed fatalism of Islam's holy book.[25] Seabury evidently had no relish for such a project, for he never wrote the refutation. The first sustained attack on Edwards's treatise ultimately came from within the Congregational ranks, in a book by New Haven minister James Dana. Of Dana's response, Chandler quipped to Samuel Johnson: "If the Dissenters will confute one another, it will save us the trouble."[26]

THE NEW "LATITUDE": TEMPERING PREDESTINATION, DOWNSIZING HELL

As a sacramental protest against predestination, high-church Episcopalianism would gain new life in the Anglo-Catholic movement of the nineteenth century, which would restore more elaborate eucharistic ritual and church furnishings to many Anglican parishes on both sides of the Atlantic. Coincident with the revival of Gothic architecture, the nineteenth-century high-church revival contributed greatly to the beauty that one famous erstwhile Calvinist, Harriet Beecher Stowe, would find in the Episcopal Church, as we will see in the next chapter. Nevertheless, high sacramentalism would always remain a minority perspective among American Protestants, who tended to be suspicious of anything resembling Catholicism. A more insidious and pervasive threat to predestination would be the movement known among historians as latitudinarianism, which also entered American culture via the Anglican tradition. Originally a term of reproach among its detractors, latitudinarianism was so called because of the range of opinions it tolerated on doctrinal issues once treated as life-and-death matters.[27] Born of the backlash against Puritan radicalism in Restoration England, latitudinarianism valued moderation over zeal and morality over dogma. The movement's high priests included John Tillotson (1630–1694), whom William III appointed archbishop of Canterbury after the nonjuror William Sancroft was deposed, and Gilbert Burnet (1643–1715), the bishop of Salisbury. In contrast to the hard-edged preaching style cultivated by many Puritans, the more polite parlance of the latitudinarians referred to God as the "Supreme Architect," the visible universe as "stupendous" and "sublime," and religion as a matter of "essential truths." Where Puritan predestinarians emphasized the supremacy of biblical revelation, latitudinarians spoke of the knowledge of God that could also be gained from nature and from human reason.[28] Tillotson's sermons, in particular, enjoyed a remarkable afterlife in eighteenth-century America as colonists, even in the Calvinist citadel of New England, cultivated British refinement. Indeed, as Norman Fiering has argued, the latitudinarian sermon "was the primary medium by which New England was eased into the enlightenment."[29]

The Enlightenment's aversion to uncompromising orthodoxies shone through in the latitudinarian attitude toward predestination. The most notable statement on the subject was Bishop Burnet's *Exposition of the Thirty-nine Articles* (1699), which attempted to demonstrate that Anglicanism's founding confession permitted latitude on controversial doctrinal matters. Of all the disputed questions in divinity, Burnet explained, predestination was "one of the longest, the subtilest, and indeed the most intricate." In the Church of England, Calvinists and Arminians had long contended with each other over this issue, and each position had both advantages and disadvantages. Burnet believed that Calvinism's advantage was its tendency to ascribe all honor to God, which usually promoted a salutary humility among the faithful; its disadvantage was its adherents' occasional temptation to "false Security and Sloth" about their own election. Arminianism's advantage was its sense of personal responsibility for sin, which tended to promote virtuous action; its disadvantage was its adherents' occasional propensity for trusting their own abilities too much and God's too little. The common fault of both Calvinists and Arminians was to "charge one another with the Consequences of their Opinions, as if they were truly their Tenets." The division between the two parties admitted of no final resolution, Burnet argued. Indeed, he added, the same irreconcilable difference existed among Catholics in the division between the disciples of Augustine and the disciples of Molina. The "Knot of the whole Difficulty" was whether God elected persons with or without foresight of their conduct. Fortunately, claimed Burnet, article 17 of the Thirty-nine Articles allowed both sides to maintain their opinions. Though it was "very probable" that the framers of the confession accepted the Calvinist doctrine that predestination was absolute and not linked to foreseen merit, they did not say so explicitly in article 17, which simply stated that before the foundation of the world, God "decreed by his Counsel, secret to us" to choose certain persons for salvation. Thus, Arminians could also subscribe to the document without renouncing their commitment to conditional predestination.[30]

Though Burnet refrained from taking sides in his explication of article 17, he could not resist noting in the book's preface his own preference for "the Doctrine of the Greek Church"—a reference to John Chrysostom and others who, like the later Arminians, tied predestination to foreknowledge. Augustine, Burnet insisted, had departed from this doctrine and formed a new system. Yet despite his own disagreement with Augustinianism, Burnet appealed to his Calvinist readers to examine his *Exposition* to see if he had not represented their opinions both with "Truth and Candor" and with "all possible Advantages." "There is no part of this whole Work, in which I have labour'd with more Care, and have writ in a more uncommon Method, than concerning Predestination."[31]

Burnet's ambitions as a great conciliator were only partially realized. His fellow latitudinarians loved the *Exposition*, and in America the book was still being used a century later by presiding Episcopal bishop William White in instructing candidates for the ministry.[32] But in his own day, Burnet's commentary enraged partisans on both sides of the Calvinist-Arminian divide. The high-church Arminians, who then dominated the lower house of the Church of England's governing body, the Convocation of Canterbury, attempted unsuccessfully to push through a formal censure of the book in 1701.[33] In America the following year, Cotton Mather undoubtedly had Burnet in mind when, in an address to fellow ministers defending Calvinist predestinarianism, he complained of the "Late Attempts to make the Articles…of the Church of England consistent with the most palpable contradictions hereunto." It was "high time," Mather declared, for Christians to stand up for the Calvinist doctrines of grace and to beware of the fashionable books "scattered every where" that were trafficking in alternative theologies.[34]

Yet in seeking to neutralize the acids of old dogmatic controversies, the latitudinarians did not stop with the doctrines of grace. The doctrine of eternal torment in hell had always lent predestination its urgency. Hell raised predestination from a purely academic question to a matter that inspired palpable fear in the faithful, jolting them from complacency and goading them to make their "calling and election sure" (2 Pet. 1:10). Even the latitudinarian divines recognized hell's utility—Tillotson called it "the greatest Discouragement to Sin"[35]—but they also found the extremes of hellfire preaching to be distasteful. More fundamentally, the latitudinarians, along with a growing chorus of less orthodox thinkers, expressed doubts about the reasonability of the idea that hell torment would last forever. Tillotson, even while urging his listeners to meditate often on hell, "sabotaged [the doctrine] by indirection" (as Norman Fiering has put it) in equivocating on hell punishment's duration.[36] Tillotson admitted that the Bible spoke in various places of everlasting punishment, as at the end of Jesus' eschatological discourse (Matt. 25:46), but he insisted that God was under no obligation to make good on his threats. A threat, Tillotson explained, was different from a promise. If God chose not to follow through on his threat of eternal punishment, he would be "not worse but better than his word," which would give sinners no cause for complaint. A promise, however, made God a "debtor" to humanity. If he failed to keep his promise of salvation to all who believed, he would be denying the faithful something they were owed.[37] Tillotson also suspected that there was more "subtlety than…solidity" in the traditional argument that sin deserves infinite punishment because its ultimate object is the infinite God. If all sins deserve an infinite penalty, Tillotson maintained, then all sins would in effect be equal, which is patently absurd in light of Jesus' own implied assertions that there would be different degrees of punishment in the afterlife (Matt. 11:22; Luke 12:47–48).[38] Surely, Tillotson reasoned, God inflicted a "cooler Hell" on persons who had committed less heinous sins. And whatever the degree of punishment, surely God ordained no future retribution arbitrarily and preemptively, without foresight of a person's transgressions.[39]

Tillotson's effort to downsize hell by reducing the sentences of its occupants did not sit well with Calvinists in New England. When Jesus alluded to degrees of punishment, declared Jonathan Edwards from his Massachusetts pulpit, he was not referring to varying durations. Edwards accepted the traditional argument that sin against an infinite God required eternal recompense. In addition, he reckoned, since part of sin's punishment was the abandonment of condemned persons to a perpetual state of sinfulness, then people in hell merited never-ending punishment for their ongoing viciousness.[40] As for Tillotson's argument that God is not obligated to make good on his threats, Edwards insisted that God never would have threatened endless torment in the first place if he had not already foreseen that he would follow through. To suppose that God made idle threats was just one more "blasphemous" suggestion made by Tillotson and other like-minded "new fashioned divines."[41]

On the necessity of eternal torment, Edwards was of one mind with his grandfather Solomon Stoddard, who once delivered a sermon entitled *The Efficacy of the Fear of Hell, to Restrain Men from Sin* (1713). Yet in the midst of the revivals of the Great Awakening, Edwards went beyond his grandfather in actual hellfire preaching, which he elevated to an exquisite art.[42] Perhaps no hellfire sermon in American religious history is as notorious as Edwards's "Sinners in the Hands of an Angry God" (1741). "God has laid himself under no obligation by any promise to keep natural man out of hell one moment," Edwards declared, in seeming rebuke to Tillotson. All that preserves sinners at any given moment is "the mere arbitrary will, and uncovenanted unobliged forbearance of an incensed God." "The God that holds you over the pit of hell, much as one holds a spider, or some loathsome insect, over the fire, abhors you, and is dreadfully provoked;...you are ten thousand times so abominable in his eyes as the most hateful venomous serpent is in ours."[43]

Edwards's vehemence was that of a man whose dearest predestinarian commitments were under attack, and he knew that Tillotson was not the only enemy of the eternal torment of the damned. As the "new learning" of the Enlightenment was making inroads among intellectuals, more impudent deniers of orthodoxy were stepping forward. William Whiston, a mathematician and theologian expelled from his professorship at Cambridge for rejecting the doctrine of the Trinity, had recently denounced the "barbarous and savage" opinion that God inflicted eternal punishment on persons for the "sins of this short life."[44] Whiston echoed seventeenth-century Socinians (who likewise had been accused of heresy for denying the Trinity) on the absurdity of the notion that God should be angry forever for the finite sins of his creatures.[45] To the Socinians, perpetual anger did nothing to increase God's glory, whereas to Calvinists such as Edwards, eternal punishment not only vindicated God's "injured majesty" but also increased the pleasure of the saints in heaven. "When they see others who were of the same nature," Edwards wrote, "and born under the same circumstances, plunged in such misery,... O, it will make them sensible, how happy they are."[46] To Edwards and other Calvinists, moreover, the divine prerogative to spare only certain creatures the interminable agony that everyone deserved was an essential aspect of God's inscrutable will. Ultimately, what was at stake for Edwards in all liberal equivocations on predestination and hell was God's absolute sovereignty. Or, as the poet Alexander Pope waggishly summed up the general climate:

> Then Unbelieving Priests reform'd the Nation,
> And taught more Pleasant Methods of Salvation;
> Where Heav'ns Free Subjects might their Rights dispute,
> Lest God himself shou'd seem too Absolute.[47]

FROM ARBITRARY TO ORDERLY: DOMESTICATING PROVIDENCE

In such an environment, it was perhaps inevitable that the very nature of divine sovereignty—specifically, the doctrine of divine providence—should next be thrown open to debate. The English Enlightenment's quarrel with providence centered on the form of the doctrine inherited from Calvin and his Puritan heirs. For Calvin, the whole world was the theater of God's providence. Nothing fell outside of God's control, which he exerted either directly (through miracles such as the biblical manna from heaven) or indirectly (through kings and kingdoms and other earthly instruments). Whether working directly or indirectly, however, God engineered all historical developments toward the preservation and ultimate glorification of his church. Even the oppression and other calamities periodically endured by the church were all part of God's plan for his elect people, to whom he gave the power, through the Holy Spirit, to interpret the providential significance of events.[48] Puritans and other Calvinists thus engaged in a kind of Spirit-enabled divination in which they attempted to read everything from politics to the weather for signs of God's electing favor.[49] For persons already assured of their election, this divination could become self-confirming and even egotistical, or what Alexandra Walsham has called a "set of rose-coloured spectacles" that transformed both setbacks and successes into signs of divine approbation.[50] For individuals not blessed with assurance, any personal misfortune— illness, house fire, crop failure—could be cause for predestinarian despair. Even celestial apparitions such as comets, which affected no person directly, could be read as fearful omens of divine wrath.

To some observers, such readings of heavenly signs looked suspiciously like astrology—a connection that Calvinists (including Calvin himself) vigorously denied. Astrologers, Calvin insisted, looked only to the stars, whereas Christians looked beyond the stars to the deeper purposes of God's will. Christians should not therefore dread stars and comets but rather should stand in holy fear of the God who communicates with his elect in providential wonders.[51] Yet Calvin's disavowals of astrology did not prevent Anglicans in Restoration England from equating Puritan providentialism with occult charlatanism. Anglican critics particularly resented the readiness of Puritans to interpret "special," or out-of-the-ordinary providences as signs of God's judgment on the laxity of the established church. Thus, Restoration prelates such as Thomas Sprat, the bishop of Rochester, increasingly emphasized God's general providence, or his government of the world through predictable laws of cause and effect. Any interruption of this regularity, Sprat urged, should be interpreted with all due caution: "Whenever...a hevy calamity falls from Heven on our Nation, a universal Repentance is requir'd; but all particular applications of privat men, except to their own hearts, is to be forborn." Similarly, John Tillotson criticized as "rash" any attempts to determine God's intended meaning in special providences. He recommended instead a pious appreciation for God's general providence in the "constant course of nature": the "daily miracles" of day and night, sun and rain, the cycle of the four seasons, and the like.[52]

Tillotson's benign, orderly providence had the advantage of being congenial to the emerging scientific rationality of the day, especially the new mechanical philosophy of Sir Isaac Newton. As Newtonians such as William Whiston explained, the laws of motion and gravitation were integral to the first mover's harmonious government of the universe.[53] In exalting the predictability of the created universe, popular Newtonianism contributed to a steady cultural shift away from an earlier view of God's sovereignty as essentially arbitrary. Historian Michael Winship has aptly summed up the change: "Calvin discovered and interpreted God's power in the world's contingencies; the new Restoration piety found it in the world's regularities."[54] Yet the realization of a law-governed universe did not banish all cognitive dissonance from Enlightenment era belief in God. Troubling questions remained. Did God ever interrupt the clockwork of creation to send special divine signs? Were all scientific discoveries divinely intended, or could science become the enemy of God's providential designs?

In colonial America, such questions came dramatically to the fore in 1721, when a smallpox epidemic struck Boston. The dreaded disease had afflicted the colonies periodically, but nearly two decades had passed since the last epidemic in Boston until an infected ship arrived from South America. Efforts to quarantine the crew proved futile, and the disease began spreading among the town's residents, many of whom had been born since the previous outbreak and lacked immunity. Among these vulnerable young people were two of the children of Cotton Mather. Fearing for their safety and his own, Mather enlisted physician Zabdiel Boylston in a campaign to inoculate citizens against the disease. Mather had learned of inoculation from published accounts and from his African slave, Onesimus, whose people had practiced it. But because the technique, which involved transferring the virus from a mildly afflicted patient to a healthy person, entailed a small risk of transmitting a fatal case of the disease, many Bostonians were wary. More ominously, many people feared that inoculation interfered with God's providential judgments and that even greater catastrophe would surely follow as punishment for human presumption.[55] Inoculation, declared one anonymous pamphleteer, was a snare of the devil that violated Jesus' express command not to tempt God (Matt. 4:7).[56] Mather soon became the object of public vilification and even of attempted assassination. Late one night, someone lobbed a primitive grenade into his house. Though the device failed to detonate, it came with a note attached: "Cotton Mather, You Dog, Dam you; I'l inoculate you with this."[57]

History ultimately vindicated Mather, as inoculation would prove to be the precursor of vaccination and of smallpox's eradication. In Mather's own day, however, the inoculation controversy was a barometer of changing assumptions about human initiative in the face of providence. For Mather himself, inoculation was a question not of resisting the divine will but of assenting to the technology that God providentially made available. Moreover, Mather asked rhetorically, did not scripture command, "Do yourselves no harm" (Acts 16:28)? He charged the anti-inoculation forces with being accessories to innumerable deaths for opposing a measure that demonstrably reduced fatalities.[58] Similarly, William Cooper, the junior pastor at Boston's Brattle Street Church, insisted that though smallpox was indeed a divine judgment, it was not unlawful to use God-given means for reducing the extremity of the suffering. As for the opponents' argument that persons should not seek to prolong the divinely predetermined lengths of their lives, Cooper maintained that by this logic, humans would be forced to avoid "the Use of all Physick, nay even of Food." "I truly believe, as my Bible teaches me, that God has fix'd the Period of every ones life," Cooper added, "but I also believe that He has done it with regard to Second Causes…; the End and Means are determin'd together."[59] Cooper, like Mather, was a convinced predestinarian, but in his appeal to second causes, he was unwittingly abetting a cultural transformation that would eventually leave many Americans convinced that the First Cause would never predetermine to punish individuals with illness—or eternal reprobation. The emerging Enlightenment mind-set allowed Christians to attribute the arbitrariness of suffering—why one person contracted smallpox while his neighbor did not—to impersonal second causes rather than to the inscrutable will of a personal God.[60]

Three decades after the inoculation controversy, in the 1750s, another scientific advance reopened the debate over providence. This time, the issue was lightning rods, which were being pushed by their inventor, Benjamin Franklin. Ironically, as a 16-year-old printer's apprentice in 1722, Franklin had contributed anonymous satires of Cotton Mather to the New-England Courant, which had led the fight against inoculation. Now, after his famous kite experiments, Franklin was publishing his conclusion that pointed iron rods on the roofs of buildings could save property by conducting electricity harmlessly to the ground.[61] Lightning had always been the perfect image of an undomesticated providence. Striking without warning from heaven, lightning bolts revealed to many Christians the God who, as Calvin put it, could "by his nod alone…kindle the air with flashes" and then "at his pleasure clear them away in a moment."[62] Unpredictable enough even in our own day of satellite photos and Doppler radar, lightning in the eighteenth century still inspired a more elemental religious awe at the power of the predestining God. Not surprisingly, lightning strikes garnered mention in the limited space of colonial newspapers. In June 1755, the Boston Evening-Post reported that lightning "entirely consumed to Ashes" the glass works in Braintree, along with six other nearby buildings. A week later, lightning "shattered from Top to Bottom" Captain David Clap's house in Scituate, melting his pewter utensils.[63] Such incidents led many colonists in Massachusetts and elsewhere to consider the benefits of Franklin's lightning rods, which he had discussed in a book published in London in 1751. As in the inoculation controversy, however, some people wondered if the new technology interfered with God's sovereign judgments and might draw even greater wrath from on high.

As it turned out, the greater wrath came from below, in the form of the Cape Ann earthquake of 1755. A little after 4:00 in the morning on 18 November, a powerful temblor awakened people across coastal New England and sent them panic-stricken into the streets. Many, having read Michael Wigglesworth's Day of Doom, feared the last judgment was nigh.

"[N]ever was such a Scene of Distress in New-England before," recalled one Boston observer, who described screaming children, lowing livestock, and streets strewn with toppled chimneys and other debris.[64] In the days that followed, the clergy seized the occasion to preach on God's anger at human sinfulness and to urge general repentance and reform. The pastor of Old South Church, Thomas Prince, however, singled out the presumptuous use of Franklin's "points of iron" as a possible reason for God's wrath in the earthquake. "In Boston are more [lightning rods] erected than any where else in New England; and Boston seems to be more dreadfully shaken. O! there is no getting out of the mighty Hand of God!" Prince's sermon drew a prompt retort from John Winthrop, the great-great-grandson of the Bay colony's first governor and professor of natural philosophy at Harvard, who announced himself "surprised and concerned" that Prince would venture such a theory. Winthrop feared that Prince's comments might discourage the use of lightning rods as a means of preventing the many "mischievous and sorrowful accidents, which we have so often seen to follow upon thunderstorms."[65]

The focus of the debate soon widened, however, from the propriety of using lightning rods to the propriety of referring to natural calamities as random or chance occurrences. Were lightning strikes merely unfortunate accidents, as Winthrop suggested? He conceded that they might "justly be regarded as the tokens of an incensed Deity," though he hastened to add that lightning in general revealed God's benevolence, for it was nature's way of freeing itself of "a certain unwholesome sultriness."[66] Other people, such as Boston pastor Thomas Foxcroft, saw in lightning and earthquakes the "very legible Signatures" of God's righteous anger. "It would be Atheism to ascribe these Events to meer Casualty or Chance," thundered Foxcroft, who pointed not only to the Boston temblor but also to the truly catastrophic earthquake earlier that November, which had devastated Lisbon, Portugal, killing between 50,000 and 100,000 people. Speaking in the customary code of Protestant anti-Catholicism, he attributed the Lisbon disaster to that city's worship of "idols." Though Boston's escape from similar destruction revealed God's goodness, according to Foxcroft, the New England quake also put residents on notice that they should not be at ease in Zion.[67] Similarly, the *Boston Gazette* editorialized that divine indignation over the "Vices that abound among us" was the sole cause of the New England earthquake. Any other explanation was a slippery slope to atheism: "To ascribe these powerful Operations wholly to second Causes, and totally to disregard the Hand of Him on whom Nature and all her Laws depend, is very little, if any Thing, short of the Folly of him who saith in his Heart there is no God."[68]

Nevertheless, second causes were slowly but surely emerging as a popular means of explaining natural disasters and of thinking about divine sovereignty more generally. Boston pastor Charles Chauncy argued that though in the biblical age of miracles God had caused some earthquakes by his immediate power, now he worked by "concurring" with the second causes that he himself had established at the time of creation. Second causes might lead to short-term calamity and suffering, but God as first cause was fundamentally benevolent.[69] Indeed, Chauncy maintained that benevolence, not sovereignty (as strict Calvinists typically maintained), was God's chief attribute. He drew from this the decidedly un-Calvinist conclusion that a benevolent deity would not have brought humans into existence if he had not intended to "make them finally happy."[70] Chauncy did not deny the punishment of the wicked in the afterlife, but in an anonymous book published in 1784, just three years before his death, he laid out his theory that hell torments would not be eternal. Sooner or later, the rebellious hearts of all persons in hell would be mollified, and every last soul would attain heavenly bliss by willingly embracing Christ.[71]

THAT "HELLISH" DOCTRINE: EVANGELICALS AGAINST PREDESTINATION

Chauncy's benign deity anticipated in many respects the God of later Unitarianism and deism—liberal movements that, however influential among certain classes, were destined to remain minority perspectives in American religious culture. Rationalistic faiths, especially those that denied or downplayed eternal hellfire, were not well suited for bringing the masses into the revival tents to pray tearfully to God to save their souls. Chauncy, in fact, had earlier distinguished himself as a staunch opponent of the revivalistic enthusiasm that swept the colonies during the middle decades of the eighteenth century. He considered the terror preaching of Jonathan Edwards and other revivalists blatantly manipulative and abhorred their predestinarian theology as cruel. "A more shocking idea can scarce be given of the Deity," he wrote, "than that which represents him as arbitrarily dooming the greater part of the race of man to eternal misery."[72]

Such indictments only galvanized the awakening's propagandists, who regarded the revivals as a providential antidote to the corrosive effects of rationalism, Anglicanism, and other alleged toxins on evangelical zeal.[73] In the opinion of many revival promoters, a strong predestinarian theology was simply the logical working-out of the conversion experience. Persons who had been overwhelmed with a sense of being chosen by God's grace would naturally reach the conclusion that election was absolutely unconditional, unmerited, irresistible, and irrevocable. The awakening would therefore amount to a great revitalization of the doctrine of absolute predestination, which to its partisans was nothing more (and nothing less) than a revival of biblical Christianity.

There was only one problem. It soon became clear that the revivalists themselves were not of one mind on predestination. Contrary to Calvinists' expectations about a general renewal of five-point theology, revivalism and predestination did not everywhere go hand in hand. The most dramatic rift among the revivalists erupted in the early 1740s between John Wesley, the founder of the Methodist tradition, and George Whitefield, the "Grand Itinerant" who electrified the American colonies with his preaching tours. Both men had been ordained in the Church of England, but whereas Wesley had internalized the aversion of high-church Anglicans to Calvinism, Whitefield had embraced the predestinarianism of the church's Calvinist wing. Once the two men emerged as the leading come-outers from the Anglican fold, a struggle ensued for the soul of the burgeoning transatlantic evangelical movement.

Eleven years Whitefield's senior, Wesley was born in 1703 to a ministerial family in which his mother proved to be a decisive theological influence. Susanna Annesley was the daughter and granddaughter of prominent Puritans, but at age 13 she broke with family tradition and joined the established Church of England. Later, she clashed with her husband, Samuel Wesley, over her Jacobite sympathies and her refusal to say "Amen" to his prayers for William III. (The couple even split up for a time, with Samuel telling her, "You and I must part: for if we have two kings, we must have two beds.")[74] Like other Jacobites, Susanna disliked the king's Dutch Reformed connection, but anti-Calvinism was also for her a matter of principle, which she strongly inculcated in her son John and his younger brother Charles. In a 1725 letter to John while he was a student at Oxford, she declared her abhorrence of the Calvinist doctrine of predestination and endorsed instead the prescient, conditional view of election whereby God chose certain persons based on foreknowledge of their faith. This view, she insisted, was firmly grounded in Romans 8:29 ("For whom he did foreknow, he also did predestinate") and neither derogated God's free grace nor impaired human liberty.[75]

This perspective on predestination, emphasizing divine-human cooperation, would become John Wesley's own, even after his famous conversion experience at Aldersgate Street, London, in 1738 in which he felt his heart "strangely warmed" by the realization that Christ alone was responsible for his salvation.[76] For Wesley, the dictum of "Christ alone" did not preclude human cooperation since Christ himself provided the grace that enabled people to respond to him in faith. Wesley consistently maintained that election was conditional and that God operated according to "the known Rules of his Justice and Mercy." Though God had charged all humans with original sin, this inherited taint was by itself not enough to warrant a person's eternal damnation. A "Measure of Free-will [is] supernaturally restored to every Man," making all people genuinely responsible for accepting Christ as the condition of their salvation.[77] The Calvinist view of unconditional election was "not a Doctrine of God." It rendered insincere Jesus' own invitation ("Come unto me, all ye that labour and are heavy laden"; Matt. 11:28) and bred a lamentable "sharpness" of temper among its partisans.[78]

The accusation of sharp tempers would prove a self-fulfilling prophecy among the alumni of the so-called Holy Club of Methodists that had formed around John Wesley and his brother Charles at Oxford. George Whitefield had joined this group after matriculating at the university in 1732, and at first he and the Wesleys were united in their strict rituals of fasting and self-examination. Yet whereas John Wesley reverted to a lifelong pattern of self-doubt after his heart was strangely warmed at Aldersgate, Whitefield's own conversion experience in 1735 left him firmly convinced that he had been irreversibly chosen by Christ.[79] For Wesley, assurance was always of *present* salvation only; he echoed Jacob Arminius in insisting that a person now in a state of grace could ultimately fall away by his own free choice. For Whitefield, as for other five-point Calvinists, a person who had genuinely experienced the "new birth" could rest assured that he would persevere to the end.[80]

Thus, when Wesley first published his conclusion that the Calvinists' doctrine of predestination destroyed the comfort of Christianity and extinguished the zeal for good works, Whitefield was incensed. "This doctrine is my daily Support," Whitefield declared in a printed reply. "I should utterly sink under a Sense of my impending Tryals, was I not firmly persuaded Christ had chosen me from before the Foundation of the World, and therefore will suffer nothing to pluck me finally out of his almighty Hands." As for Wesley's charge that unconditional predestination rendered Christ's invitation insincere and the clergy's preaching useless, Whitefield dismissed this as strange "sophistry." A pastor must preach "promiscuously" to all, Whitefield argued, since he cannot be sure who is elect and who is reprobate. For all the minister knows, his preaching may be the means preordained by God to bring certain listeners into a state of grace. Yet Whitefield concluded that Wesley had greatly erred in assuming that God *universally* granted persons the ability to come to him. Eternal reprobation was no less of a reality than eternal election, Whitefield maintained, and he insisted that this was the upshot both of scripture and of article 17 of the Thirty-nine Articles. He recommended

PULPIT SCENE.

" At the tabernacle a man came up to him in the pulpit. p. 165."

George Whitefield confronted in the pulpit by an opponent of his revival preaching. From John Gillies, *Memoirs of Rev. George Whitefield* (1838).

that Wesley consult the writings of the staunch Anglican Calvinist John Edwards and of Boston pastor William Cooper, who had just published a series of four sermons defending unconditional predestination. (This was the same Cooper who two decades earlier had written in favor of smallpox inoculation.) Of unconditional predestination, Cooper declared that there was no other truth "so plainly laid down" in all of the Bible.[81] He also invoked the English nonconformist John Sladen, who had scoffed at the idea that the Arminian version of predestination was more comforting than the Calvinist version. Arminian doctrine, Sladen wrote, left people perilously dependent on their own weak wills, whereas Calvinist doctrine provided a rock of true assurance: "Ours makes the salvation of millions of the fallen children of men absolutely certain, while theirs makes the salvation of any man but barely possible."[82]

Cooper's book appeared in 1740, exposing the predestinarian rift among revivalists as the Great Awakening was reaching its height. Thus, even as evangelicals on both sides of the Atlantic were portraying the revivals as the most glorious work of God since the Reformation, the old Calvinist-Arminian battle from the Old World was replaying itself in the New, with Calvinists tarring Arminians as heretics and Arminians portraying Calvinists as killjoys.[83] The difference this time was the awakening itself, which tended amid the clamor of populist rhetoric to reduce the two positions to caricatures. Methodists in particular were contemptuous of the sort of metaphysical speculation that had subdivided Calvinists in the academy into precise supralapsarian and infralapsarian factions.[84] The characteristic Methodist medium was not systematic theology but the hymn, which the Wesleys turned into a means of clever anti-Calvinist satire. Their 1741 collection, *Hymns on God's Everlasting Love*, included a hymn by Charles, "The Horrible Decree," which lambasted the *decretum horribile* (dreadful decree) of Reformed theology. In 15 stanzas, the hymn decried as "hellish blasphemy" the idea that certain persons were damned from birth, deprived of the ability to respond to the gospel invitation:

> To damn for falling short,
> Of what they could not do,
> For not believing the report
> Of that which was not true.[85]

Other hymns in the collection expressed the Methodist embrace of prevenient (or, more archaically, "preventing") grace and the Arminian insistence that it was given universally. In "Free Grace," Charles made clear that Methodists did not deny the Protestant maxim of grace alone but taught that Christ graced all persons with the initial power of choice:

> Thou drawest all men unto Thee
> Grace doth to every soul appear;
> Preventing grace for all is free,
> And brings to all salvation near.[86]

The same hymn offered a Methodist rebuttal to the Calvinists' logical parallelism that the unmerited election of certain persons entailed the arbitrary reprobation of others: "We need no reprobates to prove/That grace, free grace, is truly free." Elsewhere in verse, Charles skewered the Calvinists for imputing their doctrine of predestination to God:

> Still shall the hellish doctrine stand,
> And Thee for its dire author claim?
> No: let it sink at Thy command
> Down to the pit from whence it came.[87]

To hell with the "devil and his doctrine," exclaimed Charles, in insolent couplets that were destined to disappear from Methodist hymnals once Methodism became comfortably mainline and polite.[88]

The Wesleys' anti-predestinarian hymn campaign irked Calvinists, especially George Whitefield. Hardly given to excessive decorum himself, Whitefield assumed the pose of one whose delicate sensibilities had been offended. In a letter to John Wesley, he complained: "Dear Brother Charles is more and more rash. He has lately printed some very bad hymns."[89] Whitefield was already on the defensive for his own public comment that another Arminian sympathizer, Archbishop John Tillotson, "knew no more about true Christianity than Mahomet."[90] Whitefield's polemics against the Wesleys had also drawn a sharp retort from their mother, Susanna, in an anonymous tract—her only publication in her lifetime, printed just months before her death. If Whitefield's doctrine of eternal reprobation were true, she wrote, "what good Man would not rather choose to be a Hangman than a minister of the Gospel?" Disproof of the "low, vile, unworthy" Calvinist doctrine of predestination could be found at the very outset of scripture, where, in Genesis, God declared to the serpent that the seed of the woman would bruise his head. In this instant, she argued (citing the interpretation of the nonjuror William Law), God broke the power of the devil and decreed that all of Adam and Eve's posterity, despite their inherited sin, would be born in "salvable Condition."[91] She denounced Whitefield for "harangu[ing] the Populace" with the false accusation that her son John was preaching sheer universalism, the idea that all persons would be saved in the end. "Mr. Wesley has said (which is true) *that all might be saved*," she wrote, "but I am sure he never said, *that all will be saved*."[92]

By 1742, the evangelical slugfest over predestination was so raucous that the *Boston Evening-Post* took the unusual step of printing on its front page an excerpt from *Veritas Redux* (1707) by John Edwards in which, as we saw earlier, the late Anglican Calvinist had speculated on the possibility of a "third sort" of persons who were neither elect nor reprobate but in a state of probation. Perhaps, the *Evening-Post* editorialized, this expedient might "have a Tendency to promote Truth and Peace" among the two warring factions of revivalists.[93] Yet Whitefield was already on record as rejecting Edwards on

John Wesley at the London grave of his mother, Susanna.
Nineteenth-century engraving, Guildhall Art Gallery,
London (Art Resource).

this particular point, which he evidently regarded as a momentary lapse in orthodoxy by an otherwise stout defender of all-or-nothing predestination.[94]

Two years after the *Evening-Post* article, 71-year-old Martha's Vineyard pastor Experience Mayhew, widely respected for his missionary work among the Indians, attempted his own reconciliation of Arminians and Calvinists. "I hope that if my Hypothesis might be admitted," Mayhew wrote, "the Way would be thereby paved for the contending Parties to come to a better Understanding." Some Arminians, he explained, underestimated the debilitating effects of original sin and mistakenly rejected the Calvinist insistence on the necessity of supernatural regeneration prior to conversion. But many Calvinists were equally mistaken in assuming regeneration to be passive and election unconditional: "Tho' we cannot regenerate our selves, yet it is not true, that we cannot apply our selves to Christ to work this great Change in us by his Spirit." God's offers of salvation in scripture are everywhere conditional, Mayhew added, revealing his underlying Arminian sympathies. Yet he hoped that Arminians could meet Calvinists halfway, recognizing in the "Calvinian scheme" a worthy sense of human depravity and of the absolute necessity of God's grace.[95]

Mayhew's middle-ground hypothesis proved to be unrealistically utopian, for in the great Arminian-Calvinist debate over predestination, both sides showed themselves equally unwilling to compromise. Even conciliatory comments could become causes of offense. When Whitefield died at age 55 while on an American preaching tour in 1770, Wesley did not help matters by delivering a memorial oration in London in which he praised his erstwhile Holy Club colleague but noted that they had "agree[d] to disagree" on certain doctrines of a "less essential" nature. To Calvinists, unconditional predestination was far from nonessential. They were incredulous, moreover, at Wesley's insistence that he and Whitefield were of one mind on the two "fundamental" truths of the new birth and justification by faith alone.[96] From a Calvinist perspective, the conditional predestination of Arminianism made justification somehow dependent on human exertion rather than on a faith that was entirely a gift of God to the elect. Wesley had already reignited the Calvinists' suspicions earlier that year when he suggested in print that Protestants had been too "dreadfully afraid" of the idea of merit and that there was but a hair's breadth separating it from his own doctrine of conditional predestination. "We are rewarded, according to our Works, yea because of our Works. How does this differ from for the sake of our Works? And how differs this from *Secundum merita operum*? As our Works deserve? Can you split this Hair? I doubt, I cannot."[97] Wesley later clarified himself, explaining that strictly speaking, only the blood of Christ was meritorious. Human works were meritorious in the "loose sense" of being rewardable because they were enabled by Christ himself.[98] But the damage had been done. Selina Hastings, countess of Huntingdon and onetime patron of both Whitefield and Wesley, banned Wesley from her pulpits and denounced him as "a papist unmasked, a heretic, an apostate." She also sponsored the anti-Wesley *Gospel Magazine*, edited by Augustus Toplady. Wesley countered with the *Arminian Magazine* whose title was an attempt to reclaim "Arminian" from the disrepute it had gained among Calvinists.[99]

The ensuing Toplady-Wesley debate in the 1770s is one of the nastiest exchanges over predestination in the history of transatlantic evangelicalism. The initial sources of the altercation were Toplady's books, *The Church of England Vindicated from the Charge of Arminianism* (1769), which followed the late John Edwards in emphasizing the Calvinist implications of the Thirty-nine Articles, and *The Doctrine of Predestination Stated and Asserted* (1769), a condensation of writings by the sixteenth-century Calvinist Jerome Zanchius. Wesley followed with an anonymous parody, written under the name "Mr. A— T—," in which he summarized Toplady's views this way: "One in Twenty (suppose) of Mankind are Elected; Nineteen in Twenty are Reprobated. The Elect shall be saved, do what they will; The Reprobate shall be damned, do what they can. Reader, Believe this, or be damned."[100] Toplady rushed to condemn the "forgery": "Blush, Mr. Wesley, if you are capable of blushing." Wesley and his "hair-brained Perfectionists," he charged, were but thinly separated from popery, like the forbidden lovers Pyramus and Thisbe attempting to kiss each other through a hole in the wall. Toplady heaped metaphor on metaphor: Wesley's Arminianism was the "Gangrene of the Protestant Churches"; it undercut the eternal security of Christians like an insane architect who built his house's foundation with tiles and laths and reserved bricks and stones for the roof.[101] Wesley and his allies shot right back. If Arminians were papists, wrote Wesley's supporter Walter Sellon, then Calvinists must acknowledge that their absolute predestination made them little different from the "Mahometans" with their doctrine of "necessitating Fate."[102] Wesley, meanwhile, fired off an anonymous pamphlet upbraiding that "young, bold Man" (Toplady) and defying anyone to prove unconditional predestination by appeal to scripture. However strenuously Toplady might deny the fatalistic consequences of his doctrine, Wesley insisted, absolute predestination in fact consigned most persons to hell, in blind disregard for their actions.[103]

Determined to have the last word, Toplady penned a yet more extensive rebuttal, decrying Wesley's attempt to "terrify old Women" with his fearmongering over reprobation. Wesley was the real "Mahometan," who, like Islam's prophet, was bent on "propagating his Religion by the sword." God had in fact chosen an "innumerable multitude" for eternal glory, and Wesley's charge that Calvinists preached the reprobation of 19 in 20 was wickedly presumptuous. God alone knew the numbers of saved and damned, just as he alone knew the date and time of each person's death. "Omniscience only can tell, which of us shall first appear before the Judge of All," wrote the 31-year-old Toplady to the 68-year-old Wesley. "I shortly may. You shortly must."[104] As it happened, Toplady miscalculated the imminence of Wesley's demise. Toplady died in 1778 at age 37, still repudiating Wesley on his deathbed; Wesley lived another 13 years.

The deaths of Wesley and Toplady only briefly silenced the controversy, for their debate of the 1770s, though it took place in England, anticipated many of the major themes of later evangelical battles over predestination in the United States. At the turn of the twenty-first century, certain segments of American evangelicalism would still be torn between factions accusing each other of naive perfectionism, on the one hand, or "Muslim" fatalism, on the other. Yet while the Arminian-Calvinist divide would prove to be the most familiar battle over predestination, the doctrine would engender conflicts far beyond the Anglican, Congregational, and Methodist confines just described. As we will see in the remaining chapters, predestination was the leaven of dissension and change across the denominational spectrum, even in traditions not normally thought of as being preoccupied with the problem. And just as we saw Augustus Toplady going to his death in London still angry with his anti-predestinarian opponents, we will see deathbed dramas played out in America in the unrelenting career of this contentious doctrine.

CHAPTER 4

From Methodists to Mormons

Attacking Predestination in the Young Republic

All the time of my conviction I used to consider what church or society I should join, whether the Baptist, Presbyterian, or Methodist; but at this time the Lord said unto me, "You must join the Methodists, for they are my people, and they are right."

—*Benjamin Abbott,* Experience and Gospel Labours *(published posthumously, 1801)*

I asked the Personages who stood above me in the light, which of all the sects was right (for at this time it had never entered into my heart that all were wrong)—and which I should join. I was answered that I must join none of them, for they were all wrong; and the Personage who addressed me said that all their creeds were an abomination in his sight.

—*Joseph Smith, Jr.,* History of the Church *1:18–19 (c. 1839)*

IN THE LATE spring of 1809, Thomas Paine lay dying and forgotten in a Greenwich Village apartment. The revolutionary pamphleteer, whose *Common Sense* (1776) reportedly sold 150,000 copies and galvanized Americans' support for war with Britain, had lost most of his public support after publishing a scathing attack on the Bible in *The Age of Reason* (1794–1795). The deist arguments of the book were by the 1790s at least a century old, but he had repackaged them in his usual pugnacious prose. The Bible, in his view, was a "book of lies, wickedness, and blasphemy." Moses was a "detestable villain" who, after capturing the Midianites, ordered his men to "butcher the boys, to massacre the mothers and debauch the daughters." The writers of the Gospels could not have been eyewitnesses to the events they related because of the many discrepancies among their accounts. And the evangelists' efforts to read Old Testament prophecies as references to Jesus, as when Matthew interpreted Isaiah 7:14 as a prediction of the virgin birth, strained credulity to the breaking point. Isaiah's prophecy, Paine quipped, "has no more reference to Christ and his mother than it has to me and my mother."[1]

Such statements did not endear Paine to orthodox Christians. Once, when he tried to catch a stagecoach near his farm in Bordentown, New Jersey, the drivers of two different coaches refused him a seat. "My stage and horses were once struck by lightning," commented one coachman, "and I don't want them to suffer again." When Paine finally caught a ride, an angry mob jeered him on the way out of town. The Federalist press denounced him as a "loathsome reptile," a "lying, drunken brutal infidel," and "that living opprobrium of humanity." Now, on his deathbed at age 72, his body wracked by pain from gangrenous ulcers, he cried out involuntarily, "Oh, Lord help me!" (Contrary to popular opinion, Paine was not an atheist: "I believe in one God, and no more," he famously said in *The Age of Reason*, "and I hope for happiness beyond this life.") His physician, in a last-ditch effort to save his soul, asked him if he believed that Jesus Christ was the Son of God. "I have no wish to believe on that subject," Paine replied. A few days later, he died.[2]

It was not until 1820 that what is believed to have been Paine's last essay appeared in a London magazine. Entitled "Predestination: Remarks on Romans 9:18–21," it was addressed to the "Ministers of the Calvinistic Church." The essay revealed that Paine was not unlike many people, then and now, who turn their thoughts to religion when death is near. But instead of falling back on one of his ancestral faiths—his mother had been an Anglican; his father, a Quaker—Paine remained an iconoclast to the end. Blasting Paul's defense of predestination ("Therefore hath he mercy on whom he will have mercy"), Paine declared the whole passage to be "presumption and nonsense." Paul's metaphor of the potter and clay revealed him to be an "unfeeling idiot" who degraded humans and impugned divine justice and wisdom in supposing that God would "treat the choicest work of creation like inanimate and insensible clay." The Calvinists and Universalists would continue to wrangle over the proper interpretation of Paul's words, Paine said, but reason compelled deists to criticize scripture if it violated

Thomas Paine by John Wesley Jarvis (c. 1806–1807).
National Gallery of Art, Washington, D.C.

God's goodness: "Nonsense ought to be treated as nonsense wherever it be found." The "absurd and impious doctrine of predestination, a doctrine destructive of morals, would never have been thought of had it not been for some stupid passages in the Bible, which priestcraft at first, and ignorance since, have imposed upon mankind as a revelation."[3]

In singling out predestination in his final essay, Paine in a sense was only continuing his career-long attack on the idea of absolute monarchy. In his view, the apostle Paul's God was the ultimate arbitrary monarch, who bestowed favor and imposed punishment for no reason other than his inscrutable will. Ironically, as historian Mark Noll has pointed out, the younger Paine of *Common Sense* was not averse to co-opting other portions of the Bible to argue against monarchy.[4] The Israelites, Paine maintained, had originally lived under "a kind of republic" until, in a fit of national delusion, they began agitating for a king (1 Sam. 8:1–22). The people's over-confidence in human kingship was a sin in the eyes of the Lord, who, at the prophet Samuel's urging, sent down thunder and rain to remind the people that he alone should be feared (1 Sam. 12:16–25). "All anti-monarchial parts of scripture," Paine concluded, "have been very smoothly glossed over in monarchial governments."[5] Paine's shrewd use of biblical evidence went a long way toward stoking popular discontent against England's George III, though as Noll speculates, *Common Sense* never would have been given a hearing among evangelical Christians if Paine had published *The Age of Reason* first. Similarly, Noll suggests, "the allegiance of traditional Christian believers to republican liberty might not have been so thoroughly cemented."[6]

The mixture of republican ideology with the idea that the Bible (if prop-erly interpreted) was a charter of liberties proved a corrosive acid of predes-tination in the years surrounding the American Revolution and throughout much of the nineteenth century. In this momentous era of nation building, a variety of upstart religious movements burst onto the scene to fill the void left by the disestablishment of the old state churches. What united these disparate groups was opposition to the monarchial God of Calvinism and confidence that a commonsense reading of scripture would bury the old Puritan specters of unconditional election and reprobation. Elite and popu-lar prophets alike preached this message of liberty and in so doing left an indelible imprint on American religion. The ferment in the republic's first 100 years would produce not only untold numbers of Methodists, both black and white (and, by the twentieth century, their Holiness and Pente-costal successors), but also a raucous din of deists and freethinkers, Univer-salists, Stone-Campbell "Christians," Adventists, Christian Scientists, and Mormons. We will see how each of these movements, despite their differ-ences, can be viewed as variations on the anti-predestinarian theme. All of the groups rejected a portion of the Augustinian doctrinal inheritance, though they varied in the radicalism of their repudiations, from Methodists, who discarded only the unconditional aspect of predestination, to Mormons, who abandoned predestination's entire substructure in original sin. While the Mormon option appeared too extreme to most other Americans in the nineteenth century, the Latter-day Saints ironically were in good company with the most prominent oldline New England Protestants of the time, the Beecher clan, several of whom reached similarly radical anti-Augustinian conclusions. These strange bedfellows, Mormons and Beechers, together shed light on a pregnant cultural moment when Augustinian assumptions about God's government of his creatures suddenly seemed at odds with the American way.

THE NEW (OLD) ORDER OF THE AGES

The great backlash against unconditional predestination had various antecedents. In the last chapter, we saw the irony of royalist Anglicans denouncing the absolute monarchy of Calvinism's God. Anglicanism was thus one vanguard of anti-predestinarian thought, even while many of its adherents remained loyal to the king and had to flee the colonies during the Revolution. (Calvinists often evinced the opposite paradox: absolute monarchists in their view of God, they were the revolutionaries who overthrew Charles I in 1649 and later, in many cases, supported America's break with George III in 1776.)[7] Anti-predestinarianism also borrowed language from more secular traditions: civic humanism, rooted in classical antiquity and revived in the Renaissance, which idealized the virtue of self-governing citizens in a republic; and natural rights theories, articulated in the Enlightenment, which opposed divine right monarchy. When the 56 signers of the Declaration of Independence announced to the world that all men were "endowed by their Creator with certain unalienable rights," namely, "life, liberty, and the pursuit of happiness," this reflected assumptions about human self-determination that at the very least were in tension with the self-abasement once cultivated by Puritan predestinarians. The language of liberty and freedom was in the air, and religion could hardly escape its influence.[8]

Yet on balance, anti-predestinarianism in the infant United States derived less inspiration from elite intellectual sources than from a simple notion— a powerful founding myth—that underlay American republican ideology: the idea of starting afresh. "[I]n the beginning all the world was America," wrote the Englishman John Locke in his *Second Treatise of Government* (1690), and such was Americans' own conception of their new nation.[9] America was the land of boundless possibility, the endless frontier where people could remake themselves by shedding, as historian Bernard Bailyn has put it, "the heavy crust of custom that was weighing down the spirit of man."[10] In religion, this meant throwing off the shackles of old scholasticisms, particularly the predestinarian orthodoxies codified in such documents as the Westminster Confession. Creeds and confessions, many Americans came to believe, were products of fallible human interpreters, whereas the Bible represented religion pure and undefiled. The idea of the Bible's purity so captivated one American founder, Charles Thomson, that he worked for nearly two decades on a new translation based on more ancient manuscripts and cast in simpler English. Earlier, as secretary of the Continental Congress, Thomson had designed the Great Seal of the United States, which included the Latin motto *Novus Ordo Seclorum* (New Order of the Ages). Based loosely on a passage from Virgil about the restoration of the reign of Saturn ("The great succession of centuries is born afresh"), it was the perfect encapsulation of the primitivist myth. America was at once new and old, a return to a primitive state of nature uncorrupted by the intellectual pretensions and obfuscations of all the intervening centuries of European tradition.[11]

Despite its anti-elitism, and even anti-intellectualism, the primitivist idea held a powerful allure for some of America's most eminent founders, including Thomas Jefferson and Benjamin Franklin. Together they sat on the committee to draft the Declaration of Independence, with Jefferson serving as the principal author. The document's famous invocation of the "laws of nature and of nature's God" hinted at Jefferson's assumption that humans in their primitive state were fundamentally good and rational, capable of self-government. But kings, with their doctrine of divine right, had duped the common people into thinking that absolute monarchy was the only way to preserve order in society. The clerical hierarchy had perpetrated similar deceptions in religion. Jefferson did not reach this conclusion for lack of churchly upbringing. Catechized in the Book of Common Prayer by his mother, he remained outwardly an Anglican his whole life and supported St. Anne's Parish near his Monticello home in Virginia.[12] Yet ever the voracious reader, he was also deeply influenced by the critiques of traditional religion by deists such as John Toland, who in *Christianity Not Mysterious* (1696) insisted that true Christianity could not require belief in mysteries, nor in things contrary to human reason. For centuries, Toland wrote, priests and theologians had shrouded the plain message of the gospel with "Litigious Disputes and vain Subtilties," enthroning themselves as the sole interpreters of the faith. True religion instead was characterized by simplicity—the "noblest Ornament of the Truth."[13] Similarly, Jefferson maintained that the "incomprehensible jargon" of the theologians had to be swept away before Jesus' straightforward ethical teachings could shine through: "when, in short, we shall have unlearned every thing which has been taught since his day, and got back to the pure and simple doctrines he inculcated, we shall then be truly and worthily his disciples."[14]

For Jefferson, unlearning doctrinal corruptions meant quite literally cutting them out of the Bible. With scissors in hand, Jefferson went to work on a pair of King James New Testaments (he needed twin copies so he could work with both sides of the printed page), along with editions in Greek, Latin, and French. In addition to excising miracle stories, including the Resurrection, and apocalyptic material, he completely eliminated the letters of Paul (the "first corrupter of the doctrines of Jesus"), thereby removing Romans 9–11 and other predestinarian proof texts. Likewise, Jefferson pruned the references to Jesus' divinity and other dogmatic passages from

John's Gospel, slicing out such predestinarian verses as 6:44 ("No man can come to me, except the Father which hath sent me draw him"). When he pasted the remaining portions in a notebook, he was left with a Bible depicting Jesus not as the divine savior of the elect but as a wise teacher who conveyed moral lessons in parables. Jefferson, like modern-day scholars of the historical Jesus, believed that he had found the gold nugget of reliable material buried in the dross of scripture. His version of Holy Writ was a book of teachings *by* Jesus, not *about* him.[15]

Jefferson's Bible was not published until 1904, 78 years after his death, but in his own lifetime his reputation for unorthodoxy was such that he was vilified as an atheist and a "French infidel" (owing to his five years as U.S. minister to France) during the election of 1800. He refused to respond to the charges publicly, but in his private letters, he unleashed his anger against the "mountebanks calling themselves the priests of Jesus." Among the greatest charlatans in his view were John Calvin and his later American disciples, such as the Edwardsean theologian Samuel Hopkins: "The strait jacket alone was their proper remedy." Calvin, declared Jefferson in a letter to John Adams, was the real atheist: "If ever man worshipped a false god, he did. The being described in his 5 points is not the God whom you and I acknolege [*sic*] and adore, the Creator and benevolent governor of the world; but a daemon of malignant spirit."[16] Earlier, Adams had expressed the same opinion to his son, the future president John Quincy Adams. Calvinistic predestination precluded human liberty and thus removed all possibility for just reward or punishment. "The Calvinists and the Atheists differ in nothing but this; the former believe in eternal Misery; the latter not," the elder Adams wrote.[17]

Benjamin Franklin was equally skeptical of the five-point Calvinism on which he was reared. Baptized by the supralapsarian Samuel Willard at Boston's Old South Church, Franklin lamented in his *Autobiography* (written in 1771–1789) that as a boy he had wasted precious hours reading his father's small library of treatises in "polemic Divinity" rather than seeking out "more proper Books" that would have satisfied his thirst for true knowledge. Later in his memoir, he confessed his doubts about the dogmas of the "Presbyterian" persuasion, particularly election and reprobation, which "appear'd to me unintelligible."[18] No doubt he had in mind a controversy that had engaged him in 1735, when he defended a Presbyterian minister, Samuel Hemphill, against charges of heterodoxy. Hired as an assistant to Philadelphia pastor Jedediah Andrews (himself a protégé of the redoubtable Increase Mather), Hemphill had aroused suspicions of deist sympathies after preaching on morality more than doctrine and downplaying original sin and other pillars of Calvinist orthodoxy. Put on trial by the Philadelphia Synod, Hemphill was found guilty and suspended, but not before Franklin lampooned in print the "Rev. Asses" in charge of the inquest.[19] In several pamphlets, Franklin anticipated the primitivism of Jefferson in criticizing the church's tendency to reify time-bound dogmatic accretions. The Presbyterians in particular, "fancying themselves infallible in their Interpretations," had "ty'd themselves down by the Westminster Confession."[20] Indeed, creeds and confessions in general perpetuated the "greatest Absurdities and Falshoods" while obscuring the simple morality of Jesus. "One solid Argument will do more than all the human Creeds and Confessions in the Universe."[21] As for scripture, Franklin believed that unlike denominational confessions, it was by and large in harmony with sound reason. Though he added that he would not hesitate to reject as spurious any passage that could be proven to support an absurd position, he was confident that the Bible, if properly understood, came down conclusively against a God who would arbitrarily damn the greater part of humanity. A "thousand" passages of scripture testified against this sort of irrational "Demonism."[22]

In treating the Bible, especially the Gospels, as the wellspring of a common-sense religion unadulterated by dogmatic artifice, Franklin and Jefferson were, in a curious way, harbingers of the next wave in American religion—the series of revivals between the 1790s and the 1830s that came to be known as the Second Great Awakening. In addition to igniting a steady increase in religious participation that would continue through the twentieth century, the Second Great Awakening was a time when untold numbers of ordinary Americans deemed themselves to be the only rightful interpreters of scripture.[23] In the earlier Great Awakening, led by Calvinists such as George Whitefield, "men and women seemed to think and speak in the passive mood, as if to underscore God's action upon them," notes historian Grant Wacker.[24] But in the revivals of the early nineteenth century, a striking biblical populism emerged. Confident of the enabling grace they had received in Christ, hosts of people in burgeoning new movements rebelled against the old-style clergy who would restrict biblical exegesis—or the saving benefit of Jesus' death—to an elect few.[25]

UNIVERSALISM: CALVINISM "IMPROVED"

One popular religious movement that emerged on the heels of the new republic was named for its perspective on eternal election. Universalism, the idea that God would save all people in the end, was probably as old as Christianity itself. Its most important early exponent was the third-century church father Origen, who, influenced partly by Neoplatonism, believed that all souls would ultimately be reunited with God after a period of purification by fire.[26] Universalism in the United States emerged in a very different social context but shared with its ancient precursor a heterodox reputation, which was one reason that the American movement never rose above minority status. As an independent religious denomination, the Universalist Church ceased to exist in 1961 with the merger that created today's Unitarian Universalist Association. Even before the merger, the Universalists had often been beaten out by the wealthier and more influential Unitarians, who could boast of deep connections to Harvard and its Boston Brahmin alumni, for the honor of carrying the banner of American liberal religion.[27] Yet of the people who came to be nicknamed UUs, the Universalists actually had the longer denominational history and were the prototype of anti-predestinarian agitation in the early American republic. A description of the movement's early days by Hosea Ballou II (1796–1861), first president of Tufts University and grandnephew of the more famous Universalist theologian of the same name, is revealing. In the first decades of the American nation, "there seems to have risen up, simultaneously, in different parts of the country, a sense of unsatisfied wants, a longing for something more than the old system of religion could give," he wrote. "Here and there were individuals" who were "painfully groping...out of the stifling atmosphere of high Calvinism, to some freer issue."[28]

Among those individuals was John Murray (1741–1815), an immigrant from England who grew up on a diet of strict Calvinism and attended Whitefield's preaching in London before falling under the influence of Whitefield's ex-colleague James Relly. A book by Relly convinced Murray that scripture taught universal salvation. Christ was the first elect, and all people were united in him: "I in them, and thou in me, that they may be made perfect in one" (John 17:23). Thus, when predestinarians quoted Ephesians 1:4 ("he hath chosen us in him before the foundation of the world"), they failed to realize that the "us" meant all of humanity.[29] Even persons who had not heard the gospel "knew" Christ by virtue of their unity with him in the flesh, Relly later argued. And as Luke 3:6 promised, "all flesh shall see the salvation of God."[30] After reading Relly's book, Murray went to hear him preach in a London meetinghouse and came away remarking that it was "the first consistent sermon I have ever heard."[31] In 1770, Murray settled in America, where he founded the nation's first Universalist society in Gloucester, Massachusetts, in 1779.

Meanwhile, another pioneer of the movement, Elhanan Winchester (1751–1797), was slowly embracing Universalist principles. A Massachusetts native with little formal education, Winchester schooled himself in

Hebrew and Greek and became a Baptist minister in the theological mold of "hyper-Calvinist" John Gill (see chapter 6) before a book by a German mystic convinced him to reject the doctrine of limited atonement.[32] When Winchester aired his newfound views in 1781, his Philadelphia congregation ousted him, and he formed a Universalist society at the University of Pennsylvania. In 1787, he began a seven-year sojourn in England, where as an itinerant preacher he spoke out against slavery and published works on universal salvation. Upon his return to the United States in 1794, he published a refutation of *The Age of Reason* by Thomas Paine, who was, ironically, a would-be ally in the fight against Calvinistic predestination.[33]

Murray and Winchester reveal the devil in the details of Universalism, for they disagreed over precisely how Christ redeemed humanity. Murray tended to speak of redemption in more predestinarian terms: election was indeed before time, as the Calvinists taught, but *all* people were elected, not some. His position resembled that of another Universalist, Joseph Huntington (brother of Samuel Huntington, governor of Connecticut and a signer of the Declaration), who argued in his 1796 book, *Calvinism Improved*, that the Calvinists were correct on everything except election's extent. The biblical passages they marshaled to prove that only some individuals were elect—for example, the references to God's loving Jacob and hating Esau (Mal. 1:2–3; Rom. 9:13)—concerned their status in this life, not the life to come. But on the absoluteness and eternity of God's electing decree, Huntington was firm: "I hold to the doctrine of predestination as fully as any man in the world ever did, and that in the supra-lapsarian sense, which is the only consistent sense."[34] In contrast, Winchester, who published an elegy on the death of John Wesley, preferred to speak in more Methodist terms of a universal grace that enabled all people to choose Christ. Unlike the Methodists, however, he extended the time of decision into the hereafter, assuming that some souls might resist Christ for thousands of years before all surrendered to God's saving designs in the end. (Biblical references to "everlasting" punishment, he insisted, were simply figures of speech indicating a long but not interminable duration.) To Murray, Winchester's intermediate state looked suspiciously like the Catholic notion of "purgatorial satisfaction," which threatened the already-accomplished redemption in Christ.[35] While both men expected the sinful to suffer before attaining heavenly bliss, "Murray thought of the suffering as merely punitive," notes historian E. Brooks Holifield, whereas "Winchester gave it redemptive meaning."[36] A related but clearer-cut controversy erupted in the next generation when the more famous Hosea Ballou (1771–1852), pastor of Boston's Second Universalist Church, began advocating an "ultra-Universalism" that denied hell punishment altogether. The hardships of this life, he concluded, were sufficient penance for finite human sins. This raised the ire of more traditional "restorationist" Universalists, who maintained that all sinners would be restored to unity with God after enduring some sort of penalty or purgation. Outright denial of future retribution, the traditionalists feared, would expose Universalism to the charge of abetting immorality.[37]

Yet for all their disagreements, early Universalists held one vital characteristic in common: a populist biblicism. The movement's largely rural and urban working-class constituents eagerly embraced Holy Writ as a plain-spoken word of comfort against the academic pretensions of New England's Calvinist-turned-Unitarian elite. It is therefore not surprising that Paine's attack on scripture in *The Age of Reason* so riled Elhanan Winchester. Here were two populists clashing head-on over whether the Bible could be trusted as a source of common sense. For Universalists, the problem was not the Bible itself but the cunning glosses put on it by Calvinistic predestinarians. Getting past these inherited interpretations, Universalists believed, normally required only a clear-headed reappraisal, although a few enthusiasts looked to more ecstatic methods of exegesis. A notable example was the itinerant preacher Caleb Rich (1750–1821). Like many of his coreligionists, Rich was reared in Massachusetts on strict Calvinism (in his case, of the Baptist variety) and endured significant bouts of predestinarian melancholy. But instead of finding relief from reading alone, Rich was seized in 1778 by a series of trances and visions. In the most remarkable episode, a luminous personage appeared, carrying a Bible, and revealed to him the correct interpretation of the story of Abraham's wife Sarah and the bondwoman Hagar, as retold by Paul (Gal. 4:22–31). All the "formal" churches were wrong, the person explained, in assuming that the apostle had in mind *eternal* election and damnation in speaking of "two covenants." The children of the bondwoman suffered only in this life. In the life to come, all people would enjoy unending happiness by virtue of their descent from Jesus Christ, the second Adam. The angelic being then instructed Rich to go out and proclaim this gospel. Evidently, he proved to be a persuasive evangelist, for he is credited with converting another onetime Baptist, the elder Hosea Ballou.[38]

HOT-BLOODED METHODISTS

The Universalists put the Methodists on the defensive. Ever since John Wesley's heart was strangely warmed, Methodists had been sensitive to the charge that their doctrine of prevenient grace, which gave all people the *potential* to be saved, amounted to Universalism. George Whitefield had accused Wesley of precisely that, prompting Wesley's mother, Susanna, to upbraid the Grand Itinerant for his "Great Mistake (I would hope it is not wilful)."[39] Indeed, the Methodists' excessive zeal to distance themselves from the stigma of heterodoxy contributed to mutual antipathy with their Universalist competitors. One Universalist in antebellum New York state, Nathaniel Stacy, recalled his encounter with a Methodist circuit rider, a Mr. Mitchell, who preached on 1 Peter 4:18 ("And if the righteous scarcely be saved, where shall the ungodly and the sinner appear?"). Mitchell soon made it clear that Methodists were the only righteous ones and even many of them would have difficulty getting into heaven. The unrighteous included persons propagating false doctrines "leading souls blindfold down to hell." At this point in the harangue, recounted Stacy, Mitchell leaned forward "so as to almost thrust his finger in my face, and raising his voice almost to a scream, he exclaimed, 'If the righteous are scarcely saved, where do *you* expect to appear'?" Stacy held his tongue but "smiled, disdainfully, in his face":

[Mitchell's countenance] instantly reddened with passion—his eyes seemed to flash fire! he leaped, it appeared to me, three feet from the floor, and smiting his fist on the Bible, his eyes steadfastly fixed on me, and mine on him with the same contemptuous smile—he exclaimed, with a voice like thunder, "I'll tell you where you'll appear—you'll appear in *hell*, with the liquid streams of fire and brimstone pouring down your throat, to all eternity!"[40]

Later, Stacy wrote of his run-in with another Methodist evangelist, "Mr. F.," who prayed that the Lord would "deliver us from atheism, from deism, from Universalism, and every other hell-hatched ism that prevails in the land." Mr. F. then turned his wrath to the Calvinists, but, as Stacy put it, "the poor fellow knew no more about Calvinism than he did about the man in the moon. He stamped, raved, and foamed a long time about ' 'lection' but finally contented himself by saying, 'but I don't believe that.'"[41]

In Stacy's eyes, Mr. F. was the most "ignorant block-head I ever heard attempt to address a congregation." For their part, however, Methodists were incredulous that Universalists could believe (as Mr. F. put it) that "everybody's 'lected." Empirical evidence seemed to suggest that some people were irredeemably sinful. Were unrepentant "thieves, robbers, [and] whore-mongers" all going to heaven? Mr. F. asked. "[I]f everybody's going to heaven, I don't want to go there."[42] More genteel Methodists were no less adamant than their backcountry brethren on Universalism's deleterious influence. Wilbur Fisk, who graduated from Brown University in 1815 and became the first president of Wesleyan University in Connecticut in 1831, criticized Huntington's *Calvinism Improved* for leading many people down the slippery slope to an infidelity that feared "no hell—no devil—no angry God."[43] Elsewhere, he derided the Universalists for treating time-honored theological traditions as no better than "impressions received in the nursery from our old superstitious grandmothers."[44]

Yet as we saw in the last chapter, the original and chief opponents of the Methodists were not the Universalists but the Calvinists. By the first decades of the nineteenth century, this battle was erupting on a wider front both in the revival tents and in print. The Methodist-as-recovering-Calvinist became a familiar figure, thanks to oft-reprinted texts such as the *Experience and Gospel Labours* of Benjamin Abbott (1732–1796), a New Jersey farmer turned itinerant preacher. Abbott was arguably more influential in death than in life: his memoir, posthumously published in 1801, went through at least a dozen antebellum editions. In addition to revealing the depth of anti-Calvinism in the Methodist movement, Abbott's case also shows the importance of ecstatic experience, which would assume a central role by the twentieth century wherever Methodism evolved into Pentecostalism. Abbott began his odyssey as a Presbyterian; his wife was a strict "praying woman" of the same denomination. He recalled that his visions began with a dream of himself in hell, where giant scorpions repeatedly stung him with tails nearly six feet long. A few weeks later, he dreamed of standing before God in heaven and hearing him say, "Benjamin, this place is not for you yet." After these wake-up calls, he backslid into his sinful ways, which caused him to revert to his familiar anxiety. He became increasingly desperate: "Being brought up in the doctrine of election and reprobation, I concluded that I should be damned, do what I could." He imagined the devil lurking at every turn: "my hair arose on my head through fear." Days passed, and losing all appetite, he threw his food to the dog. The turning point came one day in October 1772, when Christ himself appeared to him and said, "I died for you." In that moment of tearful catharsis, "the Scriptures were wonderfully opened to my understanding." Christ further instructed him that "[y]ou must join the Methodists, for they are my people, and they are right."[45]

Emboldened by such a miraculous refutation of Calvinism, Abbott went back to his wife and told her that "she had no religion, and was nothing more than a strict Pharisee." This indelicate announcement prompted her to seek advice from her pastor, who sent her back with a copy of "Bellamey's New Divinity," namely, *True Religion Delineated* (1750) by Jonathan Edwards's disciple Joseph Bellamy. "I read it about half through and found him a rigid predestinarian," Abbott noted.[46] The next day, Abbott reluctantly agreed to the minister's request for a meeting, which left him mired anew in anxiety about his eternal state. Progressing once more to a spiritual climax, Abbott heard the Lord speak to him: "Why do you doubt? Is not Christ all-sufficient?" This new theophany turned Abbott's distress into raptures of joy: "I then sprang upon my feet, and cried out, not all the devils in hell, nor all the predestinarians on earth, should make me doubt; for I knew that I was converted." Amazingly, however, Abbott found himself a few days later succumbing yet again to temptations until finally he resolved to compare the Bible with the Westminster and Baptist confessions until he settled his doubts. "I found the Bible held out free grace *to all*, and *for all*, and that Christ tasted death for every man, and offered gospel salvation to *all*: therefore, I could not bear those contracted partial doctrines of unconditional election and reprobation." He threw the confessions aside and continued reading the Bible straight through, from Genesis to Revelation, "by which time, I was well armed with arguments against the predestinarians." Confirmed at last in his decision to become a Methodist, he continued to take his wife to the new sect's meetings until, under the influence of another preacher, she repented of her pharisaical ways and became a willing Methodist too, restoring the couple to wedded bliss. "These were the beginning of days to us," Abbott exulted.[47]

While Abbott's memoir enjoyed a remarkable shelf life among a popular readership, some Methodist leaders began to see the need to confront the Calvinists in the academic arena. Nathan Bangs (1778–1862), who rose to become head of the Methodist Book Concern in New York City, typified this new concern for scholarly respectability as the Methodist movement gained institutional strength after 1800.[48] Though not a college graduate himself, he took a dim view of the "ill-digested effusions" of unlettered exhorters and recognized the polemical advantage that Calvinists gained from their long tradition of an educated ministry.[49] Calvinists could portray their predestinarianism as grounded in cool reason, whereas Methodists too often appeared hot-headed and irrational. Consequently, in his early polemical efforts, Bangs turned the tables. In a reply to an attack on the Methodists by the Congregational minister Daniel Haskel, a Yale graduate who would serve three years as president of the University of Vermont before suffering a mental breakdown, Bangs insisted that the unconditional predestination taught by Haskel and other Calvinists was neither scriptural nor rational. Bangs invoked John Wesley's claim that no passage of scripture could prove Calvinism's "horrible decree," which rendered Christ a hypocrite and Paul a liar for claiming that God "will have all men to be saved" (1 Tim. 2:4). Bangs also ridiculed Haskel's argument, standard among Calvinists, that humans were free, and therefore responsible for their sins, even while their eternal destinies were fixed. This was like saying that both the earth-centered and sun-centered models of the solar system were true and "we must all believe it."[50] The worst offenders in perpetuating this dubious compatibilism were "those rigid predestinarians, who inhabit the eastern and northern sections of our country," by which Bangs meant the New Divinity successors of Jonathan Edwards: Joseph Bellamy, Samuel Hopkins, and their disciples. Haskel had internalized the vocabulary of this school as a student at Yale under president Timothy Dwight.[51] Bangs attacked the tradition more fully in *The Errors of Hopkinsianism* (1815), which sold 3,000 copies in six months—a testament to the New Divinity's wide currency at the time among college-educated ministers and their flocks.[52]

METHODISTS VERSUS NEW ENGLAND CALVINISTS

Indeed, the "New England theology," as the evolving New Divinity came to be known by the mid-nineteenth century, emerged as a classic American attempt to reconcile human freedom with divine determinism, and it became a major target of Methodist anti-Calvinism.[53] The New England project extended for a century, from its leading light, Jonathan Edwards, to his namesake Edwards Amasa Park (1808–1900), professor at the Congregationalists' Andover Seminary (founded in 1807 in opposition to Unitarian-dominated Harvard).[54] Central to this "consistent Calvinism" (another nickname of the movement) was Edwards's distinction, developed in *Freedom of the Will* (1754), between natural and moral ability.[55] Under normal circumstances, people had a *natural ability* to obey God and repent, meaning that in the absence of physical or mental impairment or some external coercion, their minds and bodies were fully capable of turning to Christ. *Moral ability* referred to what people did by free choice of their wills, which was inseparable from the psychological inclinations or dispositions governing their choices. A person inclined toward sin lacked the moral ability to choose Christ. But because the sinner's refusal to convert was entirely due to his own unwillingness, and not due to any natural inability, he was fully responsible for his actions. As one New England theologian put it, "sinners *can* do what they certainly *will* not do."[56]

This ingenious formula begged many technical questions, among them how exactly the will related to the inclinations and how these in turn related to original sin and the operation of God in inclining elect sinners toward Christ. Out of these questions, a rift developed in the New England theology between the "exercisers" and the "tasters."[57] The exercisers, intent on emphasizing human accountability for sin, avoided talk of inclinations or dispositions, which seemed to let individuals off the hook, and maintained that the will simply *was* as a person chose to exercise it. To old

Calvinists—those conservatives who refused to join the consistent Calvinist bandwagon—this looked suspiciously like a denial of original sin (understood in the traditional way as an innately depraved nature or inclination toward sin). The exercisers insisted that they still believed in the T (total depravity) of the five-point Calvinist TULIP, only they understood depravity not as an inherited or imputed trait but as the "moral exercises" produced in each person individually by God's immediate power.[58] Meanwhile, the tasters, intent on quelling the old Calvinists' murmurings that the New England theology was soft on original sin, preferred to speak of "taste" (or "feelings" or "heart") as a separate faculty that governed the will. A person's taste was depraved by nature until God regenerated it, setting in motion the will's actions in conversion.

No succinct summary can do justice to the full positions carved out by the two sides in this indigenous scholastic dispute. (The leading exerciser, Nathanael Emmons, literally carved out his position: said to spend 10–16 hours a day in his study, he left a gouge in the wainscoting where he propped up his feet.)[59] Yet for all their technical differences, the two parties were equally committed to the paradox, however imperfectly understood on this side of the eschaton, that though the human will was absolutely free, it was also absolutely determined by God. Thus, Edwards A. Park, the New England theology's first historian, explained in a triumphant retrospective that the movement "insisted on an eternally decreed liberty, and a free submission to the eternal decrees." It was precisely because the New England theologians had "secured human liberty" that they "preached more than others on predestination, because they have prepared the way for it by showing that man's freedom has been predestined."[60]

Such thinking on predestination—that it was fully compatible with liberty, which Americans had come to expect as their birthright—influenced none other than the young Charles Finney (1792–1875), the most famous revivalist of the Second Great Awakening. His spectacular 1830–1831 revival in Rochester, New York, which occurred amid the social and economic ferment created by the new Erie Canal, helped to give the region its nickname, the Burned-Over District. Originally trained as an attorney, Finney's lawyerly preaching style combined "hot passion and cold logic."[61] Logically speaking, Finney was an exerciser in the mold of Emmons. Any notion of sin as an inherited taste or nature, he believed, could become an excuse for laxity. He used techniques such as group prayer in hopes that the regenerate (those already properly exercising their wills) would influence others to do the same.[62] Eventually, as a professor and later as president of Oberlin, he came to regard the Edwardsean dichotomy of natural ability and moral inability as unhelpful. (Finney, like his contemporary the Yale professor

Nathaniel William Taylor, feared that moral inability in effect made God the author of sin.) But by then, Finney the revivalist had cemented in many people's minds the connection between the New England theology and what Allen Guelzo has called the "double vocabulary of radical free-willism and radical Calvinism."[63]

This vocabulary became a favorite subject of parody by the no-nonsense Methodists, who regarded it as a peculiarly obstinate form of doublespeak. King of the satirists was "Crazy" Lorenzo Dow (1777–1834), who barnstormed across the country and even in the British Isles, attracting greater throngs to camp meetings than any other Methodist preacher of the day. With his long hair, intense eyes, and hard-edged manner, Dow regaled audiences with anti-Calvinist jingles that later appeared in his many popular publications.[64] In his journal, *History of Cosmopolite* (1814), he ridiculed Calvinists for talking out of both sides of their mouths: "You can and you can't—You shall and you shan't—You will and you won't—And you will be damned if you do—And you will be damned if you don't."[65]

From a Methodist perspective, Calvinists shot themselves in the foot by embracing a theology that forced them to reconcile the open invitations of the revivals with the closed system of absolute predestination.[66] The seemingly straightforward free-willism of Arminian theology struck Methodists as the obvious solution. (In reality, as we saw in chapter 1, technical Arminianism, with the Molinist questions it suggested about God's foreknowledge, could be just as labyrinthine.) Yet as Nathan Hatch has pointed out, the quarrel of Dow and other frontier preachers with Calvinism was at least as much about social class and politics as it was about doctrine. A radical Jeffersonian, Dow shared the third president's hostility to "priestcraft" and was not averse to quoting Tom Paine alongside the Bible in his sermons. The untrained Dow typified a widespread anticlericalism in the decades following the Revolution, when, as Hatch has described, a motley crew of Protestant populists rebelled against what they regarded as the "self-appointed aristocracy trying to control the soul of the nation." This populism enshrined the right of private judgment in Bible reading and it privileged scripture as the supreme authority that trumped the pious pronouncements of clerical and professorial elites.[67]

Calvinist predestination thus became the perfect emblem of academic self-importance, though not all the populists who railed against it were themselves aliens to academe. Wesleyan University president Wilbur Fisk, whom we met earlier, co-opted many populist themes in attacking the New England theologians. He accused them of espousing a two-faced system that cleverly couched the doctrine of moral inability in the language of free will, while keeping the harshness of reprobation out of sight altogether.

"[H]onest John Calvin" himself would have been appalled at such "disingenuousness and cowardice," Fisk declared. The New England theology's duplicity was crassly opportunistic. Its "metaphysical abstrusities and distinctions," he maintained, were calculated to appeal to students of theology, while its commonsense talk of free will duped ordinary people into thinking that the system offered them genuine hope.[68] New England's Calvinists advertised themselves as champions of the "doctrines of grace," Fisk added, but Methodists were the true defenders of grace alone and grace for all. The Calvinists' repeated insistence that humans had the *natural* ability to repent denied the necessity of prevenient grace, which Methodists recognized must precede any move toward Christ: "To say a fallen man has a natural power to make a right choice, because he has the faculties of his mind entire, is the same as to say that a paralytic man has the natural power to walk, because he has his limbs entire." The Bible abundantly confirmed humans' absolute dependence on grace, which New England's counterfeit Calvinists ignored. Fisk's coup de grâce was John 6:44, that shibboleth for unconditional predestinarians, which he turned against the New Englanders. "No man can come to me, except the Father which hath sent me draw him": this proved conclusively to Fisk that humans had no abilities of any sort without God's prevenient assistance.[69]

In the end, however, Methodism's theological drawing card was not prevenient grace per se. No Calvinist worth his salt, not even the subtle New Englanders, denied the Reformation's grace alone. What inspired Methodism's antebellum converts was rather the simple, empowering message that God gave prevenient grace to *all*, without exception, and that this good news was plainly evident in scripture. This gospel drew converts from across the social spectrum. Because Methodists tended to value inspiration over formal theological training, they left the door ajar for leadership by women and African Americans, who lacked access to the elite credentialing centers of the oldline Protestant establishment. To be sure, Methodism often succumbed to the same gender and racial prejudices operative in society at large. America's first independent black denomination, the African Methodist Episcopal Church, was born in the crucible of racism, after its leaders rebelled against the second-class treatment they endured from white Methodist authorities. Yet there was no denying the attraction of a tradition that seemed to offer a more robust egalitarianism than Calvinism.[70]

Methodism's appeal is strikingly evident in the case of Richard Allen (1760–1831), the founding bishop of the AME Church, who was drawn into the Wesleyan orbit by circuit riders while he was still a slave in Delaware. Later, after Allen became an itinerant himself, he crossed paths with Benjamin Abbott, whose own conversion had occurred about a dozen years earlier. "He was one of the greatest men that ever I was acquainted with," Allen wrote of Abbott in his autobiography. Transcending the racial divide, the two men became close, sometimes preaching together. "He was a friend and father to me," Allen wrote. "I was sorry when I had to leave West Jersey, knowing I had to leave a father."[71] It seems likely that Allen titled his autobiography, *Life Experience and Gospel Labors* (1833), after Abbott's similarly named memoir. And Allen's text, like Abbott's, testified powerfully to Methodism's populist dimension. The Methodists, he wrote, "were the first people that brought glad tidings to the colored people. I feel thankful that ever I heard a Methodist preach. We are beholden to the Methodists, under God, for the light of the Gospel we enjoy; for all other denominations preached so high-flown that we were not able to comprehend their doctrine."[72]

Allen's own preaching converted the female itinerant Jarena Lee (1783–1850?), who first found solace in Methodism after negative experiences in three other denominations and who became famous for her unsuccessful battle in the AME Church for full ordination rights for women. Born to free black parents in New Jersey, she began work early as a servant and landed first in a Presbyterian church, where the preacher's sermon on original sin plunged her into suicidal despair. Finding a job next with a Catholic family, she took to reading scripture until, one day, the lady of the house, "observing this, took the Bible from me and hid it, giving me a novel in its stead." From there, she wound up in Philadelphia, where she briefly attended the Episcopal church of the English rector Joseph Pilmore. It soon became apparent to Lee that "there was a wall between me and a communion with that people, which was higher than I could possibly see over." Finally, in Allen's Bethel Church, she experienced an emotional conversion, though wrenching doubts about the state of her soul soon returned. As she recounted, with Edwardsean echoes, "the awful gulf of hell seemed to open beneath me, covered only, as it were, by a spider's web, on which I stood." The ultimate catharsis came when she obeyed a voice whispering in her heart, "Pray for sanctification." "That very instant," she recounted, "as if lightning had darted through me, I sprang to my feet, and cried, 'The Lord has sanctified my soul!'" Then came the confirming voice from heaven: "Bow down for the witness," it told her, "thou art sanctified!"[73]

In Lee's sudden, overwhelming sanctification, we catch a glimpse of American religion's future, when millions of Pentecostal and other charismatic Christians would bypass the intellectualism of predestination entirely and find ecstatic confirmation of their salvation. Holiness pioneers, such as the Methodist Phoebe Palmer (1807–1874), paved the way with their idea of a "Spirit baptism," or an unmediated, instantaneous proof of sanctification.[74]

From this, it was but a short step to the restoration of speaking in tongues—the fire from heaven described in Acts 2—as the sure sign of the Spirit's blessing.[75] Foretold, its adherents believed, by Joel 2:23, the "latter rain" of the modern Pentecost mirrored the "former rain" of the biblical outpouring, rendering all the complicated doctrinal developments between the first and the twentieth centuries essentially irrelevant. This is classic primitivism, the end result of a Wesleyan-Arminian trajectory that ignited the populist fires of biblical revival.[76]

To be sure, the long history of American religious awakenings proves that it would be a serious mistake to equate all revivalism with the Arminian lineage.[77] In the First Great Awakening, unconditional predestinarians such as George Whitefield and even the more bookish Jonathan Edwards moved many people to ecstatic fears or joys no less remarkable than those inspired by the later Arminians. Nor were the antebellum Methodists the only Protestants who succeeded in converting persons other than white males. The black Congregational minister and former indentured servant Lemuel Haynes (1753–1833) was a New Divinity man who once delivered a sermon, "Divine Decrees," that repeated the double vocabulary that Methodists loved to hate: "The agency and government of God is [sic] perfectly consistent with the liberty and freedom of men."[78] Nevertheless, in sheer numbers of converts, pride of place in the antebellum period belongs to the Methodists. Between 1776 and 1850, Methodists increased from an estimated 3 percent of all church members to 34 percent, making them "the most extensive national institution other than the Federal government."[79] By contrast, Presbyterians and Congregationalists lost ground in the same period, declining from 39 to 15 percent of adherents. Even allowing for error in the notoriously difficult science of religious demographics, these numbers strongly suggest that the first eight decades of the republic were not kind to unconditional predestinarians.[80]

THE BIBLE AS CHARTER OF LIBERTIES: MORE VARIATIONS ON A THEME

Successful as Methodism was, its popular Arminian theology was hardly the only version of anti-Calvinism that caught fire in the republic's first century. Opposition to unconditional predestination, combined with a thoroughgoing biblicism, helped to give birth to four uniquely American traditions: Stone-Campbell "Christians," Adventists, Christian Scientists, and Mormons.[81] Surveying them in that order will reveal the progressively more radical conclusions they drew from repudiating "invented" predestinarian doctrines in favor of the presumably uncorrupted word of God. Each group believed it had discovered a key to the scriptures that would prove how other groups had perverted their meaning and obscured the genuine freedom God gave to all people.

Stone-Campbell Christians

For those in the Stone-Campbell movement—many of whom preferred to be known simply as "Christians"[82]—the key to scripture was common sense. Because the Bible's meaning was assumed to be clear and unambiguous, unlocking it required no special training. Indeed, ordinary people were thought to be more reliable interpreters than the theologians, whose dogmatic hobbyhorses inevitably skewed their perceptions of the text. "I have endeavored to read the Scriptures as though no one had read them before me," declared the movement's co-founder, Alexander Campbell (1788–1866), an immigrant from Ulster.[83] Campbell's tabula rasa was not entirely blank, however. As a young man, he attended classes at the University of Glasgow, where he internalized the Scottish "common sense" philosophy of Thomas Reid (1710–1796) and Dugald Stewart (1753–1828), themselves disciples of a pioneer of the modern scientific method, Francis Bacon. The Scottish version of Baconianism arose in opposition to the skepticism of David Hume, and its significance for Campbell was twofold. First, it privileged an inductive, rather than deductive, method. Conclusions should proceed from the specific to the general, from sense experience and observation of particular facts to more general conclusions. Second, and in opposition to Hume's doubts about the absolute reliability of general conclusions drawn from limited human observations, Scottish philosophy insisted that people could trust their intuitions—their common sense—in evaluating observable data.[84] Every perception involved certain basic presuppositions (for example, that a sensing self existed), and these implicit judgments could be accepted as what Reid called "first principles" of the mind.[85]

Applied in somewhat simplistic fashion to predestination, this meant the following. The Bible was Christianity's chief repository of observable "facts." (Campbell and his colleagues did not question the historical accuracy of the biblical accounts.) Observation of scripture revealed a variety of passages claiming, as Campbell put it, that "whosoever will, may, can, and ought" to accept Christ in order to be saved. Everyday perception of the world, moreover, suggested that humans have the power of free choice. (Even the Calvinists agreed that from a purely human standpoint, we freely choose our actions.) Common sense thus seemed to corroborate the biblical evidence that people are genuinely free to accept or reject Christ.

Campbell believed that Calvinism violated the inductive method by building its system of unconditional predestination largely on rash speculation rather than on a preponderance of observable facts. Where did the Bible mention supralapsarians and infralapsarians? Where did it spell out the five points of Dort or Westminster? For that matter, where did it discuss the prevenient grace of Arminianism? Even the word for "predestine" occurred in New Testament Greek only a handful of times. "From the frequent use of this word in theological and controversial works, one would imagine that it must have occupied a large space in the sacred original," Campbell wrote.[86] The passages typically used to justify Calvinistic predestination were, he believed, "either wrested, perverted, or misapplied." He was content to accept scripture's assurances of "whosoever will" and leave it at that. "This may be called any *ism* men please," but it "is in accordance with the whole scope, design, and letter of the inspired volume."[87] Campbell believed strongly that creeds and confessions had served only to divide Christians. A former Presbyterian himself, he offered a backhanded compliment to his Calvinist brethren: "the more thinking, inquisitive, and intelligent the community which owns a creed, the more frequent their debates and schisms."[88] The solution was to accept "no creed but the Bible." This "Bibleism," as he elsewhere called it, became a rallying cry for Campbell's followers. He admitted that clearing away the sediment of invented doctrines had been difficult even for him. "[W]e found it an arduous task, and one of twenty years' labour, to correct our diction and purify our speech according to the Bible alone; and even yet we have not wholly practically repudiated the language of Ashdod."[89]

Campbell's movement eventually joined forces with that of another former Presbyterian, Barton Stone, whose commitment to Bible-only voluntarism was forged in the white heat of revival. From 6 to 12 August 1801, Stone, then pastor of the Presbyterian congregation at Cane Ridge, Kentucky, hosted a massive camp meeting that has been dubbed "America's Pentecost" by one historian.[90] Stone welcomed participation by other ministers, including Methodists and Baptists, who "all preached the same things—free salvation urged upon all by faith and repentance." Many laypeople were slain in the Spirit, experiencing ecstatic jerking, barking, dancing, and laughing, according to Stone's account.[91] Meanwhile, some of his colleagues in the Presbyterian Synod of Kentucky, while hesitant to question the mighty work of revival, were perturbed by his failure to adhere to the Westminster Confession and his fraternization with Methodists and Baptists. By 1804, Stone and his allies announced their secession from the Presbyterian Church, declaring themselves denominated only by the name "Christian." Later, Stone wrote in his memoir that the Westminster doctrine that Christ died only for the elect belied the "whole tenor of Scripture."[92]

Independently of Stone and Campbell, two lesser-known prophets of Bible-onlyism were spreading the message in New England. Elias Smith (1769–1846) and Abner Jones (1772–1841), both former Calvinistic Baptists, founded churches in Vermont and New Hampshire before creating the loose fellowship that would come to be known as the Christian Connection. From 1806 to 1817, Smith edited the *Herald of Gospel Liberty*, which reprinted in its first issue Stone's declaration of independence from Presbyterianism. The newspaper also trafficked in popular verse against Calvinism and its "horrible decree," including this earthy stanza:

> That ALL if they choose,
> May enjoy the GOOD NEWS,
> May embrace Jesus Christ and Salvation;
> Then with all he must pass
> For a dull, senseless ass,
> Who depends upon predestination.[93]

Smith's later career was unusually fluid, even in an era marked by religious instability. Twice, he left the Connection to join the Universalists, only to return to the fold each time, before finally fading into obscurity as a dabbler in herbal medicine.[94]

Adventists

The New England circles of the Christian Connection helped to provide converts for the Adventists, the second of the four uniquely American traditions that emerged out of antebellum anti-Calvinism.[95] Originally known as Millerites after their founder, William Miller (1782–1849), in 1860 they took the name Seventh-day Adventists, inaugurating a steady rise into their familiar presence in today's denominational pantheon. Born in Massachusetts but reared in upstate New York on the Vermont border, Miller learned Calvinism from his mother, a strict Baptist, and his maternal grandfather and paternal uncle, both Baptist preachers. Not formally educated, he eagerly frequented a local library. As a young married man, he kept company with a band of village deists enamored of Paine and of Jeffersonian politics. In an act of rebellion that cut his mother to the heart, he ridiculed his grandfather's and uncle's piety in their presence. His life changed after a series of sobering events: the death of his father in 1812, a serious illness during a fever epidemic in 1813, and bloody fighting witnessed during his service as a captain in the Battle of Plattsburgh in 1814. Returning from the war chastened of his infidelity, he began the religious quest that would make him one of the most famous (and infamous) prophets in U.S. history.[96]

Rejecting his earlier view of the Bible as rank superstition, Miller embarked upon a systematic survey of Holy Writ. "I determined to lay aside all my pre-possessions, to thoroughly compare Scripture with Scripture, and to pursue its study in a regular and methodical manner," he recalled. "I commenced with Genesis, and read verse by verse."[97] His later description of his rules for biblical interpretation revealed that common sense, with its confidence in the Bible's perspicuity and the discernment of ordinary folk, was Miller's key just as it had been for Stone and Campbell. Miller learned that "the Bible contained a system of revealed truths, so clearly and simply given that the 'wayfaring man, though a fool,' need not err therein." Exegesis required no special expertise: "If I depend on a teacher to expound it to me,...then his guessing, desire, creed, or wisdom is my rule, not the Bible." Obscure passages would be made plain by comparison with other passages. Careful collation would indicate certain recurring figures of speech, as when "day" was used to mean "year."[98] In applying this chronological axiom, however, Miller revealed his common sense to be a little less common than most. Daniel 8:14 ("Unto two thousand and three hundred days; then shall the sanctuary be cleansed") meant 2,300 years from the "seventy weeks" (Dan. 9:24), which, according to Miller, "the best chronologers dated from B.C. 457." Thus, the math: –457 + 2,300 = 1843, which would be the date of the cleansing of the sanctuary, which Miller interpreted as the Second Coming. This was Baconianism in the extreme, treating every verse of scripture as a potentially momentous "fact."[99]

When Christ did not appear, and Miller's revised calculation of 1844 also failed to pan out, his followers suffered the "great disappointment." This storied episode has overshadowed the undercurrent of anti-predestinarianism that would become more explicit as the Millerite movement was reincarnated as Adventism. Miller himself once drafted a statement of his theology, which revealed his belief in an essentially Arminian election based on divine foreknowledge. Elsewhere, in a self-deprecating moment, he wrote to a correspondent that the apostle Paul "must have been as crazy as Bro. William" for rashly speaking of becoming "all things to all men" that he might save "some" (1 Cor. 9:22; cf. Rom. 11:14), which helped to spawn the endless debate between Universalists and Calvinists about the extent of the atonement. "O, how many long arguments it would have saved," Miller mused, if Paul "had not said anything about two classes of mankind."[100] But Miller was no Universalist, and his successor, Ellen G. White (1827–1915), who was given to trances and visions, made clear the truth as it had been revealed to her: "God sets before man life and death. He can have his choice."[101] In her book *The Great Controversy* (1858), which depicted history as a cosmic battle between Christ and Satan, she denounced the "monstrous" Calvinist doctrine of perseverance of the saints and praised John Wesley for showing that God gave all people the means to respond to Christ.[102]

The same free-will doctrine carried over into the Jehovah's Witnesses-movement, founded by Charles Taze Russell (1852–1916), a onetime Presbyterian, who was drawn into apocalypticism by an Adventist preacher. Ironically, the Witnesses' own Baconian fact mining led them full circle to a modified predestinarianism. Though God did not foreordain the fates of individuals, he did predetermine that a "little flock" of 144,000 (Luke 12:32; Rev. 14:1) would reign with him in heaven, while other saved persons would enjoy an earthly paradise. The specific members of the little flock would be determined later based on their conduct in life.[103] The idea of an open-ended decree may have been planted in part by Adventism, which appeared to entertain the possibility that God's power was temporarily circumscribed by the cosmic contest of good and evil. "Compared to the sublime immutability of Calvin's deity," note two scholars of the movement, "Adventism's God has always worked with numerous restrictions on his freedom of action."[104] In the late twentieth century, the question of divine indeterminacy came to the fore dramatically when Richard Rice, a professor at the Seventh-day Adventists' Loma Linda University, published *The Openness of God* (1980), a controversial manifesto of "open theism"—the idea that God's knowledge of future contingents is in some sense limited.[105] Though the Adventist publishing house backed away from reprinting the book after its initial run, the episode revealed the surprising willingness of some apocalyptic Protestants to tackle tough questions that many other Christians—despite their endless mantra that God grants people real freedom—have been afraid to ask.

Christian Scientists

Revisionism of a radically different kind became the hallmark of the third American original to spring forth from the nineteenth-century rebellion against predestination. For Mary Baker Eddy (1821–1910), the founder of Christian Science, the key to scripture was not common sense because the usual human rationality was flawed. "To mortal sense Christian Science seems abstract," Eddy wrote, "but the process is simple and the results are sure if the Science is understood."[106] The key to the Bible was understanding that the material world is an illusion. Sickness and death do not truly exist because only mind is real, and it is immortal. Mind is God, and humans are the "full and perfect expression" of this deity.[107] Salvation comes when we understand matter's unreality, a message that Jesus came to impart: "Atonement is the exemplification of man's unity with God."[108]

The antecedents of Eddy's ideas, and her breakthrough "discovery" after a serious fall on ice, are extensively documented.[109] What is intriguing is predestination's prominence in her early biography. During her childhood in rural New Hampshire, Eddy sometimes chafed under the strict Calvinist piety of her father, who led the family in lengthy, extemporaneous prayer every morning. (Shortly before her death, she confided to a secretary that once, as a child, she took a shawl pin from a pincushion and stabbed her father in the behind while he was praying!)[110] Her first intellectual defiance of Calvinism occurred at age 12, when, as she later wrote in her memoir, "the doctrine of unconditional election, or predestination, greatly troubled me." Already beset with chronic illness, young Mary was now seized by a variant strain of *tentatio praedestinationis*—the dreaded New England "melancholy." None of her older siblings had yet made the public profession of conversion required for Congregational church membership, and she was "unwilling to be saved" if her brothers and sisters "were to be numbered among those who were doomed to perpetual banishment from God." Wracked with a literal fever brought on by her "father's relentless theology," Eddy followed her mother's urgings to go to God in prayer. Soon, her fever was gone, and the "'horrible decree' of predestination—as John Calvin rightly called his own tenet—forever lost its power" over her. Five years later, after the family had moved to a new town and Eddy had presented herself for examination by her minister, she confessed her rejection of predestination and said that while she was willing to trust God, she would take her chances with her brothers and sisters if her doubts prevented the church from granting her full membership. The people in attendance were so moved by her earnestness that the pastor received her into communion.[111]

Eddy would remain officially a Congregationalist for the next four decades until she obtained a charter for the First Church of Christ, Scientist, in Boston in 1879. As scholars have pointed out, she also remained a lifelong Calvinist in certain respects, as in her acceptance of a rigid spirit-flesh dualism and her Edwardsean conviction that religion is a matter of the affections and must thereby transform a person's perception of the world.[112] Yet Calvinism as a system was fundamentally wrong, in her view, not only because of unconditional predestination but also because of the doctrine of original sin, which posits a will enfeebled by wickedness and a mass of humanity fit only for destruction. "The crudest ideals of speculative theology have made monsters of men," Eddy once declared in a sermon. "The eternal roasting amidst noxious vapours—the election of the minority to be saved and the majority to be eternally punished; the wrath of God to be appeased by the sacrifice and torture of his favorite Son; are some of the false beliefs that have produced sin, sickness, and death."[113] Liberation from these errors still depended on scripture—Eddy insisted that the Bible was her only authority—but its interpretation required a metaphysical lens. She was confident that more and more people were awakening to their own powers of mind and rejecting the old doctrines. Indeed, in the quasi-sacred text she bequeathed to her followers, *Science and Health with Key to the Scriptures* (1875), Eddy predicted that the "time is not distant when ordinary theological views of atonement will undergo a great change—a change as radical as that which has come over popular opinions in regard to predestination and future punishment."[114]

Mormons

The transformation foretold by Eddy had, in fact, already occurred among the Mormons, whose uniquely radical revision of predestination and original sin reflected their boundless faith in human potential. The Latter-day Saints belong last in the progression of distinctively American groups we have just surveyed because they took the back-to-the-Bible mentality to its logical conclusion. For Mormon founder Joseph Smith (1805–1844), the Bible was not simply a source but a paradigm. To some extent, this was true for other figures we have examined. Barton Stone and Alexander Campbell, for example, were rebaptized as adults in obedience to Jesus' paradigmatic baptism by John the Baptist in the Jordan River. But Smith made the Bible *itself* the paradigm when he concluded that if scripture could be revealed in the apostolic age, the same could happen in his own time. God could also disclose the correct interpretation of existing biblical passages. Ongoing revelation, in other words, was Mormonism's interpretive key.

The revelations to Smith began early. He received his first vision around 1820, at age 14, while his family was living in Palmyra, New York, in the heart of the Burned-Over District. Thanks to the Erie Canal, the village had a bustling economy and a thriving religious scene. Within a few miles of the Smiths' house, there were four churches: Baptist, Methodist, Presbyterian, and Quaker. Joseph's mother, Lucy, was a member of the Presbyterian congregation, but his father, Joseph Sr., who was given to prophetic dreams himself, attended no church. Joseph Jr.'s paternal grandfather, meanwhile, was a Universalist.[115] All of this religious diversity left young Joseph bewildered: "In process of time my mind became somewhat partial to the Methodist sect, and I felt some desire to be united with them; but so great were the confusion and strife among the different denominations, that it was impossible for a person young as I was ... to come to any certain conclusion who was right and who was wrong."[116] Determined to follow the injunction of James 1:5 and take his uncertainty to God, he retired to the woods (Jonathan Edwards's own favorite refuge for meditation and prayer). Gripped by satanic temptation to despair, he suddenly saw two personages appear to him out of the sky in blinding light. One personage motioned to the other, "This is my beloved Son. Hear him!" Joseph asked him which of the sects was right, and the famous answer came: they were all wrong. "[A]nd the Personage who addressed me said that all their creeds were an abomination in His sight."[117]

As in Benjamin Abbott's strikingly similar experience almost a half century earlier, anti-predestinarianism was an important subtext. But whereas Abbott learned that the Methodists, with their Arminian theology, were right, Smith's first vision foreshadowed Mormonism's more radical break with Calvinism and indeed with the whole Augustinian tradition. All the sects were wrong, the Son explained to Smith, in the words of 2 Timothy 3:5, because they had "a form of godliness, but they deny the power thereof."[118] The Latter-day Saint tradition not only would restore humans' full powers of godliness, denying original sin, but also would read human free agency backward into a premortal existence and forward into a postmortal spirit world. All of this would be made known to Smith in an ancient trove of writings engraved on gold plates and in subsequent revelations given to him directly by God.

The plates that became in translation the Book of Mormon (1830) will always be the most dubious aspect of the Latter-day Saint tradition to out-siders. Yet "hunting for deception can be a distraction," argues eminent historian and practicing Mormon Richard Bushman, because it "throws us off the track of Joseph Smith the Prophet."[119] From the standpoint of U.S. history, it hardly matters whether the gold plates were real or whether the stories they conveyed about Christ and other ancient characters really happened. What matters is the extraordinarily industrious culture, symbol-ized by the Mormon beehive on the Utah state flag, that belief in Smith's revelations produced. Mormon industry, unlike the predestinarian work ethic famously analyzed by Max Weber, arose from the idea that humans are radically free, indeed godlike, in their ability to choose and that their choices will determine which degree of glory they attain in the afterlife. Thus, Mormonism engendered its own kind of striving—not the Weberian anxiety about a fait accompli but worry over doing one's utmost for Christ in a probationary period that is not over until the last judgment.[120]

The Book of Mormon is replete with assurances of free will. The uni-verse, we learn, consists of things that act and things that are acted upon. Humans, like God, are free "to act for themselves and not to be acted upon, save it be by the punishment of the law at the great and last day."[121] Echo-ing Genesis 3:5, the book speaks of humans "becoming as Gods, knowing good from evil."[122] Later, in revelations that were canonized as part of the ongoing Doctrine and Covenants, Smith spoke in the language of "agency" that had dominated American theological debates since Edwards. Man is an "agent unto himself"; he has "moral agency" and is "accountable for his own sins."[123] This agency is not, as one later Mormon scholar explained it, "the freedom of perversity, the freedom to will only evil," but rather "full freedom of alternative action."[124] Though Adam's sin brought death into the world, it imposed no genetic taint of sinfulness on his posterity. In the Latter-day Saints' 13 Articles of Faith, first composed by Smith in 1842, number 2 spells this out clearly: "We believe that men will be punished for their own sins, and not for Adam's transgression."[125] Smith's successor, Brigham Young (1801–1877), who led the Mormons on the trek to Salt Lake City, was equally explicit: "The volition of the creature is free; this is a law of their existence and the Lord cannot violate his own law."[126]

Though Mormons believe that the miraculous disclosures to Smith and to subsequent prophets transcend merely human teaching, the revelations also serve the earthly, time-bound purpose of refuting the supposed errors on predestination that were rife in the Saints' initial nineteenth-century context. Nehor, a character in the Book of Mormon, is a thinly veiled Universalist who teaches that the Lord "redeemed all men; and, in the end, all men should have eternal life." In a debate with the orthodox Gideon, Nehor draws a sword and slays him, for which the false prophet is taken to the top of a hill and hanged, to show that "what he had taught to the people was contrary to the word of God."[127] The Book of Mormon also dispels the countervailing Calvinist doctrine of limited atonement when, in a telling aside in the book of 2 Nephi, we read of "the atonement, which is infinite for all mankind." This verse once prompted Alexander Campbell to quip that "the Calvinists were in America before Nephi."[128] Another instance of anti-Calvinism occurs in Joseph Smith's "translation" of the Bible—his unfinished effort, guided by direct revelation, to revise certain passages in the King James Version that were either mistranslated or that required doctrinally substantive revision or amplification. The old Calvinist favorite, John 6:44, was an obvious target for revision based on the progressive unfolding of divine wisdom. Smith's inspired version removed the implication of predestination ("except the Father...draw him") and changed the verse to read: "No man can come unto me, except he doeth the will of my Father who hath sent me."[129] Likewise, Smith modified 1 Corinthians 1:24 ("But unto them which are called") to read, "But unto them who believe," thereby replacing a predestinarian implication with a voluntaristic one.[130]

The doctrine of ongoing revelation ensures that Mormon theology will never be static. Because Mormonism teaches that God speaks through prophets in all ages, the Book of Mormon was only the beginning of an inexorable stream. "As well might man streatch forth his puny arm to stop the Missouri River," Smith once wrote (in his untutored spelling), as "hinder the Almighty from pooring down knoledge from heaven upon the heads of the Latter day saints."[131] Indeed, as an oracle of evolving wisdom, Smith departed ever more dramatically from Calvinist orthodoxies in the 14 years between the Book of Mormon's publication and his martyrdom at the hands of an angry mob. In 1832, he received a vision, elaborating 1 Corinthians 15:40–42, that disclosed the tripartite hierarchy of celestial, terrestrial, and telestial kingdoms constituting the realms of glory in the afterlife. While not everyone will earn a place in the highest, or celestial, heaven, very few people will fail to inherit one of the three. Even visible sinners, after enduring a period of punishment in hell, will attain the lowest, or telestial, kingdom. Only those people who deny the Son at the last, even after learning the truth of his divine mission from the Father, will be abandoned to everlasting punishment. This revelation, Bushman notes, moved Mormonism toward acceptance of a remedial hell that is virtually indistinguishable from that taught by many Universalists.[132]

Arguably the most dramatic departure from Calvinism came in 1844, less than three months before Smith's murder, when he elaborated the doctrine of preexistence. Adam's choice in Eden was neither the beginning nor the end of human free will. In premortal life, all persons were radically free, self-existent intelligences. "God was a self exhisting being, [and] man exhists upon the same principle," Smith declared. "God never had the power to create the spirit of man, God himself could not create himself. Intelligence is Eternal & it is self exhisting." God was not the sovereign creator of the universe out of nothing, Bushman explains, but instead was an intelligence who *learned* to become God and instituted laws to help weaker intelligences do the same. As the fifth president of the LDS Church, Lorenzo Snow (1814–1901), put it, "as man now is, God once was; as God now is, man may become."[133]

Such speculation has ancient, Platonic roots. In the third century, Origen spoke of preexistent intelligences, though he regarded them as creatures of God, not as self-existent entities. Once the Fifth Ecumenical Council of 553 condemned the "fabulous" doctrine of the preexistence of souls, Origenism forever acquired the taint of heresy.[134] Mormonism suffered under a similar stigma, which paradoxically only strengthened its adherents' conviction that they were a peculiar people, chosen for a special mission by God. Mormons may have shattered all predestinarian constraints on free will, but they were good Puritans in at least this respect. When Brigham Young marked the location for the Salt Lake Temple in 1847, he was confident that this was the foreordained Zion, where the Saints could realize their divine destiny.

Mormonism met with unmitigated hostility from the beginning, even from other Christians committed to what Alexander Campbell called the "restoration of the ancient order of things."[135] Critiquing the Book of Mormon in 1831, Campbell wrote that Joseph Smith was "as ignorant and as impudent a knave as ever wrote a book."[136] Later, Mark Twain unleashed his incomparable wit, dismissing the book as "chloroform in print" and mocking Smith's frequent use of certain phrases from the King James Bible. "'And it came to pass' was his pet," Twain observed. "If he had left that out, his Bible would have been only a pamphlet."[137] Other critics were more vicious. Methodist minister C. P. Lyford, who served four years as a missionary in Utah, cited the doctrines of preexistence and the plurality of gods as evidence of Mormons' perverse acceptance of "whatever trash a lecherous priesthood may be pleased to pronounce divinely inspired."[138]

Yet in flirting with ancient heresies, especially Pelagius's denial of original sin and Origen's doctrine of preexistence, Mormonism was in some ways simply the culmination of a much wider cultural rebellion against Augustinianism. Joseph Smith was far from a systematic theologian—he described himself as a "rough stone"[139]—but his elimination of original sin was nevertheless a shrewd tactical maneuver because it deprived predestination of its foundation. Without an inherently damnable humanity, God's sovereign election of some and reprobation of others could hardly appear to be anything else but arbitrary. Preexistence, meanwhile, not only extends human agency into the indefinite past but also throws open the plan of salvation, suggesting that this short life is but a fraction of the time in which humans can realize their divine aspirations.

Though it is likely that the rough-hewn Smith was unaware of the anti-Augustinian implications of his theology, other more polished thinkers of Smith's day actually named the bishop of Hippo as the culprit in the corruption of simple, biblical Christianity. The most notable attacks came from the educational reformer Catharine Beecher (1800–1878), eldest child of the prominent New England minister Lyman Beecher and his wife, Roxana Foote.[140] Reared on the Westminster Confession and Edwardseanism, she gradually turned against predestinarian orthodoxy, especially after her fiancé, Yale mathematician Alexander Metcalf Fisher, was killed in a shipwreck. Like Catharine, Fisher was unregenerate, despite the strenuous efforts of his pastor, Nathanael Emmons. The tragedy plunged Catharine into a prolonged period of anxiety over Fisher's, and her own, eternal destinies. Lyman, in an attempt to comfort his daughter, poured salt on her wound when he wrote to her that many people "did and will indulge the hope" that Fisher had experienced a last-minute conversion. Catharine was so tortured by this uncertainty that on an extended visit with Fisher's family, she combed through his remaining papers, searching for evidence of regeneration, only to conclude that Fisher had tried mightily "to yield that homage of the heart to his Maker which was required; but he could not."[141] Amid her grief, Catharine slowly abandoned the Augustinian system in which innately sinful humans were left utterly dependent on an uncertain hope of election.

Catharine would not air her most contentious theological views for many years, not until, as Stephen Snyder points out, Lyman had become safely senile.[142] Then, in 1857, she published the first of two companion theological works, *Common Sense Applied to Religion; or, The Bible and the People.* In addition to articulating 11 "intuitive truths" about human free agency,

Alexander Metcalf Fisher by Samuel Finley Breese Morse (1822). Yale University Art Gallery.

the reliability of the senses, and the like, *Common Sense* threw down the gauntlet against Augustine, condemning his doctrines of original sin and the enslaved will as the chief impediments to the reform of American society. The Augustinian system, Catharine believed, left the laypeople largely incapable of independent thought or right action and instead elevated the authority of fallible clerics and church institutions to promulgate doctrine and regulate behavior by coercion. If only Pelagius, whose theology she unabashedly claimed as her own, had possessed "the power and adroitness of Augustine," the churches throughout the ages would have been focused on the proper training of the human mind in obedience to God's laws rather than on the curing of hopelessly diseased and miseducated minds.[143]

Catharine continued her attack in *An Appeal to the People in Behalf of Their Rights as Authorized Interpreters of the Bible* (1860), in which she charged that the Augustinian theory of the depravity of human nature was based on "a few misinterpreted passages of the Bible," especially Romans 5:12–19. Augustine, she insisted, had mistakenly taken this passage as proof of the *spiritual* death of all humans in Adam, whereas it referred only to natural death.[144] Yet she buried her most provocative rhetorical flourish, as one might conceal a dagger, in the last endnote on the last page of the second volume. Seizing upon the African context of Augustine's career as a metaphor for his deleterious influence on Christian theology, she concluded that reasonable people have a duty to resist the "African enslavement of Anglo-Saxon minds" no less than to combat the "Anglo-Saxon enslavement of African bodies."[145]

Ironically, while Catharine found no salvation in the African Augustine, two of her seven clergyman brothers, Edward and Charles, relieved their own Augustinian anxieties by rehabilitating an earlier African father of the church, the Alexandrian-born Origen. Like their sister Catharine, and Joseph Smith before her, Edward and Charles recoiled at a God who would impute Adam's sin to all humanity. Origen's doctrine of preexistence allowed them to explain human sin (and vindicate God) by claiming that individuals implicated themselves in an existence prior to birth. The present life was a remedial stage in which a just and loving God intervened to save his creatures.[146] Edward's and Charles's books detailing their proposal won quick and nearly universal disapproval. Edward was forced to resign his post as editor of the *Congregationalist* newspaper, and Charles was found guilty of heresy by his local Congregational ministerial conference, though the conviction was later rescinded. Even their Beecher siblings were mystified by the brothers' preexistence theory, though they were in general agreement that the Augustinian doctrine of original sin was, as the most famous brother, Henry Ward Beecher, put it, so much "stale yeast."[147]

From Catharine's unapologetic embrace of Pelagian free will to Charles and Edward's Mormon-like resort to preexistence, then, the Beechers represented the radical conclusions that dissatisfaction with predestinarianism could elicit. Yet at least one Beecher, the celebrated novelist Harriet Beecher Stowe (1811–1896), followed a more sacramental religious path that would lead her away from the questions of human volition that so preoccupied her siblings.[148] Like her sister Catharine, Stowe became obsessed with questions of election and damnation after losing a loved one who had not yet experienced the requisite Calvinist conversion—in this case, her son Henry, a student at Dartmouth College, who drowned in 1857 while swimming in the Connecticut River. Grief-stricken and haunted by the uncertainty of Henry's eternal destiny, Stowe penned *The Minister's Wooing* (1859), which, along with *Oldtown Folks* (1869) a decade later, concluded that Augustinianism failed to take into account the experience of women as mothers of the human race. "[W]oman's nature has never been consulted in theology," she wrote, but if it had, the Augustinian view of woman as mere temptress would have yielded to a different kind of theology.[149] Unlike the male system builders, "women are always turning from the abstract to the individual, and feeling where the philosopher only thinks."[150] A theology informed by a mother's

The Beecher Family by Matthew Brady (c. 1859). *Standing, left to right*: Thomas, William, Edward, Charles, Henry Ward. *Seated, left to right*: Isabella, Catharine, Lyman, Mary, Harriet. *Insets*: James (*left*), George. Harriet Beecher Stowe Center, Hartford, Conn.

grief would have long ago downplayed the tortured intricacies of election and reprobation and would have focused instead on the love of Christ.[151]

In portraying Augustinianism as, at times, coldly calculating and fatalistic, Stowe contributed, along with her siblings, to the nineteenth-century assault on old orthodoxies. She took special delight in satirizing the hedged bets of New England's latter-day Augustinians, the New Divinity theologians. As one of the characters in *The Minister's Wooing* observes of the Congregational minister Dr. Hopkins (based on Samuel Hopkins): "One Sunday he tells us that God is the immediate efficient Author of every act of will; the next he tells us that we are entire free agents." Yet in her own complicated religious quest, she also found at least one salvageable element in Augustine's thought: his high regard for the sacrament of baptism. For all its ambiguity and its despairing attitude toward infants who did not receive the sacrament, Augustine's doctrine of baptism still enfolded the baptized child "in some vague sphere of hope and protection." The New England Congregationalists of her upbringing had deprived baptism of much of its efficacy. Their insistence on the necessity of conversion—of discerning one's election even while admitting the awful uncertainty of God's decree—consigned Christians to constant despair, without the "protecting shield" of a more robust view of the church's sacraments.[152]

Stowe's solution was to abandon her native Congregationalism in 1864 for the Episcopal Church—a "nice old motherly Church" that under the influence of the Oxford movement had revived elements of a medieval sacramentalism. Though she believed that Puritanism, in its least separatist mode, had also retained a relatively high view of baptismal regeneration, she claimed that this perspective had been dethroned by Jonathan Edwards, who departed from his predecessors in enforcing a stricter standard of conversion as the requisite for church membership. In her view, Congregationalists ever since Edwards had suffered under the tyranny of this unattainable standard of conversion, which she likened to climbing a rungless ladder. Instead of being "recognized from infancy as a member of Christ's Church, and in tender covenant relations with him," Edwards's New England inheritors were estranged from both God and church.[153]

Stowe's attraction to the Episcopal Church was also aesthetic, as John Gatta has noted. The Oxford movement had transformed the whitewashed, unadorned Episcopal parishes of the colonial era into the more luxuriant, neo-Gothic creations of the later nineteenth century. Though Stowe still evinced a lingering Puritan suspicion of things Catholic—she once contrasted the "active-minded" religion of New England to the supine Catholicism of Spain, awash in the "sentimental paraphernalia of ritualism"—she also discovered on her three European tours an unrealized affinity for the religious art of medieval Europe. As a painter herself, who filled her Hartford, Connecticut, home with her own artwork, she found in the Victorian era Episcopal Church an untapped well of aesthetic sustenance.[154]

Even the Catholic idea of prayers for the dead, a practice that Protestants typically reviled as superstitiously medieval or crypto-Mormon (because of the temple ritual of baptism for the dead), struck Stowe as an aspect of Augustine's own thought that zealous predestinarians had jettisoned too hastily. The bishop of Hippo, who had offered up fervent petitions on behalf of his departed mother, Monica, "solaced the dread anxieties of trembling love by prayers offered for the dead," Stowe noted in *The Minister's Wooing*. In Augustine's day, "the Church above and on earth presented itself to the eye of the mourner as a great assembly with one accord lifting interceding hands for the parted soul."[155] For Stowe, sacramental intercession, whether for the living or the dead, relieved the impossible burden of solving the predestinarian riddle, which the New England theologians had vainly tried to solve. "All systems that deal with the infinite are, besides, exposed to danger from small, unsuspected admixtures of human error, which become deadly when carried to such vast results," she wrote. "The smallest speck of earth's dust, in the focus of an infinite lens, appears magnified among the heavenly orbs as a frightful monster."[156]

Stowe's eloquence on behalf of sacramentalism was remarkable for any daughter of Lyman Beecher, who in his nativistic *Plea for the West* (1835) had fomented suspicions that wily Catholic educators were brainwashing Protestant youth with prayers for the dead and other means of "arbitrary clerical dominion over trembling superstitious minds."[157] In recognizing the potential of the sacraments to blunt predestination's sharp edge, she recovered an insight that had all too often been lost in Protestantism. Yet in her zeal to banish the monster of the old Puritan melancholy, she averted her eyes from the predestinarian anxieties to which even sacramental Christians could fall prey. In the next chapter, we will consider predestination's career among Augustine's other American heirs—immigrants far removed from the world of New England Calvinists and their discontents. Within their world, we will also encounter a few native-born New England converts who, like Stowe, found sacramental relief from predestinarian angst.

CHAPTER 5

Domesticating a Doctrine

Catholics and Lutherans

[W]e can never be sufficiently thankful to God for having called us to a religion whose maternal care, charity and zeal goes beyond the confines of our earthly pilgrimage and follows us even after our eyes have been closed in death.

—*Monsignor John A. Nageleisen,* Charity for the Suffering Souls *(1895)*

I have been baptized. I believe in Jesus Christ. I have received the Sacrament. What do I care if I have been predestined or not?

—*Martin Luther,* Tischreden, *no. 2631b*

A YOUNG GIRL LAY dying, her mother keeping watch by her side. The girl knew from her Catholic catechism that her soul would likely soon be in purgatory, and she was frightened. "You are so very, very poor," she said to her mother, "that you cannot have masses said for my soul." Fighting back tears, her mother tried to reassure: "Yes, my dear child, I am very poor, but I'll work day and night and earn money to get your soul out of purgatory. Do you think your poor mother could rest until she knew you were delivered from your purgatorial pains?"

But the girl's unease only grew: "Dear mother, I so often think of my cousin Catherine. She was so happy before she died, and she never confessed to a priest nor received absolution, and she did not believe in purgatory, yet she believed she was going straight to heaven."

At this, the mother's countenance hardened: "Catherine was a heretic, my child; she was not of the true church. It is better for you to be troubled than to die in error like her."

Seized by grief, the mother hurried out of the room, and the girl's brother came in to resume the vigil. The girl asked her brother why cousin Catherine had been so happy.

"Dear sister," he replied gently, "it was because she loved God and believed in the Lord Jesus Christ. She had no reason to fear. Jesus himself spoke to her soul and comforted her by the assurance of his love and forgiveness of her sins. What need [had] she of a priest to assure her of all this?"

"What, brother!" the startled girl replied. "Are you also a heretic?"

"Dear sister, do not alarm yourself. I do not deny the truth. I have read the word of God for myself, and I found it so full of love for poor sinners that it has become more precious to me than all the world."

"Have you then a Bible?" the girl inquired. "How did you procure it? Did you ask the priest for it? Does he know that you have it?"

"No, no! I assure you, I did not ask him for it. I met a Bible reader and thought I would like a Bible for myself, and I asked for one, and the good man gave it to me....I have found pardon and am happy."

"Oh! my brother, why did you not come sooner to tell me this? But tell me, brother, quick, is there anything in the Bible about purgatory?"

"I have searched from beginning to end of the book, and I could not find one single word about purgatory; the priest knows it is not there and that is the reason he will not let us read it."

Hastily taking out his Bible, the brother read to his sister a series of consoling verses he had marked, including the promise in John 3:16 that whoever believed in Christ would not perish but have eternal life and the declaration in 1 Timothy 2:5 that Christ was the only mediator between God and men. Finally, the brother closed the book and, taking his sister's hands in his, asked with unwavering voice: "Could you think for one moment, dear sister, that Jesus would have suffered half the chastisement and leave us to suffer the other half? That is the teaching of the priest, but not the word of God."

A wave of relief flooded his sister's face. "Oh! dearest brother, now I understand it all. I, too, am happy!" And with that, she settled down on her pillow again, serenely confident that she would soon meet her God.[1]

The preceding account would have been ideal ammunition for Protestant apologists, were it only substantiated. In fact, it was an old canard that had circulated, reportedly first in French, in the scurrilous world of anti-Catholic literature. The chief purveyor of the English version of the story was the self-styled "Luther of the West," L. J. King, an active Klansman and "ex-Romanist" who founded the Protestant Book and Tract House in Toledo, Ohio. King distributed the story in an oft-reprinted tract, *Testimony of a Dying Catholic Girl*, one of many such publications issued by his firm in the early 1950s. Another tract offered a $50 reward to "any Romish priest or layman for Bible proof that there is such a place as a 'Purgatory after death.'"[2] The tract did not mention that Protestantism stacked the deck against Catholicism since the chief scriptural proof of purgatory came from the deuterocanonical book of 2 Maccabees, which only the Episcopalians among Protestants accepted as part of the Bible.

To King and other Protestant apologists, purgatory epitomized Catholicism's alleged culture of gloom. The doctrine also brought to mind Luther's protest against Tetzel's indulgence peddling, in which purgatory became, as another anti-Catholic tract put it, the goose that laid "so many golden eggs" for Rome.[3] In contrast to the angst-ridden system of purgatorial satisfaction, the predestinarian framework accepted by some Protestants purported to offer a blessed assurance in the face of death. Catholic apologists, meanwhile, regarded absolute predestination as comforting only to those audacious enough to conclude they were among the elect. The middle state of purgatory was a means of domesticating the werewolf of predestination by involving the living in the pious task of praying for their dead relatives' swift purification on the way to heaven. Ironically, when Catholic devotional writers were not using images of purgatorial fire as a means of instilling holy fear, they described purgatory in the same way that Calvinist Protestants typically described predestination—as a consoling doctrine. For Catholics, the consolation came from the realization that the faithful departed were never outside of the sacramental protection of mother church.

This chapter is about Catholics and Lutherans, seemingly strange bedfellows who nevertheless both attempted to domesticate the undomesticated God of predestination in sacramental as well as scholastic ways. Neither group found predestination in its unmitigated form to be as obviously consoling as it was for true-believing Calvinists. Indeed, another striking similarity between Catholics and Lutherans was their vehement anti-Calvinism. Catholic and Lutheran theologians did not deny predestination—some, as we will see, were as ardently Augustinian as their Calvinist brethren—but both traditions also developed subtle qualifications of the doctrine that became the subject of serious internal controversies. Those disputes are as much a part of predestination's American story as the famous self-scrutiny of New England Puritans, yet because Catholics and Lutherans both resided in ethnic enclaves, their non-Anglo accents on election have gone unnoticed in wider surveys of religion in the United States. Similarly, Catholics and Lutherans for centuries remained largely ignorant of each other until the modern ecumenical movement finally revealed some of the underlying affinities between the two groups on the doctrines of grace.

CATHOLIC SCHOLASTIC CONTROVERSIES

The late historian Heiko Oberman once wrote that a theologian's opinion of predestination is a most revealing indicator of his position on justification, and the converse is also true in the history of debates since the Reformation.[4] The Council of Trent's Decree and Canons on Justification (1547) decried the "erroneous" notions then spreading among Christians, which had led to the "loss of many souls." The council noted that the Protestant notion of "faith alone" (a faith viewed by the reformers as entirely the result of the unmerited grace bestowed on the elect) had led many believers to the "rash presumption" that they were surely predestined for salvation. "[A]part from a special revelation," Trent declared, "it is impossible to know whom God has chosen for himself." Similarly, persons could never know with "absolute and infallible certitude" whether they would persevere in faith to the end. Rather than presuming themselves permanently numbered among the elect, individuals should "work out their own salvation with fear and trembling, in labors, watchings, almsdeeds, prayers and offerings, in fastings and chastity." The bishops at Trent took pains to stress that such good works could not by themselves justify a person. To teach that regeneration was possible without divine grace, according to the council, was heresy. But it was equally heretical to maintain that a person's free will, once "moved and roused" by God's grace, did not need to cooperate with God in the process of salvation. Cooperation through good works was the lifelong task of Christians as they grew in grace through the sacraments.[5]

Trent established for Catholics the primacy of God's grace and the necessity of the will's cooperation, yet the council left unanswered some of the knottiest questions of predestination. The church's theologians taught that God was all-knowing, but did he predestine certain persons for salvation based on his foresight of the merit they would accrue through grace-enabled, freely willed good works? And in what sense were human works genuinely free if God foresaw them? Soon after the conclusion of Trent in 1563, these old problems again came to the fore, summoning the church's theologians to what one later American priest characterized as a "great battle" over predestination that remains unresolved to this day.[6]

The battle lines were drawn in Europe, particularly in Spain. On one side were conservative Thomists such as Domingo Báñez (1528–1604), a Dominican theologian at Salamanca who was the spiritual director and confessor of St. Teresa of Ávila. Like his younger English Puritan contemporary William Perkins, Báñez invoked Aquinas to argue that predestination was antecedent to foreknowledge of human merits in God's eternal logic. Aquinas had insisted that the apostle Paul "ruled out" the prescient view of election by his comment on Jacob and Esau in Romans 9:11 ("the children being not yet born, neither having done any good or evil, that the purpose of God according to election might stand, not of works, but of him that calleth").[7] Aquinas, and Báñez following him, regarded divine foreknowledge as causal: in foreseeing Jacob as elect, God *caused* it to be. Nothing in God's knowledge of humans was passive or determined in any sense by creatures' own willing. From their own limited perspective, humans still experienced freedom, but it was the free will granted to them as secondary causes by the first cause, God himself. As Aquinas put it, "what is from freewill and what is from grace are not distinct, no more than what is from a secondary cause and what is from the first cause."[8]

On the other side were the Molinist theologians, named for Luis de Molina (1535–1600), a Spanish Jesuit who challenged the seeming determinism of stricter Thomists in a famous work, *The Compatibility of Free Choice with the Gifts of Grace, Divine Foreknowledge, Providence, Predestination and Reprobation* (1588). Better known by its Latin short title, *Concordia*, it was in part a commentary on Aquinas's *Summa*, though it went beyond it in many respects. Molina theorized that predestination was subsequent to divine foreknowledge of human merits, but this foreknowledge was of a special kind: *scientia media* (middle knowledge). Determined to preserve the genuine freedom of humans while still upholding the all-knowing aspect of God, Molina argued that middle knowledge was in between God's *natural* (or necessary) knowledge of all possibilities and causal relations, and his *free* knowledge of things he actually willed to be. *Scientia media* thus stood in between God's knowledge of the merely *possible* and his knowledge of the *actual*. Applied to predestination, it was the means whereby God knew which persons would unfailingly (yet freely) have faith, given a particular set of circumstances.[9]

The full logic of Molina's position, especially as developed by his followers, such as the Jesuit Francisco Suárez (1548–1617), was complex and difficult to understand. Because Molina maintained that God still determined the particular circumstances into which each creature would be put, some theologians wondered if middle knowledge really left any more room for free choice than did the traditional Thomist position. Other critics found it simply nonsensical to speak of contingent choices that humans *definitely* would make, given a certain set of circumstances. At best, God could know only what humans *probably* would do in a genuinely contingent situation. Molina himself admitted that divine foreknowledge of free human choices was "inscrutable."[10] But like Jacob Arminius, he was motivated by the belief that God gave all humans prevenient grace, or enough assistance to enable them to choose freely whether to accept or reject Christ. God's *scientia media* in a certain sense *depended* on this free creaturely choice.[11]

Opponents of the Molinists recoiled at the suggestion that humans could in any way determine something in God. So arose the quintessentially scholastic *De Auxiliis* controversy, referring to the help or assistance (*auxilium*) given to humans by God's grace. The upheaval of the Reformation, still fresh in the theologians' minds, heightened the defensiveness of both sides and contributed to the polemical name calling. Thus, the Jesuit Molinists branded the Dominican Thomists as Calvinists, while the Dominicans accused the Jesuits of being Pelagians. A Roman commission appointed in 1597 by Clement VIII did not finish its work before Molina, Báñez, and the pope himself all died. Finally, in 1607, Pope Paul V declared a truce. Though he admitted that an intellectual resolution would have been desirable, he deemed a settlement unnecessary since neither side actually taught the heresies alleged by the other. "[T]he opinion of the Dominican fathers differs very much from Calvin's; for the Dominicans say that grace does not destroy but perfects free will, and its power is such that man acts in his own way, which is freely," the pope wrote. "But the Jesuits differ from the Pelagians, who declared the beginning of salvation originated from us, whereas the former hold quite the contrary." Paul V's decision was later confirmed by Benedict XIV in 1748 and has remained in force ever since.[12]

In the end, the only seventeenth-century predestinarian innovation condemned as heresy by the church (though esteemed by many Calvinists) was Jansenism, named for Flemish theologian Cornelius Otto Jansen (1585–1638), a vigorous opponent of Molinism and author of the posthumously published *Augustinus* (1640). Though Jansen hailed the bishop of Hippo as his master, he actually resembled Calvin as much as Augustine in denying the universal saving will of God. Passages such as 1 Timothy 2:4, in Jansen's view, did not mean that Christ died for all but that he died for all *types* of people.[13] Yet the church's condemnation of Jansenism in 1653 and again in 1713 may have had less to do with Jansen's actual ideas than with the movement's popularity in France, which had perennially challenged papal authority.[14]

Both Thomism and Molinism (and their various neo- reincarnations) endured as viable options among Catholic theologians in the United States, though traditional Thomism clearly enjoyed greater visibility, thanks in part to the publication of U.S. editions of works by conservative neo-Thomists such as the Dominican Reginald Garrigou-Lagrange (1877–1964).[15] Yet on the whole, Catholic disputes over predestination remained far less conspicuous than Protestant battles, for several reasons. One was the highly academic and sometimes forbidding nature of the Catholic discussions. On the eve of the Second Vatican Council in the early 1960s, one American Thomist, the Iowa-born priest William G. Most, penned a lengthy Latin treatise proposing technical modifications of Garrigou-Lagrange's views. When he sent out 500 privately lithographed copies of his work to solicit comments from fellow theologians, only about 100 replied. (Not long before Most's death in 1999, his treatise was reprinted in English by Christendom College in Virginia—one of a number of conservative institutions that sought to reinvigorate traditional Catholic teaching in the wake of Vatican II.)[16] Another reason the Thomist-Molinist dispute remained relatively cloistered was the heavy hand of papal authority, which prevents ivory-tower debates from spilling over as frequently into the world of the laity as is the case among Protestants. (Recall the anti-Calvinist jingles that became popular Protestant fare on the antebellum frontier.) A third factor was the common commitment among Catholic theologians, even among the most predestinarian Thomists, to the idea that righteousness is gradually *actualized* in the elect, not immediately imputed as many Protestants teach, and involves the ongoing cooperation of the will with God's grace.[17] But the most important reason for the comparatively muted debates over predestination among Catholics is the centrality of the church's sacramental system, which eclipses strictly doctrinal concerns in the everyday lives of most laypeople and diocesan priests. To low-church Protestants, doctrine—informed by Bible reading and preaching—is everything. Disputes over predestination and the associated doctrines of grace could, and did, become church dividing. But to Catholics and higher-church Protestants, ritual could cover a multitude of speculative uncertainties. The sacramental economy, extended into the afterlife by the doctrine of purgatory, thus became the central front of Catholic apologetics in the struggle with Protestant predestinarians.

PURGATORY AND THE HOUSEHOLD OF FAITH

Catholic sacramentalism developed over the centuries into a rich complex of beliefs and practices, including (as we saw in chapter 1) a strong commitment to eucharistic real presence and the idea that communion with Christ's true body is the sine qua non of the faith. (Vatican II declared the Eucharist "the source and the culmination of all Christian life.")[18] Another kind of communion—the *communion of saints*, or the mystical union of the faithful on earth, in purgatory, and in heaven—was essential to the Catholic view of predestination. As historian Ann Taves has shown, the doctrine of the communion of saints contributed to the domestication of American Catholic ritual, particularly in the nineteenth century, as laypeople prayed from home devotional manuals to the saints in heaven and on behalf of the souls in purgatory. In the Catholic household of faith, the living stood in solidarity with the dead.[19] The doctrine of purgatory did not deny predestination. Indeed, any soul experiencing purgatorial purification was presumed to be destined for heaven but not yet sufficiently cleansed of temporal sins. Yet in actual practice, purgatory removed predestination's air of finality by enlisting the entire Catholic household in praying for the dead and hastening their passage through the middle state.

Purgatory played a vivid role in medieval piety, inspiring an occasionally lurid iconography.[20] In the face of Protestant objections, the Council of Trent reiterated the doctrine but cautioned preachers against "uncertain speculation" or anything that "panders to curiosity and superstition." The council nevertheless made clear that souls detained in purgatory "are helped by prayers of the faithful and most of all by the acceptable sacrifice of the altar."[21] Later, the Douay-Rheims Bible, with notes by English bishop Richard Challoner (1691–1781), glossed 2 Maccabees 12:46 as "undeniable proof of the practice of praying for the dead," a "holy and wholesome" discipline that the faithful ought to observe.[22] John Carroll (1735–1815), consecrated the first Catholic bishop for the United States in 1790, complained of the hypocrisy of Protestants, who pointed to the questions raised in some patristic sources about the authority of 2 Maccabees. If the "doubts of a few early fathers" were enough to reject the book, he insisted, then other controversial portions of the canon—including Hebrews, 2 Peter, James, and Revelation—should be abandoned. In a pointed letter to the ex-Jesuit Charles Wharton in Maryland, Carroll claimed that no doctrine had stronger patristic backing than purgatory: Augustine, Cyril, and Chrysostom were just a few who endorsed the idea along with prayers for the dead.[23] Carroll's defense anticipated the much later reconfirmation of the doctrine by Vatican II, which also invoked 2 Maccabees 12:46, and by the Catholic Catechism (promulgated by John Paul II in 1992), which again quoted the 2 Maccabees verse as the principal scriptural locus.[24]

Far more compelling to Catholic apologists than any single proof text, however, was the argument that the pious devotions of the communion of saints not only helped the dead but brought hope and comfort to the living. A leading U.S. spokesman for this idea was Monsignor John A. Nageleisen, who was born to a German immigrant family in Piqua, Ohio, in 1861 and wrote a book defending purgatory in the same era when German Lutherans in the Midwest were assailing each other over predestination. A priest of the Missionaries of the Precious Blood, he originally taught at the congregation's St. Joseph's College in Rensselaer, Indiana, before becoming pastor of St. Nicholas German Catholic Church in New York City. In *Charity for the Suffering Souls* (1895), Nageleisen criticized Protestants for rejecting purgatory and thereby disrupting "one of the most sacred bonds with which faith has encircled mankind, viz. the communion of saints." The "misguided innovators have only the darkness of the grave to place between the human heart and its departed loved ones," whereas for Catholics, prayers for the dead embraced all the faithful in the constant "maternal care" of the church, assuring them that they always had "friends at the throne of God." Just as St. Monica urged her son, St. Augustine, to pray for her at the altar of God, and just as Jews prayed the mourner's Kaddish, Nageleisen noted, Catholic ritual preserved the loving connections between living and dead.[25]

Books such as Nageleisen's helped to popularize the devotion to the poor souls in purgatory, which was promoted by various popes, including Leo XIII, pontiff from 1878 to 1903, who offered indulgences for prayers for the dead.[26] In the late twentieth century, Nageleisen's book and other preconciliar manuals on purgatory were reprinted by the traditionalist Catholic publishing house TAN Books, founded in 1967 by Thomas A. Nelson in Rockford, Illinois. Among the titles still in print at the turn of the twenty-first century was *Purgatory*, from the larger text *All for Jesus* (1853) by the English Catholic convert Frederick William Faber (1814–1863), who came to Rome via the high-church Tractarian movement in the Church of England.[27] TAN also still listed *Purgatory* (1888) by the Jesuit professor at Liège, François Xavier Schouppe (1823–1904). In a 1986 publisher's preface to the latter book, Nelson argued that purgatory "sums up, from its own perspective, all of Catholic teaching," but he lamented that many Catholics no longer believed the doctrine.[28] Similarly, Karl Keating, who founded the lay apostolate Catholic Answers in 1979, has insisted that unlike limbo (believed by some medieval theologians to be the afterlife abode of unbaptized infants), purgatory is not an optional doctrine for faithful Catholics. "As a Catholic, you *must* believe in it," he wrote. Though the word *purgatory* does not appear in scripture, Keating added, neither does the word *Trinity*, "yet Scripture squares with both."[29]

Present-day conservative apologists such as Keating are not alone in defending the benefits of purgatory. Cambridge historian Eamon Duffy has written movingly of his Catholic childhood in Ireland, where he absorbed the preconciliar devotion to the poor souls that many Irish immigrants brought to the United States. The Protestant reformers, in his view, unintentionally "drove a wedge between the living and the dead" in eliminating purgatory, which they turned into a "bogey-man" for Rome's perceived abuses of power. In their iconoclastic zeal, however, Protestants lost sight of the pastoral advantages of the doctrine. Behind purgatory "lay a piercing perception, that even for those who love God, death leaves unfinished business—damaged and damaging relationships, misunderstandings unresolved, words of love or apology or explanation unspoken, the need to forgive, and to be forgiven." In silencing prayer for the dead, the reformers left no intercessory room for the gnawing realities of things left undone. "Prayer for the dead is neither fear nor fire insurance," according to Duffy. "It is an exercise in the virtues of faith and hope and love."[30]

PREDESTINATION AND ANTI-PROTESTANT POLEMIC

Though purgatory was one of Catholicism's chief means of domesticating predestination, Catholic writers also confronted Protestant doctrines of election head-on, arguing that Rome's teachings were better suited to promote a virtuous laity. The American pioneer of this apologetic line was the Irish-born prelate Francis Patrick Kenrick (1796–1863), bishop of Philadelphia and later archbishop of Baltimore, whom one historian has identified as the foremost theologian among the nineteenth-century bishops in the United States.[31] In an important 1841 treatise defending the Catholic doctrine of justification, Kenrick criticized Protestants' once-and-for-all certainty that they were irrevocably chosen by God. "Presumption is too mild a term for this daring flight of human fancy," he declared. "It is madness, impiety, blasphemy." Christian joy must always be "tempered with holy fear." After the hereditary stain of original sin was washed away in baptism, a Christian needed to be continually fed by the Eucharist and absolved through the sacrament of penance for sins committed after baptism. Protestants, in assuming that as elect persons they were justified immediately upon believing in Christ, abandoned the progressive idea of justification, which Kenrick regarded as the moral strength of Catholicism. "It requires little discrimination to judge which system presents greater facilities of pardon, and greater incentives to sin," he concluded.[32]

Kenrick's onetime assistant Augustine Francis Hewit advanced a similar critique after his conversion to Catholicism in 1846. Hewit was born in 1820 to a prominent Protestant family in New England. His father, Nathaniel, was a Congregational minister, and his mother, Rebecca, was daughter of the Connecticut senator James Hillhouse. After graduating from Amherst College, Hewit eventually found his way to Catholicism by way of high-church

Archbishop Francis Patrick Kenrick, from John J. O'Shea, *The Two Kenricks* (1904).

Anglicanism. As co-founder with Isaac Hecker of the Paulist Fathers, who were dedicated to winning American converts to the church, Hewit published an oft-reprinted work on the Catholic view of salvation, *The King's Highway* (1874), in which he condemned the Lutheran doctrine of justification as "false and absurd." Yet he reserved particular invective for those who, reading scripture with "Calvinistic spectacles," erroneously concluded that God antecedently reprobates certain persons apart from their conduct. Reprobation is wholly based on the committed sins of the unrepentant, Hewit argued, whereas election is due to grace. Both Catholics and Protestants taught the gratuity of God's grace, he insisted, but they differed on the "instrumental causes" through which grace is communicated. The "Calvinistic heresy" subverts instrumental causes, which for Catholics begin with baptism (the "laver of regeneration") and continue throughout the sacramental life of the believer, even in the postmortem process of purgation.[33] Later, in the Paulist magazine *Catholic World*, Hewit praised the Methodists for throwing off the "shackles of Calvinism" and boldly proclaiming "the universality of the love and grace of Christ toward men" and "the freedom and ability of the will to use efficaciously the means of grace." The Calvinists' theory of predestination, by contrast, forces them to believe that even some infants die as reprobates, a fatalistic conclusion that translates into "passivity and determinism in the moral order."[34] (Ironically, three decades later, Max Weber would claim the opposite in his famous *Protestant Ethic*—that Catholics and, to a lesser extent, Lutherans are the morally passive ones because they are locked in the "hand to mouth" existence of the sacramental economy.)[35]

Hewit's convert's zeal led him to paint Calvinism as almost the antithesis of Catholicism. Calvinists, in his view, in acquiescing to an absolute scheme of double predestination, denied the church's central mediating function. Hewit's fellow New England convert Orestes Brownson agreed but went further than Hewit in pressing the traditional Catholic claim that there is no salvation outside of the church. Not only are Calvinists separated from the saving confines of the true *ecclesia*, Brownson declared, they also traffic in "the most thoroughly satanic form of Protestantism." (Elsewhere, he identified Presbyterianism in particular as the "most odious" of the sects.)[36] Other Catholic apologists echoed Hewit's and Brownson's indignant anti-Calvinism. Monsignor Patrick O'Hare, author of an anti-Protestant biography of Martin Luther, singled out Calvin's predestination as even more "gruesome" than that of the German reformer.[37] C. F. Donovan, editor of the archdiocesan newspaper in Chicago, clearly had Calvinists in mind when he charged in a popular encyclopedia for Catholic laity that double predestination was a "monstrous" doctrine. Reprobates, he explained, are simply foreknown as such by God, not predestined.[38]

The persona of the "recovering Calvinist" is perhaps most familiar today in the popular Catholic apologetics of Scott Hahn, who has recalled that as a staunchly Presbyterian student at Gordon-Conwell Theological Seminary in the early 1980s, he believed that sacraments were peripheral to life-and-death matters of salvation: "I was hungry for dynamic biblical teaching and preaching; and sacraments suggested, to my mind at least, the exact opposite: a mechanical way of approaching religion—ritualistic, ceremonial, bordering on superstitious."[39] Hahn's book on the sacraments, in which he explains his change of heart, bears the imprimatur of Cardinal Edward Egan, archbishop of New York—a remarkable churchly blessing for an author who once insisted that the Presbyterians should never have eliminated the Westminster Confession's original condemnation of the pope as the Antichrist.[40]

To some extent, of course, the attack on Calvinism running from Hewit to Hahn failed to recognize that Calvinists are hardly uniform in their attitudes toward the sacraments. Baptist Calvinists, for example, demote baptism to an "ordinance" and refuse to administer it to infants. Calvin himself, admitted Hewit's contemporary James F. Loughlin, chancellor of the archdiocese of Philadelphia, still had the "shadow of Rome" enough upon him that he "lacked the audacity to carry his erroneous opinions to their legitimate, practical conclusions." Thus, by a "fortunate neglect" of logical consistency, Calvin "held fast to the ancient practice of infant baptism."[41] The attack on Calvinism also perpetuated the misconception that Calvin was unique among the reformers in his predestinarianism. Hewit said as much when he claimed that Calvin's double predestination pressed naturally toward the conclusion that election and reprobation were radically prior to all other divine decrees: "The only consistent Calvinist is the merciless supralapsarian, who asserts only the sovereignty of God, and reduces his goodness to a mere arbitrary will of bringing the elect to glory, all the rest of the rational creation being wholly excluded from the love of God."[42]

Some Catholic apologists conceded that Luther could sound just as deterministic as Calvin. Monsignor O'Hare denounced the German reformer's comparison of the human will to a beast of burden, which reduced man to "a mere tool, a machine, an automaton." Yet Catholics also reserved a measure of grudging respect for the softening of Luther's predestinarianism in later Lutheran scholasticism. As O'Hare put it, Luther's "mild, gentle and most obsequious friend" Philipp Melanchthon broke with his master and "came to a more correct view, making no secret of his rejection of Luther's determinism."[43] The Irish-born O'Hare, longtime rector of St. Anthony of Padua Church, Brooklyn, likely did not know that even as he was publishing his book on Luther in 1916, Lutherans in the heartland were embroiled in a protracted struggle over whether Melanchthon and his heirs ever should have dared to domesticate Luther's God.

THE LUTHERAN LANDSCAPE

Far from the cosmopolitan mix of O'Hare's Brooklyn, a more isolated subculture had arisen on the prairies of the American Midwest. Between 1820 and 1890, some 4.5 million Germans and over 100,000 Scandinavians, many of them Lutheran, immigrated to the United States, where they built ethnic enclaves stretching from the Mississippi port of St. Louis to the northern reaches of Minnesota and Wisconsin. Determined to preserve their linguistic and religious particularity, these Lutherans—with names like Fürbringer, Jørgensen, Rölvaag, and Ylvisaker—soon organized into a dizzying array of ethnic synods, each with its own theological and liturgical heritage.

The new Lutheran immigrants also founded colleges and seminaries whose names—Gustavus Adolphus, St. Olaf, Augsburg, and Wartburg—signaled an Old World culture that stood apart from the mainstream of Anglo-American Protestantism.

Though generally low church in ritual practice, the new Lutheran immigrants shared a higher sacramental understanding than that which had usually prevailed in Reformed America. Lutheran belief in the real presence meant that Christ's words of institution—"this is my body"—could be taken at face value and remained true even for unbelievers.[44] Reformed thinkers rejected this *manducatio impiorum*—the eating (of Christ's body) by the godless. But for Luther, who like Augustine based the formula on the notion that Judas, along with the other disciples, partook of the true body, it became another means of emphasizing the objective reality of the sacrament.[45] To be sure, Luther taught that faith was necessary for the recipient to grasp the benefits conveyed by Christ; yet confidence in the corporeal presence set Lutherans apart from less sacramental Protestants and provided something of a hedge against predestinarian anxiety. Luther's own pastoral counsel to the laity not to worry about predestination stemmed in no small part from his lingering medieval commitment to sacramental efficacy.[46] He denounced the "epicureans who say: 'I do not know whether I am predestined to salvation. If I am elected to eternal life, I shall be saved no matter what I do. On the other hand, if I am not elected, I shall be damned no matter what I do.'" "Although these opinions are true," he explained, "nevertheless the Passion of Christ and his Sacraments are thereby made of no effect." Such "poisonous speculations" about election were "weapons of the devil."[47] Indeed, the practical assumption of Lutheran piety—that grace, if lost, could be won back through trust in God's saving work in word and sacrament—was why Weber wrote of the relative "moral feebleness" of Lutheranism as compared to Calvinism.[48] Whereas Calvinists, Weber thought, were impelled by predestinarian uncertainty to "prove" their elect status through hard work and systematic moral reflection, Lutherans tended to be more comfortable in their own skins and less concerned about the ideal of building a holy commonwealth.

One might therefore conclude that Lutherans were constitutionally incapable of engaging in the same wrenching battles over predestination that perennially troubled Reformed Protestants of every stripe in the United States. In Michigan in the late nineteenth century, for example, the theologians of the Christian Reformed Church, a small denomination of Dutch Calvinist heritage, divided along supra- and infralapsarian lines, mirroring factions back in Holland.[49] Yet a major predestinarian battle did erupt among immigrant Lutherans in the late 1870s, and its consequences for the future of

American Lutheranism were far reaching. Known to its combatants by the German mouthful *Gnadenwahlslehrstreit* (literally, election-of-grace doctrine controversy), this struggle over the grounds of God's choice of humans dragged on for more than four decades, severing synodical alliances and setting the limits of future denominational mergers. No church body was more affected than the Lutheran Church–Missouri Synod, today the second largest Lutheran denomination, with 2.3 million members. Its staunch opposition to any rationalistic soft-pedaling of predestination alienated Missouri from other Lutheran groups, even as the denomination's insistence that an inerrant Bible is the only infallible source on predestinarian questions drew the synod ever closer to the mainstream of conservative American evangelicalism. The long *Gnadenwahlslehrstreit* is thus an episode with important implications not only for the history of Lutheranism but also for the wider career of predestination in American Protestant culture.[50]

BEFORE MISSOURI: BACKGROUND TO THE CONTROVERSY

Luther's inclination to discourage predestinarian inquiry by laypeople did not mean he rejected the doctrine or was averse to defending it against its humanistic detractors. Indeed, the vehemence of his arguments against free will in his protracted debate with Erasmus shocked the more conciliatory Melanchthon, who confided to a correspondent his long-standing wish that "some prudent person" such as Erasmus would oppose Luther on the matter.[51] Melanchthon avoided direct mention of predestination in drafting the Augsburg Confession (1530), the chief doctrinal statement of the infant Lutheran movement. But within two decades, the themes of the Luther-Erasmus debate resurfaced in the synergist controversy (Latin *synergismus*: "a working together"), which pitted the "Philippist" supporters of Melanchthon, who argued for a measure of human cooperation with God in the process of salvation, against the "Gnesio-Lutherans" (Greek *gnesios*: "genuine"), who excluded all human initiative in God's predestinarian designs. The battle resulted in much academic infighting and even the house arrest of one theologian, who refused to go along with an order from the duke of Saxony, then a Gnesio-Lutheran sympathizer, to renounce synergism.[52]

The warring factions finally reached a truce in the Formula of Concord (1577), which reflected the Gnesio-Lutheran view that the salvation of the elect lay "exclusively in God's mercy and the most holy merit of Christ," without any human cause. The human will was "neither totally, halfway, somewhat, nor in the slightest and smallest bit" responsible for conversion, which was entirely God's action through the Holy Spirit.[53] Yet the Formula distanced Lutheranism from Calvinism's seemingly arbitrary notion of predestination. God's grace was not irresistible, as the Calvinists taught; persons who were called by Christ could still "fall away" and return again through repentance, absolution, and the sacraments. Because God instituted these "regular means and instruments for drawing people to himself," no one should "expect to be drawn by the Father apart from Word and sacrament." Likewise, the Formula distinguished between God's foreknowledge of all things and his predestination of certain persons for salvation. Predestination applied only to the elect, not the damned; the latter sealed their own fate through sin. Nor was predestination to be "conceived of as a military muster, in which God said, 'this one shall be saved, that one shall be damned; this one will remain faithful, that one will not remain faithful.'" God instead extended a genuine offer of salvation to all people through the gospel. Finally, the Formula echoed Luther in its insistence that laypeople "should not concern or torture themselves with thoughts about the secret counsel of God." When considered rightly, predestination offered "beautiful, wonderful comfort" because it relieved humans of the burden of saving themselves through their own merit. The salvation of the elect was effected through the merit of Christ.[54]

The latent tension in the Formula between predestination and the universal grace of the gospel left a door ajar for future debates. Moreover, Melanchthon's nagging question remained: was human faith of absolutely no consequence in God's choice of the elect? In struggling with this issue, Lutherans faced a particular dilemma. If faith were of no consequence, then God seemed to loom as a fearfully arbitrary monarch. But if faith—conceived of as a human "work"—did matter, then the cardinal Lutheran principle of *sola gratia* (grace alone) was compromised. Ongoing discussions of this dilemma ultimately led Lutheran dogmaticians such as Aegidius Hunnius (1550–1603) and Johann Gerhard (1582–1637) to suggest that God elected persons *intuitu fidei*, or in view of faith. As with most scholastic distinctions, volumes of debate stood behind these two unassuming Latin words. Yet explained in a sentence, *intuitu fidei* was a clever logical construct: God elected persons in view of the faith that he himself granted to them. Though God's choice was conditional upon faith, this faith, like the predestinarian decree itself, belonged solely to God.[55] The Lutheran orthodox took pains to stress that foreseen *faith* was not the same as the foreseen *merit* typically spoken of by Catholic scholastics. (Molina had argued that God elected individuals *post praevisa merita*—after foresight of their merits, as apprehended through divine middle knowledge.)[56] The Lutheran *intuitu fidei* supposedly escaped the taint of synergism by avoiding "merit" talk (which implied the

Catholic view of freely willed cooperation) and by attributing human faith entirely to Christ. The suspiciously circular quality of locating both the decree and its condition in God did not deter the seventeenth-century theologians. They widely adopted *intuitu fidei* as an apparent middle way between the absolutely unconditional election of Calvinism and the fully conditional election of Arminianism. As one later American Lutheran writer boasted, "we steer clear of the Scylla of Calvinism on the one hand, and also escape the Charybdis of Arminianism on the other."[57]

Dogmatic formulas nevertheless were partially eclipsed in the eighteenth century as Lutherans, influenced by Pietism, emphasized the heart over the head in religion. Such was the outlook of the greatest figure of colonial American Lutheranism, Henry Melchior Muhlenberg (1711–1787), who was dispatched by the Pietist leadership at Halle, Germany, for Pennsylvania in 1742. Over the next four decades, Muhlenberg traveled extensively in British America, occasionally encountering colonists seeking counsel on predestination. On one trip off the coast of South Carolina, the skipper of the boat shared his predestinarian anxieties with Muhlenberg, who urged him to stick to scripture and "not be swayed by useless scholastic controversies." On another occasion, Muhlenberg advised "a distinguished Dutchman," whose friends were disputing with him over the divine decree, to seek an "inward experience of the clear words of Scripture which were revealed for his soul's salvation." Muhlenberg lamented in his journal the absolute version of predestination espoused by some colonial clergy, especially the Presbyterians, whom he judged "tipped with steel."[58] Meanwhile, such criticisms of Calvinist absolutism were finding their way into print among German colonists. An anonymously authored pamphlet, issued in Philadelphia by the prominent German printer Christopher Sower, denounced the Calvinist clergy as "perverse scribes" for turning God into a tyrannical monarch. The pamphlet also implicitly endorsed *intuitu fidei*, noting that God chose Jacob rather than Esau because he foreknew that Jacob would "keep close to Christ." The pamphlet's author mirrored Muhlenberg's pastoral approach in repeating to the laity Christ's own words of universalism: "Come unto me, all ye that labour and are heavy laden, and I will give you rest."[59]

The anti-Calvinism of Muhlenberg and other Lutheran Pietists revealed their unwillingness to obliterate all confessional distinctions for the sake of Christian charity.[60] Yet in the wake of the American Revolution, which cut the churches loose from state oversight and unleashed a torrent of reforming zeal, some Lutherans too were caught up in the drive to build a pan-denominational evangelical empire. Out of this crusade emerged a new leader, Samuel Simon Schmucker (1799–1873), who was born in Hagerstown, Maryland, and exemplified the desire of many American-born Lutherans to assimilate with the dominant evangelical culture. After graduating from a Presbyterian seminary (Princeton), he helped to establish the Lutheran seminary at Gettysburg, Pennsylvania, where he taught for most of his career. From 1828 until 1845, he served as president of the General Synod, which by the eve of the Civil War encompassed nearly two-thirds of Lutheran congregations in the United States. Impelled by his own Pietistic commitments and his desire to build a genuinely American Lutheranism, Schmucker advocated a theology that, while still loosely based on the Lutheran confessions, resembled the standard evangelical voluntarism of the early republic. In his *Elements of Popular Theology*, for example, he lamented Luther's own lingering attachment to the "Augustinian error" of an unconditional divine decree. Borrowing a phrase from the Congregationalist Nathaniel William Taylor, Schmucker argued that God's "moral government" required that election be in view of a person's divinely foreseen actions. God "from eternity decreed to distribute happiness or misery according to the voluntary conduct of each individual." To imagine God's decree otherwise would be "the height of absurdity."[61]

The extent of Schmucker's unease with traditional Lutheran confessionalism became clear in 1855 when he and his associates issued anonymously the Definite Synodical Platform, which included an "American Recension" of the Augsburg Confession. In a nod to the Presbyterians and other Reformed Protestants with whom he had associated, Schmucker eliminated from the confession its approval of the ceremonies of the Mass, its acceptance of private confession and absolution, and its affirmation of that traditional badge of Lutheran identity, the real presence in the Eucharist. Schmucker also watered down the confession's language on baptismal regeneration, deleting the condemnation of the Anabaptist view that children are saved without baptism.[62] Reaction among more traditional Lutherans was immediate and furious. Only three small Ohio synods (constituent bodies of the General Synod) adopted the revisions, while many other groups strenuously opposed the changes or ignored them altogether. Even Schmucker's longtime ally and brother-in-law, Samuel Sprecher, president of Wittenberg College in Ohio, came to regret the overreaching by the so-called American Lutherans, whose confessional revision he called "the culmination of Melanchthonianism."[63]

ZION ON THE MISSISSIPPI: THE MISSOURI HAVEN FROM RATIONALISM

The upheaval over Schmuckerism in the 1850s was in many respects a reprise of a debate in Germany four decades earlier. In 1817, Prussian king

Friedrich Wilhelm III, whose ruling house had been Calvinist for about 200 years, enacted a union between Lutheran and Reformed Protestants in his realm. Influenced by the Pietistic zeal for Christian fellowship and by the widespread rationalist emphasis on a "reasonable," tolerant Christianity, the king hoped to strengthen the state through a strong centralized church. Accordingly, he celebrated the union in a joint Lutheran-Reformed Eucharist in Berlin on 31 October 1817, the tercentennial of Luther's Ninety-five Theses. Though the union enjoyed much support, it also galvanized conservative opponents of rationalism in the churches. Lutheran theologian Claus Harms, archdeacon at Kiel, posted a new "Ninety-five Theses" that blasted rationalism and defended Lutheranism's traditional view of the sacraments. The controversy soon spilled over into neighboring Saxony, where it awakened antirationalist sentiment.[64]

Carl Ferdinand Wilhelm Walther (1811–1887), the eventual leader of the Missouri Synod, was just a boy of six in Saxony when the Prussian Union was consummated, but the event would permanently shape his outlook. Descended from several generations of Lutheran clergy, Walther attended the University of Leipzig, which he later recalled had but three faculty members who were not "coarse Rationalists." During his student days, he sought counsel from Dresden pastor Martin Stephan, who had dropped out of Leipzig to form a circle of like-minded clergy and laity. Like many of their unionist opponents, Stephan's followers were Pietistic in outlook; yet the Stephanites were so strongly antirationalist that the Dresden newspaper derided them as "very ignorant boneheads" and "crazy fanatics."[65] For their part, the Stephanites believed that they were simply returning to the vigorous antirationalism of Luther himself, who had condemned the "Babylonian captivity" of the Catholic Church to Aristotelian logic as a means of rationally explaining the mode of Christ's presence in the Eucharist. Indeed, Walther would later rally his American faithful with the cry "Back, you Lutherans, back to Luther, to his Reformation church and doctrine!"[66]

Feeling besieged by the Saxon establishment, the Stephanites eventually devised an elaborate plan to build a new Lutheran Zion along the Mississippi River near St. Louis. In November 1838, Stephan and more than 600 followers, including Walther, left Germany aboard five ships. One ship was lost at sea, but the rest arrived safely at the port of New Orleans, where Walther disembarked on 5 January 1839. Yet immediately upon the group's arrival upriver in Missouri, there was trouble in Zion after Stephan declared himself "bishop" and alienated both clergy and laity with his autocratic style. Within five months, he was deposed and banished from the *Gesellschaft*, or society, he had founded. Soon emerging as the group's new leader, Walther consolidated his influence in 1844 by founding a newspaper for the laity, *Der Lutheraner,* whose slogan, "God's Word and Luther's doctrine shall never pass away," bespoke his own brand of Lutheran restoration-ism.[67] In 1847, he became the founding president of the German Evangelical Lutheran Synod of Missouri, Ohio, and Other States—better known as simply the Missouri Synod. Two years later, Walther was appointed professor of theology and, by 1854, president of the synod's recently founded Concordia Seminary in St. Louis, where he established an academic journal, *Lehre und Wehre* (Doctrine and Defense), as the synod's official theological organ.

Meanwhile, the decade of the 1850s brought the largest number of Germans yet (almost a million) to the United States, and these new immigrants helped to swell the ranks of Missouri and other synods, prompting occasional talk of how the various groups might cooperate for the sake of Christ. Despite his disgust for promiscuous "unionism," Walther retained a Pietistic fervor for rightly ordered Christian fellowship. Consequently, in 1872, he became the founding president of the Synodical Conference, a loose federation of synods dominated by Missouri. United by the unpleasant memory of Schmucker's Definite Synodical Platform and a common allegiance to the entire Book of Concord (the collected volume of Lutheran confessions), the conference's membership included the Joint Synod of Ohio, led by the powerful Matthias Loy (1828–1925), professor of theology at the Lutheran seminary at Columbus. The other member bodies were the Illinois, Minnesota, Wisconsin, and Norwegian synods. (The Norwegian Synod, originally known as the Norwegian Evangelical Lutheran Church in America, was an immigrant body centered in the upper Midwest.)[68]

The conference was a triumph for Walther, who viewed it as an antidote not only to the General Synod, whose founders included Schmucker, but also to the General Council, a synodical alliance dominated by Philadelphia theologian Charles Porterfield Krauth and other confessionalist opponents of Schmucker. The latter group might have been natural allies for Missouri. Krauth, who, like Walther, was an outspoken defender of traditional Lutheran sacramental theology, in 1874 wrote a significant rebuttal to Presbyterian Charles Hodge on the subject of infant damnation. In a footnote to his *Systematic Theology,* Hodge had criticized Krauth's own contention that the Westminster Confession taught that only some who died in infancy were saved. Krauth challenged "all defenders of Calvinism to produce a solitary classical Calvinistic source that asserts or implies that all who die in infancy are certainly saved." He also upbraided Hodge and other Calvinists for rejecting the "objective force of baptism," an idea so taken for granted in ancient church tradition that even Augustine, whose predestinarian logic suggested that only elect infants and adults were saved, regarded baptism as necessary.[69] Walther shared Krauth's strong anti-Calvinism and his high valuation of the sacraments, but he believed that the General Council had compromised Lutheran purity by not unequivocally condemning pulpit and altar fellowship with Reformed clergy.[70] Walther's repudiation of the General Council was an example of the Missouri Synod's growing insistence on complete doctrinal agreement as a condition of church fellowship. To Missouri's partisans, this resistance to compromise was always a virtue. Yet this attitude would all too soon threaten the unity of the newly formed Synodical Conference.

TROUBLE IN ZION: SCHOLASTIC DISPUTES

The first few years of the Synodical Conference passed largely without incident, save for a tempest stirred up by another footnote. The source of the offending passage was Gottfried Fritschel, a reputedly shy, mild-mannered professor at Wartburg Seminary in Iowa. The German-born Fritschel and his brother Sigmund were the leading theologians of the Iowa Synod, Missouri's perennial, more liberal rival, which had refused to join the Synodical Conference. Two years before the conference's formation, in a footnote to an article in the *Theologische Monatshefte* (the organ of the General Council), Fritschel criticized the "strange and offensive statements about the doctrine of predestination" that had been made by theologians at a meeting of the Missouri Synod's Northern District in 1868. The issue, Fritschel contended, was Missouri's "slavish dependence" on Luther, even when he "obviously erred" in *De servo arbitrio* (his famous attack on Erasmus) by teaching "natural man's complete and entire spiritual inability" to respond to God's grace. Missouri's dogged defense of the early Luther, Fritschel concluded, had led the synod to embrace an unnecessarily rigid doctrine of predestination.[71]

If Fritschel thought that Walther and his Synodical Conference allies might not notice a criticism buried in the margin of his article, he was mistaken. The footnote touched a nerve that had been raw since the days of Melanchthon, and months of arguments and counterarguments ensued in the *Monatshefte* and *Lehre und Wehre* in the early 1870s over the merits of Luther versus the later dogmaticians on predestination.[72] Such debates were not unusual among immigrant Lutherans, who still relished a good scholastic brawl. Synodical district meetings were frequently occasions for colloquies on prearranged theological topics, and the proceedings were often published. Yet just when it appeared that the disputation had run its course, Walther, in a tactically curious move at the Western District meeting in 1877, invoked Johann Gerhard against the "newer theologians" who would teach that predestination "rests on divine foresight of human conduct." Satan, Walther charged, had blinded some people into thinking that "eternal life is something much too big, much too glorious for man to obtain it without doing a great deal." In reality, Walther declared, God from eternity elected "a certain number" in whom he "foresaw nothing, absolutely nothing" that might be worthy of salvation.[73] Walther's "newer theologians" included Friedrich Adolph Philippi (1809–1882), professor at Rostock and a Jewish convert to Lutheranism, who had argued that a certain degree of synergism ought not to be excluded from Lutheran thinking about the process of salvation. Though Missouri theologians prided themselves on avoiding such unapologetic rationalism from the old country, some of Walther's brethren in the Synodical Conference had become accustomed to teaching election in view of faith and knew that Gerhard himself had used that formula, partly as an antidote against the perceived absolutism of the Calvinists. Walther's apparent rejection of *intuitu fidei*—and his selective reading of Gerhard—therefore did not sit well with some of his colleagues in the synod.[74]

The fateful challenge to Walther soon came, though from an unlikely source. Friedrich August Schmidt (1837–1928) was secretary of the Synodical Conference and Walther's beloved former student. Born in Germany, Schmidt came to St. Louis with his family as a child and eventually attended Concordia Seminary. After a brief stint as a parish pastor, he won an appointment, on Walther's recommendation, to the faculty of Luther College in Decorah, Iowa. Because the college had been founded by Norwegian immigrants, Schmidt changed his ministerial affiliation from the Missouri to the Norwegian Synod and mastered the art of theological disputation in a language other than German. From 1872 to 1876, he served in a coveted position as the Norwegian Synod's professor at Concordia Seminary before being transferred to the Norwegians' newly established Luther Seminary at Madison, Wisconsin. Two years later, a new chair in theology opened at Concordia Seminary, and by some accounts, Schmidt was eager to return to his alma mater. When the Missouri Synod's convention elected Franz A. O. Pieper instead, Schmidt may have blamed Walther for the outcome. Missouri's partisans later charged that this was the reason for Schmidt's attack on Walther.[75]

Whether or not he was motivated by his wounded ego, Schmidt informed Walther by letter in early 1879 that he could no longer abide by the Missouri Synod's doctrine of election. At Walther's request, Schmidt summarized his grievances in four "antitheses" to Missouri's position. Predestination, Schmidt insisted, was not "an election without rules" but rather the "determination to eternal life of all those of whom God foresaw that they will persevere in faith."[76] After Schmidt distributed his statement to a handful of other pastors, Walther proposed to meet privately with the group after the Synodical Conference gathering in Columbus in July 1879. As Walther explained to a friend, the meeting would afford discussion "in all quietness without causing any sensation and without any disturbance."[77]

The meeting was indeed held, with Walther, then 67 years old, likely assuming his former role of teacher to the 42-year-old Schmidt. No reconciliation occurred, however, and the following January Schmidt lobbed a grenade when he inaugurated a new theological journal, *Altes und Neues* (Old and New), for the sole purpose of engaging the predestinarian battle. On the first page of the new journal, Schmidt cited recent Western District reports as evidence of Missouri's allegiance to a theology that seemed indistinguishable from the "Calvinistic error."[78] Reacting to Walther's charge that those in disagreement with the Missouri doctrine of election were heretics, Schmidt resolved to "defend our Lutheran skin to the best of our ability." He went on to blast Missouri's diminution of human faith, which the new crypto-Calvinists had turned into a "necessity which God wants to accomplish himself," even in the face of the most wanton resistance on the part of the elect. In Schmidt's view, Missouri's strong predestinarianism undermined the sincerity of the gospel's call to faith in Christ.[79]

Walther was furious, especially at the charge of "crypto-Calvinism," which for a purebred Lutheran was scarcely better than being branded a papist. Wasting no time, he published a formal response to Schmidt's "scandal sheet" in *Der Lutheraner*, for the benefit of lay readers. In his Thirteen Theses, which the Missouri Synod adopted at a meeting in Fort Wayne, Indiana, in May 1881, Walther repeatedly denounced Reformed doctrines, including the idea of a limited atonement: "We believe, teach, and confess that the Son of God came into the world for all men... and that He fully redeemed all men, none excepted; we therefore reject and condemn the contrary Calvinistic doctrine with all our heart." Walther further contended that those whom God had particularly elected could not ultimately fall away. This assertion, as he later explained, meant that persons were elected by God's "unfailing necessity" rather than by the "absolute necessity" claimed by the Calvinists. As for the disputed shibboleth of *intuitu fidei*, he declared again that Christ's merit alone was the cause of election, not any faith or other good conduct foreseen in the elect themselves.[80]

To his opponents, Walther's salvo betrayed his misrepresentation of *intuitu fidei*, which its defenders insisted *was* about Christ's merit (obtained through the God-given gift of faith) rather than human merit. Walther's distinction between "unfailing" and "absolute" necessity, moreover, looked suspiciously ethereal to some observers and raised a host of abstruse questions about justification, perseverance, and other issues connected to election.

The complexity of the dispute became almost comically apparent in January 1881, when the warring factions within the Synodical Conference met for a colloquy at Milwaukee. The participants resolved to debate all the key biblical passages on predestination, but in 10 sessions, the discussion barely moved beyond Romans 8:29 ("For whom he did foreknow, he also did predestinate"), in which the correct sense of the verb "foreknow" prompted days of disagreement.[81]

Out of such mind-numbing deliberations, it was perhaps inevitable that the positions of the two sides would finally be condensed into warring slogans. The anti-Missourians' election "in view of faith" emerged as a rival to the Missourians' election "unto faith," with the latter formula intended to remove any implication that God's choice was conditional. Both sides vehemently maintained that they taught in accordance with true Lutheranism, which in their view meant teaching in accordance with the scriptures. Each faction loudly resisted the other's charge of innovation—decidedly a term of abuse for Lutherans. Indeed, even the allegedly more liberal Schmidt was, like Walther, a dyed-in-the-wool traditionalist whose doctrine was, according to one later observer, scholastic and antiquated, "as if a Kant had never existed."[82]

Ohio Lutheran leader Matthias Loy had called the Milwaukee conference as a last-ditch attempt to reconcile the two sides. Loy, like Schmidt, had once admired Walther and was hoping to avoid an outright schism in the Synodical Conference. Loy later wrote in his autobiography that although Walther was a man sincerely devoted to the Lord, he had "become a dictator by habit" who was accustomed to having his own doctrinal assertions accepted as indisputable facts. Regarding the predestination controversy, Loy also recalled his growing horror at the inroads made by the "poison of Calvinism" within the Lutheran church. He found stark evidence of this at one meeting when a Missouri Synod speaker answered yes to the question of whether an elect person was "necessitated" to accept the grace offered by God.[83]

Loy finally resolved that he could no longer remain neutral, and thus in February 1881, he too began a new publication, the *Columbus Theological Magazine*, dedicated to articulating the Ohio position on predestination. In the magazine's inaugural editorial, Loy ridiculed the Missouri attempt to reconcile its "new doctrine" with the explication of predestination in the Formula of Concord. Suddenly, he quipped, after three centuries of Lutheran theology, the Formula's true meaning had been "discovered in St. Louis." Loy then offered his own recommendation of *intuitu fidei*, invoking the Lutheran dogmatician August Pfeiffer (1640–1698), who wrote that God elected "only those whom He foresaw and foreknew that they would in true faith accept and employ the grace which was intended for all." This faith, Loy explained in a later editorial, should never be construed as a work carrying its own inherent virtue; otherwise, *intuitu fidei* would be unscriptural and false. Yet the potential for synergistic misinterpretation of "in view of faith" was less worrisome in Loy's view than the danger posed by Missouri's crypto-Calvinism, which he warned could all too easily lead to "Calvinistic consistency" in denying the full efficacy of the sacraments.[84]

As an inoculation against a Calvinistic Lutheranism, Loy resurrected Pfeiffer's classic work, *Anti-Calvinismus* (1699), publishing it in 1881 at Columbus in a new English translation. This text had once captivated the patriarch of Lutheran liturgy, Johann Sebastian Bach, who had jotted a recommendation of it on a musical manuscript prepared for his wife, Anna Magdalena. Conservative Lutherans ever since had occasionally invoked Pfeiffer as a weapon against promiscuous unionism with Reformed groups. In the introduction to the new edition, Loy, ironically echoing Walther, mocked the modern fashion of emphasizing points of agreement among differing church bodies. The desire for unity, Loy maintained, should never be allowed to stand in the way of exposing doctrinal error.[85]

THE LUTHERAN CIVIL WAR

The most troublesome church union, at least to its opponents, now appeared to be the Synodical Conference itself. The Joint Synod of Ohio, under Loy's leadership, was the first to cut its ties. Meeting at Wheeling, West Virginia, in September 1881, the synod adopted the Four Theses, which asserted that election took place "*in view of Christ's merit apprehended by faith*, or, more briefly stated but with the same sense, *in view of faith*."[86] The synod then voted to withdraw from the conference, which, though dealing a stinging blow to Walther, ironically made possible an Ohio-Iowa alliance that eventually contributed to the birth of a new denomination, the American Lutheran Church (ALC). A more dramatic rift occurred when delegates to the Synodical Conference's 1882 meeting, after adopting Walther's Thirteen Theses, demanded an apology from Schmidt (who was there representing the Norwegian Synod) for his vehement polemics. When he refused, the delegates unseated him, pronouncing him "spiritually dead" and no longer a "brother in Christ." Schmidt left Chicago in disgrace, and in 1883, an internally divided Norwegian Synod withdrew from the Synodical Conference in protest.[87]

With the Synodical Conference now bereft of two of its key constituent bodies, the midwestern turmoil attracted the attention of Lutherans in the East. Leaders of the New York Ministerium, worried by the recent defections of several of their member clergy over predestination, solicited a formal opinion on election from Charles Porterfield Krauth and his conservative confessional colleagues at the Philadelphia seminary. Cautious in tone, the faculty's statement discouraged the use of *intuitu fidei* as potentially misleading but nevertheless seemed to lean toward an anti-Missourian view of predestination. Krauth himself, in a manuscript penned in a shaky hand not long before his death in 1883, suggested that the question at issue ("Is our faith a cause of God's election or an effect of it?") needed to be "carefully defined before men can wisely take sides upon it." He detected a dialectic in history: Luther, against the "Pelagianism of Rome," emphasized the pure grace of God in election, while the later Lutheran orthodox, against the "absolutism of Calvinism," emphasized election's relation to human responsibility. Present-day Lutherans, Krauth concluded, should seek to balance these two emphases.[88]

Krauth's plea for the middle way did not stanch the increasing defections by individual clergy from one synod to another. One later observer counted 27 clerical defections from Missouri to Ohio and 19 from Ohio to Missouri in the years 1880–1885 alone.[89] Secessions of pastors elsewhere are not well documented, though at least one southern synod, Tennessee, which encompassed part of western North Carolina, suffered the loss of 4 clergy to Missouri, including a theologian from Lenoir College (later, Lenoir-Rhyne University) in Hickory, North Carolina, where a pastoral conference on predestination had been convened.[90] Defections by clergy of course drew laypeople into the conflict, so much so that Walther's early biographer, D. H. Steffens, described a scene of virtual civil war: "Not only congregations, but families and households were divided, the husband communing at one church, the wife at another."[91]

Several battles over church property suggest that Steffens's claim was not entirely overblown. One Missouri Synod breakaway congregation in Dearborn, Michigan, appealed to the state supreme court after its former pastor, who had remained loyal to Missouri, tried to lay claim to the church building. The court ruled against the pastor on the grounds that he had never had the parish formally incorporated. Meanwhile, a pastor who had resigned from the Ohio Synod because of its doctrine of *intuitu fidei* was barred from entering his parish building after Ohio loyalists in the congregation won a temporary restraining order. The pastor responded by securing the church doors with a padlock, which the Ohio loyalists, backed by Matthias Loy himself, circumvented by breaking a lock on a side door. Walther reported this incident in *Der Lutheraner* as a warning to other congregations not to bind themselves in their constitutions to any synod, much less to a heretical one.[92]

Such legal fights notwithstanding, the *Gnadenwahlslehrstreit* was chiefly a war of words. The principal historian of the controversy, Hans Haug, conservatively estimated that it produced upward of 25,000 printed pages.[93] The rhetorical volume of the many articles, tracts, and books was equally elevated. "May God have mercy on our American Lutheran Zion," Walther exclaimed in one tract, for God has imposed upon Lutherans the difficult task of contending for one of the "most mysterious doctrines of His Word." This divinely appointed mission was particularly perilous because of the temptation to reconcile biblical teachings with human reason. "O beware! then, dear reader," Walther warned, "of such desire to reconcile!"[94] Rhetoric on the other side was similarly overwrought. "Beware, O Lutheran Church of America, beware!" declared an unsigned statement by several prominent pastors who had jumped ship from Missouri to Ohio: "Missouri, so highly favored and blessed...has fallen into great error," an error "which in very fact annuls the universal love of God."[95]

The statement's warning was noteworthy given its publication fully two decades after the outbreak of the initial controversy. It appeared in 1897 in an 802-page indictment, *The Error of Modern Missouri*, largely authored by Schmidt and by Friedrich W. Stellhorn, a leading defector from Missouri to Ohio and the husband of Walther's niece. The book included nearly 250 pages of quotations from dozens of sixteenth- and seventeenth-century dogmaticians to back up what Schmidt lauded as the "orthodox shibboleth" of *intuitu fidei*. Containing little that was new, the book echoed New England's Beecher clan in lamenting the "unevangelical onesidedness and harshness" of the Augustinian doctrines of absolute predestination and irresistible grace. "It was likewise a strange self-deception," Stellhorn wrote, "when Augustine imagined that his doctrine agreed with the Scriptures." The anonymously written conclusion of *The Error* leveled the more novel and inflammatory charge that Missouri was like the "Israel of old" in rejecting Christ. The alleged proof was in the Missourians' fixation on God's decree of election in eternity, rather than on the merits of Christ, as given in and apprehended by faith.[96]

Outside of midwestern enclaves, the *Sündfluth* (literally, sin flood: the biblical deluge), as one waggish tract described the torrent of polemical publications, was bewildering if not amusing to the few Protestants who noticed the controversy.[97] The Congregational *Andover Review* carried a report on the conflict by "a Lutheran observer" who noted that the Formula of Concord "contained the shibboleth of neither party, and its wording is such that both claimed it for their views." The author also pointed out that most of the controversy's key battles had already been fought in New England decades earlier.[98] Lutheran editors in Germany, influenced by the more pervasive rationalism of theology on the Continent, could barely conceal their disdain for Walther and his allies. A Bavarian church newspaper concluded that Missouri had debased itself by becoming a sect rather than a church. A north German periodical ridiculed Missouri's theology as a "Talmudically-petrified Lutheranism," a charge reflecting some critics' perception that Walther was a *Zitatentheologe* (quotation theologian).[99]

Yet more striking than the barbs from across the Atlantic were the efforts by Walther and his opponents to win the hearts and minds of the laity back home. To achieve this goal, linguistic barriers had to be overcome. While the Missouri Synod's constitution required the exclusive use of German in synodical proceedings, the older and more assimilated Joint Synod of Ohio had a large English-speaking constituency.[100] In order to reach fence-sitting English congregations in the feud over predestination, Missouri theologians felt compelled to make their case in English as well as German. Consequently, the most important Missouri tracts appeared in both languages. The use of Latin terminology in the controversy also became a bone of contention, with Walther accusing his foes of deliberately seeking to confuse "poor farmers" with scholastic distinctions resembling those of the papists.[101]

Indeed, theologians on both sides took pains to dispel the assumption that predestination was a subject too esoteric for the average layperson to comprehend. "Nothing is easier for a pious Christian than to know and to decide this," Walther wrote. "He only must take care not to leave his Lutheran castle and not to be decoyed upon the slippery soil of human reason." Walther, whose tract promised on its title page "plain, trustworthy advice for pious Christians," insisted that laypeople should memorize key passages from the Formula of Concord as a ready defense against both Calvinism and rationalism.[102] On the other side, in a tract similarly billed as a "plain and clear answer for every Lutheran Christian," Stellhorn retorted that the Missourians were the real rationalists in spurning Lutheran dogmatic tradition in favor of their own idiosyncratic interpretations of scripture. "Even the humblest Christian," he declared, could understand that Missouri's election "unto faith" made God into an arbitrary sovereign who blindly rescued a few persons from the fallen mass of humankind.[103]

CONSEQUENCES OF THE CONTROVERSY

Ironically, predestination, which Walther once called "the most consolatory of all doctrines," deprived him of comfort in the last decade of his life as he fretted over the future of Lutheran confessionalism.[104] He confided to a layman in 1881 that "since the deplorable predestination controversy has arisen, I cry and plead day and night upon my knees to God, that He will not suffer me to fall into error."[105] Walther's preoccupation with the controversy was probably the main reason for his failure to produce the multivolume systematic theology that colleagues had urged him to write.[106] Besides sapping his energy, the controversy left him bitter and alienated from many of his onetime allies. He was especially grieved and angered that Schmidt, his former student, had lumped the Missourians together with the Calvinists, "the vilest heretics that ever lived."[107] Walther's intense revulsion at being labeled a Calvinist stemmed in part from his youthful opposition to unionism with Reformed Protestants in Germany, but beneath this lay his abiding suspicion that Calvinism and rationalism were of a piece in seeking, through "sophistry" and "subtlety," to explain the glorious mysteries of predestination and the Eucharist.[108] To his dying day on 7 May 1887, he believed that true Lutheran theology rested not on human reason but on the divine light of scripture. His parishioners in St. Louis honored his commitment to scripture in the mausoleum they erected, at the substantial cost of $9,000, five years after his death. Above his tomb, a life-size, Italian marble statue of him holds the Book of Concord, resting it on a Bible situated atop a pillar.[109] The monument is a fitting memorial to Walther's public persona, which, despite any self-doubt that may have plagued him in private, projected unwavering confidence in his absolute conformity to the scriptures.

To his opponents, however, Walther's self-assurance had been his least endearing quality. He had once declared of his critics that insofar as "they are inimical to me, they are also inimical to God and His truth."[110] Even Walther's sympathetic biographer August Suelflow conceded that the predestination controversy brought about a "radical change" in the attitude of the Missourians toward other Lutherans.[111] Walther's dogged insistence on reine Lehre—pure doctrine, defined on his terms—fostered a spirit of isolationism that continued after his death. This attitude significantly limited the ecumenical potential of the Missouri-dominated Synodical Conference.[112] Though the conference enjoyed some notable successes in the twentieth century, especially in mission work among African Americans in the Deep South, it was never able to repair the ties to Lutherans outside of Missouri's immediate orbit that had been broken over predestination during the 1880s. It was finally dissolved in 1967 by its sole remaining members, the Missouri and Slovak synods (the latter a member from 1908).[113]

A more pragmatic climate ultimately prevailed elsewhere in U.S. Lutheranism. The Norwegians are an important case in point, though peace among them did not come without more fighting over predestination. Even after withdrawing from the Synodical Conference in 1883, the Norwegian Synod was left sharply divided between a pro-Missouri faction, led by synod president

THE WALTHER MAUSOLEUM
Saint Louis, Missouri

Dr. Carl Ferdinand Wilhelm Walther
Born October 25, 1811 - Died May 7, 1887

Dedicated to the members of the Southern District Synod of Missouri, Ohio
and other states, by a greatful pupil of his sainted teacher.　　G. J. W.

Tomb of C. F. W. Walther, Concordia Cemetery, St. Louis, Mo.
Nineteenth-century engraving, Lutheran Historical Institute,
Concordia Seminary, St. Louis.

Herman Amberg Preus (1825–1894), and an anti-Missouri faction, led by
Schmidt. The controversy became so animated on Good Friday 1883 that
Schmidt loyalists in Preus's own Wisconsin parish physically removed him
from the building.[114] By 1886, Schmidt, who had by then discontinued *Altes*

und Neues to focus on the internal Norwegian conflict, established an anti-Missouri seminary at Northfield, Minnesota, in conjunction with St. Olaf College. The following year, Schmidt and approximately one-third of the Norwegian Synod's clergy seceded to form the Anti-Missourian Brotherhood, which united in 1890 with two other Norwegian groups to form the United Norwegian Lutheran Church in America. This left most Norwegian immigrants belonging to either the United Church (with some 152,000 members) or to the old Norwegian Synod (with approximately 94,000 members).[115]

Two factors—one cultural, the other theological—eventually helped to bring these two groups together. On the cultural side, fraternal organizations such as the Norwegian Society of America contributed to a sense of ethnic solidarity, even amid religious disagreements. (German immigrants, who were more numerous, were also more fragmented, both into different Protestant factions and between Protestants and Catholics.) On the religious side, the Church of Norway had never officially subscribed to the Formula of Concord, the interpretation of which so confounded Missouri's relations with Ohio. Norwegians instead shared a common heritage of religious education centering on the teaching of Bergen bishop Erik Pontoppidan (1698–1764), a Danish-born Pietist theologian whose commentary on Luther's Small Catechism taught, in agreement with Johann Gerhard, that election was in view of faith. Pontoppidan's authority helped to assure even many pro-Missouri Norwegians that *intuitu fidei* was not a Christ-denying heresy.[116]

By 1912, Norwegian calls for reunion resulted in the historic Madison Agreement, which declared both "in view of faith" and "unto faith" to be valid forms of the doctrine of election. This paved the way for the merger in 1917 of the two major church bodies to form the Norwegian Lutheran Church of America. The denomination's founding was celebrated at a large convention at St. Paul, which was held in conjunction with the 400th anniversary of Luther's Ninety-five Theses.[117] The new church, which represented over 90 percent of Norwegian Lutherans in the United States, eventually was absorbed in successive mergers to become part of the Evangelical Lutheran Church in America (ELCA), which in the early twenty-first century was the largest and most liberal Lutheran denomination, with 4.7 million members.

The Norwegian merger, however, did not put an end to the theological debate. Prominent ELCA theologian Carl Braaten recalled that as a student at Luther Seminary in the early 1950s, he and fellow student Robert Jenson, who would become one of the denomination's most prolific theologians, were caught up in a campus-wide controversy over whether election was "in view of" or "unto" faith. As Braaten explained the issue at stake,

"[T]here is a significant difference between 'foreseeing' something will happen and 'seeing to it.' The orthodox side stressed the preeminent priority and efficacy of divine grace; the pietist party stressed the role of free will and the necessity of human decision." Braaten began seminary committed to the pietistic view, but by graduation, he had joined Jenson and Professor Herman Amberg Preus (grandson of the late synod president of the same name) in defending election unto faith.[118] Decades later, as a leading voice for confessional renewal in the ELCA, Braaten continued to argue that the Lutheran scholastics of the seventeenth century had gone astray in linking predestination to divine foreknowledge: "The *intuitu fidei* form of doctrine places the burden of salvation on human good will, and at best is a form of semi-Pelagianism. It leaves us with no assurance of salvation."[119]

Meanwhile, a minority of Norwegian Lutherans who did not accept the Madison Agreement persisted as a small, separate denomination. Organized in 1918, the Evangelical Lutheran Synod, which presently claims about 22,000 members, continues to regard election unto faith as an important litmus test of orthodoxy. In a 1997 book on predestination, John A. Moldstad, Jr., the synod's president, warned that "if one capitulates on election," other fundamental biblical teachings inevitably "fall by the wayside." "The current liberalism prevailing in the ELCA today," he added, "bears witness to this irrefutable fact."[120]

The Missouri Synod took an equally dim view of the Madison Agreement and its ecumenical consequences. Franz A. O. Pieper, Walther's successor as president of Concordia Seminary, insisted in a 1913 book that only election unto faith was faithful to scripture and the Lutheran confessions and could therefore be the basis of church unity. He found particularly compelling proof of unto faith in 2 Thessalonians 2:13 ("God hath from the beginning chosen you to salvation through sanctification of the Spirit and belief of the truth"). This verse, he maintained, demolished not only *intuitu fidei* (which made faith a condition, or at least an antecedent, of election) but also the Calvinists' "absolute" decree (which made faith and the "operation of God through the Gospel" meaningless in the face of arbitrary divine election).[121]

In 1932, the synod adopted a Brief Statement of its doctrinal position, authored largely by Pieper, which again condemned "in view of faith" as unscriptural.[122] By this time, in the wake of Schmidt's death in 1928, more than a generation had passed since the outbreak of the predestination controversy. Younger Missouri pastors who picked up the Brief Statement may not have realized the complicated history behind its section on election, which was the lengthiest portion of the document—three and a half times longer than the section on the more characteristically Lutheran doctrine of justification. Nevertheless, the Brief Statement, with its polemical section on predestination intact, was reaffirmed in 1947 by Missouri's centennial convention and has remained authoritative to the present day.

In addition to its boundary setting on predestination, the statement's condemnation of "unionism, that is, church-fellowship with the adherents of false doctrine," has significantly limited Missouri's ecumenical engagement, with one notable exception.[123] In 1969, the synod narrowly approved pulpit and altar fellowship with one of the ELCA's predecessor bodies, the American Lutheran Church, which by then had absorbed the old Norwegian Lutheran Church of America.[124] In the preceding three decades, the ALC, caught up in the headiness of the twentieth-century ecumenical movement, had made a series of overtures to Missouri, even declaring *intuitu fidei* to be a "human construction" that should be avoided. Yet in 1981, only a little more than a decade after entering into fellowship with the ALC, the Missouri Synod pulled out, concluding that the two churches were not in complete doctrinal agreement after all.[125] By that point, the Missouri Synod was firmly controlled by a faction committed to biblical inerrancy (similar to the Southern Baptist inerrantists described in the next chapter). Led by brothers Jacob A. O. and Robert Preus (sons of Minnesota governor J. A. O. Preus and great-grandsons of the original Herman Amberg Preus), the inerrantists not only purged Missouri's seminaries of theological moderates but also insisted that the Bible admitted only one correct interpretation on predestination—election *unto* faith.[126] Missouri's triumphant conservatives echoed the certitude of Franz Pieper, who in a hyperbolic moment once argued that the perfect balance between the grace alone of predestination and the universal offer of salvation in the gospel had been struck only three times in Christian history: in the decrees of the Second Council of Orange (which condemned semi-Pelagianism), in the Formula of Concord, and in the Missouri Synod's Thirteen Theses.[127]

THE CATHOLIC-LUTHERAN JOINT DECLARATION

As Missouri was circling the wagons around an inerrant Bible and Luther's undomesticated version of divine election, the more moderate Lutherans in the ELCA's predecessor bodies were taking ecumenical steps toward Rome that scarcely any observers could have imagined even a few decades before. For centuries, anti-Catholicism had been inscribed in Lutherans' DNA. The date of 31 October, when Luther posted his Ninety-five Theses in 1517, had become Reformation Day, an annual occasion for boisterous renditions of Luther's militant hymn, "A Mighty Fortress," and sermons on the Reformation rallying cry of "faith alone." Yet in the wake of Vatican II in 1965, the

Lutheran World Federation (which included the largest U.S. Lutheran bodies, save for Missouri) had initiated wide-ranging talks with Rome in hopes of capitalizing on the dramatic openness ushered in when John XXIII called the council.

In 1978, a series of more formal talks began on the doctrine of justification, which resulted by 1986 in a detailed, 381-page study authored by two dozen Catholic and Lutheran theologians. The document conceded Luther's legitimate grievances with indulgence peddling and acknowledged that money paid for masses for souls in purgatory had once "provided the main support for a large proportion of priests."[128] At the same time, the document noted that the primacy of divine grace was a theme not exclusive to Protestantism but was also found in leading Catholic authorities such as Aquinas. The statement quoted the *Summa*'s assertion that "it is impossible that the total effect of predestination in general have any cause on our part."[129]

Talks continued for another decade, making clear to all involved that neither Catholic nor Lutheran theologians had lost their zest for scholastic disputation. Finally, in June 1998, the breakthrough moment arrived when the Lutheran World Federation and the Catholic Church (represented by Edward Cardinal Cassidy, head of the Pontifical Council for Promoting Christian Unity) announced the Joint Declaration on the Doctrine of Justification, which lifted the mutual condemnations dating back to Trent. Hailed on the front page of the *New York Times*, the statement declared a "consensus on basic truths," especially on the doctrine that by "grace alone, in faith in Christ's saving work and not because of any merit on our part, we are accepted by God and receive the Holy Spirit, who renews our hearts while equipping and calling us to good works."[130] The declaration stressed that salvation depends "completely" on God's saving grace and noted that when Catholics speak of the will's cooperation with God, they regard this "personal consent as itself an effect of grace, not as an action arising from innate human abilities." Conversely, the document added, the Lutheran emphasis on justification by faith is not meant to exclude the idea of a gradual growth in grace, which would bear fruit in good works.[131]

Amid great fanfare, Catholic and Lutheran representatives signed the Joint Declaration on Reformation Day, 31 October 1999, in Augsburg, Germany. Not surprisingly, the agreement met with unqualified scorn from the Missouri Synod, whose president, A. L. Barry, placed a full-page advertisement in *USA Today* and 15 other major newspapers explaining why Missouri was not among the signatories. In 2001, the Missouri Synod convention declared that the ELCA was not "an orthodox Lutheran body."[132] Barry and other critics in St. Louis felt that the ELCA not only had ignored unresolved differences between Catholics and Lutherans but also had engaged in ecumenical promiscuity in approving nearly simultaneous full-communion agreements with five Protestant denominations: the Presbyterian Church (U.S.A.), the United Church of Christ, and the Reformed Church in America (all in 1997); and the Episcopal Church and the Moravian Church (in 1999). These ecumenical alliances, pursued in seemingly contradictory theological directions, proved to the Missourians that doctrinal distinctions no longer mattered in the ELCA.[133]

Missouri's leaders thus reassumed their familiar role as naysayers, though some of their concerns were eventually echoed by one of the most celebrated veterans of the Catholic-Lutheran dialogue: the Jesuit theologian Avery Dulles of Fordham University. Son of Secretary of State John Foster Dulles and his wife, Janet Pomeroy Avery, he was a convert to Catholicism by way of Presbyterianism. Created cardinal by John Paul II in 2001, Dulles was the only career theologian in the United States ever to receive such an honor, which is typically reserved for archbishops. In a 2007 retrospective on the ecumenical movement, Dulles wondered aloud if the Joint Declaration had "exaggerated the agreements" between the two sides. Could humans "merit an increase of grace and heavenly glory with the help of grace they already have?" he asked. "Do sinners, after receiving forgiveness, still have an obligation to make satisfaction for their misdeeds?" On such questions, he continued, "Lutherans and Catholics seem to give incompatible answers. Nothing in the Joint Declaration persuades me that such differences are mere matters of theological speculation or linguistic formulation."[134]

Yet despite the apparent second thoughts by Cardinal Dulles, the successful passage of the Joint Declaration suggests that beneath their time-worn shibboleths on justification, Catholics and Lutherans are temperamentally similar on predestination. For all of Luther's own skepticism about fine-spun philosophy, the later Lutheran scholastics resembled their Catholic counterparts in struggling, through the most exacting intellectual labor, to banish the specter of arbitrary predestinarianism. Moreover, theologians on both sides—including those in Missouri—recognized that in the end, the best antidotes to predestinarian angst are sacramental. In the final installment of his *Systematic Theology*, published in the same year that the Joint Declaration was signed in Augsburg, Robert Jenson rejected the common predestinarian picture of "God in solitary eternity arbitrarily sorting future persons into two heaps." Drawing on the logic of the Swiss Reformed theologian Karl Barth, Jenson argued that election and reprobation properly applied not to humans individually but to Christ himself, who was both reprobate (in the Crucifixion) and elect (in the Resurrection). The sacraments, Jenson continued, bring the church's people into the election side of this dialectic: "Baptism *is* the Father's giving of sheep to the Son's fold."[135]

Such a credo, had it been more widely and wholeheartedly accepted (even by Lutherans and Catholics themselves), might have neutralized centuries of predestinarian conflict among the dogmaticians. But purely sacramental solutions to the problem of election went against the American grain. In the next chapter, we will return to more characteristically American contexts in which God's eternal decrees loom larger than any grace conveyed through water, bread, or wine.

CHAPTER 6

Debating a Doctrine

Presbyterians and Baptists

"I never heard enough damnation from your pulpit. Many mornings I had to strain to take hold of what you were saying, Reverend. I couldn't figure it out, and got dizzy listening, the way you were dodging here and there....Take away damnation, in my opinion, a man might as well be an atheist. A God that can't damn a body to an eternal Hell can't lift a body up out of the grave either."

"Mr. Orr, to relieve your mind—"

"Young man, don't worry about relieving my mind. I told you, I can face it. I can face the worst, if it was always ordained. God's as helpless in this as I am."

—John Updike, In the Beauty of the Lilies *(1996)*

There is no essential difference between the unbelieving fatalism of Calvinists and the fatalism of Moslems or other heathen people. Essentially Calvinism would teach that there is no real right or wrong, no moral responsibility for men and women.

—John R. Rice, Predestined for Hell? No! *(1958)*

AN UNPLEASANT SURPRISE awaited former U.S. president Benjamin Harrison when he sat down with his morning newspaper at his Indianapolis home on Saturday, 26 May 1900. His eyes landed on an article announcing that he had been appointed by the Presbyterian General Assembly to serve on a new committee to revise the Westminster

Confession. A similar effort to amend the confession's pointed predestinarianism had failed seven years earlier amid much strife. Now the assembly's pro-revision moderator, Philadelphia pastor Charles Dickey, was enlisting some heavyweights, including Harrison and Supreme Court justice John Harlan, for what promised to be another protracted controversy. Harrison, a Union general during the Civil War, was no stranger to rough-and-tumble politics or electoral setbacks. In a disastrous midterm election during his presidency, his party lost the House of Representatives to the Democrats. In 1892, he became the only president deprived of a second term by his predecessor, when voters returned Grover Cleveland to the White House in a landslide. Most recently, he had come out of retirement to represent the Venezuelan government in a boundary dispute with British Guiana, a case in which he delivered 25 hours of closing arguments over several exhausting days.[1] Yet despite his proven endurance, Harrison knew one thing for sure: church battles were the worst, and he wanted no part of this one.

Harrison immediately penned a letter to his onetime secretary of state and fellow Presbyterian layman, John W. Foster, quipping that "after the Assembly adjourns I propose to resign in your favor!"[2] (Harrison's inner circle had been known as the "Presbyterian cabinet" because of his policy of appointing coreligionists to top posts.)[3] A few days later, however, the former president received a letter from Dickey urging him to accept the assignment and asking if he could attend an initial meeting of the committee at Saratoga, New York, in August. Harrison replied that "after two years of very hard work in the Venezuelan case," he wanted to enjoy the "unwonted luxury" of not taking any work with him to his summer home in the Adirondacks: "I find that work tires me more than it did when I was a younger man." But Dickey would not take no for an answer. "I know your loyalty and love for our dear old Church, and your good name would be of such value in this time of need," he responded. "You can do much, I am confident, to bring about unity of action in the Committee." Two days later, another entreaty arrived from St. Louis pastor Samuel J. Niccolls, the Presbyterian General Assembly's former moderator, who told Harrison that his presence on the revision committee would "be a guarantee to thousands that safe and conservative counsels will prevail."[4]

Harrison finally relented. Though he missed the Saratoga meeting, he attended the next session, a four-day marathon in Washington, D.C., in December, and corresponded with his fellow revisers in the weeks following. By early February, with winter lingering and several members of his household suffering from influenza, the run-down former president wrote to Niccolls that he felt "as if the monster were reaching in my direction."[5] The flu did strike him, and it soon turned to pneumonia. As his 42-year-old

President Benjamin Harrison by T. C. Steele (1900). Harrison Residence Hall, Purdue University, and National Portrait Gallery, Smithsonian Institution (Art Resource).

second wife, Mary Dimmick, and 4-year-old daughter watched in anguish, he descended into a coma. He died on 13 March 1901 at age 67. Niccolls, perhaps feeling a twinge of guilt, helped to officiate at the funeral and at the graveside, where 15,000 Hoosiers gathered to bid their beloved president farewell. Also officiating was Harrison's own trusted pastor, M. L. Haines, who probably had helped to convince him to join the confessional revision effort. Not long before Harrison had joined the committee, Haines had been quoted in the *New York Times* as supporting a "newer and shorter creed" that would eliminate "certain misleading statements...which seem to teach fatalism."[6] But Harrison did not live to see these hopes realized. His own fate, a cynic might well conclude, was to die a victim of one too many church meetings over predestination.

Harrison's brief stint on the revision committee brought him face to face with a question that had dogged American Presbyterians since the colonial era: how binding was the Westminster Confession? No other American Protestant tradition, save perhaps for Lutheranism, was so strongly associated with a founding document, and no major confession was as unequivocal on unconditional predestination. Yet even as Presbyterians named churches, colleges, and seminaries after Westminster, they disagreed over whether the confession's teachings on predestination were essential for all faithful members to believe. Similar disagreements arose among the Baptists, who, while lacking a single standard as iconic as Westminster, had a seventeenth-century confessional heritage that reemerged at the center of modern battles for the soul of the church. Presbyterians and Baptists warrant further comparison because of two factors that intensified their battles over predestination: fundamentalism (which led conservatives in both groups to insist that an inerrant Bible was univocal in its teaching) and regionalism (which in the wake of the Civil War incubated a particularly resistant strain of Calvinism in the South). Nowhere do these factors remain more vividly in play in the early twenty-first century than in the 16 million–member Southern Baptist Convention. Though home to some of the most convinced and articulate predestinarians in the United States today, the SBC also includes anti-Calvinists who are equally adamant that unconditional election is unbiblical.

PRESBYTERIANS AND CONFESSIONAL SUBSCRIPTION

The earliest American Presbyterians brought their allegiance to the Westminster Confession from Scotland and Ulster, where Calvinism lived on even after the Restoration doomed any official status for the document in England. The father of American Presbyterianism was Francis Makemie, a Scots-Irish immigrant who founded the colonies' first presbytery in Philadelphia in 1706. Nine years earlier, while ministering in Barbados, he wrote a vigorous defense of Westminster's predestinarianism against the "groundless, silly, and inconsequential" objections to it by the island's Anglicans. The Westminster position was not substantially different from the doctrine of election in the Church of England's own Thirty-nine Articles, Makemie claimed, implying that the Anglicans had lost sight of their own creed.[7] Yet whereas Anglicanism's constitution was artfully ambiguous—Bishop Burnet's *Exposition* (published the same year as Makemie's tract) insisted that the Thirty-nine Articles could accommodate both Calvinism and Arminianism[8]—the Westminster Confession stated the divine decrees more baldly. Some persons were "predestinated unto everlasting life, and others foreordained to everlasting death." Christ's redemptive death pertained only to the elect, who were predestined to eternal felicity "out of [God's] mere free grace and love, without any foresight of faith or good works." Even newborns fell under the same unconditional decree: "Elect infants, dying in infancy, are regenerated, and saved by Christ."[9] The confession's readers were thus left to assume that certain infants were not elect.[10]

These teachings had provoked criticism well before Makemie rushed to their defense. In England in the 1650s, the Anglican Laurence Womock, who was elevated to the episcopate after the Restoration, satirized infant damnation with his fictional "Mr. Fri-Babe."[11] In America in the 1680s, the Quaker George Keith, who would eventually become an Anglican priest, asked how any Presbyterian or other Calvinist could justifiably believe that certain infants were damned for Adam's sin, given the biblical assurances, as in Romans 2:6, that persons were judged according to their deeds. Keith was unimpressed by the Calvinists' attempt to soften infant damnation by claiming that children of *believing* parents were undoubtedly elect. By this logic, he said, Calvinists must conclude that Esau, "whose Parents were believers," was elect—a notion that belied the usual Reformed exegesis.[12] All the while, latitudinarian and Enlightenment currents were eroding the traditional Calvinist picture of sinners in the hands of an angry God. "That God hath from all Eternity absolutely decreed the eternal ruine of the greatest part of Mankind, without any respect to the Sins and Demerits of Men, I am as certain that this Doctrine cannot be of God, as I am sure that God is Good and Just," wrote Archbishop John Tillotson. Surely an infinitely benevolent God would not do what "no good man would do."[13]

Amid the growing doubts about predestination, Presbyterians on both sides of the Atlantic moved to enforce Westminster orthodoxy. The Scots Parliament made subscription to the confession mandatory for ministers in 1690, and the Synod of Ulster did the same in 1698. By the early 1720s, conservatives in the Synod of Philadelphia were pushing for a similar measure. But Jonathan Dickinson, who would later become the first president of the College of New Jersey (Princeton), argued that no human creed deserved the same allegiance as the Bible itself. Though Dickinson expressed no qualms about the Westminster orthodoxy himself, he crafted a compromise, enacted as the Adopting Act of 1729, which required confessional subscription but allowed ministers to voice their scruples about particular articles. The measure left it to the individual presbyteries to decide if a member's scruples concerned "essential and necessary" doctrines.[14] The stage was set for heresy hunting by presbyteries and synods, a recurring theme in Presbyterian history into the twentieth century.

The Adopting Act was soon put to the test in the 1735 heresy trial of Samuel Hemphill, whose sermons had raised suspicions about his commitment to original sin, among other doctrines. Hemphill, however, had admitted no scruples in subscribing to the Westminster Confession, first in Ulster and then after arriving in Philadelphia. He defended himself by pointing out that the church had never defined which articles were "essential and necessary." The Philadelphia Synod suspended him anyway, over the protests of Benjamin Franklin (as we saw in chapter 4). Franklin compared the synod's judicial commission to the Spanish Inquisition and mocked the Presbyterians for preferring their "darling Confession" to the "Gospel of Christ."[15]

Though Hemphill faded into obscurity, conservatives could see the handwriting on the wall. Fears that this was only the beginning of challenges to five-point orthodoxy help to explain why the College of New Jersey, the first Presbyterian institution of higher learning in America, tapped Jonathan Edwards as its third president in 1757. Though Edwards was a Congregationalist, he had recently published his predestinarian *Freedom of the Will* (1754) and had completed a major treatise on original sin. The latter, published as *The Great Christian Doctrine of Original Sin Defended* (1758), took a hard line against the heterodox English Presbyterian John Taylor, whose own *Scripture-Doctrine of Original Sin* (1740) had made great waves by denying the imputation of Adam's guilt to his posterity.[16] Edwards reasserted the Augustinian argument that the universal mortality of humanity proved the culpability of all people—including infants—in original sin. Indeed, the high rate of infant mortality confirmed that "infants are not looked upon by God as sinless" but "are by nature children of wrath." Elsewhere, Edwards explained that though children lacked the same weight of committed sins as adults, "we know they have enough to make their damnation very just." Though privately he seemed in agreement with other Reformed divines that the children of godly parents would likely be saved if they died in infancy, Edwards nevertheless upheld the rigor of Calvinist logic, which demanded that the uncertainty of election extend to everyone, regardless of age.[17]

Yet despite its logical consistency, the idea of infant damnation was, as church historian Philip Schaff would write more than a century later, "cruel and revolting to every nobler and better feeling of our nature." Present-day historian James Turner has aptly described the doctrine as "the soft underbelly of Calvinism" because of the heavy burden of justification it placed on Calvinism's defenders.[18] Indeed, by the early nineteenth century, the freighted confessional phrase "elect infants" had emerged as one of the biggest stumbling blocks for many Presbyterians in subscribing to Westminster. One of those uncomfortable Presbyterians was Lyman Beecher, patriarch of the famous New England clan. Trained in the Congregational orbit of Timothy Dwight at Yale, he became a Presbyterian upon his appointment as the first president of Lane Seminary in Cincinnati in 1832. In considering this call, he reportedly remarked—only half-jokingly—that his answer to the standard question for subscription ("Do you sincerely receive and adopt the Confession of Faith of this Church, as containing the system of doctrine taught in the Holy Scriptures?") would be, "Yes, but I will not say how much more it contains."[19] Such equivocations did not sit well with the local presbytery's conservatives, who were already on high alert because of Beecher's association with Dwight and the New Divinity. Like Dwight, Beecher hoped to have his cake and eat it too. He wanted to believe, as Marie Caskey has put it, that "God was sovereign but his sovereignty was such as befitted republican forms of government."[20] Beecher eagerly portrayed himself as a defender of the "Augustinian or Calvinistic system" even while denying some of its starkest consequences.[21]

Beecher's historical contortionism had initially landed him in trouble with liberals back in Boston when he engaged the Unitarian *Christian Examiner* on the contentious question of infant damnation and baptism. Ever since the fifth century, theologians had debated Augustine's insistence that unbaptized infants were surely lost, an opinion that in Pelagius's view only compounded predestination's harshness by further reducing the number of the saved.[22] Beecher insisted that the bishop of Hippo did not teach the actual damnation of unbaptized infants but only the loss of "holy enjoyment" in heaven. In a scathing reply in the *Examiner*, the Unitarian Francis Jenks accused Beecher of never having read Augustine directly but instead adulterating two secondhand quotations of him from Thomas Ridgley's *Body of Divinity* (1731–1733), a favorite among Congregationalists and Presbyterians, which had been published in a four-volume U.S. edition in 1814–1815. Had Beecher examined Augustine directly, Jenks wrote, he would have discovered that though Augustine believed that unbaptized infants would experience a milder punishment than that of other condemned souls, they would still be damned because of original sin. Moreover, Jenks pointed out, Augustine maintained that even some *baptized* infants who were not among the elect would be damned. Augustine thus deserved the epithet *durus pater infantum* (stern, or hard, father of infants), and Beecher's attempt to exonerate him from this charge was, in Jenks's view, a "total failure."[23]

Beecher's soft-pedaling of Augustinianism won him no friends among Presbyterian traditionalists who, after his arrival in Cincinnati, accused him of Pelagianism and other deviations from the Westminster Confession. In 1835, he was hauled before the local presbytery on heresy charges brought by Joshua Lacy Wilson, pastor of the city's First Presbyterian Church, whom the *Christian Examiner* derided as "the *malleus hereticorum* [hammer of heretics] of the West."[24] In a published exposition of his views, Beecher denied any taint of Pelagian perfectionism and professed his allegiance to original sin: "I scarce ever attended the funeral of an infant without an express recognition of these views upon infant depravity, and the atonement and regeneration as the only ground of hope that they are saved." As for predestination and human volition, he insisted that even Augustine had believed in free will, though to be sure, the Fall had "biased" the human will in favor of sin. "[I]f I am a Pelagian," he declared, "Augustine was a Pelagian."[25]

Beecher was acquitted, though not before the presbytery "goaded" him (according to the *Examiner*) into promising to use the Westminster Confession as a textbook at Lane. He also pledged that he would never support any revision of the confession. Should he renege on his promise, he intoned, "may my right hand forget its cunning and may my tongue cleave to the roof of my mouth."[26] Meanwhile, heresy proceedings were under way for a second time against another pastor, Philadelphia's Albert Barnes, who had denied limited atonement and the imputation of Adam's guilt. Initially convicted of heresy by the presbytery in 1831, Barnes appealed to the synod and then to the General Assembly, which let him off with a slap on the wrist. But in 1835, his *Notes on the Epistle to the Romans* raised conservatives' suspicions anew. Suspended by the synod until he agreed to recant, Barnes refused. He won reinstatement by the 1836 General Assembly.[27] The following year, the enmity between the advocates of strict subscription (the faction known as the Old School) and the more liberal evangelicals, such as Beecher and Barnes (known as the New School), resulted in all-out war. By that point, the revivalist Charles Finney, a New School sympathizer who had been serving a Presbyterian congregation in New York City, had jumped ship for the Congregationalists. "No doubt there is a jubilee in hell every year about the time of the meeting of the [Presbyterian] General Assembly," he concluded.[28]

The Old School–New School schism, finalized when the two groups withdrew into rival conventions amid a chaotic General Assembly in May 1838, occurred just two months before Ralph Waldo Emerson, in his famous address to the graduating class at Harvard Divinity School, declared that truth is intuition and announced his emancipation from all orthodoxies: "All attempts to contrive a system are as cold as the new worship introduced by the French to the goddess of Reason."[29] Historian Mark Noll has noted that while Emerson's Romantic manifesto has overshadowed the Presbyterian debacle in history textbooks, the Old School–New School split was more revealing of American religion's future. In the schism, Noll argues, "the power of self-interpreting axioms faltered"—that is, the Bible, which Protestants heretofore believed would be interpreted in the same way by all people of common sense, had ceased to unify.[30] The initial breakdown occurred, as it had among eighteenth-century evangelicals, over the broad complex of doctrines touching on predestination. For the leading Old School theologian, Charles Hodge, who was a professor at Princeton Seminary from 1822 until his death in 1878, the Westminster Confession articulated what he regarded as the patently obvious sense of scripture: Adam was the federal head of all humanity, who received his guilt by imputation; Christ died for the elect only, who received his righteousness by imputation. To Hodge, this federal plan of salvation was a divinely engineered machine. Remove one part, such as original sin, and the whole system failed.[31] New School theologians read the same Bible but found in it no deterministic scheme of imputation. To Albert Barnes, "men sin in their own persons, sin themselves—as indeed, how can they sin in any other way?"[32] The issue for him was far from merely semantic. In failing to emphasize the scriptural thread of individual responsibility, the Westminster Confession risked tempering the moral zeal required of citizens in a virtuous republic. Indeed, the more radical New Schoolers such as Barnes concluded that a strong sense of moral agency was the necessary starting point for eradicating all social ills. For Barnes and other northerners, the greatest societal evil of the day was slavery.[33]

NORTH AND SOUTH: REGIONAL VARIATIONS

The problem of slavery precipitated what Noll has identified as a theological crisis in the Civil War era as American Christians debated whether the Bible justified human bondage.[34] Partly as a result of this crisis, predestination found a more hospitable climate in the South, though the doctrine was never without its strong northern defenders. The Presbyterian case shows how theology and regional concerns could become mutually reinforcing. Regarding the "peculiar institution," the proslavery forces clearly had the easier task in appealing to scripture. In the Old Testament, slaveholding was taken for granted among the Hebrew patriarchs, and God sanctioned the enslavement of Israel's vanquished enemies. Similarly, in the New Testament, Jesus never spoke directly against slavery, and Paul enjoined servants to obey their masters.[35] The strict predestinarianism of Old School Presbyterians also lent to the proslavery cause an important doctrinal resource: a broad and pliable sense of divine determinism. Old School stalwarts in the South freely drew parallels between individual predestination and God's providential plan for whole peoples. In a famous sermon delivered on a Confederate fast day two months after the war's outbreak at Fort Sumter, Benjamin Morgan Palmer, pastor of the First Presbyterian Church of New Orleans, declared that "nations are in a weighty sense *persons* before God" and "are held to account for their fidelity to their trusts," even as they live out a foreordained mission.[36] Palmer drew out the analogy in the story of Noah and his sons, two of whom (Shem and Japheth) averted their eyes when they found their father drunken and naked in his tent, while the third (Ham) looked upon Noah in his shame. In the fates pronounced upon the three brothers, Palmer found "the fortunes of mankind presented in perfect outline." Ham's posterity, which Palmer identified with the African race, was condemned to perpetual servitude: "a servant of servants shall he be unto his brethren" (Gen. 9:25). To Shem's descendants, the Semites, God bequeathed a destiny "primarily religious." The Hebrews and Christ himself issued from this pure line, though Palmer saw its perversion in "the Mohammedan imposture." Japheth's stock constituted the "hardy and aggressive families" of Greeks and Romans, English and Germans, and others who gave the world its scientific, political, and artistic culture.[37]

Palmer later cautioned against reading all biblical pronouncements of divine favor as references to groups rather than to particular persons. (Calvinists had often accused Arminians of precisely this error.) The apostle Paul made clear, Palmer wrote, that the blessing of Jacob and the cursing of Esau were meant to demonstrate individual, unconditional election.[38] Nevertheless, Palmer and other conservatives continued to argue that the diverse fortunes of whole nations mirrored God's electing purposes on the micro level. Indeed, Princeton's Charles Hodge, who sympathized with his southern colleagues and never unequivocally denounced slavery in principle, found in the inequalities among the world's peoples unmistakable empirical confirmation of unconditional predestination.[39] Writing in the Baconian language that had come to dominate American theological reflection, Hodge insisted, "We must conform our theories to the facts, and not make the facts conform to our theories." It was a fact that God did not treat people equally: "It cannot be believed that the lot of the Laplanders is as favourable as that of the inhabitants of the temperate zone; that the Hottentots are in as desirable a position as the Europeans; that the people of Tartary are as well off as those of the United States." Clearly, in Hodge's view, God did not give sufficient grace to all, as Arminians claimed. Only one theory explained the grave disparities in national and individual fortunes: "Augustinianism accords with these facts of providence, and therefore must be true."[40]

Hodge's logic could have been a recipe for a crisis of confidence in the Confederacy, which after 1865 lacked compelling evidence of national election. Yet providentialism is infinitely malleable, and the South's defeat paradoxically yielded an even more enduring brand of Christian "fatalism"—the religion of the Lost Cause.[41] This was emphatically not fatalism of the secular variety, for the Confederate religious press had been vocal in denouncing the "creeping atheism" that the horror of war inevitably caused in some of its victims.[42] Instead, the South resurrected the idea of the persecuted, elect remnant, which had steeled the refugees in Calvin's Geneva, the Huguenots in Louis XIV's France, and the Puritans in colonial New England. Fundamental to this ideology was Theodore Beza's old notion that God's elect were like an anvil that had worn out many hammers. Providence sent hostile armies to hammer away, but God's anvil withstood them, harder than before. Similarly, some preachers imagined the South as a metal bar heated in the forge by the divine blacksmith. As James I. Vance, pastor of Nashville's First Presbyterian Church, summed up the war, "the period of struggle was the period of discipline. It was providence placing the idle ore in flame and forge."[43] Though the trial by fire was unquestionably severe, partisans for the Lost Cause never doubted the South's ultimate vindication. *Deo vindice* (God will avenge): so proclaimed the Great Seal of the Confederacy. A decade after Confederate president Jefferson Davis died, his wife and daughter placed on his tomb an inscription from the Sermon on the Mount: "Blessed are they which are persecuted for righteousness' sake: for theirs is the kingdom of heaven."[44]

Davis was an Episcopalian, but his epitaph aptly expressed the postwar mood of many southern Presbyterians, who saw themselves as a righteous remnant in a wider tradition increasingly swayed by theological liberalism. The war had forced the sectional division of both the Old School and New School bodies, but by 1869, the four churches again became two.[45] The southern denomination, the Presbyterian Church in the United States (PCUS), was dominated by the former Old School and resisted calls from a handful of clergy to soften the Westminster Confession's statements on predestination. As one southern church newspaper declared, confessional revision had few advocates in Dixie, "and this is the glory and the strength of our Southern Church—that it is the soundest Presbyterian Church in the world." Another periodical editorialized: "Our church is recognized as the exponent of conservatism. We cannot afford to set the example of remodeling our doctrinal standards at a time when the tendency in the world is towards an abandonment of strong doctrinal positions."[46] On predestination, the only "remodeling" approved in the South actually appeared to sharpen the church's stance. In adopting the Westminster Confession as its doctrinal summary, the PCUS changed the heading of chapter III from "Of God's Eternal Decree" (the original 1647 reading) to "Of God's Eternal Decrees." The plural construction connoted for some observers the parallelism of double predestination—that the election of some persons necessarily entailed the reprobation of others.[47]

Meanwhile, in the northern denomination, known as the Presbyterian Church in the United States of America (PCUSA), a rift soon emerged between leaders of the former New School, such as the theologian and historian Henry Boynton Smith, and former Old School figures such as Charles Hodge. Smith, influenced as a graduate student in Germany by Hegelian idealism, came to regard historical development as the key to Christian faith. Like a living organism, the church gradually manifested the glory of the incarnation. Because doctrine is never static, Smith believed, the unfolding history of ideas reveals God's evolutionary purposes.[48] Hodge sensed danger in such views. If Jesus Christ was the same yesterday, today, and forever, as the Bible claimed (Heb. 13:8), then surely the essential doctrines did not change. Christianity was not so much an organic "life" as a system of truths revealed "in a definite and complete form for all ages."[49]

Within a few years of the PCUSA's formation in 1869, these conflicting perspectives helped to resurrect the practical question of whether subscription to unvarying confessions should be required. "Adaptation to the times in which we live, is the law of Providence," Henry Ward Beecher declared in 1873. A son of Lyman Beecher and Roxana Foote, he had pastored a New School congregation in Indianapolis before accepting his better-known Congregational pulpit at Plymouth Church in Brooklyn. In his view, the five-point Calvinism codified by the Westminster divines had become a procrustean bed. Doctrines such as total depravity were "so gross and so undiscriminating" as to be utterly useless in a modern age that appreciated humanity's evolutionary potential.[50] Similarly, David Swing, pastor of Chicago's Fourth Presbyterian Church, pleaded with his ministerial colleagues in 1874 to emancipate themselves from what he regarded as Westminster's grim calculus of election and reprobation: "Not one of you, my brethren, has preached the dark theology of Jonathan Edwards in your whole life. Nothing could induce you to preach it, and yet it is written down in your creed in dreadful plainness. Confess, with me, that our beloved church has slipped away from the religion of despair."[51] Swing's cri de coeur came during his trial for heresy by the Chicago presbytery, which reflected the divided mind of the northern church as a whole. Though he was acquitted by a vote of 48–13, a threatened appeal by the conservatives prompted him to withdraw from the denomination. His chief antagonist, Francis Patton, who would eventually become president of Princeton University, represented the defenders of creedal subscription when he insisted that dogmas such as eternal punishment were ironclad rules: "I cannot help it if that is a doctrine which is unpleasant to the feelings. It is in the Confession of Faith."[52] Patton and his allies feared that the continual revision of the church's creedal standards implied that God himself was contingent rather than eternal in his decrees.

THE REVISION CONTROVERSY

Despite conservatives' fears, revision was in the air on both sides of the Atlantic. In 1879, the United Presbyterian Church of Scotland adopted the Declaratory Act, which tempered the Westminster Confession's controversial chapter III with what amounted to a qualifying footnote invoking the words of 2 Peter 3:9, long a favorite of Arminians. The doctrine of the divine decrees was to be "held in connection and harmony with the truth that God is not willing that any should perish, but that all should come to repentance."[53] In 1883, a commission of Congregational churches in the United States issued a revised creed that, unlike Westminster (whose doctrinal provisions colonial Congregationalists had adopted as their own), was conspicuously silent on election. Instead, it asserted that "those who through renewing grace turn to righteousness, and trust in Jesus Christ as their Redeemer, receive for His sake the forgiveness of their sins, and are made the children of God."[54] Two years later, the Presbyterian Synod of England appointed a committee that would eventually overhaul Westminster and refer to election only in the broadest terms as God's choosing "unto Himself in Christ a people, whom He gave to the Son."[55] All the while, the nascent ecumenical movement was pushing liberal Protestants toward the adoption of statements of faith that lacked the church-dividing particularities of older confessions. Leaders of the cumbersomely named Alliance of Reformed Churches throughout the World Holding the Presbyterian System, founded in 1875, envisioned a consensus creed that might one day unite all latter-day Calvinists who were weary of ecclesiastical infighting.[56]

It was not a complete surprise, therefore, when 15 presbyteries asked the PCUSA General Assembly in 1889 to consider revising the Westminster Confession. Because the Adopting Act of two centuries earlier required support from two-thirds of the presbyteries for any confessional emendation, the General Assembly voted to send two questions back to all of the church's districts: "1. Do you desire a revision of the Confession of Faith? 2. If so, in what respects, and to what extent?"[57] A heated debate soon engaged Presbyterians from coast to coast and dominated the denominational press for the next four years. The hundreds of articles published in church newspapers revealed that a large number of clergy and laypeople had grown increasingly uneasy with their doctrinal past. A vocal minority, however, feared that confessional revision would hasten the emergence of a lowest-common-denominator Christianity devoid of theological substance. At the center of the dispute, like a heavy piece of antique furniture inherited by a grandchild with no place to put it, was the doctrine of predestination.

As in the debate a decade earlier in Scotland, the most contentious portions of Westminster were chapter III, the fullest statement on predestination, which asserted that the number of the elect "is so certain and definite that it cannot be either increased or diminished," and chapter X ("Of Effectual Calling"), which contained the infamous reference to "elect infants."[58]

To many northern Presbyterian clergy, these chapters were an embarrassment and a needless stumbling block for would-be converts. A columnist for the *New York Evangelist* complained that these sections went "beyond the wise reserve of Scripture" and had become "a favorite weapon against us in the hand of other denominations." "We were recently told by a non-Presbyterian clergyman," the writer recounted, "that 'the Confession of Faith is fit only to be put up in a glass-case and hermetically sealed.'"[59] Ohio minister James Monfort lamented that chapter III's statement on the unchangeable number of the elect had driven away "thousands of our people" and "hindered thousands from coming to us." He recalled from his young adulthood hearing boys in the street repeating Lorenzo Dow's "damned if you do, damned if you don't" jingle and listening to evangelists preach mock funeral sermons for Calvinism, which they claimed had committed suicide by stubbornly clinging to chapter III.[60] Other contributors to the Presbyterian press expressed similar exasperation with the intransigence of conservatives, who treated the confession "with an almost superstitious awe, as though it were the very ark of God," according to an observer from "a Hoosier Front Porch." Another writer, the prominent Philadelphia layman and type foundry executive Thomas MacKellar, argued that the time had come to update a confession dating from an epoch that was "cruel, harsh, and unduly vindictive," when people were "put to death for what are now regarded [as] comparatively trivial offenses."[61]

Among the most noted advocates of revision was the Swiss-born church historian Philip Schaff (1819–1893), who had transferred his ministerial credentials to the Presbyterian Church after joining the faculty of the denomination's Union Seminary in New York in 1870. Schaff, who shared Henry Boynton Smith's organic view of doctrinal development, saw the "finger of God" in the revision movement, which was calling Presbyterians to "a higher, broader, and more liberal position in theory and practice." In his view, the problem with Westminster was that it went beyond even the Canons of Dort in broaching the subject of reprobation. Whether interpreted as fully parallel to election, as section III.3 ("foreordained to everlasting death") seemed to imply, or as preterition, or a mere "passing by" of the non-elect, as section III.7 suggested, Westminster was needlessly explicit, Schaff maintained, in speaking of God's wrath. "These doctrines are no longer believed by the majority of Presbyterians, nor preached by any Presbyterian minister as far as I know," he declared in a meeting of the presbytery of New York. "What cannot be preached in the Church and taught in the Sunday-school, ought not to be put into a Confession of Faith." The Westminster divines had gotten stuck in the "darkness" of Romans 9, "the strong fortress of supralapsarianism," without moving on to the "glorious light" of Romans 11, which promised the salvation of all Israel. Schaff commended the Congregationalists' solution of 1883—the adoption of a simpler creed that avoided "all the knotty and disputed points of the scholastic Calvinism of a by-gone age."[62] Such a creed would aid the causes of evangelism and ecumenism, just as the new translation of the Bible, the Revised Version of 1881–1885, had done. Schaff, who chaired the U.S. company of translators, had once remarked that it "might be well to revise the Bible every fifty years, to induce the people to read it."[63] He regarded translations and confessions as similarly time-bound and subject to the Holy Spirit's guidance in every era.

To leading conservatives such as Benjamin Breckinridge Warfield (1851–1921), however, the danger of updating the language of the confessions was that fundamental doctrines might be altered or abandoned in the process. Warfield, who had recently succeeded Charles Hodge's son, Archibald Alexander Hodge, as professor of theology at Princeton Seminary, suspected that some of the proponents of revision were intent on "emasculating" the confession of doctrines they privately no longer believed. He wondered aloud if Schaff's comments on preterition betrayed the elder historian's denial of the doctrine, a position that would be "fundamentally heretical." Preterition is the unavoidable consequence of election, Warfield insisted, and Christians dare not shrink from it: "The very essence of heresy consists in so emphasizing one truth as consciously to deny the complementary truth."[64] Warfield's colleague across the street at Princeton University, President Francis Patton, feared that preterition was the least of the doctrines doubted by some of the revisers, whom he accused of abandoning the more central idea of unconditional election. "They go on speaking of election on the ground of holiness, or election on the ground of foreseen faith, and are unconsciously using the Shibboleths of Arminianism in advocating the cause of the Westminster divines," he maintained in a speech before the Presbyterian Social Union in New York City.[65]

The charges of creeping unorthodoxy did not sit well with the advocates of revision. Henry J. Van Dyke, Sr., pastor of Brooklyn's First Presbyterian Church, assailed Warfield's "very bad taste" in accusing Schaff of heresy. The conservatives arrogantly regarded themselves as the only guardians of orthodoxy, Van Dyke added, and wrongly assumed that the Westminster Confession could not err. "May I be excused for frankly expressing what rises to my lips and saying with the boys, 'this is *rot*,'" he exclaimed. Similarly, Samuel Niccolls, who would eventually enlist Benjamin Harrison in the revision effort, insisted that the church's desire to "revise a fallible Confession, and make it conform more clearly and fully to the teachings of the Word of God, is surely no evidence that it is about to abandon its ancient faith."[66]

Yet Warfield's and Patton's concerns were not entirely unfounded, for some pro-revision clergy had no qualms about assailing the cardinal tenets of Calvinist orthodoxy. Howard Crosby, pastor of New York's Fourth Avenue Presbyterian Church and the former chancellor of New York University, had been a zealous partisan for Bible revision, once making the impolitic prediction that the Revised Version would win universal acceptance as soon as the "old grannies and croakers" were dead.[67] Likewise, he looked to confessional revision to sweep away the encrusted dogmas that had obscured commonsense biblical truths. He believed that the Westminster divines had uncritically followed Calvin's and Augustine's error in making divine grace "arbitrarily discriminate between man and man." The onus of responsibility was on freely willing humans, as numerous scriptural passages clearly taught: "'Whosoever will' is the style of them all."[68]

Crosby's apparent Arminianism was increasingly the norm among rank-and-file Presbyterians, for whom the Westminster Confession was a "heavy burden for their consciences," according to the New York clergyman and professor of biblical theology Charles Augustus Briggs. In his inaugural in 1891 after being named to a new chair at Union Theological Seminary, Briggs ignited his own denominational firestorm when he denied the verbal inspiration of the scriptures. In the same address, he complained that "Presbyterians have too often limited redemption by their doctrine of Election." Indeed, he believed that Protestants in general had erred in restricting the process of redemption to this life and not recognizing the possibility that nearly all persons will be saved through progressive sanctification during the middle state between death and resurrection.[69] Briggs's manifesto prompted the PCUSA General Assembly to defrock him on grounds of heresy, for which Union Seminary retaliated by severing its ties to the denomination. Briggs remained at Union and took refuge in a communion where liturgical correctness trumped confessional subscription: the Episcopal Church.

The Briggs affair revived the old bugbear—earlier seen in connection with Catholics, Mormons, and the Beechers—of probationary existences beyond this mortal life. His case also revealed again the perennial willingness of many Protestants to thumb their noses at aspects of confessional orthodoxy they judged to be in violation of humanitarianism and common sense. On one such point—the intractable problem of infant damnation—even the conservatives among Presbyterians seemed ill at ease in the company of the Westminster divines. No less of a traditionalist than Charles Hodge once declared that "he never saw a Calvinistic theologian who held that only a certain part of those who die in infancy are saved." Henry Van Dyke, who quoted Hodge's comment with glee, argued that the church should therefore change the Westminster assertion that "*elect* infants, dying in infancy," are saved, to "all" infants.[70] Warfield retorted that no revision was necessary, so long as people correctly understood the confession's intent. The disputed phrase, he pointed out, occurred not in chapter III on God's eternal decree but in chapter X on the effectual calling of the elect. Westminster's framers thus were distinguishing not between elect and non-elect infants but between two classes of elect infants—those dying in infancy, who are saved apart from "the intermediation of the word," and those reaching the age of accountability, who are saved through normal means. The confession left open the question of whether any non-elect infants die in infancy. "For myself," he hastened to add, "I believe with all my heart that all dying in infancy are saved," though he conceded that some conservatives might regard this as more of a "pious hope" than an established fact.[71] Schaff, meanwhile, rejected Warfield's suggestion that Westminster needed no revision here. The church should eliminate the troublesome phrase "elect infants," he argued, since the "inevitable logical inference" was the existence of those who are non-elect, which needlessly lessens the comfort provided by Calvinism—that *anyone* might, in theory at least, be born elect. "This is the great advantage of the Calvinistic Reformed over the Augustinian Catholic system," he added. Calvinists, unlike strict Augustinians, did not insist that baptism was a prerequisite of salvation, which removed the necessity of emergency administration of the rite for dying infants.[72]

Indeed, the elect-infants clause stirred up like a hornet's nest the entire swarm of age-old uncertainties surrounding predestination, including the questions of original sin, conversion, and sacramental efficacy. (Regarding the similar debates in Augustine's own day, historian Elizabeth Clark once quipped that at no time before or since had a group of celibate men been so concerned about babies.)[73] The complexity of the issue was such that some proponents of revision, including Samuel Niccolls, began to see the wisdom of a declaratory statement, similar to the act adopted by the Scottish church, that would stress God's loving intention without attempting the arduous work of actually amending the confession. Ardent liberals like David Swing scoffed at this proposed compromise: "The Mercy of God in a footnote! The Sermon on the Mount might also be added as an appendix!"[74]

LIBERAL AND CONSERVATIVE DIVERGENCE

In the end, the initial revision effort of the 1890s collapsed in disarray. The General Assembly of 1890 had appointed a revision committee after 63 percent of the presbyteries registered their desire for some sort of confessional change, but the two-thirds vote required for any actual emendation proved too high a bar to overcome. The committee received dozens of suggestions for revision—some major, some minor—and forwarded 28 of them to the church's 220 presbyteries, with the instruction that each proposal be considered separately. When all the localities reported back to the General Assembly of 1893, none of the revision overtures received the support of more than 115 presbyteries—32 votes shy of the 147 needed.[75]

The revision question did not die, however, and debate continued as Presbyterians marked the 250th anniversary of the Westminster Assembly. The turn of the twentieth century brought a renewed flurry of calls for revision, and, accordingly, the General Assembly of 1900 appointed a Committee of Fifteen to revisit the issue. The panel included two pro-revision veterans of the previous effort, Herrick Johnson of McCormick Seminary and Samuel Niccolls, and the clergyman and Princeton University literature professor Henry J. Van Dyke, Jr., whose father had locked horns with Benjamin Warfield. On the conservative side, Warfield was appointed to the committee but soon resigned, calling it an "inexpressible grief" to him that the church was "spending its energies in a vain attempt to lower its testimony to suit the ever changing sentiment of the world."[76]

With the 1893 debacle still fresh in everyone's memory, the committee's pro-revision chair, Charles Dickey, scored the public relations coup mentioned earlier when he convinced Benjamin Harrison to join the effort. Harrison was a lifelong friend and Miami University (Ohio) fraternity brother of David Swing, which perhaps contributed to the former president's reluctance to view creed revisers as heresiarchs.[77] Though Harrison's death in March 1901 cut short his involvement, his name proved useful to Dickey, who reported on behalf of the committee to the General Assembly later that year that Harrison "would have joined us" in recommending a change to the confessional standard. The revision was destined to be modest, however. At the 1901 assembly, 63 presbyteries voted for actual emendation of the text, while 68 supported some sort of supplemental statement. In light of these results, the committee recommended a change that would "in no way impair the integrity" of Westminster's doctrine but would somehow make clear that "God is not willing that any one should perish."[78]

Ultimately, after a larger committee was appointed to coordinate the revision process with the presbyteries, the General Assembly of 1903 adopted a Declaratory Statement, which remains in force in the twenty-first-century Presbyterian Church (U.S.A.)—the successor to the old PCUSA. While leaving the disputed predestinarian language in chapters III and X unchanged, the statement became the official interpretation of these articles. It stressed that "the doctrine of God's eternal decree is held in harmony with the doctrine of his love to all mankind" and "his readiness to bestow his saving grace on all who seek it." The divine decree, moreover, "hinders no man from accepting" God's offer of salvation. The statement also declared that "all dying in infancy are included in the election of grace, and are regenerated and saved by Christ through the Spirit."[79]

These disclaimers passed comparatively easily the second time around, in part because of another movement afoot by 1903—an attempt to merge the PCUSA with the smaller Cumberland Presbyterian Church. Born on the antebellum Kentucky-Tennessee frontier amid the anti-Calvinist fervor of the Second Great Awakening, the Cumberlands had always bucked Presbyterian tradition by repudiating what they regarded as the fatalism of the Westminster Confession. As the denomination's principal founder, Finis Ewing, proclaimed in 1812, "We do not believe in the doctrine of eternal reprobation. We do not believe that Christ died for a part of mankind only. We do not believe that a part of the infants who die in infancy are lost."[80] Nearly a century after the Cumberlands seceded from their parent presbytery, the confessional revision by the PCUSA cleared the way for a reunion of the two denominations, which was finally consummated in 1906.[81] The late Philip Schaff's great hope—that a revised confession would prove a boon to ecumenism—was at last being realized.

Yet reactions to the 1903 Declaratory Statement from outside church circles seemed to portend the eventual outcome feared by many conservatives, that in their ecumenical retreat from hard-edged particularities, mainline Presbyterians were sliding into comic irrelevance. The New York *Daily Tribune* hailed the end of the "tedious dispute" among the Presbyterians and concluded that they were finally embracing a de facto Arminianism. The *New York Times*, in an editorial prompted by the death of Pope Leo XIII in July 1903, grudgingly praised the top-down bureaucratic structure of the papacy, which allowed the Catholic Church to amend doctrine with an agility and decisiveness missing from the ponderous deliberations of Protestant assemblies. Thus, observed the *Times*, the Presbyterians continued to claim "up to 1903, that unelect infants were necessarily born to be damned, and, in 1903, that this was not necessarily so." Similarly, Mark Twain quipped that "it has taken a weary long time to persuade American Presbyterians to give up infant damnation and try to bear it the best they can." Even the Mormons, meeting in their own General Conference in Salt Lake City, issued a "we told you so" response to the Presbyterians through John W. Taylor, a member of the Quorum of the Twelve Apostles, who pointed out that the prophet Joseph Smith had long ago declared infants to be sinless.[82]

In the South, traditionalists in the PCUS looked upon the amendment saga in the PCUSA with a mixture of disgust and alarm. "The Confession does not need revision, nor does it need any such weak prop as a 'foot-note.' The Confession needs nothing," declared Alabama pastor John Weldon Stagg, whose book *Calvin, Twisse and Edwards on the Universal Salvation of Those Dying in Infancy* attempted to refute the "slander" that Presbyterians taught the hell punishment of babies.[83] Southern conservatives had earlier reacted angrily to liberals in their midst, such as Nashville's James Vance, who argued in an 1898 sermon on predestination that God intended to save all people. Vance's view struck George A. Blackburn, pastor of Second Presbyterian Church in Columbia, South Carolina, as hopelessly naive: "It is love, love, love, nothing but love; no justice, no righteousness, no holiness." Similarly, editor James R. Bridges of the *Presbyterian Standard* in North Carolina derided Vance's diluted "milk and water" theology, which provided no real nourishment for the soul.[84]

Yet unease over Westminster's elect-infants clause was widespread enough among southern Presbyterians, who felt the sting of criticism from the region's more numerous Methodists and Arminian-leaning Baptists, that the PCUS adopted its own explanatory statement on the confession's chapter X in 1902. Unlike the PCUSA's statement, it was not formally appended to the confession—it remained "buried in the Minutes of the Assembly," according to historian Ernest Trice Thompson—but nevertheless it made clear that "the Holy Scriptures, when fairly interpreted, amply warrant us in believing that all infants who die in infancy are included in the election of grace."[85] The statement was not exactly an official footnote, as Stagg had feared, but like his book, it unwittingly highlighted the awkward disjunction between the era's increasingly benevolent view of God and the less sentimental outlook of the Westminster divines. The novelist John Updike captured the poignancy of this cultural shift with his fictional Presbyterian minister Clarence Wilmot, who loses his faith in part over the "clifflike riddle of predestination." One of the books on Wilmot's shelf is Stagg's volume, which "Clarence now saw as so much flotsam and rubble, perishing and adrift, pathetic testimony to belief's flailing attempt not to drown."[86]

Ultimately, conservative minorities in both the North and the South decided that the only way to stem the tide of liberalism was to secede from their denominations. In the North, J. Gresham Machen and a group of other conservative faculty members at Princeton Seminary resigned in 1929 after moderates gained the upper hand on the board. Their withdrawal led to the founding of Westminster Theological Seminary and, in 1936, a new denomination, the Orthodox Presbyterian Church (OPC). In the South, ongoing discussion in the PCUS about reunion with the northern Presbyterians, who in 1967 adopted a supplemental confession of faith that avoided predestination entirely, led a group of conservatives to withdraw and form the Presbyterian Church in America (PCA) in 1973. Though the biggest factor in the birth of the OPC and the PCA arguably was scripture—specifically, the liberals' rejection of biblical inerrancy—both denominations were staunchly confessional, adopting Westminster unaltered by any qualifications of pre-destination. To conservatives, the liberal retreat from predestination was symptomatic of what one OPC minister called the "state of indifference and doctrinal disintegration" plaguing the Presbyterian mainline.[87]

Since 1983, when the northern and southern mainline bodies reunited to form the Presbyterian Church (U.S.A.), strict predestinarianism among Presbyterians has continued to find its strongest advocates in the OPC, the PCA, and other constituencies committed to biblical inerrancy. Conserva-tives in these circles typically insist that scripture unambiguously affirms the unconditional election taught by Westminster. "I believe there is only one correct interpretation of the Bible," explains theologian R. C. Sproul, a best-selling author and radio evangelist who abandoned mainline Presbyterian-ism in the mid-1970s to join the PCA. "There may be a thousand different applications of one verse," he adds, "but only one correct interpretation."[88] For Sproul, the law of noncontradiction also means that two separate Bible verses cannot support two fundamentally different theologies since all bib-lical books had the same divine superintendent—the Holy Spirit. When rightly interpreted, scriptural passages that seem to authenticate Arminian-ism in fact affirm only Calvinism. Thus, in his *Chosen by God* (1986), prob-ably the most popular evangelical defense of Calvinistic predestination in print today, Sproul denies any Arminian reading of 2 Peter 3:9 ("The Lord is...not willing that any should perish"). "What is the antecedent of *any*? It is clearly *us*," Sproul writes. "Peter is fond of speaking of the elect as a special group of people. I think what he is saying here is that God does not will that any of us (the elect) perish."[89]

Similarly, Robert A. Peterson and Michael D. Williams, theologians at the PCA's Covenant Theological Seminary in St. Louis, insist that the Arminian doctrine of conditional election "is not taught by a single passage of Scripture." Their popular text, *Why I Am Not an Arminian*, issued by the evangelical InterVarsity Press, reflects the urgency and certitude with which advocates of biblical inerrancy typically approach the predestination question. (The publisher, not wanting to limit its market share to Reformed consumers, simultaneously issued a companion volume, *Why I Am Not a Calvinist*, by two professors at Asbury Theological Seminary.)[90] Six decades earlier, OPC writer Loraine Boettner set the all-or-nothing tone of the argu-ment in his *Reformed Doctrine of Predestination* (1932), a text still in print in the early twenty-first century. "The Bible unfolds a scheme of redemption which is Calvinistic from beginning to end," he declared, "and these doc-trines are taught with such inescapable clearness that the question is settled for all those who accept the Bible as the Word of God."[91] Boettner, a veteran come-outer with Machen, was not only addressing fellow fundamentalists who had fallen into the alleged error of Arminianism. Mainline liberals loomed much larger for him as a target because they viewed the Bible as a composite of multiple authorial agendas and consequently saw little possibility (or necessity) of determining the one "correct" biblical doctrine of predestination. As Charles Briggs wrote in 1889, three years before his heresy trial, "We have to learn the great principle of Unity in Variety. That variety we find in the sacred Scriptures."[92]

BAPTISTS AND PREDESTINATION: HISTORICAL BACKGROUND

In no branch of American Protestantism would fundamentalism—defined here as the militant adherence to biblical inerrancy and infallibility—so sharpen predestinarian debates as in the Baptist tradition. Yet Baptist fights over the doctrine long predated twentieth-century conflicts over the Bible. Unlike the Presbyterians, who in the early days were more or less united behind the Calvinistic standard of Westminster, Baptists were divided almost from the beginning between General (or Arminian) and Particular (or Calvinistic) factions. Both groups emerged in England out of seventeenth-century Puritanism. General Baptists (so named because of their belief in the general, or universal, saving potential of the atonement) made clear in a 1611 confession of faith by Thomas Helwys that God did not predestine certain individuals to wickedness but instead elected and damned people based on whether they believed.[93] In a later creed, General Baptists also declared that babies dying in infancy, whether born to believing or unbelieving parents, were saved.[94] Particular Baptists, meanwhile, adopted the Westminster Confession's unconditional predestinarianism as their own. Their Second London Confession of 1689 reproduced Westminster's chapters III and X almost verbatim, reiterating the controversial statements on the unchangeable number of the elect and the salvation of "elect infants dying in infancy."[95]

The earliest Baptist association in America adopted the Second London Confession in Philadelphia in 1742. By the next century, however, weariness among some Baptists with the Arminian-Calvinist struggle led one state convention to approve a middle-of-the-road alternative, the New Hampshire Confession of 1833, which avoided the most contentious predestinarian issues. It stated that while "election is the eternal purpose of God, according to which he graciously regenerates, sanctifies, and saves" fallen humans, "nothing prevents the salvation of the greatest sinner on earth but his own inherent depravity and voluntary rejection of the gospel."[96] The New Hampshire Confession was, as Baptist historian Bill Leonard has observed, "an effort to 'have it both ways,' retaining election but extending it to all who chose to believe."[97]

In the South, such moderate views competed with theologies at both ends of the Arminian-Calvinist spectrum, often sparking intense controversies in local Baptist associations and even within single congregations. Journalist Hal Crowther has quipped that "the Bible Belt likes its religion the same as its whiskey—strong, homemade, and none too subtle."[98] Strong views on predestination particularly flourished in the backcountry, where as early as the 1760s, Anglican itinerant Charles Woodmason found rough-hewn Baptists in Carolina who "Divide and Sub divide, Split into Parties—Rail at and excommunicate one another" over the "Knotty Points" of speculative theology. It was, in his judgment, "a scene so farcical, so highly humoursome as excels any Exhibition of Folly that has ever yet appear'd in the World."[99] More than a century later, Baptist church records from across the South revealed that the predestinarian strife had hardly abated. A Tennessee congregation voted in 1890 that members espousing the "doctrine of fatality" should be expelled. A Virginia church demanded that brethren entangled in the "Arminian net" cease and desist from "such heresies." An Alabama association displayed a talent for understatement when it concluded that Baptists were "not the same people so far as doctrinal points are concerned."[100]

Adamant views on predestination crossed racial boundaries. Andrew Marshall, a former slave and pastor of the oldest independent black Baptist congregation, the First African Church of Savannah, Georgia, once impressed a Presbyterian observer by preaching a "clear and decided" testimony to the "precious though unpopular [Calvinistic] doctrines of Grace." Ironically, Marshall almost lost his pulpit after he welcomed the visiting Alexander Campbell as a guest preacher. The furor within his flock subsided after he renounced Campbell's "new doctrines."[101] Another historic black Baptist congregation, Dexter Avenue Church in Montgomery, Alabama, is best known for the twentieth-century tenure of Martin Luther King, Jr. But before the civil rights movement displaced strictly doctrinal concerns, one of the church's early pastors, former slave Charles Octavius Boothe, defended election and reprobation in his book *Plain Theology for Plain People* (1890). God's discrimination among persons is not for humans to judge: "If we ask why they were chosen and others left, we find that no answer has been given by him who alone can explain his reasons."[102]

The strongest predestinarianism developed among the Primitive Baptists, who flourished in Appalachia and the wiregrass and pine barrens regions of the southern coastal plains. Named for their desire to replicate the uncorrupted purity of the New Testament church, Primitive Baptists drew their energy in part from class antagonisms, specifically populist resentment of the perceived overlordship of denominational mission societies, theological seminaries, and other elite institutions.[103] The antebellum antimission movement also partook of the starkly predestinarian conviction that because God had already divided elect from reprobate, organized missionary efforts were futile. Responsibility for this "hyper-Calvinist" conclusion is often laid at

John Gill, engraving by George Vertue (1748), after Joseph Highmore. National Portrait Gallery, London.

Cushing Biggs Hassell, undated photograph. Southern Historical
Collection, University of North Carolina, Chapel Hill.

the feet of the English Particular Baptist John Gill (1697–1771), who was
influenced by the Independent (Congregational) minister Joseph Hussey
(1660–1726). Hussey, a supralapsarian in the mold of William Perkins and
William Twisse, argued in *God's Operations of Grace but No Offers of
His Grace* (1707) that preachers should not "offer" salvation to sinners
because this implied that humans have the innate power to accept or reject
God's grace. Even the elect are powerless before God's irresistible grace,
according to Hussey, who insisted that offer-language is a "Man's Device"

not grounded in the gospel.[104] Several decades later, Gill adopted a similar line against John Wesley's Methodist doctrine that prevenient grace gives all persons the ability to choose. "[T]hat there are universal offers of grace and salvation made to all men, I utterly deny; nay, I deny they are made to any; no, not [even] to God's elect," he declared.[105]

Antimission sentiment and no-offers theology were hallmarks of the Kehukee Primitive Baptist Association, a group of congregations in eastern North Carolina that led the Primitive movement in splitting from missionary Baptists in 1827. The association's moderator from 1859 until his death in 1880 was Cushing Biggs Hassell, a businessman and sometime county government official who was ordained a minister in 1842.[106] His greatest contribution to the movement was his giant doorstop of a book, the 1,008-page *History of the Church of God, from the Creation to A.D. 1885*, which was completed after his death by his son Sylvester. Significantly, the volume hailed Gill as "the most able Baptist theologian since the death of the apostle John" and the only man who ever "hunted and drove out Arminianism from the explanation of every verse in the Bible." Arminianism was not only the product of false exegesis, the Hassells maintained. It was also greatly inferior to predestinarianism in its moral results, "as may be seen by comparing the Waldenses with the other Italians, the Huguenots with the other French, the Jansenists with the Jesuits, the Puritans with the Cavaliers, and the Scotch with other Europeans." Sounding a populist note that belied any notion of the elect as a spiritual aristocracy, the Hassells insisted that predestination promotes civil and religious liberty by representing God "as absolute and supreme" and making "all men equal before Him." The doctrine "develops the power of self-government and a manly spirit of independence, which fears no man, though seated on a throne, because it fears God, the only real sovereign."[107]

The Primitives' prostration before God's absolute sovereignty—a predestinarian stance described by two contemporary ethnographers as "elegant in its very hardness, impressive in its tragic solemnity"[108]—made sense amid the hardscrabble life on the Appalachian frontier, where the movement established an enduring presence. Among the early faithful were Thomas and Nancy Hanks Lincoln, parents of the future U.S. president Abraham Lincoln, who steeped their son in what one biographer described as "a Calvinism that would have out-Calvined Calvin."[109] Though Lincoln never joined a church himself, his early exposure to "hard-shell" thought (one derogatory name for Primitive doctrine) contributed to his lifelong belief in fate or necessity. An abject surrender to God's will also appealed to some African Americans, who formed their own Primitive Baptist associations. Even the more mainstream black Baptist Andrew Marshall confessed his admiration for John Gill.[110] While the largest African-American subgroup, the National Primitive Baptist Convention, moved beyond a strict antimission stance in the twentieth century, its Articles of Faith still refer to the "eternal and particular election of a definite number of the human race."[111] Indeed, the overwhelming sense that God chose his elect from before the foundation of the world has persisted as a hallmark of both black and white Primitive Baptists, for whom the very word *predestination* has a unique resonance. (Many Primitives were incensed in 1952 by the Revised Standard Version of the Bible, which in Ephesians 1:5 replaced the King James Bible's "predestinated" with "destined.")[112]

The predestinarian aesthetic remained a constant of the movement even as Primitive subgroups disagreed, sometimes mightily, over the precise nature of the forces governing human destiny. The most colorful schism occurred early on when Daniel Parker (1781–1844) founded the Two-Seed-in-the-Spirit Predestinarian Baptists, who taught that the elect are the children of God and the non-elect the offspring of Satan. The Two-Seeders, never numerous to begin with, dwindled to near-extinction by the last half of the twentieth century, but not before trying to convince their Primitive brethren that the Bible taught a dual-bloodline predestination. "I am able to take the word of God and prove fatalism as strong on the goats as I can on the sheep," wrote a Two-Seeder in North Carolina to Sylvester Hassell in 1898. "[A]ll whose names that was [*sic*] not written in the Lambs Book from the foundation of the world are the Devils Seed."[113]

While most Baptists dismissed Two-Seed ideology as a bizarre aberration, the no-offers theology of the nineteenth-century antimission movement—and the ghost of John Gill—would continue to haunt Baptist discussions of predestination, even outside of Primitive circles, into the twenty-first century. Yet in the Southern Baptist Convention, organized in 1845 as a result of a split with northern Baptists over slavery, the early leaders subscribed to the more conventional Calvinism of what one theologian called "our Confession (The Westminster)," or rather, the slightly revised version of the 1689 London Confession adopted in Philadelphia in 1742.[114] The most notable early exponent of this tradition was John Leadley Dagg (1794–1884), a Virginia native and largely self-taught theologian who would become president of Mercer University in Georgia. In his *Manual of Theology* (1857), Dagg anticipated Charles Hodge's argument (quoted above) that the unequal fortunes of individuals and nations indirectly confirmed God's election of only certain people for salvation. Just as one person enjoys lifelong health while another endures chronic illness, so God is "sovereign in the dispensations of his grace," Dagg insisted. "He is not bound to give to every one an equal measure of undeserved favor." God is bound only by his justice, which "limits the exercise of his benevolence," in effect compelling him to abandon at least a portion of humanity to the punishment that all justly deserve.[115] (Liberals as far back as the seventeenth-century latitudinarians had effectively maintained the reverse, that God's benevolence trumps his vindictive justice.) Dagg also believed that logic demolished the Arminian doctrine of election based on foreseen faith: "Faith and good works do not exist, before the grace consequent on election begins to be bestowed; and therefore a foresight of them is impossible."[116]

In the next generation, James Petigru Boyce (1827–1888), the founding president of what would become the flagship SBC theological school, Southern Seminary in Louisville, Kentucky, extended Dagg's defense of predestinarianism, arguing that people who railed against the divine decrees misunderstood the intent of the term. A decree was not so much "an edict" or "some compulsory determination" but a wise plan or purpose "tending both to [God's] own glory and the happiness of his creatures." God's plan encompasses "all things whatsoever that come to pass; not some things, but all things."[117] The divine plan of predestination is infralapsarian. Following the Westminster divines, Boyce spoke of the preterition of the non-elect, explaining it as a negative act of God's passing by certain humans and leaving them in their inbred depravity. The final condemnation of persons results from actual sins committed; thus, God remains blameless in the affair.[118] Benjamin Warfield, complaining about liberal Presbyterians' cavils against Westminster, applauded Boyce's vindication of God's honor: "I do not know where this necessary distinction between the sovereignty of preterition and the grounding of the consequent condemnation on sin is better put." "These are not theological subtleties," Warfield added, "they are broad, outstanding facts of God's dealing with men."[119]

Warfield's praise of Boyce's exposition of the biblical "facts" was not surprising, given that Boyce was trained at Princeton Seminary. His mentor there, Charles Hodge, had taught him that the theologian's job was simply to "ascertain, collect, and combine all the facts which God has revealed concerning himself and our relation to Him." These facts come from the Bible and together they make up a harmonious system. "All truth must be consistent," Hodge declared. "God cannot contradict himself."[120] Accordingly, much of Boyce's treatment of election in his *Abstract of Systematic Theology* (1887) was little more than a string of biblical quotations intended to disprove Arminianism. Boyce's collation was evidently persuasive. His successor as president of Southern Seminary, John Broadus, claimed that the young students were typically "rank Arminians" when they matriculated, but few studied with Boyce "without being converted to his strong Calvinistic views."[121]

Yet even as the Louisville seminary was turning out legions of card-carrying Calvinists, many Baptist leaders in the North were embracing the same evangelical liberalism that inspired the Presbyterians to revise Westminster. To William Newton Clarke of Colgate Theological Seminary, proof texting, whether from confessions or scripture itself, was the wrong way to do theology. The Bible, he wrote in 1898, should always be read alongside other sources, including the human psyche, which itself discloses something of God's nature. Self-examination reveals humans' intrinsic freedom and thus renders predestination of interest only to academic philosophers. As Clarke put it, "[I]f predestination does not affect the acts of free beings in relation to God, theology is not bound to give it further study."[122] Though this perspective was still beyond the pale for many southerners, by the 1920s, the struggle between fundamentalists and modernists—made famous in the Scopes "Monkey Trial"—was making some SBC leaders increasingly uneasy about black-and-white approaches to confessional orthodoxy and biblical interpretation.

Indeed, over the next several decades, many professors at the SBC's seminaries would follow their northern counterparts in embracing a moderately liberal theology that valued individual experience—safeguarded by what colonial Baptist Roger Williams called "soul liberty"—over doctrinal uniformity. The harbinger of this more moderate outlook in the South was Edgar Young Mullins (1860–1928), who served as president of Southern Seminary from 1899 until his death. By all accounts a man of essentially conservative temperament, Mullins nevertheless represented a shift away from the inductive method of theology favored by Hodge and Boyce. Religion, he argued in *Christianity at the Cross Roads* (1924), was not governed by the logic of science but was instead about a "personal relation" that could be confirmed only by "the immediate experience of God." Mullins's Presbyterian friend J. Gresham Machen sensed peril in such views, which he feared would expose Christianity to subjective flights of fancy. To Machen, as historian George Marsden has remarked, science and religion were both about facts: either a person saw the facts correctly or she did not.[123] What Machen could not have foreseen was how violently Southern Baptist conservatives would one day disagree among themselves over the biblical "facts" of predestination.

THE *OTHER* BAPTIST BATTLE

The predestinarian controversy that exploded in the SBC at the turn of the twenty-first century was preceded by the takeover of the denomination by an inerrantist party elected in 1979 on a platform of exterminating what one pastor called the liberal "termites" who would eat holes in God's word.[124] By the mid-1990s, as conservatives consolidated control over denominational institutions, about 80 percent of the faculty at the SBC's six seminaries had either been forced out or taken early retirement. This epic Bible battle has been thoroughly recounted and need not be retold here.[125] In the early twenty-first century, however, the pyrrhic nature of the conservative victory became clear. In making the SBC safe for inerrancy, conservatives exposed seemingly irreconcilable differences within their own ranks. The new struggle was not between fundamentalists and moderates (as the two parties of 1979 have been styled) but between an outspoken cadre of five-point Calvinists and their equally resolute non-Calvinist opponents.

Despite the frequently overheated rhetoric between the two sides, they were not exactly polar opposites. Most Southern Baptists had been influenced enough by the Calvinism of the convention's founders that they rejected the Arminian notion that a genuinely converted person could later backslide and lose his salvation. Baptists called this "eternal security" rather than perseverance, and they used it as an apologetic weapon against Methodists and Pentecostals.[126] Nevertheless, the non-Calvinist faction shared Arminians' profound unease with the Calvinist doctrines of unconditional election, limited atonement, and irresistible grace. The non-Calvinists were in many respects the heirs of a revivalistic tradition in the South, which was first institutionalized during the Great Awakening by the Sandy Creek Baptist Association in North Carolina and was anticreedal and voluntaristic in outlook. This quasi-Arminian faction was also highly biblicistic, often railing against the tyranny of "man-made" dogmas.[127] By the twentieth century, as simple biblicism gave way to the more rigid doctrine of inerrancy, anti-Calvinists hurtled headlong into a collision with Calvinists over whose system was most faithful to scripture.

Warning signs of the exegetical train wreck were visible well before 1979. In 1944, the 34-year-old W. A. Criswell was called as pastor of the SBC's First Baptist Church in Dallas, a ministry he would build into a small empire, complete with a Bible college and a 100,000-watt radio station. Not long after accepting the position, Criswell, a staunch defender of inerrancy, announced to his flock that he would preach through the entire Bible, from Genesis to Revelation. In the resulting 17-year sermon series, he left no doubt as to his own reading of the biblical facts on predestination. In a homily on Isaiah 46:9–11 (in which God announces through the prophet, "I will do all my pleasure"), Criswell declared: "That's what you call predestination. That's Calvinism. And I am a Calvinist. That's good old Bible doctrine. And I believe the Bible." Later, in preaching on 2 Thessalonians 2:13–14 ("God hath from the beginning chosen you to salvation"), he hammered home the same theme. Predestination was "woven into the very fiber of the Holy Scriptures." "You could not take it out and have the Bible left." All true confessions of faith taught unconditional election. Any other theology was "spineless and water."[128]

Yet in the same year that Criswell was haranguing his Dallas congregation on spineless non-Calvinists, another flamboyant Texas preacher, John R. Rice, was denouncing the theology of Westminster as evangelism-killing "hyper-Calvinism." Reared in a pious Southern Baptist family, he later abandoned the SBC as too moderate and became an independent Baptist. He is most remembered for his combative newspaper, *Sword of the Lord*, which regularly featured attacks on the compromises made by other evangelists. Less known, but no less militant, is his 1958 book, *Predestined for Hell? No!* in which he painted five-point Calvinism as scarcely different from the "fatalism of Moslems or other heathen people."[129] Scholars such as Loraine Boettner were wrong, Rice asserted, when they placed Baptists in the Calvinist orbit. Rice claimed that only a few "hard-shells" were strict Calvinists. The vast majority of Baptists recognized the gross errors of biblical interpretation that Calvinists had perpetuated. Among these falsehoods was the notion that Paul was speaking of eternal election in his discussion of Jacob and Esau (Rom. 9). "Salvation is not the question under discussion in this passage at all," Rice declared. "That is a perversion and misuse of Scripture."[130] Calvinists were also wrong, he added, in teaching absolute divine sovereignty. God's saving promises in the Bible actually prevented him from preemptively damning sinners to hell apart from any consideration of their conduct: "God is love and love limits absolute sovereignty."[131]

However shocking Rice's statements might have been to someone like Criswell, they proved that among Baptists at least, rock-ribbed fundamentalists and hard-nosed predestinarians were not always one and the same. Rice was so vehement in his anti-predestinarianism that he used it as a line of attack against Billy Graham after the two friends had a bitter falling-out in 1957–1958. Though early in his career Graham became a Southern Baptist, he had been reared in the Associate Reformed Presbyterian Church, a small denomination of Scottish heritage that clung to the unaltered Westminster tenets on election. After Graham accepted sponsorship of his 1957 New York City crusade by mainline Protestant leaders, Rice (along with his fellow culture warriors Carl McIntire and the Bob Joneses, Senior and Junior) publicly repudiated him as a tool of Satan for fraternizing with modernists. Rice unleashed a barrage of articles against Graham in *Sword of the Lord* and also made a thinly veiled reference to him in *Predestined for Hell? No!* "On the fringes of the fundamentalist movement," Rice warned his readers, "only one well-known man, an active defender of his modernistic denomination and a worker with the National Council of Churches...is an ardent hyper-Calvinist." The unnamed evangelist, Rice added, came out of the "Reformed Presbyterian" tradition, a brand of "sectarian" Calvinism at odds with the "fundamental Christian" perspective of true Bible believers.[132] Rice's branding of Graham as a sectarian could not have been more ironic, given Rice's own reputation as a come-outer. Graham was in reality the forerunner of contemporary figures such as Rick Warren, for whom doctrinal specificity gets in the way of winning souls for Christ.

Rice's uncompromising stance on doctrinal distinctions foreshadowed the attitude of many of the combatants in the post-1979 conservative revolution in the SBC. Battle lines began to be drawn in 1982 with the birth of the Southern Baptist Founders Conference (later renamed Founders Ministries), which was dedicated to recovering the Calvinist heritage of the 1689 London Confession. A principal architect of the movement was Florida pastor Ernest Reisinger, whose church led a campaign to distribute 12,000 free copies of Boyce's *Abstract of Systematic Theology* to graduates of the SBC's six seminaries.[133] Reisinger and his allies became convinced that the SBC had taken a wrong turn with Edgar Young Mullins, whose emphasis on

John R. Rice (*left*) and Billy Graham (*center*) with an unidentified clergyman in Scotland in 1955. Billy Graham Center Archives, Wheaton, Ill.

soul competency had opened the door for subsequent generations to deny the confessional substance of the Baptist tradition. ("Religion," Mullins had explained, "is a personal matter between the soul and God.") Some conservatives also lamented Mullins's role as chair of the committee that drafted the SBC's first official statement of faith, the Baptist Faith and Message (1925), which was based on the mediating New Hampshire Confession of 1833 rather than on the Second London Confession.[134]

When Reisinger's church began handing out its reprints of Boyce in the late 1970s, the inerrantists' housecleaning of the SBC was not yet complete. The "Boyce project" soon ran into opposition from some moderates, including Russell Dilday, president of Southwestern Seminary in Fort Worth, who barred distribution of the book on his campus, later complaining of the "enforced creedalism" that was afflicting Baptist life.[135] As the Southern Baptist Founders commenced a series of annual conferences in 1983, however, it appeared that predestination might prove to be the Achilles' heel for the internal unity of the inerrantists themselves. One ominous sign was correspondence that Reisinger received from Paige Patterson, a future president of Southwestern Seminary, expressing concern that a rift might develop between "Bible-believing conservatives" over the doctrines of election.[136] A few years later, Arizona pastor and Founders supporter Robert Selph published a little book, *Southern Baptists and the Doctrine of Election*, which argued that unconditional election was "the foundation, the heart, and the hub of all Bible truth." Selph claimed that "not one verse of scripture" supported the Arminian scheme of conditional election, and he denounced the "candy-coated appeals" made by some preachers, which "may boost per-capita baptism ratios but will fill the pews of hell with the self-deceived."[137] Selph's local Baptist association did not take kindly to his accusations and charged him with heresy, though the association later repented of its actions.[138] In the meantime, theologian and Founders board member Thomas J. Nettles issued a longer book on the Baptist doctrines of grace in which he devoted a whole chapter to rehabilitating the reputedly hyper-Calvinist John Gill from the "calumny and disparagement" he had long suffered. Nettles endorsed Gill's view that the bestowal of grace was God's sovereign prerogative and therefore not something that human preachers could, properly speaking, "offer."[139]

Tensions escalated in the 1990s. Memphis megachurch pastor Adrian Rogers, whose election as the SBC president was engineered by the inerrantists in 1979, issued a popular tract, *Predestined for Hell? Absolutely Not!* that did not criticize the Calvinists by name but nevertheless seemed directed against their growing influence. Much of the problem, as Rogers saw it, was misinterpretation of Romans 9, "one of the hardest chapters in the entire Bible."

Regarding Jacob and Esau, "God is not talking about two little babies, one born for heaven and one born for hell," he insisted. "This is national, not personal." As for the vessels of wrath fitted to destruction, Rogers contended that the Bible said only that God *formed* them; he did not *create* them for the express purpose of damning them. "God has a plan and a purpose. The Bible says God is molding these, that He is longsuffering with them." "What potter in his right mind would be making vessels so he could turn around and destroy them?" Rogers asked. "That sounds more like a madman."[140]

The board of Southern Seminary, by then controlled by conservatives, in 1993 named R. Albert Mohler, Jr., a 33-year-old theologian and former church newspaper editor, as the school's ninth president. Known as an unabashed partisan of inerrancy, Mohler was appointed with the expectation that he would purge the school's faculty of moderates. A bloodbath ensued: 96 percent of the seminary's professors left after he announced that anyone paying mere lip service to inerrancy was unwelcome. In rebuilding the faculty, he also instituted another litmus test: subscription to the school's unmistakably Calvinistic 1858 Abstract of Principles, which had been drafted originally by James Boyce and which defined election as "God's eternal choice of some persons unto everlasting life—not because of foreseen merit in them, but of his mere mercy in Christ." Mohler went on to hire Nettles and others friendly to the Southern Baptist Founders' confessional agenda. As journalist Collin Hansen has put it in his book *Young, Restless, Reformed*, Southern Seminary became "ground zero" in an upsurge of Calvinism in the SBC.[141]

Mohler's transformation of the SBC's flagship seminary was accompanied by a wider cultural development—the dramatic explosion of the Internet—that would further fuel debates over Calvinism in Baptist life. Not since the invention of the printing press in the fifteenth century had theological disputation received such a shot in the arm. The Southern Baptist Founders Conference went online in 1996 and two years later hired as executive director Tom Ascol, a Florida pastor who eventually began a lively blog that would become the Web's chief clearinghouse of information on Baptists and the doctrines of grace. Unlike old-style theological colloquies, whose proceedings appeared in print only after a time lag, blogs and other Web sites keep disputes alive 24 hours a day, turning any computer user into an armchair theologian.

Not surprisingly, then, when retired Southwestern Seminary professor William Estep declared in the Texas *Baptist Standard* in 1997 that the "Calvinizing" of the SBC risked turning the denomination into a "perfect dunghill," his words sparked an online firestorm. Estep was quoting the eighteenth-century English Baptist Andrew Fuller, who had warned that adoption of John Gill's no-offers theology would reduce the Baptist tradition to a dunghill. But Estep did not stop there. Calvinism, he insisted, "is a system of theology without biblical support." Borrowing a move from Rice's playbook, Estep cast the opposition in terms of the Muslim other: "Calvinism's God resembles Allah, the god of Islam, more than the God of grace and redeeming love revealed in Christ." The Calvinist vanguard in the SBC, Estep implied, threatened to sap the denomination's missionary zeal and subject non-Calvinists to the sort of heresy hunting that Calvin himself led against Bolsec.[142] Ascol immediately responded that Estep's editorial bordered on blasphemy in suggesting that the "impersonal, unconcerned" God of Islam bore any resemblance to the loving Father revealed by scripture and taught by John Calvin. To the extent that Estep denied the Calvinist God, Ascol intimated, he was denying the Bible. Calvinism "is not embarrassed by biblical words like predestine, elect and purpose. Nor is it afraid of biblical words like choose, repent and believe."[143]

Prominent South Carolina pastor Frank Page came to Estep's defense in *Trouble with the TULIP* (2000), which pointed to what Page saw as the dissimilarities between the misbegotten system of five-point theology and the "beautiful flower" for which it was named. Dismissing Calvinism as a "manmade system of logic," he urged his readers to remember that God "predestined the how, not the who." The "how" was conditional election: God promised salvation to all who would accept it, which meant that he could not distinguish elect from damned apart from their conduct. This Arminian stance notwithstanding, Page insisted that he was advocating neither Arminianism nor Calvinism but "scriptural soteriology." Its chief difference from Arminianism was eternal security, which Page grounded in John 10:27–28 ("My sheep hear my voice…neither shall any man pluck them out of my hand").[144]

Page's book might have been lost amid the rising tide of polemics, but in June 2006, he was voted president of the SBC, a surprise development that some observers in the Baptist press interpreted as a rebuke to the faction allied with Mohler. The double meaning in one headline said it all: "Election Could Prove Troubling to Calvinists in SBC." A few days before the vote, at the denomination's annual Pastors' Conference, Mohler and Patterson (who by then had taken the reins at Southwestern) presented their opposing views on predestination at two identical forums, each attended by standing-room-only crowds of more than 2,500. The event broke no new intellectual ground but showcased the colorful personalities of the SBC's two leading seminary executives—Mohler, who on the side hosts a popular radio talk show, and Patterson, who hunts big African game in his spare time. Though they lavished praise on each other, their fundamentally different theologies—both grounded in a cocksure acceptance of biblical inerrancy—had never been clearer. Mohler declared his allegiance to the TULIP: "If you are counting points, there are five of them, and I affirm all five." Patterson took issue with the middle three points—unconditional election, limited atonement, and irresistible grace. Calvinists, he lamented, inevitably fall back on the idea of a "secret will" in God that predetermines the elect in spite of scriptural assurances that those who believe in Christ will be saved. The biblical evidence against this scheme, he insisted, is "absolutely overwhelming." Mohler retorted that his own five-point Calvinism did not prevent him from affirming without hesitation the "whosoevers" and the "alls" of scripture.[145]

The Mohler-Patterson colloquy, however, was restrained compared to the all-out brawl that erupted four months later when a planned debate between Calvinist and anti-Calvinist bloggers fell through amid a flurry of recriminations. The event had been slated for Thomas Road Baptist Church in Lynchburg, Virginia, pastored by fundamentalist stalwart Jerry Falwell until his death in 2007. (Founded as an independent congregation, Thomas Road had affiliated with the SBC after the inerrantist takeover.) The scheduled speakers on the anti-Calvinist side were Ergun Caner, president of Falwell's Liberty Theological Seminary, and his brother Emir, dean of the College at Southwestern Seminary. Representing the Calvinists were the Southern Baptist Founders' Ascol and James White, a prolific apologist and director of Alpha and Omega Ministries in Phoenix. The prominence of the speakers and the venue heightened the pre-debate anticipation. But in an eleventh-hour dispute over ground rules, the event was canceled, leaving the contending parties to duke it out online.[146]

Ergun Caner, a Turkish-born Muslim convert to Christianity who once suggested that the prophet Muhammad was a pedophile, trotted out the time-worn, anti-Muslim similitude linking Calvinism with Islam. On his Web site, he charged his opponents with waging a "Calvinist Jihad." "[J]ust like Muslims," he explained, Baptist Calvinists were determined to defend the honor of their theology at all costs. "Dr. Falwell and I have laughed about it, because they are so insistent, and they miss the point completely," he added. "There are plenty of schools to which the neo-Calvinists can go, but Liberty [Seminary] will be a lighthouse for missions and evangelism to the 'whosoever wills.' Period." Ascol, in a lengthy series of posts on his blog, concluded that Caner had "discredited himself" by mischaracterizing Calvinism: "An untruth is an untruth no matter the credentials of the man who speaks it." Far more was at stake, he insisted, than simply the recovery of Calvinism in the SBC. The future of "biblical Christianity" itself was on the line.[147]

Amid the polemical torrent, new evidence emerged that the Calvinism controversy was trickling down to the grassroots. A poll of SBC pastors found that nearly half (47 percent) preached on the subject of Calvinism "several times a year or more."[148] To some observers, this was a sign of a denomination that had become too contentious. Church historian Timothy George, dean of Beeson Divinity School and a Southern Baptist Founders supporter, said as much in a 2007 address on Baptist identity: "let us banish the word 'Calvinist' from our midst. It has become the new n-word for some, and an unseemly badge of pride for others....Let us confess freely and humbly that none of us understands completely how divine sovereignty and human responsibility coalesce in the grace-wrought acts of repentance and faith."[149]

If the previous four centuries of Baptist battles were any indication, George's modest proposal to abandon divisive nomenclature seemed destined to go unheeded, at least by seminary faculty members and other leaders with a vested interest in denominational identity. Even so, in other parts of the Southern Baptist empire, particularly in Sunbelt subdivisions of pristine McMansions, the antique terminology of predestinarian debates had already become as scarce as old housing stock. In these vast, treeless tracts of postmodern suburbia, SBC megachurches had sprouted in which even the label *Baptist* was avoided as too denominationally encrusted. And yet, as we will see, the ghost of predestination haunted still.

The Purpose-Driven Life?

Predestination and the Decline of Mystery

Dogma is the guardian of mystery. The doctrines are spiritually significant in ways that we cannot fathom.

—*Flannery O'Connor, letter (1959) in* The Habit of Being *(1979)*

IN OCTOBER 2002, as I was deeply immersed in the vast sea of print generated by predestinarian controversies, a major phenomenon burst onto the scene of U.S. religious publishing. Virtually overnight, it seemed, the whole media world was abuzz over *The Purpose-Driven Life* by the southern California pastor in the Hawaiian shirt, Rick Warren. President George W. Bush reputedly owned a dog-eared copy, and on the other side of the political divide, 2004 Democratic vice presidential nominee John Edwards carried a leather-bound edition, embossed with his name, on the campaign trail. The book garnered such staggering royalties that Warren stopped taking a salary from his Saddleback Church and reimbursed the congregation for his previous two decades on the payroll. He also began donating 90 percent of his annual income to the church. By 2008, at least 30 million copies of *The Purpose-Driven Life* were in print, and the title was listed along with J. K. Rowling's seven *Harry Potter* novels as among the 20 top-selling books of the previous 15 years.[1]

The "purpose" in Warren's book title, vaguely connoting the doctrine of providence, immediately caught my attention, and when I picked up a copy, I discovered that the scriptural hallmarks of predestination were there too, though the actual word never appeared. The epigraph on the dedication page was Ephesians 1:11, one of only six verses in the Bible containing the Greek verb translated in the King James Version as "predestinate." Yet Warren cited the version of the verse from *The Message*, Eugene Peterson's paraphrase, which referred to God's "designs on us" without using any form of the term *predestination*. Later in his book, Warren emphasized another classic predestinarian proof text, Romans 8:28–29, this time from the New Living Translation, which also avoided explicit mention of predestination.

Nevertheless, the idea of divine foreordination could not have been stronger in Warren's book. "Nothing in your life is arbitrary," he declared. From the moment of a person's birth, God is behind every seeming twist of fate: "God prescribed every single detail of your body. He deliberately chose your race, the color of your skin, your hair, and every other feature." Even life's inevitable suffering is divinely directed to awaken people from spiritual lethargy. "Pain is God's megaphone," wrote Warren, quoting C. S. Lewis. Warren added his own metaphor: "We are like jewels, shaped with the hammer and chisel of adversity. If a jeweler's hammer isn't strong enough to chip off our rough edges, God will use a sledgehammer. If we're really stubborn, he uses a jackhammer. He will use whatever it takes."[2]

Such a thoroughgoing sense of providence was not unusual among evangelicals, but what struck me was the ghostly presence of predestination, like an erasure still visible on a manuscript page. Warren glossed Romans 8:29 by saying that the divine promise of salvation is "only for God's children," but what was his stance on the classic predestinarian question?[3] Did God choose his children apart from any foreknowledge of their faith, or was predestination somehow linked to human decision? I decided to seek clarification by traveling to the source.

I found Warren's Saddleback Church atop a hill in Lake Forest, California, a well-heeled Orange County enclave of palm trees, eight-lane boulevards, and tile-roofed houses perched precariously above desert canyons. A recent rash of seismic activity (a small earthquake occurred during my visit in June 2005) contributed to the sense that life there, for all its wonders, was somehow fragile—a sentiment that America's most famous predestinarians, the New England Puritans, would have readily understood. Yet if judged by the standard of Puritan simplicity, Saddleback was no "city upon a hill." The centerpiece of Warren's megachurch complex was the Worship Center, an auditorium whose glass facade had verities from *The Purpose-Driven Life* etched in large letters. Though the Worship Center seated 3,800, the sermon during the six weekend services was broadcast live to other worship venues in semi-permanent tents, each with different music, from Hawaiian luau to heavy metal. The main service could also be heard across campus through loudspeakers disguised as rocks, as well as in the Terrace Café, which, when I peeked in, was full of members sipping lattés while taking notes on the sermon. Average weekend attendance at that time topped 21,000.

The Saturday afternoon service I attended in the Worship Center began with loud pop music, flashing colored lights, and congregational hand clapping. When this opener died down, Pastor Rick, as everyone called him, entered from backstage and immediately launched into his sermon. Warren deserved the average-guy persona he had gained in the press. With his casual demeanor and ready laugh, he was the antithesis of the stereotypically gaunt and stern-faced Puritan minister. As I listened to his sermon, though, I could not shake the feeling that I was looking at Jonathan Edwards in the guise of a huggable, high school coach of a man. The subject, "Making the Most of Your Time" (part of a series, "Use It or Lose It"), was, for all its self-help, motivational tone, thoroughly Edwardsean, echoing that last great Puritan's urgent pleas to his parishioners to "redeem," or make better use of, their time. Warren's opening illustration, comparing people's ages and life expectancies to times in a 24-hour day, drove the point home: "If you're 32, it's 11:20 in the morning. If you're 42, it's 3:20 in the afternoon. If you're 52 [Warren was then almost 52 himself], it's 6:20 P.M." (This last one elicited groans from the audience.) "Whatever you intend to do with your life," he urged, "you'd better get on with it, because time is running out." Similarly, Edwards in 1734 warned his Massachusetts congregation of the clock's inexorable ticking: "If we have lived fifty, or sixty, or seventy years, and han't improved them, it now can't be helped. 'Tis all eternally gone from us. All that we can do is to improve the little that remains." Both Warren and Edwards warned of the danger of procrastination. Stop telling yourself, Warren advised, that you will finish undone tasks "when things settle down." Life never settles down. Conditions are always imperfect. "Perfectionism creates paralysis, which creates procrastination," he warned. So too Edwards: "Don't talk of more convenient seasons hereafter, but improve your time whilst you have it."[4]

Warren came closest to questions of predestination when he insisted that the wise use of one's time was a grave responsibility: "God has given you a great gift. That gift is the freedom to choose. It's what makes you like God." I wondered how he would explain the old conundrum of human free will versus divine sovereignty, and whether he would resist my comparison of him to Edwards. Though the casual visitor would never know it,

Saddleback Church is a congregation of the Southern Baptist Convention, whose Calvinist wing in the late twentieth and early twenty-first centuries has enthusiastically promoted Edwards as a spiritual forefather. Would Warren consider himself an Edwardsean? a Calvinist?

Warren's office had declined my request for an interview, but I continued my fact-finding mission the next evening in Class 101, which is required of all prospective members. On this day, 199 people filled an air-conditioned tent for a four-and-a-half-hour crash course, complete with free dinner, in the congregation's history and basic beliefs. Three of the church's other pastors led the class through a 32-page curriculum covering, among other things, the main points from *The Purpose-Driven Life*, as well as the church's fundamental doctrines, including the claim that the Bible is "the truth without any mixture of error." The curriculum also emphasized the belief in a literal heaven and hell, as well as the characteristically Southern Baptist adjunct to predestination—eternal security. "If you have been genuinely saved," the handout explained, "you cannot 'lose' it."[5]

The presentation again came close to addressing predestination when Pastor Gerald Sharon professed his own faith in providence. "Before the foundation of the world, God knew you'd be here today," he told us. "He even saw the color of the tablecloth for the table you're sitting at." Everything, Sharon explained, was integral to God's plan for creation: "Every plant has a purpose. Every rock has a purpose." He did not mention the fundamentalist conclusion that Saddleback pastors draw from this—that Darwinian evolution is a slippery slope to atheism. The congregation's allegiance to creationism was a topic covered in the more comprehensive *Foundations* curriculum co-authored by Saddleback pastor Tom Holladay and Rick Warren's wife, Kay. There, even "theistic evolution" was dismissed as an affront to God's providential control of all things at every moment.[6]

After the class, I watched as 33 people availed themselves of the opportunity to be baptized on the spot in a heated outdoor pool. Part of the class had been devoted to the topic of baptism and why Saddleback insisted on following the biblical precedent of believers' baptism by immersion. I watched as three of the people from my table at dinner were baptized: a dentist (a former Catholic), his wife (a former Episcopalian), and a onetime lay minister in the largest African-American Pentecostal denomination, the Church of God in Christ, who had found his way back to religion after a long absence. The dentist, a tanned, bearlike man, was particularly forthcoming. "Apparently the sprinkling I had as a Catholic didn't count," he told me, referring to his first baptism as an infant. I asked if it bothered him to be baptized again. "Absolutely not," he replied. He and his wife went on to explain their attraction to Saddleback, including the practical advice offered in weekly sermons and the church's welcoming stance toward Christians of all backgrounds. To this couple, Saddleback seemed to transcend denominational exclusivity. I wondered if they knew they had just joined a congregation of the Southern Baptist Convention, since Saddleback's affiliation was never mentioned in Class 101, at least not in my hearing. But I suppressed my desire to press questions of denominational identity, which suddenly seemed ponderously retro.

I finally got some answers to my doctrinal questions when I sat down two days later for an hour with Pastor Tom Holladay in his spacious office overlooking the dry southern California hills. Like his brother-in-law Warren, Holladay had an irrepressible smile and a disarmingly warm personality. I asked him about Saddleback's Baptist connection. He explained that the congregation did not call itself Baptist because the term was a needless barrier to unchurched persons unfamiliar with theological distinctions. Though I knew that a seeker-friendly avoidance of denominational shibboleths was typical of megachurches, my historian's skepticism told me that doctrinal distinctions must lurk below the surface.[7] I pressed Holladay on where Saddleback stood in the ongoing conflict in the Southern Baptist Convention between Calvinists and non-Calvinists:

We wouldn't want to take sides in that. We would rather help both sides see the truth in God's word and how it applies to God's purpose for their lives. Where I would take sides is [against] any form of Calvinism that prevents somebody from clearly, dramatically, emphatically sharing their faith with somebody else. When Calvinism gets to that point where I don't have this urge to share my faith with somebody else, that's clearly outside the bounds of the Bible.[8]

What about Rick Warren himself? Would he call himself a Calvinist? "No," Holladay said emphatically. "I can clearly speak for that. Nor would he want to embrace the Arminian label. Labels are labels. That's the problem." He added that Saddleback's pastors were in general agreement that "both Arminianism and Calvinism are true. It's not that truth is in the middle. They just both have truth in them."

I asked him if the issue of predestination ever came up in Saddleback's more advanced classes for members. He explained that in teaching the *Foundations* curriculum, he usually reserved one night for questions and answers. Invariably, someone asks about predestination and how to reconcile it with human initiative. He described his typical response: "God's foreknowledge and election do not prohibit our choice, nor does our choice inhibit God's election. Now I know that's doublespeak. I've wrestled with it for years and years. But to me that's the best way to honor the choice that God has given us while we live on this earth."[9]

On my flight home, I pondered Saddleback's postdenominational paradigm, with its cheerful matter-of-factness about doctrinal matters that were once church dividing. In sunny tracts of southern California suburbia, a vague but pervasive sense of providence (sans the term) had replaced the old party politics wrought by the most important providential riddle—predestination. Saddleback's members still clung to the idea that, as Increase Mather once put it, "nothing comes to pass in the Earth, but what was first determined by a wise decree in Heaven."[10] And yet God's *electing* decree, which engendered so much conflict in American religious history, no longer loomed as a question of life-or-death significance. Calvinists such as Mather or Edwards had denounced the conditional predestination of Arminianism as a grace-denying heresy, while John Wesley and other Arminians had decried unconditional predestination as a monstrous affront to a loving God. In the rise of the megachurch, these old acids simply evaporated, leaving behind a residue of providential language. The "purpose" talk at Saddleback paralleled President George W. Bush's frequent but nebulous references to God's plan, which one critic derided as "mostly atmospherics," devoid of any theological substance.[11]

Warren's purpose-driven movement represented the triumph of a style pioneered by evangelists such as Dwight L. Moody (1837–1899), who also

Church sign in Hickory, N.C. Photograph by Theodore J. Thuesen (2006).

split the Calvinist-Arminian difference for the sake of converting the greatest number of souls. Moody's was an "uncomplicated soteriology," as one historian has put it, designed to cater to both sides.[12] Among more doctrinally minded conservatives, this reluctance to take sides would always smack of reductionism—a lowest-common-denominator mentality that seemed to deny the Bible itself. One of Moody's own lieutenants, Reuben A. Torrey, branded some of his fellow evangelicals as cowards because of their aversion to doctrinal conflict. Christ and his disciples, Torrey insisted, "immediately attacked, exposed and denounced error."[13] Similarly, *The Purpose-Driven Life* has spawned a small industry of rebuttals by evangelicals charging that Warren betrayed the uncompromising truths of scripture. Minneapolis pastor Bob DeWaay, for example, has criticized Warren's selective use of biblical paraphrases for passages such as Ephesians 1:11. In DeWaay's view, Warren substituted "the uninspired ideas of a man" for the hard predestinarian doctrines actually contained in the biblical text. Warren's "gospel is inoffensive, attractive, winsome, popular, and easy to believe," DeWaay notes. "The gospel of the Bible is offensive and hard to believe. It is a narrow gate and narrow path with few adherents."[14] Meanwhile, Pennsylvania pastor Marshall Davis has accused Warren of ignoring the Southern Baptist confessional standard, the Baptist Faith and Message. Saddleback's own statement of faith, according to Davis, waters down traditional doctrinal language, communicating instead "that there are lots of different theological opinions, and it really doesn't matter what we think because we cannot comprehend it anyway."[15]

Such criticisms belie Warren's own professed admiration for a fundamentalist stalwart who was anything but weak-kneed on doctrine. As a college student in the mid-1970s, Warren once drove 350 miles to hear W. A. Criswell, pastor of Dallas's First Baptist Church (then the nation's largest Southern Baptist congregation), address a convention in San Francisco. After the sermon, when Warren went up to shake Criswell's hand, the fiery evangelist unexpectedly placed his hands on Warren's head and prayed, "Father, I ask that you give this young preacher a double portion of your Spirit. May the church he pastors grow to twice the size of the Dallas church." Warren later called Criswell the "greatest American pastor of the twentieth century," but he emulated him only in bringing in the numbers. At Saddleback, there were no echoes of Criswell's militant defense of Calvinism.[16]

What, then, are we to conclude about the providence-without-predestination espoused at many megachurches today? Does Saddleback portend the death of doctrine—the final dumbing down of religion in an age of sound bites and instant messaging? Such a judgment is probably premature. As we saw in chapter 6, the technologies of the Internet age have fueled the growth of neo-confessional movements dedicated to recovering the predestinarian perspectives of the Reformation era. The Internet has also revived a measure of the bitterness and gall of sixteenth- and seventeenth-century controversies, as seen in recent charges of "Calvinist jihad" in the Southern Baptist blogs. One might fault Rick Warren for doctrinal fuzziness but one can hardly blame him for steering clear of such poisonous rhetoric.

It is not primarily confessional precision that has been lost in the cultural transition from the Puritans to Warren. Outside of Saddleback, zealous Arminians and Calvinists are still to be found, and confessionalists of other stripes still thrive in some quarters. What has declined for many Christians in the modern United States, however, is the mystical dimension of their experience of divine grace. This erosion of mystery happened in two ways. First, the preoccupation with predestination weakened the hold of *sacramental* mystery over the Christian imagination. To the extent that Americans emphasized the immemorial decree of God's electing choice, the grace offered here and now through the sacraments was correspondingly deemphasized, despite what some predestinarians have claimed. High-church defenders of sacramental regeneration and the real presence have always recognized this correlation: witness the Laudians' intense hostility toward rigid predestinarians in Caroline England.[17] To be sure, there are exceptions to this general rule. Missouri Synod Lutherans, for example, were adamant defenders of the real presence even while insisting on Luther's unflinching doctrine of unconditional election. Yet even so, the Lutheran controversy over precise predestinarian formulas always threatened to erode the more mystical confidence in the sacraments that was characteristic of Luther himself.

In the more natively anti-sacramental culture of American evangelicalism, predestination's corrosive effect was much starker. During the colonial period, as Arminians and Calvinists slugged it out over whether election was conditional, both sides came to prize what historian Randall Balmer has called "an instantaneous, datable experience of grace akin to St. Paul's conversion on the road to Damascus."[18] Consequently, religious experience in the infant evangelical movement was between the believer and the electing God; churchly intermediaries and liturgies rarely intervened. The same outlook, only without the old doctrinal debates, has been passed down into the modern megachurch. Thus, when Rick Warren abandoned Criswell's card-carrying Calvinism, there were no sacraments or rituals to take the place of sharply defined doctrines. The poet Robert Lowell once wrote of the contrasting religious styles of sacramental Catholics and predestinarian Calvinists. His oversimplification contained an important kernel of truth:

"Catholicism notices things, the particular, while Calvinism studies the attenuated ideal."[19] A high-church critic might well conclude that in the predestinarian progression from the Reformation to the megachurch, the sacramental substance of Christianity attenuated to almost nothing.

Second, predestinarian controversies contributed to the decline of *dogmatic* mystery. In fighting so strenuously for particular doctrines of grace, the various contending denominations turned predestination into something logical and rational, unwittingly depriving grace of the miraculous all-sufficiency they were trying to preserve. This effect was particularly evident in America, where the Reformation and the Enlightenment profoundly shaped theological debates. The Reformation subordinated the church to the Bible, and the Enlightenment reinterpreted the Bible through the lens of empirical science. As a result, predestinarian debates often became sterile exercises in the collection of evidence and "proof." Princeton Seminary's Charles Hodge epitomized this method: "The Bible is to the theologian what nature is to the man of science. It is his store-house of facts."[20] Such an attitude naturally led many Protestants to conclude that the debate between Calvinists and Arminians *could* be settled through the collation of sufficient biblical evidence.

Premodern Christians such as Augustine sought scriptural justification too, but amid the modern preoccupation with scientific proof, the traditional Christian *credo* (I believe) gradually gave way to the more empirical "I know." The Bible became pure data, which many Americans naively believed they could mine apart from any cultural or theological preconceptions. Protestants in particular, in their biblicist zeal, lost sight of the sociological primacy of the church over the book. Precisely defined predestinarian dogmas have always been inseparable from the churchly traditions (or individual predilections) that have colored readings of the biblical text. Whether one reads the Bible with "Calvinistic spectacles" (to use Augustine Hewit's phrase) or Arminian ones, or some other, the reading glasses make all the difference. The Bible states no abstract doctrine of predestination, and even if it did, it would still be refracted differently through each community's lens.

The modern tyranny of "proof" in religion made predestination deadly—and sometimes deadly boring. The doctrine no longer inspired what scholars have called the *mysterium tremendum et fascinans*—a mystery before which one both trembles and is fascinated, or a mystery that simultaneously repels and attracts. To be sure, this special awe defies description, but as the late Rudolf Otto pointed out, we glimpse it in St. Paul, who seemed to approach predestination more through the direct intuition of God's all-sufficient grace than through the development of any abstract theory.[21] We glimpse it in

Aquinas, who in the final months of his life laid aside his pen, concluding that the ecstatic visions he had received made his intellectual labor superfluous: "I can write no more. I have seen things which make all my writings like straw."[22] We glimpse it in Luther, who lamented the intellectual hubris that led humans to probe the depths of predestination: "We disregard the Word and will of the Father which is revealed in Christ and inquire into the mysteries which ought only to be adored."[23] We glimpse it too in the young Jonathan Edwards, whose mind had been "full of objections" to the doctrine of absolute predestination until one day, in contemplating the sky and clouds on his walk, he yielded to unlimited divine sovereignty. "[T]here came into my mind," he wrote, "a sweet sense of the glorious majesty and grace of God, that I know not how to express."[24]

Yet at some point between Edwards's day and the present, the empirical temperament of American theology all but extinguished the *mysterium tremendum* of predestination. More often than not, theologians tacitly ceded mystery to artists and novelists, whose fiction tended to convey doctrines more powerfully than did logical prose. Particularly memorable is Catholic writer Flannery O'Connor's character O. E. Parker, who tries in vain to please his pious but severe wife, a latter-day Puritan iconoclast, by having a Byzantine Pantocrator (Christ as almighty ruler and judge) tattooed on his back. In choosing the image from the tattooist's book of samples, Parker feels himself "brought to life by a subtle power"; his throat becomes "too dry to speak." Though O'Connor never mentions predestination by name, Parker's "flat stern Byzantine Christ with all-demanding eyes" might well symbolize the electing God, who seizes people in ways we cannot fathom. When Parker finally reveals his newly adorned back to his wife, however, she sees only an idolatrous image. She beats Parker senseless with a broom handle, leaving him broken, like the scourged Christ of the passion.[25]

The mystery of predestination is like the tattoo on Parker's back, clothed in doctrinal garb and bared to rare individuals in flashes of divine intuition. The historian can only imagine what persons given to this mystical apprehension have seen, but their experiences are as much a part of the career of this contentious doctrine as the debates of the dogmaticians. "God? God don't look like that!" Parker's wife cried as she eyed his tattoo. " 'What do you know how he looks?' Parker moaned. 'You ain't seen him.' "[26]

Glossary of Theological Terms

ECAUSE PREDESTINATION IS entangled in such a complex web of related questions of Christian theology, debates over the doctrine have often involved a great deal of technical vocabulary. While this terminology is familiar to theologians, it can leave the average reader mystified. Moreover, even theologically trained scholars disagree on how to define certain key predestinarian concepts. I therefore provide the glossary below not only for nonspecialists but for anyone curious about how I use certain disputed terms in this volume. Most of the words below are also defined, at least briefly, within the chapters, but this glossary consolidates fuller explanations (along with a few additional endnote citations) in one place. In devising this tool, I have consulted several standard resources. The most useful and technically detailed one-volume work is Richard A. Muller, *Dictionary of Latin and Greek Theological Terms Drawn Principally from Protestant Scholastic Theology* (Grand Rapids, Mich.: Baker, 1985). For more general purposes, standard references include F. L. Cross and E. A. Livingstone, eds., *The Oxford Dictionary of the Christian Church*, 3rd ed. (Oxford: Oxford University Press, 2005); Richard P. McBrien et al., eds., *The HarperCollins Encyclopedia of Catholicism* (San Francisco: HarperCollins, 1995); and Donald K. McKim, *Westminster Dictionary of Theological Terms* (Louisville, Ky.: Westminster John Knox, 1996).

Anglican. The adjective used here to describe the transatlantic theological tradition that includes, among others, the Church of England and the Episcopal Church. Because of its gradual evolution as a "middle way" between

Protestant and Catholic extremes, Anglicanism has long encompassed both Calvinist and Arminian perspectives on predestination, with the latter predominating since the Restoration in 1660. To its New England Puritan opponents, Anglicanism was virtually synonymous with Arminianism.

Arminianism. Calvinism's leading rival in American Protestant theology, often used as a synonym for belief in conditional election. Named for the Dutch theologian Jacob Arminius (1559–1609), Arminianism posits that God grants prevenient grace to all people, enabling them to choose or reject Christ, and elects persons conditionally, according to his foresight of their faith. In the United States, the Methodists were the most numerous Arminians and led the anti-Calvinist charge in the eighteenth and nineteenth centuries. Arminianism also influenced a wide variety of other groups, including many Baptists, Episcopalians, and Pentecostals.

calling. Latin, *vocatio*. God's summons to his children through the Holy Spirit and the proclamation of the gospel. Reformed scholastics taught that though the gospel is proclaimed to all people, only the elect are *effectually* called by God. The Reformed thus conceived of calling as one of the unbreakable links in the *golden chain* of salvation. In a more general sense, calling may also refer to any divine summons, e.g., to a particular career or vocation.

Calvinism. In American Protestantism, the most influential system of belief in unconditional election; contrast with Arminianism. Named for the French-born Reformed theologian John Calvin (1509–1564) but sometimes only loosely grounded in his own writings, Calvinism posits that God elects certain persons for salvation apart from any consideration of their future faith. Calvinists have typically been either *infralapsarian* or *supralapsarian*, though Calvin himself predated this technical distinction. In America, groups rooted in Calvinistic (or Calvinist; both forms are used as an adjective) theology include the New England Puritans, the Presbyterians, many Baptists, and various other Reformed denominations.

conversion. From the Latin *conversio* (literally, a turning round), the Holy Spirit's inclining of a person's mind, will, and heart toward Christ through repentance and faith. In present-day parlance, conversion often refers to switching from one religious tradition or denomination to another, but for the groups treated here, conversion means the initial transformation wrought in a person by God's grace. The New England Puritans required a conversion relation (often given as public testimony) for church membership; conversion, if judged to be genuine, thus became an indirect sign of election.

creabilis et labilis. Latin, "creatable and fallible": the human object of election in the supralapsarian view.

creatus et lapsus. Latin, "created and fallen": the human object of election in the infralapsarian view.

decree(s), eternal. Particularly in Reformed theology, God's willing and ordering of the plan of salvation; often synonymous with predestination. Though seventeenth-century Reformed scholastics debated the order of the decrees of the creation, the Fall, and predestination (see infralapsarian and supralapsarian), this order was always understood as logical rather than temporal, since all knowledge and willing were regarded as simultaneous in the divine mind.

decretum horribile. Latin, "dreadful (or terrifying) decree": term from Calvin referring to the awe- or fear-inspiring aspect of predestination, especially for unconverted persons. As Richard Muller has argued, it does *not* translate as "horrible decree" and "in no way implies that the eternal decree is somehow unjust."[1] Nevertheless, "the horrible decree" became a common nickname for unconditional predestination among Calvinism's opponents, including Charles Wesley, who wrote a polemical hymn by that title.

double predestination. The idea that both election and reprobation are in some sense decreed by God. Sometimes equated with supralapsarianism, double predestination is really a separate issue. Calvin, for example, insisted that there could be no election without reprobation, but he never spelled out the precise order of God's decrees, as his later followers did in the supralapsarian-infralapsarian debate.[2] Yet reprobation always created a logical burden for theologians who were intent on preserving human culpability for sin. To place reprobation on the same plane with election (as equally decreed by God) seemed to many thinkers to foreclose all possibility of human responsibility or guilt. Some theologians therefore preferred to speak of single predestination (election only), referring to the reprobate as "foreknown" rather than decreed, as such, by God. Other theologians, especially the Reformed, spoke of double decrees of election and reprobation but disagreed on whether they were logically parallel. Infralapsarians typically spoke of reprobation as a negative, or passive, act whereby God simply left certain fallen humans in their sin. Supralapsarians taught "fully double predestination" whereby election and reprobation were "positive, coordinate decrees."[3]

election. The positive side of predestination: God's eternal choice, in Christ, of certain persons for salvation.

eternal security. The term preferred by some Protestants, especially Southern Baptists, for the doctrine of perseverance.

evangelical. A term with various meanings in U.S. history. Among some non-Anglo groups such as Lutherans, evangelical was often simply synonymous with "Protestant." In this volume, evangelical most often denotes the transatlantic tradition of revivalistic Protestantism, which was rooted in the eighteenth-century Great Awakening. It includes both Calvinist and Arminian factions and stresses the importance of a "new birth" conversion experience. Many nineteenth-century Protestants who debated predestination were heirs of this broadly evangelical tradition, even as some developed liberal views (for example, of biblical interpretation).

five points. See TULIP.

foreknowledge. God's eternal knowledge of all things before they occur in human time. Predestinarian debates in the Christian tradition and in U.S. history have typically hinged on whether God elects persons unconditionally, i.e., apart from his foreknowledge of their faith (Augustine, Aquinas, Luther, Calvin), or conditionally, i.e., because of (or, at least, in view of) their future faith (Molina, Arminius, some later Lutheran scholastics, Wesley). Though divine foreknowledge is logically distinct from foreordination, theologians, particularly those who taught conditional election, were always at pains to explain how God could infallibly know future human choices without in some sense determining them.[4]

Foxtrot by Bill Amend (2003). Universal Press Syndicate.

fundamentalist. Adjective used here to denote an insistence on the inerrancy and divine inspiration of scripture—the idea that the Bible is the literal word of God, uncorrupted by error or human invention. Fundamentalism naturally exacerbates predestinarian conflicts because it promotes the assumption that the Bible contains just one, divinely inspired doctrine of election.

godly. Nickname for the strongly Calvinist party in the Elizabethan Church of England, the people who would later be known as Puritans.

golden chain. Name used by Reformed theologians for the unbreakable sequence of salvation spelled out by the apostle Paul in Romans 8:30—predestination, calling, justification, glorification. Reformed scholastics later amplified this *ordo salutis* (order of salvation) to include additional stages.

infralapsarian. Latin, "below the fall"; sometimes called *sublapsarian.*[5] (Contrast with supralapsarian.) Among Reformed scholastics, the most common view of the order of God's eternal decrees, placing predestination after the Fall in the sequence of divine logic. Thus, God is said to have decreed unconditionally (1) to create humans in his image, (2) to permit the Fall (*lapsus*), and (3) to elect certain fallen people to salvation in Christ while passing over the rest and leaving them in their lapsed state to suffer eternal damnation. (Though most infralapsarians preferred the passive language of "passing over," some spoke of reprobation as a "double" decree with election.)[6] The objects of election in infralapsarianism are therefore future humans envisioned as already created and fallen (*creatus et lapsus*).

intuitu fidei. Latin, "in view of faith": the predestinarian formula favored by some Lutheran scholastics, including Aegidius Hunnius (1550–1603) and Johann Gerhard (1582–1637), that God elects persons in view of the faith that he himself grants to them. Because "in view of faith" rested both election and its condition in God, the formula was said by its supporters to avoid the alleged taint of synergism. But to its opponents, *intuitu fidei* appeared only a hair's breadth away from Arminianism. In American Lutheranism, the doctrine became the source of a major controversy between the Missouri Synod (whose leaders opposed it in favor of Luther's own unconditional election) and more liberal synods.

justification. God's gracious act of making sinful persons righteous or, as Protestants came to define it, God's reckoning (or counting) sinful persons as righteous. The question of whether justification requires the cooperation of human free will (the Catholic view) or whether it is by grace alone through faith (the Protestant view) was one of the central doctrinal debates of the Reformation. Protestants' emphasis on grace alone (*sola gratia*) naturally led many to embrace an unconditional view of the closely related doctrine of predestination as a safeguard against any hint of synergism.

liberal. Adjective used here to denote the view that scripture and doctrinal tradition are conditioned by time and circumstance and are therefore neither infallible nor above reassessment.

limited atonement. The Reformed doctrine that Christ died for the elect only. Reformed theologians insisted that though the atonement remained of infinite value, God decreed eternally that Christ's death would actually be effectual only for the elect.[7] By contrast, Catholics, Arminians, and Lutherans regarded limited-atonement language as an unwarranted restriction on the saving potential of Christ's death.

modernist. Essentially a synonym here for liberal, though with the additional connotation of a Darwinian-influenced, evolutionary view of Christian doctrinal development. Many nineteenth- and twentieth-century liberal

Protestants (e.g., the Presbyterian advocates of confessional revision) argued that Christianity had evolved beyond the predestinarian formulas of the sixteenth and seventeenth centuries.

Molinism. Named for the Spanish Jesuit Luis de Molina (1535–1600), perhaps the most sophisticated attempt, at least since the Reformation, to theorize how God could unfailingly foreknow the contingent acts of his free creatures. Molina called this special type of divine foresight *scientia media* (middle knowledge): God's infallible awareness of what creatures would certainly do in a particular set of circumstances. Molina linked divine election to foreknowledge of human conduct; he spoke of election as being *post praevisa merita* (after foresight of merits). Both the Molinism of the Jesuits and the more conservative Thomism of the Dominicans were deemed acceptable by the Catholic Church when Pope Paul V declared a truce between the warring factions in 1607.

original sin. The Western Christian (Catholic and Protestant) doctrine, originating with Augustine, that in Adam's disobedience humans fell from grace and human nature itself was tainted by an inherent sinfulness. Belief in original sin allows predestinarians to argue that unconditional election is merciful since all people are born corrupt and therefore (according to Augustinian logic) deserving of damnation.

Pelagianism. The chief rival (declared heretical by the church in the fifth century) to the Augustinian doctrine of original sin. Pelagius (c. 350–c. 425) taught that Adam's sin tainted only Adam; humans by nature remain essentially good and able to choose a life of virtue. Pelagianism thus removes the absolute dependence on God's electing grace that is the cornerstone of Augustinian predestinarianism.

predestinarian. Of or relating to the doctrine of predestination. When used as a noun in reference to persons, it denotes one strongly committed to a particular doctrine of predestination (often, unconditional election).

predestination. Latin, *praedestinatio*. In Christian tradition, the eternal decree of God appointing humans to their ultimate ends, with the elect (the saved) manifesting divine mercy and the reprobate (the damned) manifesting divine justice. Though predestination (the divine foreordination of each person's eternal destiny) is to be distinguished from providence (God's more general ordering of all things), the distinction has often been blurred in popular understanding.

preexistence. The doctrine, taught by a Christian minority from the early church father Origen (c. 185–c. 254) to the Mormons in the United States, that humans prior to their births existed spiritually in heaven with God and were endowed even then with the free will to choose Christ. In rebelling against the seeming determinism of Calvinism, the Mormons (Latter-day

Saints) radically extended human free agency into both premortal and postmortal existence. Outside of the Latter-day Saint tradition, the preexistence of souls is regarded as heretical, owing to the condemnation of the doctrine by the Fifth Ecumenical Council (553).

preterition. Latin, *praeteritio*: "a passing by." Term favored by infralapsarians for God's passing over the non-elect and leaving them in the fallen mass of humankind. Preterition, conceived as a negative, or passive, act of God's will (as opposed to his positive willing in election) was thought to remove the implication that God preemptively damned persons for no cause of their own.

prevenient grace. Latin, *gratia praeveniens*: grace that "comes before" any human response to God; sometimes called "preventing grace" in older sources. It is associated especially with Arminianism, which taught that God gives prevenient grace to all people, enabling them to accept or reject Christ. To Calvinists, prevenient grace is simply the first in a series of graces given irresistibly to the elect.[8]

providence. God's continual ordering of all things, or the divine direction of all things toward foreordained ends. It is related but not identical to predestination, which may be defined as the aspect of providence pertaining to the eternal destinies of individuals. Thoroughgoing predestinarians have often been the strongest advocates of God's providential superintendence of even life's smallest details.

purgatory. From the Latin verb *purgo*, "to clean (or cleanse)": in Catholic doctrine, the intermediate state (between heaven and hell) of purification for persons insufficiently cleansed of venial sins at their deaths. Though persons in purgatory are presumed to be already elect, the practical effect of the doctrine is to temper predestination's absoluteness by involving the living church in praying for the swift release of the suffering souls. Purgatory thus reinforces a sacramental and intercessory, rather than a purely predestinarian, view of salvation. Protestants rejected purgatory and with it the Apocrypha (or deuterocanonical books), the source of the doctrine's principal proof text (2 Maccabees 12:46).[9]

Puritan. Of or related to the zealously Calvinist faction, also nicknamed the godly, that originated in the Elizabethan Church of England. Puritans— British historians often lowercase the term—were so called because of their desire to purify the church of the alleged impurities (both doctrinal and ritual) left over from Catholicism. Puritan theologians such as William Perkins (1558–1602) were among the most thoroughgoing predestinarians in Anglo Protestantism and contributed, along with Dutch and German Calvinists, to the tradition of Reformed scholasticism. Though Puritanism as a political force in England was routed at the Restoration in 1660, the transatlantic tradition of Puritan theology extended in America through the career of Jonathan Edwards (1703–1758).

Reformed. The Protestant theological tradition often called "Calvinist" but predating Calvin to include the first-generation reformer Huldrych Zwingli (1484–1531). In the last half of the sixteenth century, two major traditions of Protestant scholasticism emerged: Reformed and Lutheran. Both theorized predestination in considerable technical detail, but the Reformed tradition (which included Puritanism) came to be more popularly associated with predestinarianism, owing in part to the minority supralapsarians, who devised the most absolute version of the doctrine.

Remonstrants. The Arminian (anti-Calvinist) party in the Netherlands, whose *Remonstrance* (1610) was confuted by the Synod of Dort (1618–1619), which enshrined five-point Calvinism (see TULIP) as Reformed orthodoxy.

renate. From the Latin *renatus*, "born again": an obsolete term occasionally used (as by the American Puritan poet Michael Wigglesworth) to refer to the elect.

reprobation. The negative side of predestination: God's eternal choice of certain persons for damnation. Whereas all Catholic and Protestant theologians spoke of election, many were uncomfortable with talk of reprobation, preferring instead to speak of preterition, or God's merely "passing over" the non-elect.

scholasticism. Originally the term for the school-based (university) theology of Aquinas and other medieval theologians who systematized Christian doctrine using the logic of Aristotle and other classical thinkers. Scholasticism also refers to the traditions of Protestant orthodoxy developed by Reformed and Lutheran dogmaticians between the latter half of the sixteenth century and the early eighteenth century. American Puritans such as Samuel Willard (1640–1707) and Jonathan Edwards (1703–1758) were conversant in the writings of continental Protestant scholastics thanks to the movement's lingua franca, Latin. Both medieval Catholic and early modern Protestant scholasticism theorized predestination with considerable technical sophistication.

scientia media. Latin, "middle knowledge": the Molinist theory of God's infallible foreknowledge of individuals' merit (or, as Arminian Protestants would have it, faith). Middle knowledge was in between God's *natural* (or necessary) knowledge of all possibilities and causal relations and his *free* knowledge of things he actually willed to be. *Scientia media* thus stood between God's knowledge of the merely *possible* and his knowledge of the *actual*—an elusive middle ground that many critics doubted really existed.

semi-Pelagianism. The doctrine, often associated with John Cassian (c. 360–c. 435), that, while not denying original sin (as in full-blown

FRAZZ   BY JEF MALLETT

Frazz by Jef Mallett (2005). United Feature Syndicate.

Pelagianism), taught that the human will's ability to cooperate with God was injured but not destroyed by Adam's sin. Humans thus retain enough God-given natural ability to take the initial step toward Christ. After the Council of Orange (529) condemned this notion, *semi-Pelagian* became a favorite term of abuse among strict Augustinians (and, later, Calvinists) for any theology hinting of synergism.

supralapsarian. Latin, "above the fall"; sometimes called *prelapsarian*.[10] (Contrast with infralapsarian.) Among the Reformed scholastics, the minority view of the order of God's eternal decrees, placing predestination before the Fall in the sequence of divine logic. Thus, God was said to have decreed unconditionally (1) to elect certain individuals and reprobate others, (2) to create humans in his image, and (3) to permit the Fall (*lapsus*). The objects of election in supralapsarianism were therefore future humans envisioned as creatable and capable of falling (*creabilis et labilis*). To its proponents, such as the American Puritan Samuel Willard (1640–1707), supralapsarianism best safeguarded the absolutely unconditional nature of predestination. God's primal purpose was to glorify himself, manifesting his mercy in election and his justice in reprobation. Even the creation was merely a means to this end. To its infralapsarian opponents, however, supralapsarianism was logically nonsensical because it seemed to make a nonentity (the not yet created person) the object of election.[11] To many later American theologians, supralapsarianism came to symbolize the alleged rigidity and absoluteness of Calvinism.

synergism. From the Latin *synergismus*: "a working together." Term used for theologies, such as Arminianism and the Lutheranism of Philipp Melanchthon, that posited some form of cooperation between the human will and divine grace in the process of salvation. Opponents often equated

Arminian and Melanchthonian synergism with semi-Pelagianism, but their "evangelical synergism," according to one contemporary Arminian theologian, insisted that prevenient grace must still precede any human move toward Christ.[12]

tentatio praedestinationis. Latin, "predestinarian temptation or trial." A term used in the Second Helvetic Confession (1566), written by Zwingli's successor Heinrich Bullinger, for excessive anxiety about one's eternal election. The New England Puritans sometimes spoke of this as predestinarian "melancholy."

Thomism. The theology of Thomas Aquinas and his later disciples; the dominant school among Catholic theologians through much of U.S. history. Unlike Molinism, which long prevailed among the Jesuits, the more conservative Thomism of the Dominicans taught that God elects persons apart from any foreseen merit. Consequently, in the controversy between the two sides that began in the late sixteenth century, the Jesuits sometimes accused the Dominicans of being "Calvinists." Pope Paul V in 1607 forbade further fighting between the two sides, in effect declaring the teaching of each to be acceptable.

TULIP. Acronym popular among Calvinists for the five-point Reformed orthodoxy based loosely on the Canons of Dort (1618–1619): total depravity, unconditional election, limited atonement, irresistible grace, and perseverance of the saints. The five points taught that (1) humans in their natural state are dead in sin, incapable of any saving good; (2) election is based on nothing foreseen in humans; (3) Christ's atoning death, though infinite in value, is efficacious only for the elect in God's eternal plan; (4) Christ's saving purpose for the elect cannot be thwarted; and (5) the elect cannot fall away but will be preserved in saving grace unto the end. The same five points correspond loosely to the teaching of the Westminster Confession and thus became the reigning orthodoxy of the New England Puritans. In the twenty-first century, TULIP has become a rallying cry for groups seeking to reinvigorate Calvinism in various traditions (e.g., in the Southern Baptist Convention).

universalism. The doctrine, taught in early Christianity by Origen (c. 185–c. 254) and in America by the Universalist Church (later merged into the Unitarian Universalist Association), that God intends to save all people in the end. American Universalists disagreed over whether a period of hell punishment for the wicked would precede universal salvation. Calvinists, meanwhile, sometimes falsely accused Methodists of teaching universalism, even though the Methodist doctrine of prevenient grace posited only that all people *could* be saved if they believed.

Notes

Introduction

1. Fortunately, the tornado in Shelby County, Indiana, on the night of 31 March 2006, killed no one. Less than five months earlier, the residents of Evansville, Indiana, had not been so lucky. A more powerful tornado there killed 25 people and damaged or destroyed some 400 homes.

2. Julia Keller, "A Wicked Wind Takes Aim," *Chicago Tribune*, 5 December 2004, p. 1 (series continued on 6 and 7 December 2004).

3. Frequently cited confessional Protestant studies include G. C. Berkouwer, *Divine Election*, trans. Hugo Bekker (Grand Rapids, Mich.: Eerdmans, 1960); Loraine Boettner, *The Reformed Doctrine of Predestination* (1932; reprint, Grand Rapids, Mich.: Eerdmans, 1951); Harry Buis, *Historic Protestantism and Predestination* (Philadelphia: Presbyterian and Reformed Publishing, 1958); and Paul K. Jewett, *Election and Predestination* (Grand Rapids, Mich.: Eerdmans, 1985). One exception to the dearth of secular historical studies is the wealth of scholarship on Puritan predestinarianism, though the focus is usually on the other side of the Atlantic; I will engage this literature in chapters 1 and 2.

4. On predestination in literature, see, e.g., Perry D. Westbrook, *Free Will and Determinism in American Literature* (Rutherford, N.J.: Fairleigh Dickinson University Press, 1979); and Paul F. Boller, Jr., *Freedom and Fate in American Thought: From Edwards to Dewey* (Dallas: Southern Methodist University Press, 1978). On national election as a theme in U.S. politics, see Conrad Cherry, ed., *God's New Israel: Religious Interpretations of American Destiny*, rev. ed. (Chapel Hill: University of North Carolina Press, 1998), and Anders Stephanson, *Manifest Destiny: American Expansionism and the Empire of Right* (New York: Hill and Wang, 1995).

5. 1 Tim. 6:20 (KJV); John Calvin, *Institutes of the Christian Religion*, ed. John T. McNeill and trans. Ford Lewis Battles (Philadelphia: Westminster, 1960), I.16.8, p. 207.

6. Allen C. Guelzo, *Edwards on the Will: A Century of American Theological Debate* (Middletown, Conn.: Wesleyan University Press, 1989), 10. Guelzo's book

is the standard history of the perennial debate in American theology over free will and determinism. See also his updated account, "The Return of the Will: Jonathan Edwards and the Possibilities of Free Will," in *Edwards in Our Time: Jonathan Edwards and the Shaping of American Religion*, ed. Sang Hyun Lee and Allen C. Guelzo (Grand Rapids, Mich.: Eerdmans, 1999), 87–110.

7. An accessible overview of the ongoing debates is Robert Kane, *A Contemporary Introduction to Free Will* (New York: Oxford University Press, 2005). A controversial compatibilist account, which sees free will as itself the product of evolution, is Daniel C. Dennett, *Freedom Evolves* (New York: Viking, 2003).

8. See, e.g., the almost complete absence of Augustine from Dennett, *Freedom Evolves*, and from his earlier account, *Elbow Room: The Varieties of Free Will Worth Wanting* (Cambridge, Mass.: MIT Press, 1984).

9. The eucharistic hymn "O Salutaris Hostia" (O Saving Victim), attributed to Thomas Aquinas; see chapter 1.

10. On the earliest years of Dutch settlement, see Gerald F. De Jong, *The Dutch Reformed Church in the American Colonies* (Grand Rapids, Mich.: Eerdmans, 1978), and on the Dutch struggles with the neighboring English, see Randall Balmer, *A Perfect Babel of Confusion: Dutch Religion and English Culture in the Middle Colonies* (New York: Oxford University Press, 1989).

11. Thomas M. McCoog, "Andrew White," in *Oxford Dictionary of National Biography*, http://www.oxforddnb.com. Soon after White and the first settlers landed in Maryland, Massachusetts Bay founder John Winthrop, notified by a traveler of the new colony's establishment, complained in his journal that "those [persons] which came over were many of them papists, & did sett vp masse openly." *The Journal of John Winthrop, 1630–1649*, ed. Richard S. Dunn, James Savage, and Laetitia Yeandle (Cambridge, Mass.: Belknap, Harvard University Press, 1996), 119.

12. The recognition of pluralism (not just on predestination) in colonial America has rightly prompted scholars to "de-center" religious history from its earlier focus on Puritanism; see Charles L. Cohen, "The Post-Puritan Paradigm of Early American Religious History," *William and Mary Quarterly*, 3rd ser., 54 (1997): 695–722. In keeping with this newer paradigm, one of the goals of this book is to show the importance of predestinarian debates both inside and outside the Anglo-Puritan theological lineage.

13. Elaine Pagels, *Adam, Eve, and the Serpent* (New York: Vintage, 1988), 146.

Chapter 1

1. Quoted in T. H. L. Parker, *John Calvin: A Biography* (Philadelphia: Westminster, 1975), 108; cf. 56 on Werly. See also Bernard Cottret, *Calvin: A Biography*, trans. M. Wallace McDonald (Grand Rapids, Mich.: Eerdmans, 2000), 190–91; and Carter Lindberg, *The European Reformations* (Oxford: Blackwell, 1996), 264–65.

2. On Gruet's views, see Max Gauna, *Upwellings: First Expressions of Unbelief in the Printed Literature of the French Renaissance* (Cranbury, N.J.: Associated University Presses, 1992), 78–80; and on the proceedings against him, Philip Schaff, *History of the Christian Church*, vol. 8, *Modern Christianity: The Swiss Reformation* (1910; reprint, Grand Rapids, Mich.: Eerdmans, 1994), 501–3.

3. John Calvin, "Articles Concerning Predestination," in *Calvin: Theological Treatises*, ed. and trans. J. K. S. Reid (Louisville, Ky.: Westminster John Knox, 1954), 179–80.

4. Quoted in Parker, *John Calvin*, 154. On the glancing mentions of predestination in the first edition of the *Institutes* of 1536, see François Wendel, *Calvin: Origins and Development of His Religious Thought*, trans. Philip Mairet (1963; reprint, Grand Rapids, Mich.: Baker, 1997), 265.

5. Kenneth P. Minkema, "Old Age and Religion in the Writings and Life of Jonathan Edwards," *Church History* 70 (2001): 684.

6. Jonathan Edwards, "A Farewell Sermon Preached at the First Precinct in Northampton, after the People's Public Rejection of Their Minister... on June 22, 1750," in *The Works of Jonathan Edwards*, vol. 25, *Sermons and Discourses, 1743–1758*, ed. Wilson H. Kimnach (New Haven, Conn.: Yale University Press, 2006), 466, 476, 486.

7. Edwards, "Farewell Sermon," 477; Calvin quoted in Parker, *John Calvin*, 153.

8. Edwards, "Farewell Sermon," 483–84.

9. The standard reference on the language of the New Testament is Frederick William Danker, ed., *A Greek-English Lexicon of the New Testament and Other Early Christian Literature*, 3rd ed. (Chicago: University of Chicago Press, 2000). See also Gary S. Shogren, "Election: New Testament," in *The Anchor Bible Dictionary*, ed. David Noel Freedman et al., 6 vols. (New York: Doubleday, 1992), 2:441–44; as well as the helpful discussions of biblical terminology in David Lyle Jeffrey and James I. Packer, "Election" and "Predestination," in *A Dictionary of Biblical Tradition in English Literature*, ed. David Lyle Jeffrey (Grand Rapids, Mich.: Eerdmans, 1992), 228–33, 635–39.

10. Jaroslav Pelikan, *The Christian Tradition: A History of the Development of Doctrine*, vol. 1, *The Emergence of the Catholic Tradition (100–600)* (Chicago: University of Chicago Press, 1971), 280–84.

11. Justin Martyr, *Second Apology*, in *The Ante-Nicene Fathers*, ed. Alexander Roberts and James Donaldson (New York: Scribner's, 1908), 1:190. See, in the same volume, Irenaeus (c. 130–200), bishop of Lyons, who maintained that according to the "ancient law of human liberty," God held humans as well as angels responsible for their choices (1:518).

12. John Chrysostom quoted in *Ancient Christian Commentary on Scripture, New Testament*, vol. 6, *Romans*, ed. Gerald Bray (Downers Grove, Ill.: InterVarsity, 1998), 250, 261. On the Eastern churches and free will, see Timothy Ware, *The Orthodox Church*, rev. ed. (London: Penguin, 1997), 221–25.

13. Augustine quoted in *Ancient Christian Commentary on Scripture, New Testament*, 6:235. Moreover, as Augustine explained in book III of *De libero arbitrio* (written between 391 and 395), God's foreknowledge did not preclude human freedom: "Unless I am mistaken, you do not force someone to sin just because you foreknow that he is going to sin." Augustine, *On Free Choice of the Will*, trans. Thomas Williams (Indianapolis: Hackett, 1993), 78.

14. The English edition of Augustine's two commentaries is *Augustine on Romans*, ed. and trans. Paula Fredriksen Landes (Chico, Calif.: Scholars, 1982); see also Paula Fredriksen, "Paul and Augustine: Conversion Narratives, Orthodox Traditions, and the Retrospective Self," *Journal of Theological Studies*, new ser., 37 (1986): 3–34. Interestingly, at least one Gnostic text echoed Romans 8:29: "Those whose names he foreknew were called at the end." Gospel of Truth 21:25, in *The Gnostic Scriptures*, ed. and trans. Bentley Layton (Garden City, N.Y.: Doubleday, 1987), 255.

15. Quoted in James Wetzel, "Ad Simplicianum," in *Augustine through the Ages: An Encyclopedia*, ed. Allan D. Fitzgerald et al. (Grand Rapids, Mich.: Eerdmans, 1999), 798. On Augustine's change of mind, see also Wetzel's helpful article "Predestination, Pelagianism, and Foreknowledge," in *The Cambridge*

Companion to Augustine, ed. Eleonore Stump and Norman Kretzmann (Cambridge: Cambridge University Press, 2001), 49–58, esp. 53.

16. *Confessions*, 10.29.40. The phrase is alternatively translated as "Give me the grace to do as you command, and command me to do what you will," in *Confessions*, trans. R. S. Pine-Coffin (London: Penguin, 1961), 233.

17. John Ferguson, *Pelagius: A Historical and Theological Study* (Cambridge: Heffer and Sons, 1956), 45. On the beginning of the controversy, see also B. R. Rees, *Pelagius: A Reluctant Heretic* (Woodbridge, England: Boydell, 1988), 38–42; and Eugene TeSelle, "Pelagius, Pelagianism," in Fitzgerald et al., eds., *Augustine through the Ages*, 633–40.

18. Augustine, *On the Predestination of the Saints (De praedestinatione sanctorum*, written in 429), in *Four Anti-Pelagian Writings*, trans. John A. Mourant and William J. Collinge, in *The Fathers of the Church*, vol. 86 (Washington, D.C.: Catholic University Press of America, 1992), 259–60.

19. Ibid., 246.

20. Augustine, *On the Gift of Perseverance (De dono perseverantiae*, written in 429), ibid., 298.

21. On the church as the hospital of grace, see Martha Ellen Stortz, "'Where or When Was Your Servant Innocent?' Augustine on Childhood," in *The Child in Christian Thought*, ed. Marcia J. Bunge (Grand Rapids, Mich.: Eerdmans, 2001), 95.

22. On Augustine's logic of original sin, as revealed in his debate with the Pelagian theologian Julian of Eclanum, see Elaine Pagels, *Adam, Eve, and the Serpent* (New York: Vintage, 1988), 127–50; on birth defects, 135.

23. Augustine, *On the Gift of Perseverance*, 296.

24. Peter Brown, *Augustine of Hippo: A Biography*, rev. ed. (Berkeley: University of California Press, 2000), 410. Elsewhere, Brown notes that Augustine's teaching was far more egalitarian than that of Pelagius, who insisted that Christians could—and should—be perfect. Augustine "did not expect every Christian to be perfect. Yet each Christian was equal to every other, because all Christians were equally dependent on the grace of God." Peter Brown, *The Rise of Western Christendom: Triumph and Diversity, A.D. 200–1000*, 2nd ed. (Malden, Mass.: Blackwell, 2003), 89–90.

25. As Cassian explained: "[T]here are by nature some seeds of goodness in every soul implanted by the kindness of the Creator"; quoted in Pelikan, *Christian Tradition*, 1:323–24. See also the general summaries in J. N. D. Kelly, *Early Christian Doctrines*, rev. ed. (San Francisco: Harper and Row, 1978), 370–71; G. W. H. Lampe, "Christian Theology in the Patristic Period," in *A History of Christian Doctrine*, ed. Hubert Cunliffe-Jones (London: Clark, 1978), 167–69. On the problems with "semi-Pelagian," see Ralph W. Mathisen, *Ecclesiastical Factionalism and Religious Controversy in Fifth-Century Gaul* (Washington, D.C.: Catholic University of America Press, 1989), 129–30; and Conrad Leyser, "Semi-Pelagianism," in Fitzgerald et al., eds., *Augustine through the Ages*, 761–66.

26. Pelikan, *Christian Tradition*, 1:321, 325. On the debate between Gaul and Africa, see Rebecca Harden Weaver, *Divine Grace and Human Agency: A Study of the Semi-Pelagian Controversy* (Macon, Ga.: Mercer University Press, 1996).

27. Kelly, *Early Christian Doctrines*, 371–72; Pelikan, *Christian Tradition*, 1:327–29.

28. On the free-for-all, see David Knowles, "The Middle Ages, 604–1350," in Cunliffe-Jones, ed., *History of Christian Doctrine*, 243. On the ninth-century controversy, see Jaroslav Pelikan, *The Christian Tradition: A History of the Development of Doctrine*, vol. 3, *The Growth of Medieval Theology (600–1300)* (Chicago: University of Chicago Press, 1978), 80–95.

29. D. E. Nineham, "Gottschalk of Orbais: Reactionary or Precursor of the Reformation?" *Journal of Ecclesiastical History* 40 (1989): 1–18; quotation from Gottschalk on 12.

30. Pelikan, *Christian Tradition*, 3:93.

31. Decrees of Orange quoted in Henry Bettenson and Chris Maunder, eds., *Documents of the Christian Church*, 3rd ed. (New York: Oxford University Press, 1999), 67.

32. On the medieval perception of Augustine's sacramental theology as "frustratingly vague," see Margaret R. Miles, *The World Made Flesh: A History of Christian Thought* (Malden, Mass.: Blackwell, 2005), 137.

33. Augustine, *Concerning the City of God against the Pagans*, 21.13, trans. Henry Bettenson (London: Penguin, 1984), 990–91.

34. NRSV. In the Catholic Douay-Rheims version (based on the Latin Vulgate), v. 45 appeared as two (vv. 45–46).

35. Jacques Le Goff, *The Birth of Purgatory*, trans. Arthur Goldhammer (Chicago: University of Chicago Press, 1984), 61–85; on Augustine as an "intellectual aristocrat," 84. See also pp. 6–7 on the assumption that those in purgatory were already elect.

36. For the evidence supporting the tradition of Aquinas's authorship, see Miri Rubin, *Corpus Christi: The Eucharist in Late Medieval Culture* (Cambridge: Cambridge University Press, 1991), 185–89.

37. Ibid., 192.

38. Joseph P. Wawrykow, *The Westminster Handbook to Thomas Aquinas* (Louisville, Ky.: Westminster John Knox, 2005), 131.

39. Thomas Aquinas, *Summa Theologiae*, I.23.8, in the Blackfriars edition, vol. 5, *God's Will and Providence (Ia. 19–26)*, trans. Thomas Gilby (London: Eyre and Spottiswoode, 1967), 141.

40. *Summa Theologiae*, I.23.5–6, pp. 123, 129. On Aquinas's Augustinian view of predestination, see also Wawrykow, *Thomas Aquinas*, 40, 118–20. Cf. the observation that "the mature Thomas of the *Summa* teaches unambiguously Augustine's justification *sola gratia*"; Heiko A. Oberman, *The Dawn of the Reformation: Essays in Late Medieval and Early Reformation Thought* (1986; reprint, Grand Rapids, Mich.: Eerdmans, 1992), 5.

41. Max Weber, *The Sociology of Religion*, trans. Ephraim Fischoff (Boston: Beacon, 1963), 25.

42. Rubin, *Corpus Christi*, 151–52.

43. Eamon Duffy, *The Stripping of the Altars: Traditional Religion in England, c. 1400–c. 1580* (New Haven, Conn.: Yale University Press, 1992), 95–102.

44. Rubin, *Corpus Christi*, 153.

45. A point made by Keith Thomas, *Religion and the Decline of Magic: Studies in Popular Beliefs in Sixteenth and Seventeenth Century England* (New York: Oxford University Press, 1971), 48. Thus, adds Thomas, church leaders "abandoned the struggle against superstition whenever it seemed in their interest to do so" (49).

46. Technically, the church claimed jurisdiction only over the living, but it petitioned God to accept indulgences on behalf of the dead.

47. Ninety-five Theses reprinted in Bettenson and Maunder, eds., *Documents of the Christian Church*, 205–12. On the context of the Ninety-five Theses, see Patrick Collinson, *The Reformation: A History* (New York: Modern Library, 2003), 54–60; and Lewis W. Spitz, *The Protestant Reformation, 1517–1559* (New York: Harper and Row, 1985), 66–69.

48. Rubin, *Corpus Christi*, 348.

49. Quoted in Heiko A. Oberman, *Luther: Man between God and the Devil*, trans. Eileen Walliser-Schwarzbart (New York: Image, 1992), 232.

50. Leigh Eric Schmidt, *Holy Fairs: Scottish Communions and American Revivals in the Early Modern Period* (Princeton, N.J.: Princeton University Press, 1989).

51. Martin Luther, *De servo arbitrio*, trans. Philip S. Watson and B. Drewery, in *Luther and Erasmus: Free Will and Salvation* (Philadelphia: Westminster, 1969), 121.

52. Ibid., 140. As a proof text, Luther cited Psalm 73:22: "I was stupid and ignorant; I was like a brute beast toward you." See the pugnacious observations on *De servo arbitrio* in Richard Marius, *Martin Luther: The Christian between God and Death* (Cambridge, Mass.: Harvard University Press, 1999), 456–63. Marius does not disguise his sympathy for Erasmus: Luther's treatise is "insulting, vehement, monstrously unfair, and utterly uncompromising" (456).

53. "Strong wine" is from Luther's 1522 preface to Romans, in *Martin Luther: Selections from His Writings*, ed. John Dillenberger (Garden City, N.Y.: Doubleday, 1961), 32.

54. David C. Steinmetz, *Luther in Context* (1986; reprint, Grand Rapids, Mich.: Baker, 1995), 17–21.

55. Steven Ozment, *The Age of Reform, 1250–1550: An Intellectual and Religious History of Late Medieval and Reformation Europe* (New Haven, Conn.: Yale University Press, 1980), 233–36. Aquinas taught that humans first needed a supernatural infusion of grace—a gift given only to the elect—before they could gain merit through good works (cf. Wawrykow, *Thomas Aquinas*, 119–20).

56. Biel, in contrast, equated predestination with foreknowledge and even referred to the reprobate as the *presciti* (the foreknown). Regarding the elect, Biel argued that St. Paul and the Virgin Mary were the only persons whom God had elected without the normally required foresight that they would "do their best." See Heiko Augustinus Oberman, *The Harvest of Medieval Theology: Gabriel Biel and Late Medieval Nominalism* (Durham, N.C.: Duke University Press, 1983), 187–93.

57. Oberman, *Luther*, 160–61; Spitz, *Protestant Reformation*, 64; Brown, *Augustine of Hippo*, 104–5, 276; and Paul Althaus, *The Theology of Martin Luther*, trans. Robert C. Schultz (Philadelphia: Fortress, 1966), 9–11. On Luther's "rediscovery" of Augustine, see Alister E. McGrath, *Reformation Thought: An Introduction*, 2nd ed. (Grand Rapids, Mich.: Baker, 1993), 93–97.

58. Luther, *Tischreden*, no. 5658a, quoted in Martin Luther, *Letters of Spiritual Counsel*, trans. Theodore Tappert (Philadelphia: Westminster, 1955), 131, 133.

59. Oberman, *Luther*, 237.

60. McGrath, *Reformation Thought*, 120–22; Collinson, *Reformation*, 72–78.

61. Wendel, *Calvin*, 131–34; David C. Steinmetz, *Calvin in Context* (New York: Oxford University Press, 1995), 172–83; Collinson, *Reformation*, 92–93.

62. Collinson, *Reformation*, 97.

63. William J. Bouwsma, *John Calvin: A Sixteenth-Century Portrait* (New York: Oxford University Press, 1988), 171–73, 183–85. On the political context in the 1540s and 1550s, see Diarmaid MacCulloch, *The Reformation* (New York: Viking, 2003), 262–65.

64. Heiko A. Oberman, *The Two Reformations: The Journey from the Last Days to the New World*, ed. Donald Weinstein (New Haven, Conn.: Yale University Press, 2003), 165. Oberman spoke of three successive Reformations: the Reformation initiated by Luther and the princes, the Reformation of the cities, and the Reformation advanced by the persecuted refugees. Calvin, he argued, is a transitional figure between the second and the third Reformations, and his stress on providence and predestination must be seen in this context (146–49).

65. On the practical nature of Calvin's predestinarian reflections, see Wendel, *Calvin*, 269–70.

66. John Calvin, *Institutes of the Christian Religion*, ed. John T. McNeill and trans. Ford Lewis Battles (Philadelphia: Westminster, 1960), III.21.1, pp. 921–23.

67. Ibid., III.21.4, pp. 925–26.

68. Ibid., III.22.11, p. 947; III.23.2, p. 949.

69. Ibid., III.23.1, pp. 947–49. Nevertheless, in Calvin's view, the decrees of election and reprobation are not in all aspects parallel (e.g., Christ is the ground of election but not of reprobation). See the discussion in Fred H. Klooster, *Calvin's Doctrine of Predestination*, 2nd ed. (Grand Rapids, Mich.: Baker, 1977), 75–79.

70. Wendel, *Calvin*, 280; McGrath, *Reformation Thought*, 124–25. On Calvin and reprobation, see also Bernard M. G. Reardon, *Religious Thought in the Reformation*, 2nd ed. (London: Longman, 1995), 178–80. On Augustine's view, see Mathijs Lamberigts, "Predestination," in Fitzgerald et al., eds., *Augustine through the Ages*, 678. Augustine sometimes appeared to advocate a double view; see John M. Rist, "Augustine on Free Will and Predestination," in *Augustine: A Collection of Critical Essays*, ed. R. A. Markus (Garden City, N.Y.: Doubleday, 1972), 227–28; cf. Pelikan, *Christian Tradition*, 1:297–98, 329.

71. McGrath, *Reformation Thought*, 125. Calvin also rejected the idea that God merely permitted the Fall: "But why shall we say 'permission' unless it is because God so wills?" (Calvin, *Institutes*, III.23.8, p. 956).

72. Calvin, *Institutes*, III.24.13, pp. 979–81.

73. Ibid., III.24.16, pp. 983–84.

74. Ibid., III.21.1, p. 921; "dreadful" decree: III.23.7, p. 955. The Latin original, *decretum horribile*, is sometimes mistranslated as "horrible decree" but means dreadful, terrifying, or awe inspiring.

75. Ibid., III.21.7, p. 931.

76. John Calvin, *Concerning the Eternal Predestination of God*, trans. J. K. S. Reid (1961; reprint, Louisville, Ky.: Westminster John Knox, 1997). The original 1536 edition of the *Institutes* included no separate section on predestination; see the English edition, *Institutes of the Christian Religion*, trans. Ford Lewis Battles (London: Collins, 1975). On Calvin's revisions of the *Institutes*, see Wendel, *Calvin*, 264–69.

77. Cottret, *Calvin*, 210–11.

78. Ibid., 211; cf. 322–24 on Calvin's reaction to these criticisms in the 1550s.

79. Ibid., 212. Calvin's criticism of "those who are so cautious or fearful that they desire to bury predestination" was probably a reference to the Bern policy; Calvin, *Institutes*, III.21.4, p. 926n14.

80. Cottret, *Calvin*, 323.

81. Diarmaid MacCulloch, *Thomas Cranmer: A Life* (New Haven, Conn.: Yale University Press, 1996), 614.

82. *Assertio Septem Sacramentorum*, translated as *An Assertion of the Seven Sacraments: Against Martin Luther* (London, 1688), 3, 29. On the context of this work, see Richard Marius, *Martin Luther: The Christian between God and Death* (Cambridge, Mass.: Belknap, Harvard University Press, 1999), 339–43.

83. For a good summary of the complicated politics of this event, see the appendix to David L. Holmes, *A Brief History of the Episcopal Church* (Valley Forge, Pa.: Trinity Press International, 1993), 179–97.

84. MacCulloch, *Thomas Cranmer*, 211–12, 428. On Bucer and Peter Martyr, see W. P. Stephens, *The Holy Spirit in the Theology of Martin Bucer* (London: Cambridge University Press, 1970), 23–41; Frank A. James, *Peter Martyr Vermigli and Predestination: The Augustinian Inheritance of an Italian Reformer* (Oxford:

Clarendon, Oxford University Press, 1998); and John Patrick Donnelley, S.J., *Calvinism and Scholasticism in Vermigli's Doctrine of Man and Grace* (Leiden: Brill, 1976), 124–69.

85. *Articles Agreed on by the Bishoppes, and Other Learned Menne in the Synode at London* (London, 1553). Cf. the comparative edition of the 1553, 1563, and 1571 articles in Gerald Bray, ed., *Documents of the English Reformation* (Minneapolis: Fortress, 1994), 284–311.

86. On the Marian exiles and predestination, see Dewey D. Wallace, Jr., *Puritans and Predestination: Grace in English Protestant Theology, 1525–1695* (Chapel Hill: University of North Carolina Press, 1982), 19–28. Wallace's fine book remains the standard treatment of Puritan predestinarianism on the English side of the Atlantic. Much of my own account of the background prior to the Great Migration relies on his narrative framework.

87. See the facsimile of the 1602 edition, *The Geneva Bible: The Annotated New Testament,* ed. Gerald T. Sheppard (Cleveland, Ohio: Pilgrim, 1989), 67, along with the introductory comments on Beza's notes by Marvin W. Anderson, 12–13.

88. Quoted in Wallace, *Puritans and Predestination,* 31.

89. Ibid., 19–24, 30–31. The King's Bench dispute is detailed in D. Andrew Penny, *Freewill or Predestination: The Battle over Saving Grace in Mid-Tudor England* (Woodbridge, England: Royal Historical Society, Boydell, 1990), 103–24.

90. Historians have debated the usefulness of the term *Puritan* because of the difficulties, especially in the Tudor age, of identifying a coherent Puritanism or Anglicanism. For this reason, British scholars tend to lowercase "puritan." I have adopted the more typical American capitalization of Puritan, which I use as a term of convenience for what one Elizabethan pamphleteer called the "hotter sort of protestants" on the temperature spectrum of the English church. Some early Puritans were hot for reforms in church governance (e.g., the presbyterian agitators of the 1570s and 1580s). Others, equally hot theologically and spiritually, were moderates on conformity who worked within established church channels (e.g., the Cambridge theologians and staunch predestinarians William Perkins and William Whitaker); see Peter Lake, *Moderate Puritans and the Elizabethan Church* (Cambridge: Cambridge University Press, 1982), 1–15. What united Puritans, in addition to the predestinarian preoccupations described in this and the next chapter, was a commitment to three "interlinked agendas," defined by Dwight Bozeman as: (1) *moralism,* or "a stress upon the moral transformation, performance, and purity of individuals and their communities"; (2) *pietism,* or "a preoccupation with the self and its subjective states, particularly with its inner controls"; and (3) *primitivism,* or "a reversion, undercutting both Catholic and Anglican appeals to a continuity of tradition, to the first, or primitive, order of things narrated in the Protestant Scriptures." See Theodore Dwight Bozeman, *To Live Ancient Lives: The Primitivist Dimension in Puritanism* (Chapel Hill: University of North Carolina Press, 1988), 3–12. On the problem of defining "Puritan," see Patrick Collinson, *The Elizabethan Puritan Movement* (Berkeley: University of California Press, 1967), 21–28 ("hotter sort" quotation on 27).

91. Dewey D. Wallace, Jr., "George Gifford, Puritan Propaganda and Popular Religion in Elizabethan England," *Sixteenth Century Journal* 9 (1978): 43. On the context of the godly writers, see Wallace, *Puritans and Predestination,* 36–55.

92. Quoted in Timothy Scott McGinnis, *George Gifford and the Reformation of the Common Sort: Puritan Priorities in Elizabethan Religious Life* (Kirksville, Mo.: Truman State University Press, 2004), 149; cf. 147–53 on Gifford's logic of assurance.

93. On the practical and technical aspects of Perkins's work, see Wallace, *Puritans and Predestination*, 55–61. Regarding Perkins's wide influence, one historian has claimed that no author was more often found on the shelves of later generations of Puritans; see William Haller, *The Rise of Puritanism; or, The Way to the New Jerusalem as Set Forth in Pulpit and Press from Thomas Cartwright to John Lilburne and John Milton, 1570–1643* (1938; reprint, New York: Harper and Brothers, 1957), 65.

94. Thomas Fuller, *The Holy State* (Cambridge, 1642), 90; see also Michael Jinkins, "William Perkins," in *Oxford Dictionary of National Biography*, online at http://www.oxforddnb.com.

95. William Perkins, *A Golden Chaine; or, The Description of Theologie Containing the Order of the Causes of Salvation and Damnation, According to Gods Woord: A View of the Order Whereof, Is to Be Seene in the Table Annexed* (London, 1591), originally published in Latin as *Armilla Aurea* (1590).

96. On Perkins's table and its relationship to Beza's, see Richard A. Muller, "Perkins' *A Golden Chaine*: Predestinarian System or Schematized *Ordo Salutis?*" *Sixteenth Century Journal* 9 (1978): 68–81. On Beza, see John S. Bray, *Theodore Beza's Doctrine of Predestination* (Nieuwkoop, Netherlands: de Graaf, 1975); and Richard A. Muller, "The Use and Abuse of a Document: Beza's *Tabula Praedestinationis*, the Bolsec Controversy, and the Origins of Reformed Orthodoxy," in *Protestant Scholasticism: Essays in Reassessment*, ed. Carl R. Trueman and R. Scott Clark (Carlisle, England: Paternoster, 1999), 33–61.

97. The distinction between supralapsarian (or "prelapsarian") and infralapsarian (or "sublapsarian") has occasioned a great deal of confusion, partly because of anachronistic attempts to classify earlier thinkers, such as Calvin, by using these later Protestant scholastic categories. Though supralapsarianism is often equated with "double" predestination and infralapsarianism with "single" predestination, these are separate issues. The double-single distinction arose from the question of whether God actively decreed reprobation in the same way he decreed election, while the infra-supra distinction concerned how predestination fit into the logical order of God's decrees. It is therefore possible to speak, for example, of predestination that is both double and infralapsarian, meaning that from out of the mass of fallen humanity, God actively decreed the election of some and the reprobation of others. Infralapsarianism can also be single, meaning that God decreed to elect some and merely passed over others, leaving them to reap the consequences of their sinfulness. Calvin may thus be identified anachronistically as double/infra in his view (at least judging from some of his language), whereas the Second Helvetic Confession (1566), to take another example, is single/infra. See Richard A. Muller, *After Calvin: Studies in the Development of a Theological Tradition* (New York: Oxford University Press, 2003), 11–12; though see his qualification about Calvin's occasional "supralapsarian accents" in Richard A. Muller, *Post-Reformation Reformed Dogmatics: The Rise and Development of Reformed Orthodoxy, ca. 1520 to ca. 1725*, vol. 1, *Prolegomena to Theology*, 2nd ed. (Grand Rapids, Mich.: Baker Academic, 2003), 127. For a source identifying Calvin as a supralapsarian, see William Stacy Johnson and John H. Leith, eds., *Reformed Reader: A Sourcebook in Christian Theology*, vol. 1, *Classical Beginnings, 1519–1799* (Louisville, Ky.: Westminster John Knox, 1993), 107–8. Johnson and Leith, like Muller, nevertheless stress that Calvin did not explicitly identify a particular order of the decrees. This development came with later scholastic figures, such as Perkins and his successors.

98. Thomas J. Davis makes this point about unintended consequences in reference to Beza's earlier table. See his "Hardened Hearts and Hardened Words: Calvin, Beza, and the Trajectory of Signification," in Davis, *This Is My Body:*

The Presence of Christ in Reformation Thought (Grand Rapids, Mich.: Baker Academic, 2008), 169–96.

99. Richard A. Muller, *Christ and the Decree: Christology and Predestination in Reformed Theology from Calvin to Perkins* (1986; reprint, Grand Rapids, Mich.: Baker, 1988), 164–65, 172. Calvin stated his view against mere "permission" in *Institutes*, III.23.8. Perkins explained that God willed sin insofar as he determined by his "wonderfull wisedome from thence to draw foorth that which is good." But God neither willed nor approved "sinne in it selfe in regard of the creatures that offend." God willed sin in itself "not simplie" but "only by willing to permit that it may be." William Perkins, *A Christian and Plaine Treatise of the Manner and Order of Predestination and of the Largenes of Gods Grace* (London, 1606), 52 (hereafter *Manner and Order*); originally published as *De Praedestinationis Modo et Ordine* (1598).

100. Perkins, *Manner and Order*, 6–31; Muller, *Christ and the Decree*, 164–73.

101. Puritanism's heretofore neglected roots in Protestant orthodoxy are discussed in Theodore Dwight Bozeman, "Forum: Neglected Resources in Scholarship," *Religion and American Culture* 7 (1997): 14–20.

102. On Perkins and God's simplicity, see Muller, *Christ and the Decree*, 164. Muller has vigorously denied the charge, often repeated in historical literature, that the Protestant orthodox made predestination the controlling principle of their systems. See Richard A. Muller, "The Myth of 'Decretal Theology,'" *Calvin Theological Journal* 30 (1995): 159–67; and Muller, *After Calvin*, 63–72.

103. Published posthumously as *Examen modestum libelli quem D. Gulielmus Perkinsius* (Leiden, 1612), with an English edition in vol. 3 of *The Works of James Arminius*, trans. James Nichols and William Nichols (1825–1875; reprint, Grand Rapids, Mich.: Baker, 1986).

104. The standard biography is Carl Bangs, *Arminius: A Study in the Dutch Reformation* (Nashville: Abingdon, 1971); see 231–39 on Arminius's appointment at Leiden and Gomarus's opposition.

105. Arminius, *Works*, 1:619, 623–25, 631–32.

106. Ibid., 1:653–54. For an explication of Arminius's scheme, see Bangs, *Arminius*, 350–55.

107. Augustine also spoke (against the Pelagians) of the necessity of "prevenient grace," a concept he drew from Psalm 59:10 (KJV: "The God of my mercy shall prevent me"—*prevent* here meaning "go before," as in *prevenient*). But for Augustine and later Calvinists, this first gift of grace was given only to the elect and would be followed inevitably by conversion and the grace necessary to persevere to the end. See G. W. H. Lampe, "Christian Theology in the Patristic Period," in *A History of Christian Doctrine*, ed. Hubert Cunliffe-Jones (London: Clark, 1978), 166–67; and J. N. D. Kelly, *Early Christian Doctrines*, rev. ed. (San Francisco: Harper and Row, 1978), 366–69.

108. Arminius, *Works*, 1:659–60; "freed will" from Roger E. Olson, *Arminian Theology: Myths and Realities* (Downers Grove, Ill.: InterVarsity, 2006), 142; see also 33–36, 141–46.

109. The Molinist view departed from the earlier insistence of Aquinas that no future event could be the cause of something in God. See Richard A. Muller, *God, Creation, and Providence in the Thought of Jacob Arminius: Sources and Directions of Scholastic Protestantism in the Era of Early Orthodoxy* (Grand Rapids, Mich.: Baker, 1991), 159–62. Muller makes a case for a Molinist influence on Arminius (see esp. 161–66), a perspective endorsed by Eef Dekker, "Was Arminius a Molinist?" *Sixteenth Century Journal* 27 (1996): 337–52. For a counterargument, see Olson, *Arminian Theology*, 195–97, who follows William Gene Witt ("Creation,

Redemption, and Grace in the Theology of Jacob Arminius," Ph.D. diss., University of Notre Dame, 1993) in suggesting that Arminius would have found the Molinist account of human freedom too restrictive.

110. The Reformed orthodox specifically denied Arminius's way of distinguishing between the *antecedent* and *consequent* wills of God. As Muller explains, for Arminius, "[a]ntecedently God wills that all mankind be saved on condition of belief, but in his consequent will he responds to the foreknown acts of men, thereby resting salvation on human choice" (*Christ and the Decree*, 169); cf. Richard A. Muller, *Dictionary of Latin and Greek Theological Terms Drawn Principally from Protestant Scholastic Theology* (Grand Rapids, Mich.: Baker, 1985), s.v. "voluntas Dei," 332.

111. Philip Benedict, *Christ's Churches Purely Reformed: A Social History of Calvinism* (New Haven, Conn.: Yale University Press, 2002), 305–13, quotation on 309.

112. English translation of the canons in Jaroslav Pelikan and Valerie Hotchkiss, eds., *Creeds and Confessions of Faith in the Christian Tradition*, vol. 2, pt. 4: *Creeds and Confessions of the Reformation Era* (New Haven, Conn.: Yale University Press, 2003), 569–600.

113. Two historians have been at the center of this debate. Nicholas Tyacke, *Anti-Calvinists: The Rise of English Arminianism, c. 1590–1640*, rev. ed. (Oxford: Clarendon, Oxford University Press, 1990), has argued that a Calvinist consensus existed prior to the 1590s and that "Anglicanism" (as a coherent *-ism*) was essentially a nineteenth-century creation. Peter White, *Predestination, Policy and Polemic: Conflict and Consensus in the English Church from the Reformation to the Civil War* (Cambridge: Cambridge University Press, 1992), has insisted that from the Reformation to the Civil War, the English church consisted of a broad spectrum of views held together by the Anglican ideal of a *via media* (middle way) between extremes. Tyacke and White's debate predates their respective books. See Nicholas Tyacke, "The Rise of Arminianism Reconsidered," and Peter White, "Rejoinder," both in *Past and Present*, no. 115 (May 1987): 201–29. See also the effort to sort out the issues by P. G. Lake, "Calvinism and the English Church 1570–1635," *Past and Present*, no. 114 (Feb. 1987): 32–76.

114. Quoted in Lake, *Moderate Puritans*, 228. For the text of the Lambeth Articles, see Bray, ed., *Documents*, 399–400. The Cambridge events of the 1590s are central to the historiographical debate about "Anglicanism" (as a coherent construct) during this period. See the accounts of H. C. Porter, *Reformation and Reaction in Tudor Cambridge* (Cambridge: Cambridge University Press, 1958), 344–90; Lake, *Moderate Puritans*, 201–42; Tyacke, *Anti-Calvinists*, 29–36; and White, *Predestination, Policy and Polemic*, 101–23.

115. Quoted in White, *Predestination, Policy and Polemic*, 146.

116. James I quoted in Wallace, *Puritans and Predestination*, 80. On the Vorstius affair as well as the English involvement at Dort, see Tyacke, *Anti-Calvinists*, 87–105; and White, *Predestination, Policy and Polemic*, 159–62, 175–202. White (esp. pp. 161–62) casts doubt on the assumption that James opposed Vorstius chiefly because of the professor's Arminianism. This caveat notwithstanding, James's public posturing against Arminianism is beyond dispute; Arminius himself was, in the king's words, "an enemie of God" and the "first in our age that infected Leiden with heresie" (Tyacke, *Anti-Calvinists*, 88).

117. Tyacke, *Anti-Calvinists*, 104–5. On the Thirty Years' War and the religious mood during the Caroline regime, see Francis J. Bremer, *The Puritan Experiment: New England Society from Bradford to Edwards*, rev. ed. (Hanover, N.H.: University Press of New England, 1995), 37–38.

118. James I quoted in Stephen Foster, *The Long Argument: English Puritanism and the Shaping of New England Culture, 1570–1700* (Chapel Hill: University of North Carolina Press, 1991), 128; cf. 133 on the inherent relationship between predestination and preaching. On English versus Dutch Arminianism, see Wallace, *Puritans and Predestination*, 98–99, and 70–76 on the antecedents of English Arminianism in the gradual emergence of a distinctively Anglican theology of grace (typified by Andrewes, Richard Hooker, and others) during the last years of Elizabeth's reign. See also Wallace's article "Arminianism," in *Puritans and Puritanism in Europe and America: A Comprehensive Encyclopedia*, ed. Francis J. Bremer and Tom Webster, 2 vols. (Santa Barbara, Calif.: ABC-CLIO, 2006), 2:312–13. On the fear that predestination undermined the sacraments, see Anthony Milton, *Catholic and Reformed: The Roman and Protestant Churches in English Protestant Thought, 1600–1640* (Cambridge: Cambridge University Press, 1995), 437–38, 521, 544. On Andrewes's agnostic leanings on predestination, see White, *Predestination, Policy and Polemic*, 118.

119. Tyacke, *Anti-Calvinists*, 246; cf. Wallace, *Puritans and Predestination*, 83. Charles's relationship to Arminianism as a theology remains a subject of scholarly debate. White (*Predestination, Policy and Polemic*, 238–55) questions the extent of pro-Arminian sentiment in the Caroline court. Similarly, Julian Davies, *The Caroline Captivity of the Church: Charles I and the Remoulding of Anglicanism, 1625–1641* (Oxford: Clarendon, Oxford University Press, 1992), has questioned the accuracy of labeling Charles's ideology Arminian, at least in a doctrinal sense. While these objections merit consideration, I have followed Tyacke and Wallace's use of the term *Arminian* (see Tyacke's comments in *Anti-Calvinists*, 245), partly for the sake of verbal convenience, but also for continuity with the later, post-Restoration portion of my narrative, when "Arminian" and "Anglican" were widely equated both in England and in New England.

120. Quoted in Nicholas Tyacke, *Aspects of English Protestantism, c. 1530–1700* (Manchester, England: Manchester University Press, 2001), 215 (on Calvinism), 142 (on the Eucharist).

Chapter 2

1. Robert Middlekauff, *The Mathers: Three Generations of Puritan Intellectuals, 1596–1728*, rev. ed. (Berkeley: University of California Press, 1999), 95.

2. Description of Mather and Boston based on details from Michael G. Hall, *The Last American Puritan: The Life of Increase Mather, 1639–1723* (Middletown, Conn.: Wesleyan University Press, 1988), 35, 326–38, 350–51.

3. Increase Mather, *Awakening Soul-Saving Truths, Plainly Delivered, in Several Sermons* (Boston, 1720), 68–70, 75–76, 84–87, 95, 97–99.

4. Thomas Shepard, *The Sincere Convert, Discovering the Paucity of True Believers and the Great Difficulty of Saving Conversion* (London, 1640), 94, 121, 124–25, 264. This oft-reprinted tract, published from a listener's notes, was first delivered as a sermon in Essex in 1629. See Michael P. Winship, *Making Heretics: Militant Protestantism and Free Grace in Massachusetts, 1636–1641* (Princeton, N.J.: Princeton University Press, 2002), 12; and Thomas Werge, *Thomas Shepard* (Boston: Twayne, Hall, 1987), 50–51. (The tract's initial publication is usually listed as 1641, but at least one edition lists the date of 1640.)

5. When non-English editions are included, at least 32 have appeared down to the present (Winship, *Making Heretics*, 248n3). The work is still in print with Soli Deo Gloria, an imprint of Ligonier Ministries.

6. Jasper Ridley, *John Knox* (New York: Oxford University Press, 1968), 215.

7. Cotton Mather, *Magnalia Christi Americana; or, The Ecclesiastical History of New-England, from Its First Planting in the Year 1620, unto the Year of our Lord, 1698* (London, 1702), 1.

8. On the New England innovation of a conversion relation as a test of membership, see Edmund S. Morgan, *Visible Saints: The History of a Puritan Idea* (Ithaca, N.Y.: Cornell University Press, 1963), 87–105; and the overview in Elizabeth Reis, "Seventeenth-Century Puritan Conversion Narratives," in *Religions of the United States in Practice*, ed. Colleen McDannell, 2 vols. (Princeton, N.J.: Princeton University Press, 2001), 1:22–26.

9. Thomas Prince, *Annals of New-England, Vol. II, Numb. 2* (Boston, 1755), 46–47. Shepard also mentioned the encounter in his autobiography; see Michael McGiffert, ed., *God's Plot: Puritan Spirituality in Thomas Shepard's Cambridge*, rev. ed. (Amherst: University of Massachusetts Press, 1994), 50–51.

10. Quoted in Michael P. Winship, "Were There Any Puritans in New England?" *New England Quarterly* 74 (2001): 124.

11. Ibid., 125–26.

12. Historians who note Dort's de facto official status include David D. Hall, "On Common Ground: The Coherence of American Puritan Studies," *William and Mary Quarterly*, 3rd ser., 14 (1987): 199; and E. Brooks Holifield, *Theology in America: Christian Thought from the Age of the Puritans to the Civil War* (New Haven, Conn.: Yale University Press, 2003), 38.

13. William Ames, *An Analyticall Exposition of Both the Epistles of the Apostle Peter* (London, 1641), A2r.

14. "Hammer away" verse quoted in Augustus Hopkins Strong, *Systematic Theology*, vol. 3, *The Doctrine of Salvation* (Philadelphia: Griffith and Rowland, 1909), 1054. Beza's related phrase from Philip Schaff, *History of the Christian Church*, vol. 8, *Modern Christianity: The Swiss Reformation* (1910; reprint, Grand Rapids, Mich.: Eerdmans, 1994), 859; cf. the comment in Horton Davies, *The Worship of the American Puritans, 1629–1730* (New York: Peter Lang, 1990), 26. Quotation from Canons of Dort in Jaroslav Pelikan and Valerie Hotchkiss, eds., *Creeds and Confessions of Faith in the Christian Tradition*, vol. 2, pt. 4: *Creeds and Confessions of the Reformation Era* (New Haven, Conn.: Yale University Press, 2003), 593.

15. Shepard quoted in Bremer, *Puritan Experiment*, 124. On the drafting of the Westminster Confession, see John H. Leith, *Assembly at Westminster: Reformed Theology in the Making* (Richmond, Va.: John Knox, 1973). The New England modifications of the confession appeared in the Cambridge Platform (1648); see Williston Walker, *The Creeds and Platforms of Congregationalism* (New York: Scribner's, 1893), 189–237. On the English Civil Wars, see the various books by Christopher Hill, including *God's Englishman: Oliver Cromwell and the English Revolution* (New York: Harper and Row, 1972).

16. For the five points in the Westminster Confession, see Loraine Boettner, *The Reformed Doctrine of Predestination*, 7th ed. (Grand Rapids, Mich.: Eerdmans, 1951), 61, 84, 150–51, 162, 182. For the quoted passages from the confession itself, see Pelikan and Hotchkiss, eds., *Creeds and Confessions*, 2:610–11, 619, 627.

17. Gerald J. Goodwin, "The Myth of 'Arminian-Calvinism' in Eighteenth-Century New England," *New England Quarterly* 41 (1968): 213–37; Mather quoted on 225.

18. William Perkins, *A Christian and Plaine Treatise of the Manner and Order of Predestination and of the Largenes of Gods Grace* (London, 1606), 33–35; quotation from Aquinas on 35: "Why hee electeth these unto glorie, and rejecteth those, he hath no reason but the divine will." Cf. the modern translation: "Why

does he choose some to glory while others he rejects? His so willing is the sole ground." *Summa Theologiae,* I.23.5, in the Blackfriars edition, vol. 5, *God's Will and Providence (Ia. 19–26),* trans. Thomas Gilby (London: Eyre and Spottiswoode, 1967), 129.

19. Scottish delegate Robert Baillie quoted in Leith, *Assembly at Westminster,* 51; see also William Barker, *Puritan Profiles: 54 Influential Puritans at the Time when the Westminster Confession of Faith Was Written* (Fearn, Scotland: Mentor, 1996), 18–21.

20. For a challenge to the conventional view of the Westminster Confession as infralapsarian, see Guy M. Richard, "Samuel Rutherford's Supralapsarianism Revealed: A Key to the Lapsarian Position of the Westminster Confession of Faith?" *Scottish Journal of Theology* 59 (2006): 27–44; cf. David A. S. Fergusson, "Predestination: A Scottish Perspective," *Scottish Journal of Theology* 46 (1993): 457–78, esp. 465.

21. William Twisse, *A Treatise of Mr. Cottons, Clearing Certaine Doubts Concerning Predestination, Together with an Examination Thereof* (London, 1646). Cotton's treatise survives only in Twisse's partial quotations of it; cf. Sargent Bush, Jr., ed., *The Correspondence of John Cotton* (Chapel Hill: University of North Carolina Press, 2001), 109–12.

22. David Como, "Puritans, Predestination, and the Construction of Orthodoxy in Early Seventeenth-Century England," in *Conformity and Orthodoxy in the English Church, c. 1560–1660,* ed. Peter Lake and Michael Questier (Woodbridge, England: Boydell, 2000), 79; see also Winship, *Making Heretics,* 30–32.

23. Brian G. Armstrong, *Calvinism and the Amyraut Heresy: Protestant Scholasticism and Humanism in Seventeenth-Century France* (Madison: University of Wisconsin Press, 1969), 169–70. Amyraut's was not the only version of hypothetical universalism. The English Puritan divine John Preston (1587–1628) held a similar view but developed its logic in different ways; see Jonathan D. Moore, *English Hypothetical Universalism: John Preston and the Softening of Reformed Theology* (Grand Rapids, Mich.: Eerdmans, 2007), esp. 217–29.

24. Twisse, *Treatise of Mr. Cottons,* 30.

25. Francis Turretin, *Institutes of Elenctic Theology,* trans. George Musgrave Giger and ed. James T. Dennison, Jr., 3 vols. (Phillipsburg, N.J.: P&R, 1992), 1:348. Karl Barth repeated the same dictum—*Quod ultimum est in executione, primum est in intentione*—in explaining the logic of supralapsarianism; see his *Church Dogmatics,* vol. 2, pt. 2, *The Doctrine of God,* trans. G. W. Bromiley et al. (Edinburgh: Clark, 1957), 128.

26. Turretin, *Institutes,* 1:343, 418, 428.

27. "Miscellanies," no. 704, in *The Works of Jonathan Edwards,* vol. 18, *The "Miscellanies," 501–832,* ed. Ava Chamberlain (New Haven, Conn.: Yale University Press, 2000), 317–18; cf. his citation of Turretin in "Miscellanies," no. 292, in *The Works of Jonathan Edwards,* vol. 13, *The "Miscellanies," a–500,* ed. Thomas A. Schafer (New Haven, Conn.: Yale University Press, 1994), 384.

28. Samuel Willard, *A Compleat Body of Divinity in Two Hundred and Fifty Expository Lectures on the Assembly's Shorter Catechism* (Boston, 1726), 262–64. On Willard's supralapsarianism, see Seymour Van Dyken, *Samuel Willard, 1640–1707: Preacher of Orthodoxy in an Era of Change* (Grand Rapids, Mich.: Eerdmans, 1972), 108–9.

29. Turretin, *Institutes,* 351.

30. Willard, *Compleat Body of Divinity,* 262. Elsewhere, Willard explained that although the glorification of God's own mercy and justice is the great end of predestination, election and reprobation are not acts of mercy and justice, properly

speaking, since "Election is no act of rewarding men's goodness, nor Reprobation of punishing men's sinfulness" (260).

31. Turretin, *Institutes*, 356.

32. William Twisse, *The Riches of Gods Love unto the Vessells of Mercy, Consistent with His Absolute Hatred or Reprobation of the Vessells of Wrath,* 2 vols. in 1 (Oxford, 1653), 1:6, quoting from *Summa*, I.23.5; Twisse invoked the same passage in *A Treatise of Mr. Cottons*, 46. See Turretin, *Institutes*, 351, citing *Summa* III.24.4. The significant overlap between Protestant and Catholic scholasticism on predestination is explored in Seán F. Hughes, " 'The Problem of "Calvinism" ': English Theologies of Predestination c. 1580–1630," in *Belief and Practice in Reformation England: A Tribute to Patrick Collinson from His Students,* ed. Susan Wabuda and Caroline Litzenberger (Aldershot, England: Ashgate, 1998), 229–49. Cf. Anthony Milton, who notes that Puritans were more apt to criticize Catholic doctrines of justification than of predestination; Milton, *Catholic and Reformed: The Roman and Protestant Churches in English Protestant Thought, 1600–1640* (Cambridge: Cambridge University Press, 1995), 210–11.

33. Stephen Charnock, *Several Discourses upon the Existence and Attributes of God* (London, 1682), 711–12 (cf. 718 on Rom. 9:15 in particular); Twisse, *Riches of Gods Love*, 2:145; Willard, *Compleat Body of Divinity*, 266.

34. David A. Weir, *The Origins of the Federal Theology in Sixteenth-Century Reformation Thought* (Oxford: Clarendon, Oxford University Press, 1990), 3–5. See ch. 7 ("Of God's Covenant with Man") of the Westminster Confession in Pelikan and Hotchkiss, eds., *Creeds and Confessions*, 2:615.

35. Norman Pettit, *The Heart Prepared: Grace and Conversion in Puritan Spiritual Life*, rev. ed. (Middletown, Conn.: Wesleyan University Press, 1989), 219. On the covenant of grace as both conditional and absolute, see John von Rohr, *The Covenant of Grace in Puritan Thought* (Atlanta: Scholars, 1986), 15–17; cf. Holifield, *Theology in America*, 40–41; and Hall, "On Common Ground," 209 (who refers to the Reformed tradition as "persistently dialectical"). The Puritan notion of conditionality, it should be noted, was not the same as the Arminian version. Puritans believed that the elect's inclusion in the covenant of grace was absolute and irresistible; Arminians insisted that grace could be resisted. See Roger E. Olson, *Arminian Theology: Myths and Realities* (Downers Grove, Ill.: InterVarsity, 2006), 53–54; cf. Perry Miller, *The New England Mind: The Seventeenth Century* (Cambridge, Mass.: Belknap, Harvard University Press, 1939), 387.

36. Thomas Hooker, *The Soules Vocation or Effectual Calling to Christ* (London, 1638), 40–41.

37. Von Rohr, *Covenant of Grace*, 130.

38. Mary Rhinelander McCarl, "Thomas Shepard's Record of Relations of Religious Experience, 1648–1649," *William and Mary Quarterly*, 3rd ser., 48 (1991): 443n59.

39. Ibid., 442.

40. John Milton, *The Christian Doctrine (De Doctrina Christiana)*, in *The Works of John Milton*, vol. 14, ed. Frank Allen Patterson (New York: Columbia University Press, 1933), 143. For comments on this text, see William Riley Parker, *Milton: A Biography*, rev. ed., ed. Gordon Campbell (Oxford: Clarendon, Oxford University Press, 1996), 480–83.

41. Kai T. Erikson, *Wayward Puritans: A Study in the Sociology of Deviance* (New York: Wiley, 1966), 191.

42. Perry Miller, "The Marrow of Puritan Divinity," in his *Errand into the Wilderness* (Cambridge, Mass.: Belknap, Harvard University Press, 1956), 73–74; and on Twisse, see Miller, *New England Mind*, 405.

43. Those who point out continuities between the sixteenth and seventeenth centuries include Goodwin, "Myth of 'Arminian-Calvinism,'" 216; George M. Marsden, "Perry Miller's Rehabilitation of the Puritans: A Critique," *Church History* 39 (1970): 96–98; and David D. Hall, "Understanding the Puritans," in *The State of American History*, ed. Herbert J. Bass (Chicago: Quadrangle, 1970), 333. On Miller's neglect of the biblical roots, see Marsden, "Perry Miller's Rehabilitation," 99–100; Von Rohr, *Covenant of Grace*, 20; and John S. Coolidge, *The Pauline Renaissance in England: Puritanism and the Bible* (Oxford: Clarendon, Oxford University Press, 1970), xiii, 141, 150–51. For a useful overview of the reception of Miller, see Hall, "On Common Ground." Miller's "The Marrow of Puritan Divinity" first appeared in 1935, and in *Errand into the Wilderness*, he responded to some of the essay's earlier critics: "It was never my intention to deny that in the large sweep of history there is an essential continuity between the New England theology and that of the Reformed, or as they are called, the Calvinistic churches" (49).

44. William K. B. Stoever, *"A Faire and Easie Way to Heaven": Covenant Theology and Antinomianism in Early Massachusetts* (Middletown, Conn.: Wesleyan University Press, 1978), 109–11. Stoever was commenting specifically on Miller's "The Marrow of Puritan Divinity" essay; elsewhere, Miller discusses at greater length secondary causation as a feature of Puritan thinking (*New England Mind*, 14, 224, 233–34, 288, 392). A similar notion of multiple causation allowed Thomas Aquinas to speak of humans as instrumental causes whose good works are meritorious even though they must be enabled by the grace of God as efficient cause; see Joseph P. Wawrykow, *The Westminster Handbook to Thomas Aquinas* (Louisville, Ky.: Westminster John Knox, 2005), 19–20, 92–95, 119–20.

45. Miller, *New England Mind*, 488. For his part, Miller was both unconvinced and awed by the Puritans' stark theism, which he believed could hardly be understood by "historical analysis, economic interpretation, or philosophical rephrasing" (489). For all the controversy surrounding his interpretation of the covenant, Miller's work remains unrivaled in its eloquence. See the critical reflection by James Hoopes, "Art as History: Perry Miller's *New England Mind*," *American Quarterly* 34 (1982): 3–25.

46. Max Weber, *The Protestant Ethic and the "Spirit" of Capitalism and Other Writings*, ed. and trans. Peter Baehr and Gordon C. Wells (New York: Penguin, 2002), 73–74.

47. Ibid., 77–78, 106–7, 80, 95.

48. On Weber's Protestantism, see the editors' introduction to *Protestant Ethic*, xii. On Weber and national stereotypes, see Paul Münch, "The Thesis before Weber: An Archaeology," in *Weber's Protestant Ethic: Origins, Evidence, Contexts*, ed. Hartmut Lehmann and Guenther Roth (Cambridge: Cambridge University Press, 1993), 67; on the discourse of Protestant Anglo-Saxon superiority, cf. Peter J. Thuesen, *In Discordance with the Scriptures: American Protestant Battles over Translating the Bible* (New York: Oxford University Press, 1999), 35–36.

49. David Zaret, *The Heavenly Contract: Ideology and Organization in Pre-Revolutionary Puritanism* (Chicago: University of Chicago Press, 1985), 10, 17–18. Zaret further argues (15–16) that the clerically supervised disciplines of self-examination and the like in covenant theology were a means for clergy to maintain control over their sometimes fractious flocks. For Weber's caution about one-sidedness, see *Protestant Ethic*, 122.

50. Malcolm H. MacKinnon, "Part I: Calvinism and the Infallible Assurance of Grace: The Weber Thesis Reconsidered," and "Part II: Weber's Exploration of Calvinism: The Undiscovered Provenance of Capitalism," *British Journal of Sociology*, 39 (1988): 143–210. See the sharp rebuttal to MacKinnon by David Zaret, "The Use

and Abuse of Textual Data," and the more ambivalent critique by Kaspar von Greyerz, "Biographical Evidence on Predestination, Covenant, and Special Providence," both in Lehmann and Roth, eds., *Weber's Protestant Ethic*, 245–72, 273–84. Alastair Hamilton, "Max Weber's *Protestant Ethic and the Spirit of Capitalism*," in *The Cambridge Companion to Weber*, ed. Stephen Turner (Cambridge: Cambridge University Press, 2000), 169.

51. Hamilton, "Max Weber's *Protestant Ethic*," 170.

52. Theodore Dwight Bozeman, *The Precisianist Strain: Disciplinary Religion and Antinomian Backlash in Puritanism to 1638* (Chapel Hill: University of North Carolina Press, 2004), 123, 127 ("age of anxiety"), 136, 333.

53. Aquinas (*Summa Theologiae*, I.23.7) and Bellarmine quoted in Jean Delumeau, *Sin and Fear: The Emergence of a Western Guilt Culture, 13th–18th Centuries*, trans. Eric Nicholson (New York: St. Martin's, 1990), 282–83.

54. Perkins, *Manner and Order*, 31, 33; Arthur Dent, *The Plaine Mans Path-way to Heaven: Wherein Every Man May Clearly See, Whether He Shall Be Saved or Damned* (London, 1601), 276–78. On printings of Dent, see Brett Usher, "Arthur Dent," in *Oxford Dictionary of National Biography*, http://www.oxforddnb.com. John Bunyan echoed Dent's opinion; see Christopher Hill, *A Tinker and a Poor Man: John Bunyan and His Church, 1628–1688* (New York: Knopf, 1988), 171.

55. Willard, *Compleat Body of Divinity*, 248–49.

56. Eaton, Sparrowhawk, and Haynes relations in *Thomas Shepard's Confessions*, ed. George Selement and Bruce C. Woolley (Boston: Colonial Society of Massachusetts, 1981), 55, 64, 168. On the frequency of admissions of discouragement in the relations, see Bozeman, *Precisianist Strain*, 237. See also the detailed content analysis by Patricia Caldwell, *The Puritan Conversion Narrative: The Beginnings of American Expression* (Cambridge: Cambridge University Press, 1983), who sees the New England context as a unique "pressure cooker" (140), in part because of the psychic dislocation caused by the Great Migration. On Spira, see David D. Hall, *Worlds of Wonder, Days of Judgment: Popular Religious Belief in Early New England* (Cambridge, Mass.: Harvard University Press, 1989), 132–33.

57. There is some evidence to suggest, moreover, that women were more prone to attribute their likely reprobation to their innate "vileness"—a gendered difference that was the "underside of covenant theology," according to historian Elizabeth Reis, *Damned Women: Sinners and Witches in Puritan New England* (Ithaca, N.Y.: Cornell University Press, 1997), 37–43. In examining Puritan conversion narratives, Reis found that men were more likely to focus on their specific sins rather than on their inherent depravity.

58. Miri Rubin, *Corpus Christi: The Eucharist in Late Medieval Culture* (Cambridge: Cambridge University Press, 1991), 148; cf. Delumeau, *Sin and Fear*, 506–7.

59. William Perkins, *A Golden Chaine*, in *The Whole Works of That Famous and Worthy Minister of Christ in the Universitie of Cambridge, M. William Perkins*, 3 vols. (London, 1631), 1:72; cf. E. Brooks Holifield, *The Covenant Sealed: The Development of Puritan Sacramental Theology in Old and New England, 1570–1720* (New Haven, Conn.: Yale University Press, 1974), 46.

60. Preston quoted in Holifield, *Covenant Sealed*, 51; "ambidextrous theologians," 155. On Preston and Shepard, see Werge, *Thomas Shepard*, 5–6.

61. Perkins, *Golden Chaine*, in *Works*, 1:76.

62. Hall, *Worlds of Wonder*, 157.

63. Fiske parishioner in Hall, *Worlds of Wonder*, 158; *The Diary of Michael Wigglesworth, 1653–1657: The Conscience of a Puritan*, ed. Edmund S. Morgan (New York: Harper Torchbooks, 1965), 54; Jane Turell in Hall, *Worlds of Wonder*,

158–59; Jonathan Edwards, "Self-Examination and the Lord's Supper," in *The Works of Jonathan Edwards*, vol. 17, *Sermons and Discourses, 1730–1733*, ed. Mark Valeri (New Haven, Conn.: Yale University Press, 1999), 270.

64. Eamon Duffy, *The Stripping of the Altars: Traditional Religion in England, c. 1400–c. 1580* (New Haven, Conn.: Yale University Press, 1992), 301–13; Philippe Ariès, *The Hour of Our Death*, trans. Helen Weaver (New York: Vintage, 1981), 10–13.

65. Lynn A. Botelho, "Death and Dying," in Bremer and Webster, eds., *Puritans and Puritanism*, 367–69.

66. Quoted in Delumeau, *Sin and Fear*, 513.

67. Increase Mather, *A Discourse Concerning the Uncertainty of the Times of Men, and the Necessity of Being Prepared for Sudden Changes & Death* (Boston, 1697), 13; cf. Hall, *Worlds of Wonder*, 135.

68. Richard Crowder, *No Featherbed to Heaven: A Biography of Michael Wigglesworth, 1631–1705* (East Lansing: Michigan State University Press, 1962), 120–21. Wigglesworth's health did not improve in Bermuda, leading him to conclude that God had brought him on the expensive trip to show him his vanity (124). For his confessions of lust, see Morgan, ed., *Diary of Michael Wigglesworth*, 9, 11, 31. See also Nicholas F. Radel, "A Sodom Within: Historicizing Puritan Homoerotics in the Diary of Michael Wigglesworth," in *The Puritan Origins of American Sex: Religion, Sexuality, and National Identity in American Literature*, ed. Tracy Fessenden, Nicholas F. Radel, and Magdalena J. Zaborowska (New York: Routledge, 2001), 41–55.

69. Michael Wigglesworth, *The Day of Doom; or, A Description of the Great and Last Judgment* (London, 1673), 2, 3, 4, 6–8, 13 (block quotation), 17, 18, 23–24, 32–33, 60, 61. This edition is still available in facsimile from Kessinger Publishing in Whitefish, Montana. The original 1662 Boston edition survives only in fragments.

70. Increase Mather, *A Call to the Tempted: A Sermon on the Horrid Crime of Self-Murder* (Boston, 1724), 1–2, 8, 10–11, 13–14.

71. Richard S. Dunn, James Savage, and Laetitia Yeandle, eds., *The Journal of John Winthrop, 1630–1649* (Cambridge, Mass.: Belknap, Harvard University Press, 1996), 229–30. Hett later tried to kill another of her children, for which she was whipped and imprisoned. She was excommunicated but reinstated by the church a year later (391–92, 469). See the comments on such suicidal cases in Hall, *Worlds of Wonder*, 130–31.

72. Jonathan Edwards, *A Faithful Narrative of the Surprising Work of God*, in *The Works of Jonathan Edwards*, vol. 4, *The Great Awakening*, ed. C. C. Goen (New Haven, Conn.: Yale University Press, 1972), 205; Mather, *Call to the Tempted*, 7.

73. Robert Lowell, "After the Surprising Conversions" (1946), in *Collected Poems*, ed. Frank Bidart and David Gewanter (New York: Farrar, Straus and Giroux, 2003), 61–62; cf. Edwards, *A Faithful Narrative*, 206–7. For the context of the Hawley incident, see George M. Marsden, *Jonathan Edwards: A Life* (New Haven, Conn.: Yale University Press, 2003), 163–69. On suicide more generally in colonial New England, see Howard I. Kushner, *Self-Destruction in the Promised Land: A Psychocultural Biology of American Suicide* (New Brunswick, N.J.: Rutgers University Press, 1989), 21–27; and on "melancholy," see Julius H. Rubin, *Religious Melancholy and Protestant Experience in America* (New York: Oxford University Press, 1994), 42–59.

74. Second Helvetic Confession in Pelikan and Hotchkiss, eds., *Creeds and Confessions*, 2:474–75; for context, see Cornelis P. Venema, *Heinrich Bullinger*

and the Doctrine of Predestination: Author of "the Other Reformed Tradition"? (Grand Rapids, Mich.: Baker Academic, 2002), 89–100. Bullinger's predestinarian views in relation to the wider Reformed tradition remain a subject of scholarly disagreement; see Venema's comments (29–32, 107–20) on the earlier work of J. Wayne Baker, *Heinrich Bullinger and the Covenant: The Other Reformed Tradition* (Athens: Ohio University Press, 1980). On *tentatio praedestinationis*, see Richard F. Lovelace, *The American Pietism of Cotton Mather: Origins of American Evangelicalism* (Grand Rapids, Mich.: Christian University Press, 1979), 86–89.

75. McGiffert, ed., *God's Plot*, 19. Cf. Michael Winship on the "delicate balancing act" of encouraging angst-ridden Christians while warning overly assured "carnal gospelers" (the Puritans' own term); Winship, "Weak Christians, Backsliders, and Carnal Gospelers: Assurance of Salvation and the Pastoral Origins of Puritan Practical Divinity in the 1580s," *Church History* 70 (2001): 462–81, esp. 475.

76. Bozeman, *Precisianist Strain*, 147; on the publishing boom, 129–32.

77. Ibid., 126.

78. Perkins quoted in Joel R. Beeke, *Assurance of Faith: Calvin, English Puritanism, and the Dutch Second Reformation* (New York: Peter Lang, 1991), 114.

79. Richard Baxter, *The Signs and Causes of Melancholy: With Directions Suited to the Case of Those Who Are Afflicted with It: Collected Out of the Works of Mr. Richard Baxter...by Samuel Clifford* (London, 1716), 8; Joseph Alleine, *An Alarm to Unconverted Sinners* (Boston, 1716), 20–21. Alleine's book originally appeared as *An Alarme to Unconverted Sinners* (London, 1672).

80. Dent, *Plaine Mans Path-way*, 255, 261–62. Dent's argument about the language of "Our Father" also had appeared in the Second Helvetic Confession; see Pelikan and Hotchkiss, eds., *Creeds and Confessions*, 2:475.

81. Mather and Bradstreet quoted in David D. Hall, *Puritans in the New World: A Critical Anthology* (Princeton, N.J.: Princeton University Press, 2004), 99, 138.

82. Cotton Mather, *Free-Grace, Maintained & Improved* (Boston, 1706), 36–37.

83. Benjamin Colman, *The Case of Satan's Fiery Darts in Blasphemous Suggestions and Hellish Annoyances* (Boston, 1744), 74–75; Willard, *Compleat Body of Divinity*, 270. On Perkins, see Peter Lake with Michael Questier, *The Antichrist's Lewd Hat: Protestants, Papists, and Players in Post-Reformation England* (New Haven, Conn.: Yale University Press, 2002), 264.

84. Dent, *Plaine Mans Path-way*, 259; Mather, *Free-Grace*, 13. On perseverance as the source of Puritan security, see Charles Lloyd Cohen, *God's Caress: The Psychology of Puritan Religious Experience* (New York: Oxford University Press, 1986), 116.

85. Amanda Porterfield, *Female Piety in Puritan New England: The Emergence of Religious Humanism* (New York: Oxford University Press, 1992), 62. Porterfield sees such conflicting images as in part the product of Shepard's childhood experiences with a rejecting stepmother and punishing schoolmaster, which contributed to his early emphasis on God's wrath as well as to his abiding desire both to receive and to regulate female love (55–66).

86. Allan I. Ludwig, *Graven Images: New England Stonecarving and Its Symbols, 1650–1815*, 3rd ed. (Hanover, N.H.: University Press of New England and Wesleyan University Press, 1999), 155–60.

87. Edward Taylor and Cotton Mather quoted in Richard Godbeer, *Sexual Revolution in Early America* (Baltimore: Johns Hopkins University Press, 2002), 77–78; Jonathan Edwards, "The Excellency of Christ," and "The Terms of Prayer," both in *The Works of Jonathan Edwards*, vol. 19, *Sermons and Discourses, 1734–1738*, ed. M. X. Lesser (New Haven, Conn.: Yale University Press, 2001), 780, cf. 592–93.

88. Charles E. Hambrick-Stowe, *The Practice of Piety: Puritan Devotional Disciplines in Seventeenth-Century New England* (Chapel Hill: University of North Carolina Press, 1982), 25–39.

89. McGiffert, ed., *God's Plot*, 20; Shepard quotation, 123; Dering and Perkins quoted in Peter Iver Kaufman, *Prayer, Despair, and Drama: Elizabethan Introspection* (Urbana: University of Illinois Press, 1996), 20, 58, 64–65. On Dering's sermon before the queen, see Patrick Collinson, *A Mirror of Elizabethan Puritanism: The Life and Letters of "Godly Master Dering"* (London: Dr. Williams's Trust, 1964), 16–17.

90. Kaufman, *Prayer, Despair, and Drama*, 20 (Perkins quotation), 103–43 (on *Hamlet*).

91. See these two overviews of Edwards's contributions: *The Princeton Companion to Jonathan Edwards*, ed. Sang Hyun Lee (Princeton, N.J.: Princeton University Press, 2005); and *The Cambridge Companion to Jonathan Edwards*, ed. Stephen J. Stein (Cambridge: Cambridge University Press, 2007).

92. Anne S. Brown and David D. Hall, "Family Strategies and Religious Practice: Baptism and the Lord's Supper in Early New England," in *Lived Religion in America: Toward a History of a Practice*, ed. David D. Hall (Princeton, N.J.: Princeton University Press, 1997), 62. On the Half-Way Covenant, see Robert G. Pope, *The Half-Way Covenant: Church Membership in Puritan New England* (Princeton, N.J.: Princeton University Press, 1969), 3–9; and on the idea of a "visible saint," see Morgan, *Visible Saints*, 34–35. On Stoddard, Edwards, and the communion controversy, see *The Works of Jonathan Edwards*, vol. 12, *Ecclesiastical Writings*, ed. David D. Hall (New Haven, Conn.: Yale University Press, 1994), 38–62.

93. This is a basic argument of Bozeman, *Precisianist Strain*.

94. The best study of Hutchinson and the antinomian controversy is Winship, *Making Heretics*, along with his shorter and more introductory account, *The Times and Trials of Anne Hutchinson: Puritans Divided* (Lawrence: University Press of Kansas, 2005). For primary sources, see David D. Hall, ed., *The Antinomian Controversy, 1636–1638: A Documentary History*, 2nd ed. (Durham, N.C.: Duke University Press, 1990). On the varieties of antinomian radicalism on the other side of the Atlantic, see David R. Como, *Blown by the Spirit: Puritanism and the Emergence of an Antinomian Underground in Pre-Civil-War England* (Stanford, Calif.: Stanford University Press, 2004).

95. Douglas L. Winiarski, "Souls Filled with Ravishing Transport: Heavenly Visions and the Radical Awakening in New England," *William and Mary Quarterly*, 3rd ser., 61 (2004): 3–46, and "Jonathan Edwards, Enthusiast? Radical Revivalism and the Great Awakening in the Connecticut Valley," *Church History* 74 (2005): 683–739.

96. On the Breck affair, see Hall's introduction to *Ecclesiastical Writings* in *Works of Jonathan Edwards*, 12:4–17; and Marsden, *Jonathan Edwards*, 175–82.

97. The picture of Edwards as tragic genius comes from Perry Miller, *Jonathan Edwards* (1949; reprint, Amherst: University of Massachusetts Press, 1981). H. Richard Niebuhr, "The Anachronism of Jonathan Edwards," in *Theology, History, and Culture: Major Unpublished Writings*, ed. William Stacy Johnson (New Haven, Conn.: Yale University Press, 1996), 123–33.

Chapter 3

1. Peter Bayliss, "Rock of Ages: The Story of a Well-Loved Hymn," *This England* 21 (Winter 1988): 34–37.

2. Augustus Toplady, *The Reverend Mr. Toplady's Dying Avowal of His Religious Sentiments*, 6th ed. (London, 1778), 4.

3. Arthur Pollard, "Augustus Montague Toplady," in *Oxford Dictionary of National Biography*, http://www.oxforddnb.com, calls the Burrington Combe story "very unlikely." Cf. George Lawton, *Within the Rock of Ages: The Life and Work of Augustus Montague Toplady* (Cambridge: Clarke, 1983), 163–65. Less skeptical is George M. Ella, *Augustus Montague Toplady: A Debtor to Mercy Alone* (Durham, England: Go Publications, 2000), 86–87, 169; and Thomas Wright, *Augustus M. Toplady and Contemporary Hymn Writers*, vol. 2 of *The Lives of the British Hymn Writers* (London: Farncombe and Son, 1911), 42–44. On the controversial dimensions of "Rock of Ages," see Mark A. Noll, "The Defining Role of Hymns in Early Evangelicalism," in *Wonderful Words of Life: Hymns in American Protestant History and Theology*, ed. Richard J. Mouw and Mark A. Noll (Grand Rapids, Mich.: Eerdmans, 2004), 13–15.

4. Emphasis mine; see *Hymns of the Church of Jesus Christ of Latter-day Saints*, 2nd ed. (Salt Lake City: Church of Jesus Christ of Latter-day Saints, 2002), 111.

5. The version favored by Methodists originated with Thomas Cotterill in 1815 and was revised in 1830; see John Julian, *A Dictionary of Hymnology: Setting Forth the Origin and History of Christian Hymns of All Ages and Nations*, 2 vols. (New York: Dover, 1957), 2:971; cf. *The Book of Hymns* (Nashville: United Methodist Publishing, 1966), 120.

6. Laurence Womock, *The Examination of Tilenus before the Triers; in Order to His Intended Settlement in the Office of a Publick Preacher in the Commonwealth of Utopia* (London, 1658), 84–85. See the comments on this text by Dewey D. Wallace, Jr., *Puritans and Predestination: Grace in English Protestant Theology, 1525–1695* (Chapel Hill: University of North Carolina Press, 1982), 122–23.

7. G. R. Cragg, *From Puritanism to the Age of Reason: A Study of Changes in Religious Thought within the Church of England, 1660 to 1700* (Cambridge: Cambridge University Press, 1966), 13–36.

8. Cotton Mather, *Manuductio ad Ministerium: Directions for a Candidate of the Ministry* (Boston, 1726), 98.

9. John Edwards, *Veritas Redux: Evangelical Truths Restored*, 2 vols. (London, 1707), 1:234, 237–45. Ironically, Edwards vigorously rejected as a "mere Delusion" the Catholic middle state of purgatory, where the elect endure the remaining temporal penalties for their sins; see John Edwards, *Theologia Reformata; or, Discourses on Those Graces and Duties Which Are Purely Evangelical, and Not Contained in the Moral Law* (London, 1726), 98.

10. Charles Leslie, *A View of the Times, Their Principles and Practices: In the Rehearsals*, 2nd ed., 6 vols. (London, 1750), 4:34–35, 42–43 (*Rehearsal* nos. 233–35, 9–16 August 1707); "fatal to the souls of men" quotation in Ronald N. Stromberg, *Religious Liberalism in Eighteenth-Century England* (London: Oxford University Press, 1954), 111.

11. Thomas S. Kidd, *The Protestant Interest: New England after Puritanism* (New Haven, Conn.: Yale University Press, 2004), 114–35.

12. Charles Leslie, *The Religion of Jesus Christ the Only True Religion; or, A Short and Easie Method with the Deists* (Boston, 1719).

13. John Checkley, *Choice Dialogues between a Godly Minister, and an Honest Country-Man, Concerning Election & Predestination* (Boston, 1720), 1, 8.

14. Ibid., 5; see the identical passage in Leslie, *View of the Times*, 4:29. On Checkley's thought, see John Frederick Woolverton, *Colonial Anglicanism in North America* (Detroit: Wayne State University Press, 1984), 115–22; and Jon Pahl,

Paradox Lost: Free Will and Political Liberty in American Culture, 1630–1760 (Baltimore: Johns Hopkins University Press, 1992), 63–69.

15. Henry F. May, *The Enlightenment in America* (New York: Oxford University Press, 1976), 77; cf. Woolverton, *Colonial Anglicanism*, 126–29; and Carl Bridenbaugh, *Mitre and Sceptre: Transatlantic Faiths, Ideas, Personalities, and Politics, 1689–1775* (New York: Oxford University Press, 1962), 68–69.

16. Franklin Bowditch Dexter, *Documentary History of Yale University, under the Original Charter of the Collegiate School of Connecticut, 1701–1745* (New Haven, Conn.: Yale University Press, 1916), 233.

17. Increase Mather mentioned in Samuel Sewall, *The Diary of Samuel Sewall, 1674–1729,* ed. M. Halsey Thomas (New York: Farrar, Straus, and Giroux, 1973), 2:995; on his death, see Kenneth Silverman, *The Life and Times of Cotton Mather* (New York: Harper and Row, 1984), 364–69. *Boston News-Letter* quotation from issue no. 976 (8–15 October 1722). The "apostasy" of Cutler et al. was widely blamed at the time on a trove of Arminian (many of them Anglican) books that had been given eight years earlier to the Yale College library; see Peter J. Thuesen, ed., *The Works of Jonathan Edwards,* vol. 26, *Catalogues of Books* (New Haven, Conn.: Yale University Press, 2008), 8–13.

18. On Johnson's Arminianism, see Joseph J. Ellis, *The New England Mind in Transition: Samuel Johnson of Connecticut, 1696–1772* (New Haven, Conn.: Yale University Press, 1973), 140–41.

19. Samuel Cooke, *Divine Sovereignty in the Salvation of Sinners, Consider'd and Improv'd* (Boston, 1741), 34.

20. Samuel Johnson, *A Letter from Aristocles to Authades, Concerning the Sovereignty and the Promises of God* (Boston, 1745), 3, 5, 7, 20, 22, 26.

21. Jonathan Dickinson, *A Vindication of God's Sovereign Free Grace* (Boston, 1746), 66, 68. On the Johnson-Dickinson debate, see Ellis, *New England Mind in Transition,* 127–33.

22. Woolverton, *Colonial Anglicanism,* 186.

23. The standard account of colonial fears of a resident bishop is Bridenbaugh, *Mitre and Sceptre.*

24. Quoted in Bruce E. Steiner, *Samuel Seabury, 1729–1796: A Study in the High Church Tradition* (Athens: Ohio University Press, 1971), 344; on weekly communion, 356–58. For a definition of "high church" in the peculiar context of the early American Episcopal Church, see Robert Bruce Mullin, *Episcopal Vision/ American Reality: High Church Theology and Social Thought in Evangelical America* (New Haven, Conn.: Yale University Press, 1986), xiii–xiv.

25. Steiner, *Samuel Seabury,* 123.

26. Ibid., 124 (Chandler quote). For an overview of Dana's response, see Allen C. Guelzo, *Edwards on the Will: A Century of American Theological Debate* (Middletown, Conn.: Wesleyan University Press, 1989), 155–64.

27. On the origin of the term, see W. M. Spellman, *The Latitudinarians and the Church of England, 1660–1700* (Athens: University of Georgia Press, 1993), 11.

28. On latitudinarian language, see Harry S. Stout, *The New England Soul: Preaching and Religious Culture in Colonial New England* (New York: Oxford University Press, 1986), 127–35; on latitudinarianism's American influence, see Ned C. Landsman, *From Colonials to Provincials: American Thought and Culture, 1680–1760* (Ithaca, N.Y.: Cornell University Press, 1997), 63–71.

29. Norman Fiering, "The First American Enlightenment: Tillotson, Leverett, and Philosophical Anglicanism," *New England Quarterly* 54 (1981): 343. On latitudinarianism's influence in New England, see also John Corrigan, *The Prism*

of Piety: Catholick Congregational Clergy at the Beginning of the Enlightenment (New York: Oxford University Press, 1991), esp. 9–31.

30. Gilbert Burnet, *An Exposition of the Thirty-nine Articles of the Church of England* (London, 1699), viii, 145–46, 166, 168–70.

31. Ibid., vi.

32. Robert W. Pritchard, *The Nature of Salvation: Theological Consensus in the Episcopal Church, 1801–73* (Urbana: University of Illinois Press, 1997), 44–48.

33. Martin Greig, "Heresy Hunt: Gilbert Burnet and the Convocation Controversy of 1701," *Historical Journal* 37 (1994): 569–92.

34. Cotton Mather, *A Seasonable Testimony to the Glorious Doctrines of Grace, at This Day Many Ways Undermined in the World* (Boston, 1702), 12–13.

35. John Tillotson, "Of the Eternity of Hell Torments" (1690), in *The Works of the Most Reverend Dr. John Tillotson, Lord Archbishop of Canterbury*, ed. Thomas Birch, 3 vols. (London, 1752), 1:322.

36. Norman Fiering, *Jonathan Edwards's Moral Thought and Its British Context* (Chapel Hill: University of North Carolina Press, 1981), 229.

37. Tillotson, "Eternity of Hell Torments," 2:324–25; and "The Justice of God in the Distribution of Rewards and Punishments," 2:576, both in Tillotson, *Works*.

38. Tillotson, "Eternity of Hell Torments," 2:323; "Justice of God," 2:574–75, both in Tillotson, *Works*; cf. Fiering, *Jonathan Edwards's Moral Thought*, 230.

39. John Tillotson, *Several Discourses of Death and Judgment, and a Future State* (London, 1701), 260; John Tillotson, *Sermons on Several Subjects and Occasions*, 12 vols. (London, 1742–1744), 8:3564–65.

40. Jonathan Edwards, "The Eternity of Hell Torments," in *Sermons on the Following Subjects* (Hartford, Conn., 1780), 172; cf. Fiering, *Jonathan Edwards's Moral Thought*, 230–31. Jonathan Edwards, "Miscellanies," no. 557, in *The Works of Jonathan Edwards*, vol. 18, *The "Miscellanies," 501–832*, ed. Ava Chamberlain (New Haven, Conn.: Yale University Press, 2000), 101 (cf. no. 574, p. 113).

41. Edwards, "Eternity of Hell Torments," 187–89.

42. Fiering, *Jonathan Edwards's Moral Thought*, 206.

43. Jonathan Edwards, "Sinners in the Hands of an Angry God," in *The Works of Jonathan Edwards*, vol. 22, *Sermons and Discourses, 1739–1742*, ed. Harry S. Stout and Nathan O. Hatch, with Kyle P. Farley (New Haven, Conn.: Yale University Press, 2003), 409, 411.

44. William Whiston, *The Eternity of Hell Torments Considered* (1740), quoted in D. P. Walker, *The Decline of Hell: Seventeenth-Century Discussions of Eternal Torment* (Chicago: University of Chicago Press, 1964), 99. On Edwards's response to Whiston, see Fiering, *Jonathan Edwards's Moral Thought*, 238–39.

45. Walker, *Decline of Hell*, 84. On Socinianism, see Klaus Scholder, *The Birth of Modern Critical Theology: Origins and Problems of Biblical Criticism in the Seventeenth Century*, trans. John Bowden (London: SCM, 1990), 26–45.

46. Edwards, "Eternity of Hell Torments," 192–93.

47. Alexander Pope, *An Essay on Criticism* (1711), in *Pastoral Poetry and an Essay on Criticism*, ed. E. Audra and Aubrey Williams, in *The Twickenham Edition of the Poems of Alexander Pope*, vol. 1 (New Haven, Conn.: Yale University Press, 1961), 300–302.

48. Randall C. Zachman, *Image and Word in the Theology of John Calvin* (Notre Dame, Ind.: University of Notre Dame Press, 2007), 80–91. Calvin nevertheless stressed that the full meaning of God's providential activity could not be known by the faithful until the end of time (see 80–81); cf. Ronald J. VanderMolen, "Providence as Mystery, Providence as Revelation: Puritan and

Anglican Modifications of John Calvin's Doctrine of Providence," *Church History* 47 (1978): 27–47, esp. 32–33. James Simpson has argued that early English Protestants such as William Tyndale applied a similar principle of Spirit-enabled reading to the interpretation of scripture itself. That is, for Tyndale, one needed to be among the elect to read the Bible correctly. Or, as Simpson puts it: "Lection presupposes election." James Simpson, *Burning to Read: English Fundamentalism and Its Reformation Opponents* (Cambridge, Mass.: Belknap, Harvard University Press, 2007), 106–41 (quotation on 108).

49. Michael P. Winship, *Seers of God: Puritan Providentialism in the Restoration and Early Enlightenment* (Baltimore: Johns Hopkins University Press, 1996), 13–15.

50. Alexandra Walsham, *Providence in Early Modern England* (Oxford: Oxford University Press, 1999), 17; on providence and predestinarian piety, 15–20.

51. Zachman, *Image and Word*, 85–86; John Calvin, *Institutes of the Christian Religion*, ed. John T. McNeill and trans. Ford Lewis Battles (Philadelphia: Westminster, 1960), I.16.3, p. 201. On the ironic resemblance between Calvinism and astrology, see Jon Butler, "Magic, Astrology, and the Early American Religious Heritage, 1600–1760," *American Historical Review* 84 (1979): 341–42.

52. Sprat and Tillotson quoted in Winship, *Seers of God*, 38, 48–49.

53. Jonathan I. Israel, *Radical Enlightenment: Philosophy and the Making of Modernity, 1650–1750* (Oxford: Oxford University Press, 2001), 518–19.

54. Winship, *Seers of God*, 44.

55. Kenneth Silverman, *The Life and Times of Cotton Mather* (New York: Harper and Row, 1984), 336–63.

56. *A Letter from One in the Country, to His Friend in the City: In Relation to Their Distresses Occasioned by the Doubtful and Prevailing Practice of the Inoculation of the Small-Pox* (Boston, 1721), 5.

57. Silverman, *Cotton Mather*, 350.

58. Ibid., 363.

59. William Cooper, *A Letter to a Friend in the Country, Attempting a Solution of the Scruples & Objections of a Conscientious or Religious Nature, Commonly Made against the New Way of Receiving the Small-Pox* (Boston, 1721), 7, 9; cf. the commentary on Cooper's text by Kenneth P. Minkema, "The Spiritual Meanings of Illness in Eighteenth-Century New England," in *Religions of the United States in Practice*, ed. Colleen McDannell, 2 vols. (Princeton, N.J.: Princeton University Press, 2001), 1:269–78.

60. The irony that religious people, in qualifying the scope of God's sovereignty, unwittingly made God expendable is the compelling argument of James Turner, *Without God, Without Creed: The Origins of Unbelief in America* (Baltimore: Johns Hopkins University Press, 1985). As Turner puts it: "The natural parents of modern unbelief turn out to have been the guardians of belief" (261).

61. On Franklin and lightning rods, see Edmund S. Morgan, *Benjamin Franklin* (New Haven, Conn.: Yale University Press, 2002), 11–14; on Franklin's satires of Mather, see Silverman, *Cotton Mather*, 359–60.

62. Calvin, *Institutes*, I.5.6, p. 59.

63. *Boston Evening-Post*, no. 1031 (2 June 1755): 4; no. 1032 (9 June 1755): 3.

64. "A Letter, Giving an Account of the Most Dreadful Earthquake," printed as an appendix to Thomas Prince, *An Improvement of the Doctrine of Earthquakes, Being the Works of God and Tokens of His Just Displeasure* (Boston, 1755), 15–16.

65. Thomas Prince, *Earthquakes the Works of God, and Tokens of His Just Displeasure* (Boston, 1755), 23; John Winthrop, *A Lecture on Earthquakes: Read in the Chapel of Harvard-College in Cambridge, N.E. November 26th 1755* (Boston, 1755), 36. See the comment on the Prince-Winthrop exchange in Andrew

Dickson White, *A History of the Warfare of Science with Theology*, 2 vols. (New York: Appleton, 1896), 364–66.

66. Winthrop, *Lecture on Earthquakes*, 27–28; cf. the comment on this in Conrad Wright, *The Beginnings of Unitarianism in America* (Boston: Beacon, 1955), 167–68.

67. Thomas Foxcroft, *The Earthquake, a Divine Visitation: A Sermon Preached to the Old Church in Boston, January 8, 1756* (Boston, 1756), 5, 41, 44–46.

68. *Boston Gazette, or Country Journal*, no. 34 (24 November 1755): 1.

69. Charles Chauncy, *Earthquakes a Token of the Righteous Anger of God* (Boston, 1755), 6–8; discussed in Turner, *Without God, Without Creed*, 39–40; and Wright, *Beginnings of Unitarianism*, 167–69.

70. Quoted in Charles H. Lippy, *Seasonable Revolutionary: The Mind of Charles Chauncy* (Chicago: Nelson-Hall, 1981), 113. See also Joseph Haroutunian, *Piety versus Moralism: The Passing of the New England Theology*, rev. ed. (New York: Harper Torchbooks, 1970), 134–40.

71. Wright, *Beginnings of Unitarianism*, 187, 194–96; Lippy, *Seasonable Revolutionary*, 120–21.

72. Quoted in Ava Chamberlain, "The Theology of Cruelty: A New Look at the Rise of Arminianism in Eighteenth-Century New England," *Harvard Theological Review* 85 (1992): 348–49. On Chauncy as an opponent of Edwards and other revivalists, see George Marsden, *Jonathan Edwards: A Life* (New Haven, Conn.: Yale University Press, 2003), 268–73.

73. On the Great Awakening as evangelical propaganda, see Frank Lambert, *Inventing the "Great Awakening"* (Princeton, N.J.: Princeton University Press, 1999).

74. Quoted in Charles Wallace, Jr., "Susanna Wesley"; see also Henry D. Rack, "Samuel Wesley," both in *Oxford Dictionary of National Biography*, http://www.oxforddnb.com.

75. Susanna Wesley to John Wesley, 18 August 1725, in *Susanna Wesley: The Complete Writings*, ed. Charles Wallace, Jr. (New York: Oxford University Press, 1997), 112–13.

76. For Wesley's own account of his heart's being strangely warmed, see Richard P. Heitzenrater, ed., *The Elusive Mr. Wesley*, 2nd ed. (Nashville: Abingdon, 2003), 94–99.

77. John Wesley, *Predestination Calmly Considered* (London, 1752), 9, 25, 29, 39.

78. John Wesley, *Free Grace: A Sermon Preach'd at Bristol* (Bristol, 1739), 10, 12, 23.

79. For Whitefield's own account of his conversion, see *George Whitefield's Journals* (Edinburgh: Banner of Truth Trust, 1960), 61–62, in which he also mentions the influence of a Calvinist classic, Joseph Alleine's *Alarme to Unconverted Sinners* (1672).

80. On John Wesley's recurring doubts, see Henry D. Rack, *Reasonable Enthusiast: John Wesley and the Rise of Methodism*, 3rd ed. (London: Epworth, 2002), 187, 393, 545–50. On Whitefield's lack of doubt, see Harry S. Stout, *The Divine Dramatist: George Whitefield and the Rise of Modern Evangelicalism* (Grand Rapids, Mich.: Eerdmans, 1991), 27–28. Mark Noll explains that for Wesley, assurance was of *faith*—faith that one is presently a child of God—whereas for the Reformed (such as Whitefield), assurance was of ultimate perseverance in salvation; see Noll, "John Wesley and the Doctrine of Assurance," *Bibliotheca Sacra* 132 (1975): 161–77, comment on 176.

81. William Cooper, *The Doctrine of Predestination unto Life, Explained and Vindicated* (Boston, 1740), 75. George Whitefield, *A Letter from the Reverend*

Mr. George Whitefield, to the Reverend Mr. John Wesley, in Answer to His Sermon, Entituled Free Grace (Boston, 1740), 6, 11–12, 17, 26.

82. Cooper, *Doctrine of Predestination,* 89, quoting John Sladen, "Of Particular Election," in *A Defense of Some Important Doctrines of the Gospel, in Twenty Six Sermons, Most of Which Were Preached in Lime-Street* (London, 1732).

83. Each side also tried to portray the other as the enemy of revival, even though antirevivalists hailed from both Calvinist and Arminian ranks. See Thomas S. Kidd, *The Great Awakening: The Roots of Evangelical Christianity in Colonial America* (New Haven, Conn.: Yale University Press, 2007), 124.

84. On the populist style of Methodism, see David Hempton, *Methodism: Empire of the Spirit* (New Haven, Conn.: Yale University Press, 2005), 84.

85. Charles Wesley, *Hymns on God's Everlasting Love,* in *Charles Wesley: A Reader,* ed. John R. Tyson (New York: Oxford University Press, 1989), 304–5.

86. Ibid., 307.

87. Ibid., 308, 297.

88. Ibid., 305. Unfortunately for mainline Methodism, the transition from insolence to politeness also brought a corresponding decline in energy and recruitment; see Hempton, *Methodism,* 187, 199–200, 208–9.

89. Quoted in Tyson, ed., *Charles Wesley,* 295.

90. Whitefield later claimed that John Wesley had made the comment first; see *Three Letters from the Reverend Mr. G. Whitefield* (Philadelphia, 1740), 2–3.

91. [Susanna Wesley], *Some Remarks on a Letter from the Reverend Mr. Whitefield to the Reverend Mr. Wesley, in a Letter from a Gentlewoman to Her Friend* (London, 1741), 7, 12, 16.

92. Ibid., 24–25.

93. *Boston Evening-Post,* no. 345 (15 March 1742): 1.

94. Whitefield, *Letter . . . to the Reverend Mr. John Wesley,* 6.

95. Experience Mayhew, *Grace Defended, in a Modest Plea for an Important Truth* (Boston, 1744), 194, 196–98; on his Arminian sympathies, iii–v. Guelzo, *Edwards on the Will,* 147, usefully refers to Mayhew's "quasi-Arminianism"; cf. the comment on Mayhew's views, 26.

96. John Wesley, *A Sermon on the Death of the Rev. Mr. George Whitefield* (Boston, 1771), 18, 20. On the inflammatory effect of this sermon, see Rack, *Reasonable Enthusiast,* 455.

97. *Minutes of Several Conversations between the Reverend Messieurs John and Charles Wesley, and Others* (London, 1770), 60.

98. Kenneth J. Collins, *The Scripture Way of Salvation: The Heart of John Wesley's Theology* (Nashville: Abingdon, 1997), 202–4.

99. Boyd Stanley Schlenther, "Selina Hastings," *Oxford Dictionary of National Biography,* http://www.oxforddnb.com; Rack, *Reasonable Enthusiast,* 349, 455.

100. [John Wesley], *The Doctrine of Absolute Predestination Stated and Asserted* (London, 1770), 12. On the Wesley-Toplady exchange, see Alan P. F. Sell, *The Great Debate: Calvinism, Arminianism, and Salvation* (1982; reprint, Eugene, Ore.: Wipf and Stock, 1998), 67–69.

101. Augustus Toplady, *A Letter to the Rev. Mr. John Wesley: Relative to His Pretended Abridgment of Zanchius on Predestination* (London, 1770), 5–6; and 2nd ed. (London, 1771), 20, 27; Augustus Toplady, *A Caveat against Unsound Doctrines: Being the Substance of a Sermon Preached in the Parish Church of St. Ann, Blackfryars, on Sunday, April 29, 1770* (London, 1770), 20, 23.

102. Walter Sellon, *The Church of England Vindicated from the Charge of Absolute Predestination* (London, 1771), 18. The comparison of Calvinists to

Muslims was becoming something of a staple of anti-Calvinist polemics. In his *Christian Library*, John Wesley excerpted a sermon from high-churchman Robert South (1634–1716) denouncing the "Mahometan Christians" who would interpret every misfortune as a sign of divine disfavor. Later, in attacking the views of Calvinist James Hervey, Wesley denounced the Calvinist vision of unborn souls consigned to hell: "I could sooner be a Turk, a Deist, yea an Atheist, than I could believe this." John Wesley, *A Christian Library*, vol. 43 (Bristol, 1755), 203; and *A Preservative against Unsettled Notions in Religion* (Bristol, 1758), 233.

103. [John Wesley], *The Consequence Proved* (London, 1771), 3, 10–11.

104. Augustus Toplady, *More Work for Mr. John Wesley* (London, 1772), 3, 16, 21, 103.

Chapter 4

1. Thomas Paine, *The Age of Reason: Being an Investigation of True and Fabulous Theology*, in *The Complete Writings of Thomas Paine*, 2 vols., ed. Philip S. Foner (New York: Citadel, 1969), 1:528–29, 553–55, 583.

2. Deathbed details and Bordentown story from David Freeman Hawke, *Paine* (New York: Harper and Row, 1974), 366, 397; Federalist press quotations from Craig Nelson, *Thomas Paine: Enlightenment, Revolution, and the Birth of Modern Nations* (New York: Viking, 2006), 306; Paine's "one God, and no more" statement from *Age of Reason* in Foner, ed., *Complete Writings*, 1:464.

3. Thomas Paine, "Predestination," in Foner, ed., *Complete Writings*, 2:894–97.

4. Mark A. Noll, *America's God: From Jonathan Edwards to Abraham Lincoln* (New York: Oxford University Press, 2002), 83–85.

5. Paine, *Common Sense*, in Foner, ed., *Complete Writings*, 1:10.

6. Noll, *America's God*, 84.

7. Put differently, absolute monarchism in theology and absolute monarchism in politics often did not go hand in hand. The late Alan Heimert argued that American Calvinism, particularly as manifested in the revivals of the Great Awakening, planted the seeds of revolution by uniting the colonists in the first great American mass movement. See Heimert, *Religion and the American Mind: From the Great Awakening to the Revolution* (1966; reprint, Eugene, Ore.: Wipf and Stock, 2006); and on the debate over his thesis, see Philip Goff, "Revivals and Revolution: Historiographic Turns since Alan Heimert's *Religion and the American Mind*," *Church History* 67 (1998): 695–721. Calvinism's democratizing potential was partly due to its Augustinian commitment to original sin, according to which all people are born equally depraved before God; see Rachel Wheeler, " 'Friends to Your Souls': Jonathan Edwards' Indian Pastorate and the Doctrine of Original Sin," *Church History* 72 (2003): 736–65, esp. 738–39 on the Heimert thesis.

8. On the language—and visual imagery—of liberty and freedom, see David Hackett Fischer, *Liberty and Freedom: A Visual History of America's Founding Ideas* (New York: Oxford University Press, 2005), 1–15 and passim.

9. John Locke, *Two Treatises of Government*, 2nd ed., ed. Peter Laslett (London: Cambridge University Press, 1967), 319.

10. Bernard Bailyn, *The Ideological Origins of the American Revolution* (Cambridge, Mass.: Belknap, Harvard University Press, 1967), 34.

11. On Thomson's Bible translation, see Paul C. Gutjahr, *An American Bible: A History of the Good Book in the United States, 1777–1880* (Stanford, Calif.: Stanford University Press, 1999), 93–95. On the Great Seal, see Carl J. Richard, *The Founders and the Classics: Greece, Rome, and the American Enlightenment* (Cambridge, Mass.: Harvard University Press, 1994), 195, 279n41; and on *Novus*

Ordo Seclorum and American primitivism, see Richard T. Hughes and C. Leonard Allen, *Illusions of Innocence: Protestant Primitivism in America, 1630–1875* (Chicago: University of Chicago Press, 1988), 1–2. Virgil quotation from *The Eclogues*, trans. Guy Lee (Harmondsworth, England: Penguin, 1984), 57.

12. David L. Holmes, *The Faiths of the Founding Fathers* (New York: Oxford University Press, 2006), 79–80.

13. John Toland, *Christianity Not Mysterious; or, A Treatise Shewing, That There Is Nothing in the Gospel Contrary to Reason, nor Above It* (London, 1696), 160–62. On Jefferson and human goodness and his reading of Toland and other deists, see Charles B. Sanford, *The Religious Life of Thomas Jefferson* (Charlottesville: University Press of Virginia, 1984), 19–21, 61, 85; cf., on Toland, Edwin S. Gaustad, *Sworn on the Altar of God: A Religious Biography of Thomas Jefferson* (Grand Rapids, Mich.: Eerdmans, 1996), 23–24.

14. Jefferson to Timothy Pickering, 17 February 1821, in *Jefferson's Extracts from the Gospels: "The Philosophy of Jesus" and "The Life and Morals of Jesus,"* ed. Dickinson W. Adams and Ruth W. Lester (Princeton, N.J.: Princeton University Press, 1983), 403; cf. Hughes and Allen, *Illusions of Innocence*, 18.

15. For an overview of Jefferson's biblical redactions, see Gaustad, *Sworn on the Altar of God*, 123–31; and for tables of the New Testament passages, see Sanford, *Religious Life of Thomas Jefferson*, 181–201; and Adams and Lester, eds., *Jefferson's Extracts from the Gospels*, 427–38. Quotation on Paul ("first corrupter") from Holmes, *Faiths of the Founding Fathers*, 82.

16. "Mountebanks" quotation from Jefferson to Francis Adrian Van der Kemp, 30 July 1816, in Adams and Lester, eds., *Jefferson's Extracts from the Gospels*, 375; "strait jacket": Jefferson to Thomas B. Parker, 15 May 1819, ibid., 385; "false god": Jefferson to John Adams, 11 April 1823, ibid., 410. On Jefferson and charges of atheism in the election of 1800, see Sanford, *Religious Life of Thomas Jefferson*, 1, 83; and Gaustad, *Sworn on the Altar of God*, 90–96.

17. John Adams to John Quincy Adams, 6 June 1816, quoted in James H. Hutson, ed., *The Founders on Religion: A Book of Quotations* (Princeton, N.J.: Princeton University Press, 2005), 117.

18. *The Autobiography of Benjamin Franklin*, 2nd ed., ed. Leonard W. Labaree, Ralph L. Ketcham, Helen C. Boatfield, and Helene H. Fineman (New Haven, Conn.: Yale University Press, 1964), 58, 145.

19. Franklin, *Autobiography*, 167–68, 274, 286; Kerry S. Walters, *Benjamin Franklin and His Gods* (Urbana: University of Illinois Press, 1999), 136–40; and Melvin H. Buxbaum, *Benjamin Franklin and the Zealous Presbyterians* (University Park: Pennsylvania State University Press, 1975), 93–115.

20. Benjamin Franklin, "Dialogue between Two Presbyterians" (printed in the *Pennsylvania Gazette*, 10 April 1735), in *The Papers of Benjamin Franklin*, vol. 2, *January 1, 1735, through December 31, 1744*, ed. Leonard W. Labaree, Whitfield J. Bell, Jr., Helen C. Boatfield, and Helene H. Fineman (New Haven, Conn.: Yale University Press, 1960), 32.

21. Benjamin Franklin, *A Letter to a Friend in the Country* (1735), in Labaree et al., eds., *Papers*, 2:79, 84.

22. Benjamin Franklin, *A Defense of Mr. Hemphill's Observations* (1735), in Labaree et al., eds., *Papers*, 2:114–15.

23. Daniel Walker Howe, *What Hath God Wrought: The Transformation of America, 1815–1848* (New York: Oxford University Press, 2007), 186.

24. Grant Wacker, *Religion in Nineteenth Century America* (New York: Oxford University Press, 2000), 32.

25. On populism as a key theme of the Second Great Awakening, see Nathan O. Hatch, *The Democratization of American Christianity* (New Haven, Conn.: Yale University Press, 1989), 9–11 and passim.

26. Origen connected this purification to the trial by fire in 1 Corinthians 3:12–15; see Jason M. Scarborough, "Hades," in *The Westminster Handbook to Origen*, ed. John Anthony McGuckin (Louisville, Ky.: Westminster John Knox, 2004), 119–20. The American Universalist Hosea Ballou II later invoked Origen to justify his own belief in universal salvation; see his *Ancient History of Universalism, from the Time of the Apostles to the Fifth General Council* (1829; reprint, Boston: Universalist Publishing, 1872), 69–102.

27. One example of the Universalists' relatively lower denominational profile was the Crane Theological School at Tufts University, which from its founding in 1869 struggled under the shadow of Harvard Divinity School. Crane finally closed its doors in 1968, just shy of its centennial.

28. Ballou quoted in Ann Lee Bressler, *The Universalist Movement in America, 1770–1880* (New York: Oxford University Press, 2001), 15.

29. James Relly, *Union; or, A Treatise of the Consanguinity and Affinity between Christ and His Church* (London, 1759), 39. In a response to his critics, Relly denied that he had advocated Universalism explicitly: "It is the method of salvation only, which I treat of in the doctrine of Union: and not the number of its subjects." James Relly, *Antichrist Resisted: In a Reply to a Pamphlet, Wrote by W. Mason, Intitled Antinomian Heresy Exploded* (London, 1761). On Murray's reading of Relly's book and his gradual conversion to Universalism, see Russell E. Miller, *The Larger Hope: The First Century of the Universalist Church in America, 1770–1870* (Boston: Unitarian Universalist Association, 1979), 3–10.

30. James Relly, *Epistles; or, The Great Salvation Contemplated* (London, 1776), 11.

31. Quoted in Miller, *Larger Hope*, 9.

32. Paul Siegvolck (pseudonym of Georg Klein-Nicolai), *The Everlasting Gospel, Commanded to Be Preached by Jesus Christ, Judge of the Living and Dead* (Germantown, Pa., 1753).

33. Elhanan Winchester, *Ten Letters Addressed to Mr. Paine, in Answer to His Pamphlet, Entitled The Age of Reason* (Boston, 1794). Biographical details on Winchester are from Miller, *Larger Hope*, 36–39; and David Robinson, *The Unitarians and the Universalists* (Westport, Conn.: Greenwood, 1985), 51–54, 339–40.

34. Joseph Huntington, *Calvinism Improved; or, The Gospel Illustrated as a System of Real Grace, Issuing in the Salvation of All Men* (New London, Conn., 1796), 182; cf. 80 (on Jacob and Esau) and 184 (on election's extent). See also the comments on Huntington in Bressler, *Universalist Movement*, 17–18.

35. E. Brooks Holifield, *Theology in America: Christian Thought from the Age of the Puritans to the Civil War* (New Haven, Conn.: Yale University Press, 2003), 224–26; cf. Robinson, *Unitarians and Universalists*, 52. Winchester's argument on "everlasting" punishment resembled Origen's in the third century; see Scarborough, "Hades," and Elizabeth A. Dively Lauro, "Universalism," both in McGuckin, ed., *Westminster Handbook to Origen*, 119, 213.

36. Holifield, *Theology in America*, 226–27.

37. Miller, *Larger Hope*, 111–26; Robinson, *Unitarians and Universalists*, 66–68; Bressler, *Universalist Movement*, 42–48.

38. My account of Rich relies on the retelling by Stephen A. Marini, *Radical Sects of Revolutionary New England* (Cambridge, Mass.: Harvard University Press,

1982), 72–75. On Rich's conversion of Ballou, see ibid., 85; and Miller, *Larger Hope*, 100.

39. [Susanna Wesley], *Some Remarks on a Letter from the Reverend Mr. Whitefield to the Reverend Mr. Wesley, in a Letter from a Gentlewoman to Her Friend* (London, 1741), 25.

40. Nathaniel Stacy, *Memoirs of the Life of Nathaniel Stacy, Preacher of the Gospel of Universal Grace* (Columbus, Pa., 1850), 82–83; cf. the excerpt in Ernest Cassara, ed., *Universalism in America: A Documentary History* (Boston: Beacon, 1971), 118–20.

41. Stacy, *Memoirs*, 217–18; cf. Bressler, *Universalist Movement*, 61.

42. Stacy, *Memoirs*, 217–18.

43. Wilbur Fisk, *Calvinistic Controversy: Embracing a Sermon on Predestination and Election, and Several Numbers on the Same Subject* (New York: Phillips and Hunt, 1880), 88. Previous editions of Fisk's text appeared in 1835, 1837, 1851, and 1853.

44. Wilbur Fisk, "Objections against the Doctrine of Universal Salvation," in Timothy Merritt, *A Discussion on Universal Salvation, in Three Lectures and Five Answers against That Doctrine, to which Are Added Two Discourses on the Same Subject, by Rev. Wilbur Fisk* (New York: Lane and Tippett, 1846), 321.

45. Benjamin Abbott, *Experience and Gospel Labours of the Rev. Benjamin Abbott* (1801; reprint, New York: Emory and Waugh, 1830), 6–8, 10, 12, 14–16. Abbott is widely noted in the secondary literature, e.g., Dee E. Andrews, *The Methodists and Revolutionary America, 1760–1800: The Shaping of an Evangelical Culture* (Princeton, N.J.: Princeton University Press, 2002), 91–92; Jon Butler, *Awash in a Sea of Faith: Christianizing the American People* (Cambridge, Mass.: Harvard University Press, 1990), 239–40, 249; Hatch, *Democratization*, 172, 256n95; Leigh Eric Schmidt, *Hearing Things: Religion, Illusion, and the American Enlightenment* (Cambridge, Mass.: Harvard University Press, 2000), 58; Ann Taves, *Fits, Trances, and Visions: Experiencing Religion and Explaining Experience from Wesley to James* (Princeton, N.J.: Princeton University Press, 1999), 92–95; and John H. Wigger, *Taking Heaven by Storm: Methodism and the Rise of Popular Christianity in America* (New York: Oxford University Press, 1998), 53–54.

46. Abbott, *Experience and Gospel Labours*, 17. Bellamy's widely circulated work, as Mark Valeri has noted, was designed to establish "the rational integrity and religious fidelity of Calvinism." The book's title was a deliberate swipe at *The Religion of Nature Delineated* (1722) by the liberal moral philosopher William Wollaston. See the summary of Bellamy's book in Valeri, *Law and Providence in Joseph Bellamy's New England: The Origins of the New Divinity in Revolutionary America* (New York: Oxford University Press, 1994), 49–54.

47. Abbott, *Experience and Gospel Labours*, 18–24.

48. Hatch, *Democratization*, 201–4.

49. Bangs quoted in Holifield, *Theology in America*, 257. On Bangs's career, see also James E. Kirby, Russell E. Richey, and Kenneth E. Rowe, *The Methodists* (Westport, Conn.: Greenwood, 1996), 263–65.

50. See Nathan Bangs, *An Examination of the Doctrine of Predestination, as Contained in a Sermon, Preached in Burlington, Vermont, by Daniel Haskel, Minister of the Congregation* (New York: Totten, 1817), 5, 52–54, 84–86; which was a reply to Daniel Haskel, *The Doctrine of Predestination Maintained as Scriptural, Rational, and Important* (Burlington, Vt.: Samuel Mills, 1817). On the career of Haskel (sometimes spelled "Haskell"), see William B. Sprague, *Annals of the American Pulpit* (New York: Robert Carter and Brothers, 1857), 2:526–31.

51. Bangs, *Examination*, 162. On Dwight's complex relationship to the New Divinity (and Edwards), see John R. Fitzmier, *New England's Moral Legislator: Timothy Dwight, 1752–1817* (Bloomington: Indiana University Press, 1998), esp. 116–29.

52. Publication figure from Holifield, *Theology in America*, 263. (See also his apt summary of Methodist anti-Calvinist arguments on the same page.) For a social profile of the New Divinity clergy, see Joseph A. Conforti, *Samuel Hopkins and the New Divinity Movement: Calvinism, the Congregational Ministry, and Reform in New England between the Great Awakenings* (Grand Rapids, Mich.: Christian University Press, 1981), 11–15.

53. A fine overview, with primary documents, is Douglas A. Sweeney and Allen C. Guelzo, eds., *The New England Theology: From Jonathan Edwards to Edwards Amasa Park* (Grand Rapids, Mich.: Baker Academic, 2006). Two older surveys deserve mention: the sympathetic (and wistful) account by Frank Hugh Foster, *A Genetic History of the New England Theology* (Chicago: University of Chicago Press, 1907); and the less sympathetic appraisal by Joseph Haroutunian, *Piety versus Moralism: The Passing of the New England Theology*, rev. ed. (New York: Harper Torchbooks, 1970), originally published in 1932. On the New England theology and the central problem of the human will, see Allen C. Guelzo, *Edwards on the Will: A Century of American Theological Debate* (Middletown, Conn.: Wesleyan University Press, 1989), esp. 54–139. For works on other aspects and on specific theologians of the movement, see the extensive bibliography in Sweeney and Guelzo, eds., *New England Theology*, 279–317.

54. On Park as Edwards's namesake, see Richard Salter Storrs, *Edwards Amasa Park, D.D., LL.D.: Memorial Address* (Boston: Samuel Usher, 1900), 27.

55. Paul Ramsey, ed., *The Works of Jonathan Edwards*, vol. 1, *Freedom of the Will* (New Haven, Conn.: Yale University Press, 1957), 34–47, 156–62.

56. Daniel Fiske quoted in Joseph A. Conforti, *Jonathan Edwards, Religious Tradition, and American Culture* (Chapel Hill: University of North Carolina Press, 1995), 121; for Conforti's summary of natural and moral ability, see 120–21. See also the summaries in Sweeney and Guelzo, eds., *New England Theology*, 15–16; and Holifield, *Theology in America*, 142–43.

57. My summary relies on Noll, *America's God*, 282–84; Holifield, *Theology in America*, 143–46, 349–52; Sweeney and Guelzo, eds., *New England Theology*, 70–71, 118–22, 171–86; and Bruce Kuklick, *Churchmen and Philosophers: From Jonathan Edwards to John Dewey* (New Haven, Conn.: Yale University Press, 1985), 55–59.

58. The exercisers believed that God even produced these moral exercises in infants; see Nathanael Emmons, "Man's Activity and Dependence Illustrated and Reconciled" (1842), in Sweeney and Guelzo, eds., *New England Theology*, 177–78.

59. Sweeney and Guelzo, eds., *New England Theology*, 17.

60. Park quoted in Conforti, *Jonathan Edwards*, 120.

61. Charles E. Hambrick-Stowe, *Charles G. Finney and the Spirit of American Evangelicalism* (Grand Rapids, Mich.: Eerdmans, 1996), 35. The term *Burned-Over District* gained scholarly currency from Whitney R. Cross, *The Burned-Over District: The Social and Intellectual History of Enthusiastic Religion in Western New York, 1800–1850* (Ithaca, N.Y.: Cornell University Press, 1950).

62. On Finney as an exerciser, see Allen C. Guelzo, "An Heir or a Rebel? Charles Grandison Finney and the New England Theology," *Journal of the Early Republic* 17 (1997): 72. On the significance of group prayer, see Paul E. Johnson, *A Shopkeeper's Millennium: Society and Revivals in Rochester, New York, 1815–1837* (New York: Hill and Wang, 1978), 97.

63. Guelzo, "An Heir or a Rebel?" 75, and on Finney and Taylor, 84–89. On Taylor and the fear of making God the author of sin, see Sweeney and Guelzo, eds., *New England Theology*, 195.

64. See the descriptions (and engravings) of Dow in Hatch, *Democratization*, 36–40.

65. Quoted in John H. Wigger, *Taking Heaven by Storm: Methodism and the Rise of Popular Christianity in America* (New York: Oxford University Press, 1998), 18; cf. Hatch, *Democratization*, 130.

66. This point is made by Cynthia Lynn Lyerly, *Methodism and the Southern Mind, 1770–1810* (New York: Oxford University Press, 1998), 29.

67. Hatch, *Democratization*, 36–37, 170–83; "self-appointed aristocracy": 174.

68. Fisk, *Calvinistic Controversy*, 51–53, 86–87. Fisk's remark about Calvin's honesty resembled the polemical line of the conservative "Old Calvinists," who insisted that the New England Theology had corrupted the pure predestinarianism of the Geneva Reformer. Normally, Calvin loomed as the un-American bugbear: see Thomas J. Davis, "Images of Intolerance: John Calvin in Nineteenth-Century History Textbooks," *Church History* 65 (1996): 234–48.

69. Fisk, *Calvinistic Controversy*, 25, 161, 174.

70. On the privileging of inspiration over education, see Catherine A. Brekus, *Strangers and Pilgrims: Female Preaching in America, 1740–1845* (Chapel Hill: University of North Carolina Press, 1998), 145-46, 185. Regarding women's leadership, though American Methodists were often intolerant of female preachers, local custom and occasional support from male clergy at the grassroots level allowed a number of women to become influential evangelists; see ibid., 133.

71. Richard Allen, *The Life Experience and Gospel Labors of the Rt. Rev. Richard Allen* (1833; reprint, Nashville: Abingdon, 1960), 19. See also Richard S. Newman, *Freedom's Prophet: Bishop Richard Allen, the AME Church, and the Black Founding Fathers* (New York: New York University Press, 2008), 47, 145. On Allen and the AME, see also Albert J. Raboteau, *A Fire in the Bones: Reflections on African-American Religious History* (Boston: Beacon, 1995), 72–102; and Hatch, *Democratization*, 106–10.

72. Allen, *Life Experience*, 30.

73. *The Life and Religious Experience of Jarena Lee* (1836), in *Sisters of the Spirit: Three Black Women's Autobiographies of the Nineteenth Century*, ed. William L. Andrews (Bloomington: Indiana University Press, 1986), 27–30, 34.

74. Palmer's first biographer continued what was by then a familiar polemical line, but with a feminist twist: "The iron hand of Calvinism has choked the voice of feminine witness for Christ in the churches, and tightened its deadly grip, whenever the women under its power would have proclaimed to all, the ability and willingness of Christ to save to the uttermost." Richard Wheatley, *The Life and Letters of Mrs. Phoebe Palmer* (New York: W. C. Palmer, Jr., 1876), 616.

75. On the emergence of Pentecostalism, see Grant Wacker, *Heaven Below: Early Pentecostalism and American Culture* (Cambridge, Mass.: Harvard University Press, 2001); and Donald W. Dayton, *Theological Roots of Pentecostalism* (Metuchen, N.J.: Scarecrow, 1987).

76. On Pentecostalism as a legacy of Methodism, see David Hempton, *Methodism: Empire of the Spirit* (New Haven, Conn.: Yale University Press, 2005), 208–9.

77. Calvinists and Arminians have often been at odds over which system is better suited for revival. The revival of 1857–1858, which involved Phoebe Palmer, the onetime Congregationalist Dwight L. Moody, and other actors, was an ambiguous case in point. Nineteenth-century Calvinists claimed it as their own, whereas the pioneering scholarly work of Timothy L. Smith, *Revivalism and Social*

Reform: American Protestantism on the Eve of the Civil War (Nashville: Abingdon, 1957), 92–93, portrayed Calvinism as essentially eclipsed by Arminianism by the mid-nineteenth century. Cf. the later study of William G. McLoughlin, who argued that Calvinism was "Arminianized" under Finney and his contemporaries: *Revivals, Awakenings, and Reform: An Essay on Religion and Social Change in America, 1607–1977* (Chicago: University of Chicago Press, 1978), 138. See the helpful discussion in Kathryn Teresa Long, *The Revival of 1857–58: Interpreting an American Religious Awakening* (New York: Oxford University Press, 1998), 11–25.

78. Lemuel Haynes, "Divine Decrees" (1805), in *Black Preacher to White America: The Collected Writings of Lemuel Haynes, 1774–1833*, ed. Richard Newman (Brooklyn, N.Y.: Carlson, 1990), 97. On this sermon and Haynes's New Divinity connection, see John Saillant, *Black Puritan, Black Republican: The Life and Thought of Lemuel Haynes, 1753–1833* (New York: Oxford University Press, 2003), 83–91. For a modern-day African-American Calvinist perspective invoking Haynes, see Anthony J. Carter, *On Being Black and Reformed: A New Perspective on the African-American Christian Experience* (Phillipsburg, N.J.: P&R, 2003), 76–78 (on Haynes).

79. Nathan O. Hatch, "The Puzzle of American Methodism," *Church History* 63 (1994): 178. Cf. Noll (*America's God*, 200–201), who notes that by the 1850s, the Methodists had "constructed almost as many churches as there were post offices and employed almost as many ministers as there were postal workers."

80. Percentages are from Long, *Revival of 1857–58*, 24. She and Hatch (see previous note) both cite the figures of Roger Finke and Rodney Stark, *The Churching of America, 1776–1990: Winners and Losers in Our Religious Economy* (New Brunswick, N.J.: Rutgers University Press, 1992), 55.

81. Paul K. Conkin has noted the anti-Calvinism of all four (along with Unitarian Universalists and Holiness/Pentecostal groups) in *American Originals: Homemade Varieties of Christianity* (Chapel Hill: University of North Carolina Press, 1997), 316–17. On anti-Calvinism as a widespread theme, see also Hatch, *Democratization*, 170–79.

82. In the twenty-first century, three bodies trace their roots to this movement: (1) the Christian Church (Disciples of Christ), (2) the Christian Churches/Churches of Christ, and (3) the Churches of Christ. Only the most liberal of the three, the Christian Church (Disciples of Christ), has a central denominational administration.

83. Quoted in Noll, *America's God*, 380.

84. Ironically, the Scottish philosophers' "resort to intuition" tacitly acknowledged Hume's critique of the limits of verifiable human knowledge, notes Theodore Dwight Bozeman, *Protestants in an Age of Science: The Baconian Ideal and Antebellum Religious Thought* (Chapel Hill: University of North Carolina Press, 1977), 12; cf. 4–21 for a broader summary of Scottish common sense philosophy. See also the discussions in Holifield, *Theology in America*, 174–79; and Noll, *America's God*, 233–34, 379–82.

85. Holifield, *Theology in America*, 176–77.

86. Alexander Campbell, *The Millennial Harbinger*, ser. 4, vol. 2 (Bethany, W.Va.: A. Campbell, 1852), 77.

87. Alexander Campbell, ed., *The Christian Baptist*, rev. D. S. Burnet (Cincinnati: Burnet, 1835), 254. Elsewhere, he wrote that the Bible repeatedly poses the choice of "life and death, good and evil, happiness and misery." It makes clear that "all enjoyments shall be, as respects human agency, *conditional*; and that every man, in reference to spiritual and eternal blessings, shall certainly and infallibly have his own choice." Alexander Campbell, *The Christian System, in Reference to*

the Union of Christians, and a Restoration of Primitive Christianity, as Plead in the Current Reformation, 4th ed. (1866; reprint, New York: Arno, 1969), 33.

88. Campbell, *Christian System*, 109.

89. Ibid., 6, which is a reference to the "speech of Ashdod" (Neh. 13:24), i.e., the language of the Philistines. "Bibleism" quote is in Paul M. Blowers and James O. Duke, "Calvinism," in *The Encyclopedia of the Stone-Campbell Movement*, ed. Douglas A. Foster, Paul M. Blowers, Anthony L. Dunnavant, and D. Newell Williams (Grand Rapids, Mich.: Eerdmans, 2004), 110.

90. Paul K. Conkin, *Cane Ridge: America's Pentecost* (Madison: University of Wisconsin Press, 1990).

91. John Rogers, ed., *The Biography of Eld. Barton Warren Stone, Written by Himself: With Additions and Reflections*, 5th ed. (Cincinnati: James and James, 1847), 38.

92. Rogers, ed., *Biography*, 239, 243. On Stone's secession, see D. Newell Williams, "Barton Warren Stone," in Foster et al., eds., *Encyclopedia*, 708–10. On his opposition to the Calvinistic doctrine of election, see John B. Boles, *The Great Revival, 1787–1805: The Origins of the Southern Evangelical Mind* (Lexington: University Press of Kentucky, 1972), 153–54.

93. Quoted in Hatch, *Democratization*, 228.

94. Lynn Waller, "Elias Smith," in Foster et al., eds., *Encyclopedia*, 688–89.

95. Joshua V. Himes (1805–1895), a Christian Connection minister in Boston, became the chief publicist for the Adventist tradition's founder, William Miller. James White (1821–1888), another former Connection minister, was co-founder with his wife, Ellen G. White, of the Seventh-day Adventist Church.

96. David L. Rowe, *Thunder and Trumpets: Millerites and Dissenting Religion in Upstate New York, 1800–1850* (Chico, Calif.: Scholars, 1985), 1–11.

97. Sylvester Bliss, *Memoirs of William Miller, Generally Known as a Lecturer on the Prophecies, and the Second Coming of Christ* (1853; reprint, New York: AMS, 1971), 69.

98. Wayne R. Judd, "William Miller: Disappointed Prophet," in *The Disappointed: Millerism and Millenarianism in the Nineteenth Century*, ed. Ronald L. Numbers and Jonathan M. Butler (Knoxville: University of Tennessee Press, 1993), 20–21.

99. Bliss, *Memoirs*, 74–76; Rowe, *Thunder and Trumpets*, 12; and on Miller and Baconianism, Ruth Alden Doan, *The Miller Heresy, Millennialism, and American Culture* (Philadelphia: Temple University Press, 1987), 98–99.

100. Bliss, *Memoirs*, 80, 103–4.

101. Ellen G. White, *Early Writings* (1882; reprint, Washington, D.C.: Review and Herald, 1945), 221.

102. Ellen G. White, *The Great Controversy between Christ and Satan: The Conflict of the Ages in the Christian Dispensation* (1858, 1888; reprint, Mountain View, Calif.: Pacific Press, 1950), 261–62. On the "great controversy" theme in White's writings, see Malcolm Bull and Keith Lockhart, *Seeking a Sanctuary: Seventh-day Adventism and the American Dream*, 2nd ed. (Bloomington: Indiana University Press, 2007), 24–25. Later SDA theological texts echoed White's stance on free will and criticized predestinarian interpretations of key scriptural passages: "Redemption is available to anyone—but God chooses certain persons for special assignments. Salvation was equally available to Jacob and Esau, but God chose Jacob, not Esau, to be the line through whom He would take the message of salvation to the world." *Seventh-day Adventists Believe . . .: A Biblical Exposition of 27 Fundamental Doctrines* (Washington, D.C.: General Conference of Seventh-day Adventists, 1988), 22.

103. On the Witnesses' official teaching about free will and the 144,000, see the "Beliefs" section of their Web site: http://www.watchtower.org.

104. Bull and Lockhart, *Seeking a Sanctuary*, 82.

105. Richard Rice, *The Openness of God: The Relationship of Divine Foreknowledge and Human Free Will* (Nashville: Review and Herald, 1980). Rice later collaborated with several other scholars in a key text of the open-theism perspective: Clark H. Pinnock, Richard Rice, John Sanders, William Hasker, and David Basinger, *The Openness of God: A Biblical Challenge to the Traditional Understanding of God* (Downers Grove, Ill.: InterVarsity, 1994). A spate of refutations ensued, including from Southern Baptist professor Bruce A. Ware, *Their God Is Too Small: Open Theism and the Undermining of Confidence in God* (Wheaton, Ill.: Crossway, 2003).

106. Mary Baker Eddy, *Science and Health with Key to the Scriptures* (1875; reprint, Boston: First Church of Christ, Scientist, 1994), 459.

107. Ibid., 591.

108. Ibid., 18.

109. Among the important studies are Stephen Gottschalk, *The Emergence of Christian Science in American Religious Life* (Berkeley: University of California Press, 1993); and Gillian Gill, *Mary Baker Eddy* (Reading, Mass.: Perseus, 1998).

110. Gill, *Mary Baker Eddy*, 9.

111. Mary Baker Eddy, *Retrospection and Introspection* (1891; reprint, Boston: First Church of Christ, Scientist, 1920), 13–15. Church records show that Eddy was admitted to the church at age 17, not 12, as her memoir suggests. Yet Gill (not herself a Christian Scientist) defends the basic accuracy of Eddy's recollection, which may have been conflated with memories of a revival meeting that occurred near her hometown when she was 12 (Gill, *Mary Baker Eddy*, 10–12).

112. Gottschalk, *Emergence*, 120; Stephen Gottschalk, *Rolling Away the Stone: Mary Baker Eddy's Challenge to Materialism* (Bloomington: Indiana University Press, 2006), 60; Catherine L. Albanese, *A Republic of Mind and Spirit: A Cultural History of American Metaphysical Religion* (New Haven, Conn.: Yale University Press, 2007), 284, 290.

113. Mary Baker Eddy, "The People's Idea of God, Its Effect on Health and Christianity" (1883), quoted in Gottschalk, *Rolling Away the Stone*, 52.

114. Eddy, *Science and Health*, 24.

115. Richard Lyman Bushman, *Joseph Smith: Rough Stone Rolling* (New York: Knopf, 2005), 30–41; and Bushman, *Joseph Smith and the Beginnings of Mormonism* (Urbana: University of Illinois Press, 1984), 3–6. Smith's own recollections varied regarding his age at the time of the first vision, but Bushman settles on 14 (*Rough Stone Rolling*, 570n34). On Smith's paternal grandfather Asael Smith, see Richard Lloyd Anderson, *Joseph Smith's New England Heritage: Influences of Grandfathers Solomon Mack and Asael Smith* (Salt Lake City: Deseret Book, 1971), 89–140.

116. Quoted in B. H. Roberts, ed., *History of the Church of Jesus Christ of Latter-day Saints* (Salt Lake City: Deseret News, 1902), 1:3. This passage also appears in Joseph Smith, *History* (hereafter JS-H), part of the canonical text Pearl of Great Price (often printed with the Book of Mormon); JS-H 1:8.

117. Roberts, ed., *History of the Church*, 1:4–6 (JS-H 1:13–19). On the gradual emergence of the first vision as foundational to Mormon self-identity, see Jan Shipps, *Mormonism: The Story of a New Religious Tradition* (Urbana: University of Illinois Press, 1985), 30–33.

118. Roberts, ed., *History of the Church*, 1:6 (JS-H 1:19).

119. Bushman, *Rough Stone Rolling*, 58.

120. On Mormon striving, see Richard Lyman Bushman, *Mormonism: A Very Short Introduction* (New York: Oxford University Press, 2008), 75–77. On the Weber thesis, see Douglas J. Davies, *An Introduction to Mormonism* (Cambridge: Cambridge University Press, 2003), 159–62.

121. 2 Nephi 2:14, 26. See the comment on these verses in Terryl L. Givens, *People of Paradox: A History of Mormon Culture* (New York: Oxford University Press, 2007), 8.

122. Alma 12:31. Similar statements occur in 2 Nephi 10:23, Alma 41:7, Helaman 14:30, and Moroni 7:15–16, among other verses.

123. Doctrine and Covenants 29:35 (1830), 101:78 (1833).

124. Sterling M. McMurrin, *The Theological Foundations of the Mormon Religion* and *The Philosophical Foundations of Mormon Theology* (1965 and 1959; reprinted in one vol., Salt Lake City: Signature, 2000), 77, 81.

125. The Articles of Faith were later canonized and included as part of the Pearl of Great Price.

126. Brigham Young, "Free Agency," in *Discourses of Brigham Young*, ed. John A. Widtsoe (Salt Lake City: Deseret Book, 1954), 62.

127. Alma 1:3–4, as discussed by Dan Vogel, "Anti-Universalist Rhetoric in the Book of Mormon," in *New Approaches to the Book of Mormon: Explorations in Critical Methodology*, ed. Brent Lee Metcalfe (Salt Lake City: Signature, 1993), 30–31. In highlighting this and other anachronistic mentions of nineteenth-century theological controversies in a purportedly ancient text, Vogel has drawn criticism from some who see his agenda as a naturalistic effort to debunk the Book of Mormon's supernatural origins. See Terryl L. Givens, *By the Hand of Mormon: The American Scripture that Launched a New World Religion* (New York: Oxford University Press, 2002), 166–67.

128. 2 Nephi 25:16. Campbell quoted in Dan Vogel, *Religious Seekers and the Advent of Mormonism* (Salt Lake City: Signature, 1988), 69–70.

129. Interestingly, the scribe who recorded Smith's revelation on John 6:44 was Sidney Rigdon, who, as a former Campbellite, would have been familiar with anti-predestinarianism. See *Joseph Smith's New Translation of the Bible: Original Manuscripts*, ed. Scott H. Faulring, Kent P. Jackson, and Robert J. Matthews (Provo, Utah: Religious Studies Center, Brigham Young University, 2004), 46–47, 69, 456–57. Smith's most substantive changes (including John 6:44) now appear as an appendix in the standard edition of the King James Bible published by the LDS Church in Salt Lake City. On the nature of Smith's revisions, see Philip L. Barlow, *Mormons and the Bible: The Place of the Latter-day Saints in American Religion* (New York: Oxford University Press, 1991), 46–61.

130. Robert J. Matthews, *"A Plainer Translation": Joseph Smith's Translation of the Bible: A History and Commentary* (Provo, Utah: Brigham Young University Press, 1975), 318.

131. From a letter quoted in Bushman, *Rough Stone Rolling*, 418.

132. Ibid., 198–99; cf. Doctrine and Covenants 76:43 (1832).

133. Bushman, *Rough Stone Rolling*, 533–37; quotations from Smith on 535. Snow quoted in Givens, *People of Paradox*, 89. Smith's 1844 revelation became known as the King Follett Discourse because it was delivered at a meeting following the accidental death of Elder King Follett. See a trio of articles: Donald Q. Cannon, "The King Follett Discourse: Joseph Smith's Greatest Sermon in Historical Perspective"; Stan Larson, "The King Follett Discourse: A Newly Amalgamated Text"; and Van Hale, "The Doctrinal Impact of the King Follett Discourse"—all in *Brigham Young University Studies* 18 (1978): 179–225.

134. "The Anathemas against Origen" from the Fifth Ecumenical Council (also called the Second Council of Constantinople), in *The Seven Ecumenical Councils of the Undivided Church*, ed. Henry R. Percival, in *A Select Library of Nicene and Post-Nicene Fathers of the Christian Church*, ed. Philip Schaff and Henry Wace, 2nd ser., vol. 14 (New York: Christian Literature Company, 1900), 318. Origen's doctrine is summarized in Elizabeth A. Dively Lauro, "Preexistence," in McGuckin, ed., *Westminster Handbook to Origen*, 178–79. More contemporary influences on Mormonism's doctrine of preexistence are discussed in John L. Brooke, *The Refiner's Fire: The Making of Mormon Cosmology, 1644–1844* (Cambridge: Cambridge University Press, 1994), 205–7.

135. This was the title of an article series in Campbell's *Christian Baptist*.

136. Quoted in Bushman, *Rough Stone Rolling*, 89.

137. Mark Twain, *Roughing It* (1872; reprint, New York: Harper and Brothers, 1913), 1:110–11.

138. C. P. Lyford, *The Mormon Problem: An Appeal to the American People* (New York: Philips and Hunt, 1886), 174.

139. The full quotation appears as an epigraph in Bushman, *Rough Stone Rolling*, vii.

140. Peter J. Thuesen, "The 'African Enslavement of Anglo-Saxon Minds': The Beechers as Critics of Augustine," *Church History* 72 (2003): 569–92.

141. Lyman to Catharine, 30 May 1822; Catharine to Lyman, New Year 1823; both in *The Autobiography of Lyman Beecher*, 2 vols., ed. Barbara M. Cross (Cambridge, Mass.: Harvard University Press, 1961), 1:355, 369.

142. Stephen H. Snyder, *Lyman Beecher and His Children: The Transformation of a Religious Tradition* (Brooklyn, N.Y.: Carlson, 1991), 60. On the evolution of Catharine's theological views, see Kathryn Kish Sklar, *Catharine Beecher: A Study in American Domesticity* (New York: Norton, 1973), 28–42, 244–57.

143. Catharine Beecher, *Common Sense Applied to Religion; or, The Bible and the People* (New York: Harper and Brothers, 1857), 297–300, 308–10; see also Snyder, *Lyman Beecher and His Children*, 59–64.

144. Catharine Beecher, *An Appeal to the People in Behalf of Their Rights as Authorized Interpreters of the Bible* (New York: Harper and Brothers, 1860), 4, 228–30; cf. her similar critique in *Common Sense*, 291–92. Andover Seminary biblical critic Moses Stuart made essentially the same argument about Romans 5:12–19 in an 1832 commentary; see Holifield, *Theology in America*, 350–51. Among present-day scholars, Elaine Pagels has argued that Augustine misconstrued Romans 5:12 partly because he read it in Latin rather than in the original Greek, thus misreading the last phrase as referring to Adam, "*in whom* all sinned." See Elaine Pagels, *Adam, Eve, and the Serpent* (New York: Vintage, 1988), 109. On Pagels and the continuing debate over Romans 5, see Philip L. Quinn, "Disputing the Augustinian Legacy: John Locke and Jonathan Edwards on Romans 5:12–19," in *The Augustinian Tradition*, ed. Gareth B. Matthews (Berkeley: University of California Press, 1999), 233–50.

145. Catharine Beecher, *Appeal to the People*, 380.

146. Edward Beecher, *The Conflict of the Ages; or, The Great Debate on the Moral Relations of God and Man* (Boston: Philips, Sampson, 1853), esp. 306–7, 191; and Charles Beecher, *Redeemer and Redeemed: An Investigation of the Atonement and of Eternal Judgment* (Boston: Lee and Shepard, 1864), esp. ix–x. See also Marie Caskey, *Chariot of Fire: Religion and the Beecher Family* (New Haven, Conn.: Yale University Press, 1978), 123–66, 370–73; and Snyder, *Lyman Beecher and His Children*, 67–89.

147. Quoted in Caskey, *Chariot of Fire*, 379. Catharine Beecher responded directly to Edward's book, distancing herself from his theory, in *Appeal to the People*, 15, and *Common Sense*, 305.

148. The religious complexity of Stowe's novels is ably analyzed in Charles H. Foster, *The Rungless Ladder: Harriet Beecher Stowe and New England Puritanism* (Durham, N.C.: Duke University Press, 1954); and in Caskey, *Chariot of Fire*, 169–207.

149. Harriet Beecher Stowe, *Oldtown Folks*, ed. Dorothy Berkson (New Brunswick, N.J.: Rutgers University Press, 1987), 365.

150. Harriet Beecher Stowe, *The Minister's Wooing*, ed. Susan K. Harris (New York: Penguin, 1999), 17, quoted in Joan D. Hedrick, *Harriet Beecher Stowe: A Life* (New York: Oxford University Press, 1994), 279.

151. Stowe recognized, however, that a mother's grief (as well as hope and prayers) stood behind Augustine's conversion and ordination; see the reference to St. Monica in Stowe, *Minister's Wooing*, 77.

152. Ibid., 197.

153. Stowe, *Oldtown Folks*, 265, 302–6, 385; and *Minister's Wooing*, 53–54. Prior to Harriet's conversion, Catharine had also taken refuge in the Episcopal Church—she felt that its flexible theology and open attitude toward admission to the sacraments were better suited for the religious upbringing of children—but unlike Harriet she did not give Augustine any credit as the source of Anglican sacramental piety. As she put it, the Episcopal Church, "although as strictly Augustinian in its articles as any other, has taken the lead of all others in practically renouncing that system." See Catharine Beecher, *Appeal to the People*, 321–22; on Catharine's conversion, see also John Gatta, "The Anglican Aspect of Harriet Beecher Stowe," *New England Quarterly* 73 (2000): 433; and Sklar, *Catharine Beecher*, 260.

154. Quotation about Spain from Stowe, *Oldtown Folks*, 373. See Gatta, "Anglican Aspect," 412–33; cf. Stowe's affinity for images of the Madonna, as described in John Gatta, *American Madonna: Images of the Divine Woman in Literary Culture* (New York: Oxford University Press, 1997), 53–71.

155. Stowe, *Minister's Wooing*, 197. See Augustine's prayer for his mother at the conclusion of book 9 of *Confessions*, trans. R. S. Pine-Coffin (London: Penguin, 1961), 203–5.

156. Stowe, *Minister's Wooing*, 197.

157. Lyman Beecher, *A Plea for the West*, 2nd ed. (Cincinnati: Truman and Smith, 1835), 101, 128.

Chapter 5

1. Story and quotations from L. J. King, *No Purgatory, Tract No. 9: Testimony of a Dying Catholic Girl* (Decatur, Ga.: Book and Bible House, 1951), Anti-Catholic Printed Material Collection, University of Notre Dame Archives, Notre Dame, Ind., box 5, folder 1.

2. L. J. King, *Fifty Dollars Reward: Purgatory*, undated tract, Anti-Catholic Printed Material Collection, University of Notre Dame Archives, box 5, folder 1. King eventually moved his firm, renamed the Book and Bible House, from Toledo, Ohio, to Decatur, Georgia. On his career, see Ralph Lord Roy, *Apostles of Discord: A Study of Organized Bigotry and Disruption on the Fringes of Protestantism* (Boston: Beacon, 1953), 168–69. King's self-description as the "Luther of the West" is from an advertisement for a speech he delivered in Indianapolis (also in Anti-Catholic Printed Material Collection, University of Notre Dame Archives, box 5, folder 1).

3. P. A. Seguin, *Purgatory: The Hen That Makes So Many Golden Eggs for Priests of Rome*, undated tract, Anti-Catholic Printed Material Collection, University of Notre Dame Archives, box 5, folder 9.

4. Heiko Augustinus Oberman, *The Harvest of Medieval Theology: Gabriel Biel and Late Medieval Nominalism* (Durham, N.C.: Duke University Press, 1983), 185.

5. Decree and Canons on Justification, Council of Trent, sess. 6 (1547), in *Decrees of the Ecumenical Councils*, vol. 2, *Trent to Vatican II*, ed. Norman P. Tanner (London: Sheed and Ward, 1990), 671, 676, 679–80.

6. William G. Most, *Grace, Predestination, and the Salvific Will of God: New Answers to Old Questions*, rev. ed. (Front Royal, Va.: Christendom Press, 1997), 1.

7. Thomas Aquinas, *Summa Theologiae*, I.23.5, in the Blackfriars edition, vol. 5, *God's Will and Providence (Ia. 19–26)*, trans. Thomas Gilby (London: Eyre and Spottiswoode, 1967), 123.

8. Aquinas, *Summa Theologiae*, I.23.5, p. 125. On Báñez's endorsement of this view, see M. John Farrelly, *Predestination, Grace, and Free Will* (Westminster, Md.: Newman, 1964), 6–8. Aquinas's view of the causal nature of God's knowledge is commented on in Richard A. Muller, *God, Creation, and Providence in the Thought of Jacob Arminius: Sources and Directions of Scholastic Protestantism in the Era of Early Orthodoxy* (Grand Rapids, Mich.: Baker, 1991), 158. On Aquinas, predestination, and secondary causation, see Jaroslav Pelikan, *The Riddle of Roman Catholicism* (Nashville: Abingdon, 1959), 145–46.

9. See the extensive and helpful introduction to Luis de Molina, *On Divine Foreknowledge (Part IV of the Concordia)*, trans. Alfred J. Freddoso (Ithaca, N.Y.: Cornell University Press, 1988), ix, 10–13, 23–24, 47; see also Farrelly, *Predestination, Grace, and Free Will*, 23–24.

10. Robert Kane, *A Contemporary Introduction to Free Will* (New York: Oxford University Press, 2005), 159–60.

11. Muller, *God, Creation, and Providence*, 160; Farrelly, *Predestination, Grace, and Free Will*, 22.

12. Paul V quoted in Reginald Garrigou-Lagrange, *Predestination*, trans. Bede Rose (1939; reprint, Rockford, Ill.: TAN, 1998), 151–52. For a summary of events in the *De Auxiliis* controversy, see Thomas McKay Ryan, "Congregatio de Auxiliis," in *New Catholic Encyclopedia*, 2nd ed. (Detroit: Thomson Gale, 2003), 4:110–13.

13. Alister E. McGrath, *Iustitia Dei: A History of the Christian Doctrine of Justification*, 3rd ed. (Cambridge: Cambridge University Press, 2005), 354–55; Margaret R. Miles, *The Word Made Flesh: A History of Christian Thought* (Oxford: Blackwell, 2005), 334. On Calvin's (and Augustine's) similar reading of 1 Timothy 2:4, see above, ch. 1, pp. 22, 31. One American Calvinist who took an interest in Jansenist writers was Jonathan Edwards. See Peter J. Thuesen, ed., *The Works of Jonathan Edwards*, vol. 26, *Catalogues of Books* (New Haven, Conn.: Yale University Press, 2008), 64–66.

14. Even Aquinas noted that 1 Timothy 2:4 could be read as referring to all types of people, though he further explained the passage by employing a distinction between God's *antecedent* will to save all persons and his *consequent* will to save only some, as his justice required. Aquinas, *Summa Theologiae*, I.19.6, pp. 27–31.

15. Garrigou-Lagrange's *Predestination* remains in print with TAN Books (Rockford, Ill.). On his influence, see Thomas F. O'Meara, *Thomas Aquinas, Theologian* (Notre Dame, Ind.: University of Notre Dame Press, 1997), 176–77; and on the dominance of neo-Thomism, at least until Vatican II, 192–95.

16. The treatise originally appeared as William G. Most, *Novum Tentamen ad Solutionem de Gratia et Praedestinatione* (Rome: Editiones Paulinae, 1963).

On the 500 copies distributed to other theologians, see the English edition (cited above): Most, *Grace, Predestination, and the Salvific Will of God*, v–vii.

17. This point is made by McGrath, *Iustitia Dei*, 355.

18. Dogmatic Constitution on the Church (*Lumen Gentium*), art. 11, in Tanner, ed., *Decrees of the Ecumenical Councils*, 2:857.

19. Ann Taves, *The Household of Faith: Roman Catholic Devotions in Mid-Nineteenth-Century America* (Notre Dame, Ind.: University of Notre Dame Press, 1986), 48–51.

20. See, e.g., Alice K. Turner, *The History of Hell* (Orlando: Harcourt, 1993), 126–32. The standard history of the doctrine's medieval emergence is Jacques Le Goff, *The Birth of Purgatory*, trans. Arthur Goldhammer (Chicago: University of Chicago Press, 1984).

21. Decree on Purgatory, Council of Trent, sess. 25 (1563), in Tanner, ed., *Decrees of the Ecumenical Councils*, 2:774; cf. Teaching and Canons on the Most Holy Sacrifice of the Mass, sess. 22 (1562), ibid., 2:733–34.

22. Douay-Rheims Bible (1941; reprint, Fitzwilliam, N.H.: Loreto, 2004), footnote on pp. 959–60. The verses numbered in Douay-Rheims and the Vulgate as 2 Maccabees 12:45–46 are combined as v. 45 in more recent translations (e.g., RSV Catholic Edition, Jerusalem Bible, NRSV).

23. John Carroll, "An Address to the Roman Catholics of the United States of America by a Catholic Clergyman" (1784), written in response to Wharton, in Thomas O'Brien Hanley, ed., *The John Carroll Papers*, 3 vols. (Notre Dame, Ind.: University of Notre Dame Press, 1976), 1:130–31.

24. Dogmatic Constitution on the Church (*Lumen Gentium*), art. 50, in Tanner, ed., *Decrees of the Ecumenical Councils*, 2:889; *Catechism of the Catholic Church: With Modifications from the Editio Typica* (New York: Doubleday, 1997), 291.

25. John A. Nageleisen, *Charity for the Suffering Souls: An Explanation of the Catholic Doctrine of Purgatory* (1895; reprint, Rockford, Ill.: TAN, 1982), 8–9, 10, 76. Biographical details are from Nageleisen's obituary, *New York Times*, 7 May 1952, 27.

26. Joseph Hilgers, "Purgatorial Societies," in *The Catholic Encyclopedia*, 15 vols., ed. Charles G. Herbermann et al. (New York: Encyclopedia Press, 1913), 572–75. On the devotion to the souls in purgatory, see also Taves, *Household of Faith*, 39–40.

27. Frederick William Faber, *Purgatory*, from *All for Jesus*, 23rd ed. (1854; reprint, Rockford, Ill.: TAN, 2002), originally published in 1853. On Faber's influence on the devotional world of American Catholics, see Taves, *Household of Faith*, 48–49, 71–72, 79–82, 104–6.

28. Thomas A. Nelson, "Publisher's Preface," to F. X. Schouppe, *Purgatory: Explained by the Lives and Legends of the Saints* (1888; reprint, Rockford, Ill.: TAN, 1986), xxiii–xxiv.

29. Karl Keating, *What Catholics Really Believe—Setting the Record Straight: 52 Answers to Common Misconceptions about the Catholic Faith* (San Francisco: Ignatius, 1992), 86–87, 89.

30. Eamon Duffy, *Faith of Our Fathers: Reflections on Catholic Tradition* (New York: Continuum, 2004), 129–31.

31. Gerald P. Fogarty, "Francis P. Kenrick," in *Makers of Christian Theology in America*, ed. Mark G. Toulouse and James O. Duke (Nashville: Abingdon, 1997), 167.

32. Francis Patrick Kenrick, *The Catholic Doctrine of Justification: Explained and Vindicated* (Philadelphia: Eugene Cummiskey, 1841), 116, 119, 200. On the differences between Kenrick's and Protestant accounts of justification, see E. Brooks

Holifield, *Theology in America: Christian Thought from the Age of the Puritans to the Civil War* (New Haven, Conn.: Yale University Press, 2003), 429–30.

33. Augustine F. Hewit, *The King's Highway; or, The Catholic Church the Way of Salvation, as Revealed in the Holy Scriptures*, 3rd ed. (New York: Catholic Book Exchange, 1893), x, 48, 80–81, 107–8, 159–60. On Hewit, see David J. O'Brien, *Isaac Hecker: An American Catholic* (New York: Paulist, 1992), 168–70; and Patrick Allitt, *Catholic Converts: British and American Intellectuals Turn to Rome* (Ithaca, N.Y.: Cornell University Press, 1997), 72–73.

34. Augustine F. Hewit, "The Presbyterian Revision," *Catholic World* 51, no. 304 (July 1890): 506–7. Hewit's article was prompted by the movement among Presbyterians to revise the Westminster Confession (see below, ch. 6).

35. Max Weber, *The Protestant Ethic and the "Spirit" of Capitalism and Other Writings*, ed. and trans. Peter Baehr and Gordon C. Wells (New York: Penguin, 2002), 80; on Lutherans, 78, 86–87.

36. Brownson quotations from Per Sveino, *Orestes A. Brownson's Road to Catholicism* (Oslo: Universitetsforlaget, 1970), 26. On Brownson's criticism of Hewit's more latitudinarian view of salvation outside of the church, see Patrick W. Carey, *Orestes A. Brownson: American Religious Weathervane* (Grand Rapids, Mich.: Eerdmans, 2004), 329–33.

37. Patrick F. O'Hare, *The Facts about Luther* (1916; reprint, Rockford, Ill.: TAN, 1987), 272.

38. C. F. Donovan, ed., *Our Faith and the Facts* (Chicago: Baine, 1922), 289–90. Some scholastic theologians such as Gabriel Biel (c. 1420–1495) had in fact referred to the reprobate simply as the "foreknown"; Oberman, *Harvest of Medieval Theology*, 187.

39. Scott Hahn, *Swear to God: The Promise and Power of the Sacraments* (New York: Doubleday, 2004), 3.

40. Scott Hahn and Kimberly Hahn, *Rome Sweet Home: Our Journey to Catholicism* (San Francisco: Ignatius, 1993), 25. The 1903 revision of the Westminster Confession by the Presbyterian Church in the United States of America (discussed below in ch. 6) eliminated from ch. XXV of the document the reference to the pope as the Antichrist.

41. James F. Loughlin, "The Fate of Unbaptized Infants," *Catholic World* 51, no. 304 (July 1890): 458–59.

42. Hewit, *King's Highway*, 41.

43. O'Hare, *Facts about Luther*, 269–71.

44. Martin Luther, "Confession Concerning Christ's Supper," pt. III, in *Luther's Works*, vol. 37, *Word and Sacrament III*, ed. Robert H. Fischer (Philadelphia: Muhlenberg, 1961), 367; Eric W. Gritsch and Robert W. Jenson, *Lutheranism: The Theological Movement and Its Confessional Writings* (Philadelphia: Fortress, 1976), 89; David C. Steinmetz, *Luther in Context* (1986; reprint, Grand Rapids, Mich.: Baker, 1995), 77–78; and Heiko A. Oberman, *Luther: Man between God and the Devil*, trans. Eileen Walliser-Schwarzbart (New York: Image, 1992), 242.

45. Hermann Sasse, *This Is My Body: Luther's Contention for the Real Presence in the Sacrament of the Altar* (Minneapolis: Augsburg, 1959), 30, 39–40, 103–4.

46. Richard Marius, *Martin Luther: The Christian between God and Death* (Cambridge, Mass.: Harvard University Press, 1999), 198 (on Luther's pastoral attitude toward predestination), 52–53 (on his native medievalism regarding the Eucharist); on the latter, cf. Oberman, *Luther*, 147–49.

47. *Tischreden*, no. 5658a, quoted in Martin Luther, *Letters of Spiritual Counsel*, trans. Theodore Tappert (Philadelphia: Westminster, 1955), 131.

48. Weber, *Protestant Ethic*, 72, 86.

49. Though the Christian Reformed Church Synod of 1906 declared the infra position to be more scriptural, predestination remained a subject of controversy as late as the 1980s when former missionary Harry Boer challenged what he termed the CRC's "evaded and embarrassing" doctrine of reprobation. On the earlier controversies, see James D. Bratt, *Dutch Calvinism in Modern America: A History of a Conservative Subculture* (Grand Rapids, Mich.: Eerdmans, 1984), 46–47. On the early 1980s battle, see Harry R. Boer, *The Doctrine of Reprobation in the Christian Reformed Church* (Grand Rapids, Mich.: Eerdmans, 1983), quotation on vii.

50. The only full-length treatment of the controversy is by the late Hans Robert Haug, "The Predestination Controversy in the Lutheran Church in North America" (Ph.D. diss., Temple University, 1968). Though written before the takeover of the Missouri Synod by a cadre of ardent conservatives in the early 1970s, Haug's 961-page dissertation is nevertheless invaluable for its extensive review of the polemical literature generated by the battle of the 1870s and 1880s. A summary of the controversy, written by Eugene L. Fevold and drawing on Haug, appears as "Coming of Age," in *The Lutherans in North America*, ed. E. Clifford Nelson et al., rev. ed. (Philadelphia: Fortress, 1980), 313–25.

51. Melanchthon to Georg Spalatin (1524), in Eric Lund, ed., *Documents from the History of Lutheranism* (Minneapolis: Fortress, 2002), 196.

52. Lund, ed., *Documents*, 181–84; Gritsch and Jenson, *Lutheranism*, 30–32; Eric W. Gritsch, *A History of Lutheranism* (Minneapolis: Fortress, 2002), 87–88.

53. Formula of Concord, Epitome XI:20, Solid Declaration II:25, in *The Book of Concord: The Confessions of the Evangelical Lutheran Church*, ed. Robert Kolb and Timothy J. Wengert and trans. Charles Arand et al. (Minneapolis: Fortress, 2002), 519, 549.

54. Formula of Concord, Epitome XI:2–5, Solid Declaration XI:9, 28, 34–42, 45, 70, 76, in Kolb and Wengert, eds., *Book of Concord*, 642, 645–48, 651–52.

55. See the helpful discussion of *intuitu fidei* in Richard A. Muller, *Dictionary of Latin and Greek Theological Terms Drawn Principally from Protestant Scholastic Theology* (Grand Rapids, Mich.: Baker, 1985), 158–59. On the tension between predestination and the universal grace of the gospel in Lutheran thought, see Gritsch and Jenson, *Lutheranism*, 158–63.

56. Though election, in Molina's view, was *post praevisa merita*, he argued that God ordained the *circumstances* of each person *ante praevisa merita*, or prior to any foresight. Kathryn Tanner, *God and Creation in Christian Theology: Tyranny or Empowerment?* (Minneapolis: Fortress, 2006), 146.

57. G. H. Gerberding, *The Way of Salvation in the Lutheran Church* (Philadelphia: General Council Publication House, 1918), 174. Other modern observers have been less persuaded that *intuitu fidei* avoids synergism. Reformed theologian Gerrit Cornelis Berkouwer (1903–1996), for example, cited the charge by German Lutheran theologian Paul Althaus (1888–1966) that *intuitu fidei* was scarcely different from the Molinist *post praevisa merita*. G. C. Berkouwer, *Divine Election*, trans. Hugo Bekker (Grand Rapids, Mich.: Eerdmans, 1960), 40–42.

58. Henry Melchior Muhlenberg, *The Journals of Henry Melchior Muhlenberg*, 3 vols., trans. Theodore G. Tappert and John W. Doberstein (Philadelphia: Muhlenberg, 1942), 1:59, 330; 2:181.

59. *The Fatal Consequences of the Unscriptural Doctrine of Predestination and Reprobation: With a Caution against It. Written in High-Dutch by M. K. and Translated an [sic] Desire* (Germantown, Pa.: Sower, 1753), 3, 6, 12–13.

60. On Muhlenberg's confessional brand of Pietism, see Holifield, *Theology in America*, 399–400.

61. Samuel Simon Schmucker, *Elements of Popular Theology, with Special Reference to the Doctrines of the Reformation, as Avowed before the Diet of Augsburg, in MDXXX* (New York: Leavitt, Lord, 1834), 97–102.

62. For the text of the Definite Synodical Platform, see Jaroslav Pelikan and Valerie Hotchkiss, eds., *Creeds and Confessions of Faith in the Christian Tradition*, 4 vols. (New Haven, Conn.: Yale University Press, 2003), 3:291–315. For context, see Paul P. Kuenning, *The Rise and Fall of American Lutheran Pietism: The Rejection of an Activist Heritage* (Macon, Ga.: Mercer University Press, 1988), 171–75; August R. Suelflow and E. Clifford Nelson, "Following the Frontier," in Nelson et al., eds., *Lutherans*, 221–27; Holifield, *Theology in America*, 402–8; Gardiner H. Shattuck, "Samuel Simon Schmucker," in *American National Biography Online*, Oxford University Press, http://www.anb.org (hereafter cited as *ANBO*); and Mark A. Noll, *America's God: From Jonathan Edwards to Abraham Lincoln* (New York: Oxford University Press, 2002), 409–11.

63. Quoted in Abdel Ross Wentz, *A Basic History of Lutheranism in America* (Philadelphia: Muhlenberg, 1955), 143.

64. Walter H. Conser, Jr., *Church and Confession: Conservative Theologians in Germany, England, and America, 1815–1966* (Macon, Ga.: Mercer University Press, 1984), 13–21; Walter O. Forster, *Zion on the Mississippi: The Settlement of the Saxon Lutherans in Missouri, 1839–1841* (St. Louis: Concordia, 1953), 16–24.

65. Forster, *Zion on the Mississippi*, 25; Mary Todd, *Authority Vested: A Story of Identity and Change in the Lutheran Church–Missouri Synod* (Grand Rapids, Mich.: Eerdmans, 2000), 21–27.

66. *Der Lutheraner* 5 (12 September 1848): 1, quoted in Todd, *Authority Vested*, 95.

67. Paul A. Baglyos, "Carl Ferdinand Wilhelm Walther," in *ANBO*. The slogan of *Der Lutheraner* was the same phrase stamped on some German coins during the age of Lutheran orthodoxy; see Gritsch, *History of Lutheranism*, 114 and 288n9.

68. For documents on the Synodical Conference's founding, see Richard C. Wolf, ed., *Documents of Lutheran Unity in America* (Philadelphia: Fortress, 1966), 179–98.

69. C. P. Krauth, *Infant Baptism and Infant Salvation in the Calvinistic System: A Review of Dr. Hodge's Systematic Theology* (Philadelphia: Lutheran Book Store, 1874), 10–17, 29, 72–74, 78–79. For Hodge's footnote, see Charles Hodge, *Systematic Theology*, 3 vols. (New York: Scribner's, 1871–1872), 3:605n4.

70. On the formation of the General Council, and Missouri's opposition to it, see Wolf, ed., *Documents*, 137–52, 187–96; and Suelflow and Nelson, "Following the Frontier," in Nelson et al., eds., *Lutherans*, 230–38. Representatives of the Missouri Synod attended a preliminary meeting of the General Council in 1866 but refused to attend the constituting convention the following year.

71. Quoted in Haug, "Predestination Controversy," 110–11; on Fritschel's personality, see George H. Genzmer, "Gottfried Leonhard Wilhelm Fritschel," in *Dictionary of American Biography*, vol. 7, ed. Allen Johnson and Dumas Malone (New York: Scribner's, 1931), 37–38. The subject of predestination had occasionally been debated in American Lutheran journals prior to the 1870s, but without provoking widespread controversy. For a review of this earlier literature, see Haug, "Predestination Controversy," 57–107.

72. Haug reviews this initial debate in considerable detail in "Predestination Controversy," 109–235.

73. Quoted in Theodore G. Tappert, ed., *Lutheran Confessional Theology in America, 1840–1880* (New York: Oxford University Press, 1972), 170–71, 184.

74. The confusion over Gerhard stemmed in part from his belief that *intuitu fidei* did not actually make salvation dependent on something in humans. Yet he clearly spoke of election in view of faith; see, e.g., Matthias Loy, "Is God's Election Arbitrary or in View of Faith?" (1881), in Tappert, ed., *Lutheran Confessional Theology*, 220–21.

75. The accusation about Schmidt's motivations apparently originated with Missouri Synod historian Christian Hochstetter, who is quoted in Carl S. Meyer, ed., *Moving Frontiers: Readings in the History of the Lutheran Church–Missouri Synod* (St. Louis: Concordia, 1964), 271. The charge is repeated in various places, including in John M. Drickamer, "The Election Controversy," in Arthur H. Drevlow, John M. Drickamer, and Glenn E. Reichwald, eds., *C. F. W. Walther: The American Luther: Essays in Commemoration of the 100th Anniversary of Carl Walther's Death* (Mankato, Minn.: Walther Press, 1987), 163; and in Armin W. Schuetze, *The Synodical Conference: Ecumenical Endeavor* (Milwaukee: Northwestern, 2000), 93. Neither of the standard biographical sketches of Schmidt mentions the issue of the 1878 Concordia appointment; see Darrell Jodock, "Friedrich August Schmidt," in *ANBO*; and John O. Evjens, "Friedrich August Schmidt," in *Dictionary of American Biography*, ed. Dumas Malone (New York: Scribner's, 1935), 16:440–41.

76. Quoted in Haug, "Predestination Controversy," 298.

77. Walther to J. A. Ottesen, 12 April 1879, in Carl S. Meyer, ed., *Letters of C. F. W. Walther: A Selection* (Philadelphia: Fortress, 1969), 127. See also Walther's letter to his wife (from Columbus, 18 July 1879) in the same volume, 130.

78. "Vorwort" to *Altes und Neues: Theologisches Zeitblatt vom Standpunkte des evang.-lutherischen Bekenntnisses* 1 (January 1880): 1.

79. Haug, "Predestination Controversy," 311–15.

80. Meyer, ed., *Moving Frontiers*, 272–73; Haug, "Predestination Controversy," 398. The Synodical Conference followed Missouri in adopting the Thirteen Theses in October 1882. Comment on Schmidt's "scandal sheet" from Walther to G. A. Barth, 9 May 1880, in Meyer, ed., *Letters*, 133–34.

81. August R. Suelflow, *Servant of the Word: The Life and Ministry of C. F. W. Walther* (St. Louis: Concordia, 2000), 171–72; Haug, "Predestination Controversy," 701.

82. Evjens, "Friedrich August Schmidt."

83. Matthias Loy, *Story of My Life*, 2nd ed. (Columbus, Ohio: Lutheran Book Concern, 1905), 316, 355–56, 372.

84. [Matthias Loy], "Introductory: The Burning Question," *Columbus Theological Magazine* 1, no. 1 (February 1881): 1, 7, 25. The later editorial, "Election and Justification," *Columbus Theological Magazine* 1 (1881): 273–88, is excerpted in Tappert, ed., *Lutheran Confessional Theology*, 209–22, quotation from 216.

85. August Pfeiffer, *Anti-Calvinism*, trans. Edward Pfeiffer (Columbus, Ohio: Joint Synod of Ohio, 1881), xxi. On Bach's use of Pfeiffer, see Robin A. Leaver, "Calvinism," in *J. S. Bach*, ed. Malcolm Boyd (New York: Oxford University Press, 1999), 77–78.

86. Wolf, ed., *Documents*, 203–4; emphases in the original.

87. Meyer, ed., *Moving Frontiers*, 274–75; Haug, "Predestination Controversy," 764–68.

88. Krauth's last statement was published in *Lutheran Church Review* 3 (1884): 68–71, and is reprinted in Tappert, ed., *Lutheran Confessional Theology*, 223–26.

89. Analysis by Stephen J. Carter of the Concordia Historical Institute, as cited in Haug, "Predestination Controversy," 745.

90. Raymond M. Bost and Jeff L. Norris, *All One Body: The Story of the North Carolina Lutheran Synod, 1803–1993* (Salisbury, N.C.: North Carolina Synod, Evangelical Lutheran Church in America, 1994), 217.

91. D. H. Steffens, *Doctor Carl Ferdinand Wilhelm Walther* (Philadelphia: Lutheran Publication Society, 1917), 348.

92. Both incidents were reported in the Lutheran press and are recounted in Haug, "Predestination Controversy," 736–37, 741–42.

93. Haug, "Predestination Controversy," 950.

94. C. F. W. Walther, *The Doctrine Concerning Election, Presented in Questions and Answers, from the Eleventh Article of the Formula of Concord of the Evangelical Lutheran Church*, trans. J. Humberger (St. Louis: Concordia, 1881), 7, 10–11.

95. *A Testimony against the False Doctrine of Predestination Recently Introduced by the Missouri Synod*, trans. R. C. H. Lenski and printed in *The Error of Modern Missouri: Its Inception, Development, and Refutation*, ed. George H. Schodde (Columbus, Ohio: Lutheran Book Concern, 1897), 575.

96. F. A. Schmidt, *Intuitu Fidei*; F. W. Stellhorn, *The Present Controversy on Predestination*; and *Testimony against the False Doctrine*; all in Schodde, ed., *Error of Modern Missouri*, 5, 7–8, 194, 619.

97. "Antibarbarus Logikus" (pseudonym), *Lutherthum oder Calvinismus? Populäre Beleuchtung des, als Einleitung zum 300jährigen Jubiläum der Concordia, innerhalb der Synodal-Conferenz der amerikanisch-lutherischen Kirche, ausgebrochenen Lehrstreites über die Gnadenwahl* (Oshkosh, Wis., 1880), 8.

98. "The Predestination Controversy in the Lutheran Church," *Andover Review* 3 (May 1885): 477, 479.

99. *Süddeutsche Evangelisch-Lutherische Freikirche* and *Hannoversche Pastoral-Correspondenz* cited in Haug, "Predestination Controversy," 825, 827. On Walther as a *Zitatentheologe*, see Holifield, *Theology in America*, 414; Todd, *Authority Vested*, 95.

100. On Ohio and language, see Fevold, "Coming of Age," in Nelson et al., eds., *Lutherans*, 349–50. On debates over language within the Missouri Synod, see Todd, *Authority Vested*, 92–94.

101. "Walther on Sola Scriptura: C. F. W. Walther's 1884 Synodical Conference Essay," *Concordia Journal* 14 (1988): 363–73, quotation from 366.

102. C. F. W. Walther, *The Controversy Concerning Predestination: That is, a Plain, Trustworthy Advice for Pious Christians That Would Like to Know Whose Doctrine in the Present Controversy Concerning Predestination Is Lutheran, and Whose Is Not*, trans. August Crull (St. Louis: Concordia, 1881), 6, 15.

103. F. W. Stellhorn, *What Is the Real Question in the Present Controversy on Predestination? A Plain and Clear Answer for Every Lutheran Christian*, trans. George H. Schodde (Columbus, Ohio: Trauger, 1881), 4–5, 15.

104. C. F. W. Walther, *Sermon on Predestination*, trans. August Crull (St. Louis: Concordia, 1883), 10.

105. Quoted in Steffens, *Doctor Carl Ferdinand Wilhelm Walther*, 351.

106. William J. Schmelder, "The Predestination Controversy: Review and Reflection," *Concordia Journal* 1, no. 1 (January 1975): 21–33, esp. 27.

107. Walther to the Rev. Ulrich V. Koren, 19 February 1880, in Carl S. Meyer, ed., *Walther Speaks to the Church: Selected Letters* (St. Louis: Concordia, 1973), 45.

108. Walther mentioned the effect of "sophistry" and "subtlety" not only on predestination but also on the eucharistic words of institution ("This is my body") in *Controversy Concerning Predestination*, 15.

109. Suelflow, *Servant of the Word*, 293.

110. Quoted in Baglyos, "Walther," *ANBO*.

111. Suelflow, *Servant of the Word*, 209.

112. Todd, *Authority Vested*, 91–92; and Fevold, "Coming of Age," in Nelson et al., eds., *Lutherans*, 324. For a dissenting view, see the celebratory history by Schuetze, *Synodical Conference*, 111–12.

113. On the Synodical Conference's African-American missions, see Jeff G. Johnson, *Black Lutherans: The Untold Lutheran Story* (St. Louis: Concordia, 1991), 151–58, 166–72. The deathblow to the conference came in 1963 when the Wisconsin Synod and the Evangelical Lutheran Synod (a conservative remnant of the old Norwegian Synod; see below) withdrew—ironically, because of Missouri's alleged "unionism" in cultivating ties with the American Lutheran Church (ALC). See below for more on the short-lived Missouri-ALC relationship.

114. John A. Moldstad, Jr., *Predestination: Chosen in Christ* (Milwaukee: Northwestern, 1997), 87. Moldstad's grandfather, then nine years old, witnessed this dramatic event.

115. Fevold, "Coming of Age," in Nelson et al., eds., *Lutherans*, 339–40.

116. Fevold, "Coming of Age," and Fred W. Meuser, "Facing the Twentieth Century," both in Nelson et al., eds., *Lutherans*, 322–23, 370–73.

117. Meuser, "Facing the Twentieth Century," in Nelson et al., eds., *Lutherans*, 370–72; L. DeAne Lagerquist, *The Lutherans* (Westport, Conn.: Greenwood, 1999), 96–98. For the text of the Madison Agreement, see Wolf, ed., *Documents*, 232–35. The agreement stated that the two forms of the doctrine of election "should not be cause for schism within the Church or disturb that unity of the spirit in the bond of peace which God wills should prevail among us" (233).

118. Carl E. Braaten, "Robert William Jenson—A Personal Memoir," in *Trinity, Time, and Church: A Response to the Theology of Robert W. Jenson*, ed. Colin E. Gunton (Grand Rapids, Mich.: Eerdmans, 2000), 2–3.

119. Carl E. Braaten, *Justification: The Article by Which the Church Stands or Falls* (Minneapolis: Fortress, 1990), 37–38. Similarly, Missouri Synod theologian Robert Kolb has suggested that *intuitu fidei* at least implies synergism "at the key point of admitting the Holy Spirit to the human heart and mind so that he might create the faith." Robert Kolb, *Bound Choice, Election, and Wittenberg Theological Method: From Martin Luther to the Formula of Concord* (Grand Rapids, Mich.: Eerdmans, 2005), 266.

120. Moldstad, *Predestination*, 93.

121. Franz Pieper, *Conversion and Election: A Plea for a United Lutheranism in America* (St. Louis: Concordia, 1913), 12–17.

122. *Brief Statement of the Doctrinal Position of the Missouri Synod* (1932; reprint, St. Louis: Concordia, n.d.), 15–19 (on election). In addition to repudiating election in view of faith, the statement also unequivocally rejected the Reformed doctrine of double predestination: "No man is lost because God has predestinated him to eternal damnation" (17). See the comment on this in Alister E. McGrath, *Christianity's Dangerous Idea: The Protestant Revolution—A History from the Sixteenth Century to the Twenty-First* (New York: HarperCollins, 2007), 266–67.

123. *Brief Statement*, 13.

124. The Norwegian Lutheran Church of America had been renamed the Evangelical Lutheran Church in 1946.

125. On the ALC-Missouri pact, see E. Clifford Nelson, "The New Shape of Lutheranism," in Nelson et al., eds., *Lutherans*, 530. On Missouri's withdrawal from the agreement, see "The Lutheran Understanding of Church Fellowship," typescript, Office of the President and Commission on Theology and Church

Relations, Lutheran Church–Missouri Synod (2000), 16, online at http://www
.lcms.org/graphics/assets/media/CTCR/flwshp2k.pdf.

126. See, e.g., Robert Preus, "Article XI, the Formula of Concord:
Predestination and Election," in *A Contemporary Look at the Formula of
Concord*, ed. Wilbert Rosin and Robert Preus (St. Louis: Concordia, 1978),
274–75; and John M. Drickamer, "The Election Controversy," in Drevlow et al.,
eds., *Walther: The American Luther*, 163.

127. Pieper, *Conversion and Election*, 5.

128. H. George Anderson, T. Austin Murphy, and Joseph A. Burgess, eds.,
Justification by Faith: Lutherans and Catholics in Dialogue VII (Minneapolis:
Augsburg, 1985), 23.

129. Ibid., 21 (quoting *Summa Theologiae* I.23.5).

130. *Joint Declaration on the Doctrine of Justification: The Lutheran World
Federation and the Roman Catholic Church* (Grand Rapids, Mich.: Eerdmans,
2000), 11, 15; Gustav Niebuhr, "Vatican Settles a Historic Issue with the
Lutherans," *New York Times*, 26 June 1998, A1, A12.

131. *Joint Declaration*, 17, 25.

132. Edgar R. Trexler, *High Expectations: Understanding the ELCA's Early
Years, 1988–2002* (Minneapolis: Augsburg Fortress, 2003), 158.

133. On the background to these agreements, see ibid., 110–52.

134. Avery Dulles, "Saving Ecumenism from Itself," *First Things*, no. 178
(December 2007): 25.

135. Robert W. Jenson, *Systematic Theology*, vol. 2, *The Works of God*
(New York: Oxford University Press, 1999), 173–78 (quotations on 175 and 178).

Chapter 6

1. On the Venezuelan case, see Charles W. Calhoun, *Benjamin W. Harrison*
(New York: Times Books, 2005), 162–63.

2. Benjamin Harrison to John W. Foster, 26 May 1900, Benjamin Harrison
Papers, ser. 2, reel 94, President Benjamin Harrison Home, Indianapolis.

3. Homer E. Socolofsky and Allan B. Spetter, *The Presidency of Benjamin
Harrison* (Lawrence: University Press of Kansas, 1987), 23; Lew Wallace and
Murat Halstead, *Life and Public Services of Hon. Benjamin Harrison, President of
the U.S.* (Philadelphia: Edgewood, 1892), 449.

4. Benjamin Harrison to Charles A. Dickey, 11 June 1900; Charles A. Dickey
to Benjamin Harrison, 13 June 1900; Samuel J. Niccolls to Benjamin Harrison, 19
June 1900; Harrison Papers, ser. 2, reel 95.

5. Benjamin Harrison to Samuel J. Niccolls, 7 February 1901, Harrison Papers,
ser. 2, reel 95. On Harrison's absence at Saratoga, see the revision committee's report
to the 1901 Presbyterian General Assembly, reprinted in "Presbyterian Revision,"
New York Times, 19 May 1901, 7. His participation in Washington is noted in
"Presbyterian Committee in Session," *New York Times*, 6 December 1900, 2.

6. Haines quoted in "The Presbyterian Creed," *New York Times*, 14 April
1900, 3; on the funeral, see "Gen. Harrison's Body Rests in the Tomb," *New York
Times*, 18 March 1901, 7.

7. Francis Makemie, *Truths in a True Light*, written in 1697, first published
in Edinburgh in 1699, and reprinted in Boyd Stanley Schlenther, ed., *The Life and
Writings of Francis Makemie, Father of American Presbyterianism (c. 1658–1708)*
(Lewiston, N.Y.: Mellen, 1999), 124–27, quotation on 134.

8. Gilbert Burnet, *An Exposition of the Thirty-nine Articles of the Church of
England* (London, 1699). See above, ch. 3.

9. Westminster Confession of Faith in Jaroslav Pelikan and Valerie Hotchkiss, eds., *Creeds and Confessions of Faith in the Christian Tradition*, 4 vols. (New Haven, Conn.: Yale University Press, 2003), 2:610–11, 620.

10. So Philip Schaff: "This seems naturally (though not necessarily) to imply the existence of *reprobate* infants who are not saved." Schaff, ed., *The Creeds of Christendom, with a History and Critical Notes*, 3 vols., 6th ed., rev. by David S. Schaff (1931; reprint, Grand Rapids, Mich.: Baker, 2007), 1:816.

11. Laurence Womock, *The Examination of Tilenus before the Triers; in Order to His Intended Settlement in the Office of a Publick Preacher in the Commonwealth of Utopia* (London, 1658), 6–7; on Womock, see above, ch. 3.

12. George Keith, *The Presbyterian and Independent Visible Churches in New-England and Elsewhere, Brought to the Test* (Philadelphia, 1689), 84–85, 89.

13. John Tillotson, "Concerning Our Imitation of the Divine Perfections," in *Several Discourses upon the Attributes of God* (London, 1699), 45–46.

14. Bryan F. Le Beau, *Jonathan Dickinson and the Formative Years of American Presbyterianism* (Lexington: University Press of Kentucky, 1997), 27–44; Randall Balmer and John R. Fitzmier, *The Presbyterians* (Westport, Conn.: Greenwood, 1993), 25–27; James H. Smylie, *A Brief History of the Presbyterians* (Louisville, Ky.: Geneva, 1996), 44–46.

15. Melvin H. Buxbaum, *Benjamin Franklin and the Zealous Presbyterians* (University Park: Pennsylvania State University Press, 1975), 107–8; Le Beau, *Jonathan Dickinson*, 45–63.

16. On the impact of Taylor's text, see H. Shelton Smith, *Changing Conceptions of Original Sin: A Study in American Theology since 1750* (New York: Scribner's, 1955), 10–36.

17. Clyde A. Holbrook, ed., *The Works of Jonathan Edwards*, vol. 3, *Original Sin* (New Haven, Conn.: Yale University Press, 1970), 215–16; Thomas A. Schafer, ed., *The Works of Jonathan Edwards*, vol. 13, *The "Miscellanies," a–500* (New Haven, Conn.: Yale University Press, 1994), 169; Catherine A. Brekus, "Children of Wrath, Children of Grace: Jonathan Edwards and the Puritan Culture of Child Rearing," in *The Child in Christian Thought*, ed. Marcia J. Bunge (Grand Rapids, Mich.: Eerdmans, 2001), 300–306; Brekus, "Remembering Jonathan Edwards's Ministry to Children," in *Jonathan Edwards at Home and Abroad: Historical Memories, Cultural Movements, Global Horizons*, ed. David W. Kling and Douglas A. Sweeney (Columbia: University of South Carolina Press, 2003), 41–46.

18. Schaff, ed., *Creeds of Christendom*, 1:381; James Turner, *Without God, Without Creed: The Origins of Unbelief in America* (Baltimore, Md.: Johns Hopkins University Press, 1985), 90.

19. Quoted in George M. Marsden, *The Evangelical Mind and the New School Presbyterian Experience: A Case Study of Thought and Theology in Nineteenth-Century America* (1970; reprint, Eugene, Ore.: Wipf and Stock, 2003), 67–68. Because of the conservative dominance of the Cincinnati Presbytery, Beecher wrote to the Third Presbytery of New York City, which ordained him in absentia and then released him to Cincinnati (ibid., 69). But this maneuver did not prevent the Cincinnati leaders from launching a doctrinal inquest.

20. Marie Caskey, *Chariot of Fire: Religion and the Beecher Family* (New Haven, Conn.: Yale University Press, 1978), 39. Mark Noll, following Daniel Walker Howe, has termed the perspective of Beecher and his allies the *Whig theology*: a brand of evangelicalism, allied politically with the Whig opposition to the Jacksonian Democrats, that blended Reformation themes with an emphasis on republican virtue. Mark A. Noll, *America's God: From Jonathan Edwards to Abraham Lincoln* (New York: Oxford University Press, 2002), 312–13; Daniel

Walker Howe, *The Political Culture of the American Whigs* (Chicago: University of Chicago Press, 1979), 158–61.

21. This phrase is from his son Edward Beecher; quoted in *The Autobiography of Lyman Beecher*, 2 vols., ed. Barbara M. Cross (Cambridge, Mass.: Harvard University Press, 1961), 2:436.

22. William Harmless, "Baptism," in *Augustine through the Ages: An Encyclopedia*, ed. Allan D. Fitzgerald et al. (Grand Rapids, Mich.: Eerdmans, 1999), 89–90.

23. [Francis Jenks], "Dr. Beecher against the Calvinistic Doctrine of Infant Damnation," *Christian Examiner* 5 (1828): 320–29; Jenks later published his full attack as *A Reply to the Three Letters of the Rev. Lyman Beecher, D.D., against the Calvinistic Doctrine of Infant Damnation: From the Christian Examiner, with Additions* (Boston: Christian Examiner, 1829). On Beecher's contortionism in this exchange, see Vincent Harding, *A Certain Magnificence: Lyman Beecher and the Transformation of American Protestantism, 1775–1863* (Brooklyn, N.Y.: Carlson, 1991), 258.

24. "Trial of the Rev. Dr. Lyman Beecher for Heresy," *Christian Examiner*, 3rd ser., 1 (1836): 117.

25. Lyman Beecher, *Views in Theology* (Cincinnati: Truman and Smith, 1836), 57, 192.

26. "Trial of the Rev. Dr. Lyman Beecher," 132–33.

27. Marsden, *Evangelical Mind*, 53–55, 61; Balmer and Fitzmier, *Presbyterians*, 124–25.

28. Quoted in Balmer and Fitzmier, *Presbyterians*, 47.

29. Ralph Waldo Emerson, "Divinity School Address" (15 July 1838), in *Theology in America: The Major Protestant Voices from Puritanism to Neo-Orthodoxy*, ed. Sydney E. Ahlstrom (1967; reprint, Indianapolis: Hackett, 2003), 301, 315.

30. Noll, *America's God*, 308–11.

31. Charles Hodge, *Systematic Theology*, 3 vols. (New York: Scribner's, 1871–1872), 2:333–35. Regarding original sin, the Westminster Confession asserted (ch. 6) that "the guilt of this sin was imputed" to Adam and Eve's "posterity descending from them by ordinary generation." Pelikan and Hotchkiss, eds., *Creeds and Confessions*, 2:614.

32. Quoted in Marsden, *Evangelical Mind*, 85.

33. On Barnes, the New School, and antislavery sentiment, see Marsden, *Evangelical Mind*, 101–2, 188–89; and Leo P. Hirrel, *Children of Wrath: New School Calvinism and Antebellum Reform* (Lexington: University Press of Kentucky, 1998), 134–54.

34. Mark A. Noll, *The Civil War as a Theological Crisis* (Chapel Hill: University of North Carolina Press, 2006), esp. 31–50 on the Bible.

35. See the list of biblical passages in Noll, *Civil War*, 34–35.

36. Benjamin M. Palmer, "National Responsibility before God," in *God's New Israel: Religious Interpretations of American Destiny*, rev. ed., ed. Conrad Cherry (Chapel Hill: University of North Carolina Press, 1998), 187. For an analysis of Palmer's views of the Bible and race, see Stephen R. Haynes, *Noah's Curse: The Biblical Justification of American Slavery* (New York: Oxford University Press, 2002), 125–45.

37. Palmer, "National Responsibility," 185–86.

38. B. M. Palmer, *The Threefold Fellowship and the Threefold Assurance: An Essay in Two Parts* (Richmond, Va.: Presbyterian Committee of Publication, 1902), 27–31.

39. On Hodge and slavery, see James Turner, "Charles Hodge in the Intellectual Weather of the Nineteenth Century," in *Charles Hodge Revisited: A Critical Appraisal of His Life and Work*, ed. John W. Stewart and James H. Moorhead (Grand Rapids, Mich.: Eerdmans, 2002), 47; cf. Allen C. Guelzo, "Charles Hodge's Antislavery Moment," 299–325, in the same volume.

40. Hodge, *Systematic Theology*, 2:335, 337–39.

41. Charles Reagan Wilson, *Baptized in Blood: The Religion of the Lost Cause, 1865–1920* (Athens: University of Georgia Press, 1980), 77–78.

42. Harry S. Stout, *Upon the Altar of the Nation: A Moral History of the American Civil War* (New York: Viking, 2006), 211. On the inevitable recourse to impersonal fate or blind chance, especially among some soldiers on the battlefield, see Jackson Lears, *Something for Nothing: Luck in America* (New York: Viking, 2003), 143–44.

43. Quoted in Wilson, *Baptized in Blood*, 76. See also the similar sentiments from John Adger, editor of the *Southern Presbyterian Review*, in Noll, *Civil War*, 77–78.

44. I thank my brother-in-law John Kenyon for showing me this monument in the Hollywood Cemetery in Richmond, Va.

45. Lefferts A. Loetscher, *A Brief History of the Presbyterians*, 3rd ed. (Philadelphia: Westminster, 1978), 98–100, 102–3, 110, 122–26, 128–29; Smylie, *Brief History*, 78–80, 91–93; and Sean Michael Lucas, *On Being Presbyterian: Our Beliefs, Practices, and Stories* (Phillipsburg, N.J.: P&R, 2006), 191–203.

46. *Central Presbyterian* (28 February 1883) and *Christian Observer* (4 April 1883), quoted in Ernest Trice Thompson, *Presbyterians in the South*, 3 vols. (Richmond, Va.: John Knox, 1973), 2:447.

47. Westminster Confession in *The Constitution of the Presbyterian Church in the United States* (Richmond, Va., n.d.), 25 (copy in Speer Library, Princeton Theological Seminary). The original reading appeared in *The Humble Advice of the Assembly of Divines, Now by Authority of Parliament Sitting at Westminster, Concerning a Confession of Faith* (London, 1647), 8. On the possible significance of the chapter III heading, see Kirk Bottomly, "The Skeleton in the Reformed Closet," in *The Essential Presbyterian*, ed. Mary Holder Naegeli (Louisville, Ky.: Presbyterians for Renewal, 2003), 38n8; I thank the Reverend John Allen for this citation.

48. Bruce Kuklick, *Churchmen and Philosophers: From Jonathan Edwards to John Dewey* (New Haven, Conn.: Yale University Press, 1985), 205–9.

49. Quoted in E. Brooks Holifield, "Hodge, the Seminary, and the American Theological Context," in Stewart and Moorhead, eds., *Charles Hodge Revisited*, 117.

50. Henry Ward Beecher, "The Study of Human Nature," in *American Protestant Thought in the Liberal Era*, ed. William R. Hutchison (Lanham, Md.: University Press of America, 1968), 41–42. On Beecher's career in Indianapolis, see Jane Shaffer Elsmere, *Henry Ward Beecher: The Indiana Years, 1837–1847* (Indianapolis: Indiana Historical Society, 1973).

51. David Swing, "Declaration in Reply to the Charges of Professor Patton," 4 May 1847, in Hutchison, ed., *American Protestant Thought*, 55.

52. Quoted in William R. Hutchison, *The Modernist Impulse in American Protestantism* (Durham, N.C.: Duke University Press, 1992), 61; cf. 48–75 on the Swing heresy trial.

53. Declaratory Act reprinted in William Frederick Faber, "The United Presbyterians of Scotland and Their New Service Book," *Reformed Quarterly Review* 39 (1892): 197.

54. Schaff, ed., *Creeds of Christendom*, 3:914.

55. Ibid., 3:918.

56. Lefferts A. Loetscher, *The Broadening Church: A Study of Theological Issues in the Presbyterian Church Since 1869* (Philadelphia: University of Pennsylvania Press, 1957), 41.

57. Ibid., 41; Robert Ellis Thompson, *A History of the Presbyterian Churches in the United States* (New York: Christian Literature, 1895), 245–46.

58. Schaff, ed., *Creeds of Christendom*, 3:608–11, 624–26 (English original with parallel Latin translation of 1656); cf. Pelikan and Hotchkiss, eds., *Creeds and Confessions*, 2:610–11, 619–20 (English original).

59. T. Nichols, "Shall the Confession of Faith Be Revised?" *New York Evangelist*, 25 April 1889, in *Confessional Revision: Being a Collection of 395 Articles That Have Appeared in the Religious Press between September, 1887, and October, 1890, on the Subject of Revising the Westminster Confession of Faith* (Pittsburgh, 1890), article no. 1, from microfilm of scrapbook compiled by Winthrop S. Gilman; original copies in Speer Library, Princeton Theological Seminary, and Burke Library, Union Theological Seminary (hereafter cited as *CR* and by article number).

60. James G. Monfort, "Creed Revision," *Herald and Presbyter*, 31 July 1889, *CR*, no. 8.

61. Douglas P. Putnam, "Dr. Shedd on Revision," *New York Evangelist*, 3 October 1889, *CR*, no. 61; Thomas MacKellar, "From an Elder of Forty Years," *New York Evangelist*, 24 October 1889, *CR*, no. 73.

62. Philip Schaff, "The Revision of the Westminster Confession," *New York Evangelist*, 14 November 1889, *CR*, no. 99. On Schaff's involvement in the revision movement and his view of church history, see Stephen R. Graham, *Cosmos in the Chaos: Philip Schaff's Interpretation of Nineteenth-Century American Religion* (Grand Rapids, Mich.: Eerdmans, 1995), 107–8.

63. Quoted in Peter J. Thuesen, *In Discordance with the Scriptures: American Protestant Battles over Translating the Bible* (New York: Oxford University Press, 1999), 48; cf. 43–51 on the ideology of Bible revision.

64. B. B. Warfield, "The Present Status of the Revision Controversy," *Central West*, 20 March 1890, *CR*, no. 270.

65. Francis L. Patton, "The Revision of the Confession of Faith," *Independent*, 5 December 1889, *CR*, no. 141.

66. Henry J. Van Dyke, "An Answer to Dr. Warfield," *Central West*, 3 April 1890, *CR*, no. 282; S. J. Niccolls, "The Assembly and Revision," *Independent*, 8 May 1890, *CR*, no. 311.

67. Quoted in Thuesen, *In Discordance with the Scriptures*, 49.

68. Howard Crosby, "The Good and Evil of Calvinism," *New York Evangelist*, 20 March 1890, *CR*, no. 267.

69. Charles A. Briggs, "The Westminster Standards," *Independent*, 25 July 1889, *CR*, no. 6; Briggs, *The Authority of Holy Scripture: An Inaugural Address*, 2nd ed. (New York: Scribner's, 1891), 53–56.

70. Henry J. Van Dyke, "The Revision of the Confession of Faith," *Interior*, 11 July 1889, *CR*, no. 4, quoting Hodge. Elsewhere, Hodge insisted that it was "the general belief of Protestants, contrary to the doctrine of Romanists and Romanizers, that all who die in infancy are saved"; *Systematic Theology*, 1:27.

71. Benjamin B. Warfield, "Revision of the Confession of Faith. II," *Herald and Presbyter*, 28 August 1889, *CR*, no. 38.

72. Philip Schaff, "What Is the Calvinistic System?" *Independent*, 31 July 1890, *CR*, no. 358. On Calvin's rejection of the necessity of emergency infant baptism,

see his *Institutes of the Christian Religion*, ed. John T. McNeill and trans. Ford Lewis Battles (Philadelphia: Westminster, 1960), IV.15.20, pp. 1320–21.

73. Elizabeth A. Clark, *The Origenist Controversy: The Cultural Construction of an Early Christian Debate* (Princeton, N.J.: Princeton University Press, 1992), 194.

74. Niccolls, "The Assembly and Revision"; Joseph Fort Newton, *David Swing: Poet-Preacher* (Chicago: Unity, 1909), 252n1, quoted in Hutchison, *Modernist Impulse*, 69.

75. Loetscher, *Broadening Church*, 39–47.

76. Quoted ibid., 83. On the members of the 1890 committee, see "The Revision Committee," *Presbyterian Banner*, 8 October 1890, CR, no. 382; on the 1900 committee, see "Presbyterian Assembly," *New York Times*, 26 May 1900, 7. The 250th anniversary of Westminster is noted in Smylie, *Brief History*, 99.

77. On Harrison and Swing, see Newton, *David Swing*, 43–45.

78. Dickey's committee report was reprinted in "Presbyterian Revision," *New York Times*, 19 May 1901, 7.

79. On the 1900–1903 revision process, see Loetscher, *Broadening Church*, 83–89. For the text of the Declaratory Statement, see Schaff, ed., *Creeds of Christendom*, 3:920–21; and *The Constitution of the Presbyterian Church (U.S.A.)*, pt. 1, *Book of Confessions* (Louisville, Ky.: Office of the General Assembly, 1991), 6. 191–93.

80. Quoted in Hubert M. Morrow, "A Progressive Theology," in *A People Called Cumberland Presbyterians*, ed. Ben M. Barrus, Milton L. Baughn, and Thomas H. Campbell (Memphis: Frontier, 1972), 286.

81. A portion of the Cumberlands did not accept the merger and continued as a separate denomination.

82. New York *Daily Tribune* (1 June 1903) quoted in John T. Ames, "Cumberland Liberals and the Union of 1906," *Journal of Presbyterian History* 52 (Spring 1974): 5; "The Pontificate of Leo XIII," *New York Times*, 21 July 1903, 8; Mark Twain, *Is Shakespeare Dead? From My Autobiography* (New York: Harper and Brothers, 1909), 130; "Attacks Christian Science: Mormon Apostle Taylor Also Denounces Evolution, Hypnotism, and Presbyterianism," *New York Times*, 6 October 1903, 1. Mormon statements on infant sinlessness appear in Doctrine and Covenants 29:46–47 (1830) and 93:38 (1833); cf. Mosiah 3:18 in the Book of Mormon: "the infant perisheth not that dieth in his infancy; but men drink damnation to their own souls."

83. John W. Stagg, *Calvin, Twisse and Edwards on the Universal Salvation of Those Dying in Infancy* (Richmond, Va.: Presbyterian Committee of Publication, 1902), 158; cf. 141–46 on the "present day slander."

84. Bridges quoted in Thompson, *Presbyterians in the South*, 3:223; G. A. Blackburn, "Vance's Predestination," *Presbyterian Quarterly* 13 (1898): 654; James I. Vance, *Predestination: A Sermon* (Richmond, Va.: Presbyterian Committee of Publication, 1898); Lucas, *On Being Presbyterian*, 203.

85. Thompson, *Presbyterians in the South*, 3:221. Interdenominational tension over infant damnation has had a long history in the South; see the comment in Elizabeth Fox-Genovese and Eugene D. Genovese, *The Mind of the Master Class: History and Faith in the Southern Slaveholders' Worldview* (Cambridge: Cambridge University Press, 2005), 453.

86. John Updike, *In the Beauty of the Lilies* (New York: Knopf, 1996), 7, 16. Wilmot is modeled partly after Updike's paternal grandfather, who was a Presbyterian minister (John Updike, correspondence with author, 23 January 2004).

87. Edwin H. Rian, *The Presbyterian Conflict* (Grand Rapids, Mich.: Eerdmans, 1940), 27. Ironically, Rian later rejoined the PCUSA and served for 15 years as assistant to the president of Princeton Seminary; see his obituary, *New York Times*, 25 August 1995, B7. For the confession of 1967, see the current Presbyterian Church (U.S.A.) Book of Confessions, sec. 9. On the formation of the OPC and PCA, see Lucas, *On Being Presbyterian*, 211–16, 237–40. On the birth of Westminster Seminary, see Bradley J. Longfield, *The Presbyterian Controversy: Fundamentalists, Modernists, and Moderates* (New York: Oxford University Press, 1991), 162–80. The best study of Machen as a confessionalist is D. G. Hart, *Defending the Faith: J. Gresham Machen and the Crisis of Conservative Protestantism in Modern America* (Baltimore: Johns Hopkins University Press, 1994).

88. R. C. Sproul, *Now That's a Good Question* (Wheaton, Ill.: Tyndale House, 1996), 90.

89. R. C. Sproul, *Chosen by God* (Wheaton, Ill.: Tyndale House, 1986), 197. Sproul made the same point in the Chosen by God Conference sponsored by his Ligonier Ministries, Akron, Ohio, 16 September 2007 (audio CD of question-and-answer session).

90. Robert A. Peterson and Michael D. Williams, *Why I Am Not an Arminian* (Downers Grove, Ill.: InterVarsity, 2004), 64; Jerry L. Walls and Joseph R. Dongell, *Why I Am Not a Calvinist* (Downers Grove, Ill.: InterVarsity, 2004).

91. Loraine Boettner, *The Reformed Doctrine of Predestination*, 7th ed. (Grand Rapids, Mich.: Eerdmans, 1951), 52. Originally published in 1932, the text was reissued in 1990 by P&R Publishing of Phillipsburg, New Jersey. Boettner was also noted for his virulently anti-Catholic writings; see William M. Shea, *The Lion and the Lamb: Evangelicals and Catholics in America* (New York: Oxford University Press, 2004), 142–45.

92. Charles Augustus Briggs, *Whither? A Theological Question for the Times* (New York: Scribner's, 1889), 247.

93. Thomas Helwys, "A Declaration of Faith of English People" (1611), in *A Sourcebook for Baptist Heritage*, ed. H. Leon McBeth (Nashville: Broadman, 1990), 40; cf. Bill J. Leonard, *Baptists in America* (New York: Columbia University Press, 2005), 74.

94. Bill J. Leonard, *Baptist Ways: A History* (Valley Forge, Pa.: Judson, 2003), 49.

95. *A Confession of Faith, Put Forth by the Elders and Brethren of Many Congregations of Christians (Baptized upon Profession of Their Faith) in London and the Countrey*, 3rd ed. (London, 1699), 38. On the differences between the 1689 confession and Westminster, see Schaff, ed., *Creeds of Christendom*, 738–41. Baptist historian Leon McBeth betrays his own sympathies by printing only the Particular Baptists' shorter First London Confession of 1644, in which he detects "no trace of the hyper-Calvinism which mars the Second London Confession of 1689" (McBeth, *Sourcebook*, 45).

96. Schaff, ed., *Creeds of Christendom*, 3:744–45. On the tone of the New Hampshire Confession of 1833, see William H. Brackney, *A Genetic History of Baptist Thought: With Special Reference to Baptists in Britain and North America* (Macon, Ga.: Mercer University Press, 2004), 40.

97. Leonard, *Baptists in America*, 86.

98. Hal Crowther, *Cathedrals of Kudzu: A Personal Landscape of the South* (Baton Rouge: Louisiana State University Press, 2000), 106.

99. Quoted in Richard J. Hooker, ed., *The Carolina Backcountry on the Eve of the Revolution: The Journal and Other Writings of Charles Woodmason, Anglican Itinerant* (Chapel Hill: University of North Carolina Press, 1953), 103.

100. Quotations from Paul Harvey, *Redeeming the South: Religious Cultures and Racial Identities among Southern Baptists, 1865–1925* (Chapel Hill: University of North Carolina Press, 1997), 83.

101. Marshall quoted in Gregory A. Wills, *Democratic Religion: Freedom, Authority, and Church Discipline in the Baptist South, 1785–1900* (New York: Oxford University Press, 1997), 77. On the controversy at First African, see Albert J. Raboteau, *Slave Religion: The "Invisible Institution" in the Antebellum South* (New York: Oxford University Press, 1978), 189–94.

102. Quoted in Wills, *Democratic Religion*, 77.

103. Bertram Wyatt-Brown, "The Antimission Movement in the Jacksonian South: A Study in Regional Folk Culture," *Journal of Southern History* 36 (1970): 501–29; John G. Crowley, *Primitive Baptists of the Wiregrass South, 1815 to the Present* (Gainesville: University Press of Florida, 1998), xi–17.

104. Joseph Hussey, *God's Operations of Grace but No Offers of His Grace* (London, 1707), 91. An abridged version of Hussey's book was published for Primitive Baptist use by Primitive Publications, Elon College, N.C., in 1973. On Hussey's views, see Peter Toon, *The Emergence of Hyper-Calvinism in English Nonconformity, 1689–1765* (London: Olive Tree, 1967), 70–85.

105. John Gill, *The Doctrine of Predestination Stated, and Set in the Scripture-Light: In Opposition to Mr. Wesley's Predestination Calmly Consider'd*, 2nd ed. (London, 1752), 29. Elsewhere, Gill wrote that "salvation is not offered at all by God, upon any condition whatsoever, to any of the sons of men, elect or non-elect"; quotation from Tom J. Nettles, "John Gill and the Evangelical Awakening," in *The Life and Thought of John Gill (1697–1771): A Tercentennial Appreciation*, ed. Michael A. G. Haykin (Leiden: Brill, 1997), 152. On Gill, see also Toon, *Emergence of Hyper-Calvinism*, 96–100, 129, 144.

106. Mitchell F. Ducey, "Cushing Biggs Hassell," in *Dictionary of North Carolina Biography* (Chapel Hill: University of North Carolina Press, 1988), 3:68–69. On the Kehukee Association and the early Primitive Baptist movement, see Arthur Carl Piepkorn, "The Primitive Baptists of North America," *Concordia Theological Monthly* 42 (1971): 297–314; James R. Mathis, *The Making of the Primitive Baptists: A Cultural and Intellectual History of the Antimission Movement, 1800–1840* (New York: Routledge, 2004), 83–101; Jeffrey Wayne Taylor, *The Formation of the Primitive Baptist Movement* (Kitchener, Ont.: Pandora, 2004), 33–35.

107. Cushing Biggs Hassell and Sylvester Hassell, *History of the Church of God, from the Creation to* A.D. *1885, Including Especially the History of the Kehukee Primitive Baptist Association* (1886; reprint, McDonough, Ga.: Old School Hymnal, 2002), 651, 333. On this text, see James L. Peacock and Ruel W. Tyson, Jr., *Pilgrims of Paradox: Calvinism and Experience among the Primitive Baptists of the Blue Ridge* (Washington, D.C.: Smithsonian Institution Press, 1989), 33–40.

108. Peacock and Tyson, *Pilgrims of Paradox*, 204.

109. William E. Barton quoted in Allen C. Guelzo, "Abraham Lincoln and the Doctrine of Necessity," *Journal of the Abraham Lincoln Association* 18 (Winter 1997): 67. On Lincoln's Baptist connection, see also Guelzo, *Abraham Lincoln: Redeemer President* (Grand Rapids, Mich.: Eerdmans, 1999), 36–38.

110. Wills, *Democratic Religion*, 77.

111. Arthur Carl Piepkorn, *Profiles in Belief: The Religious Bodies of the United States and Canada*, vol. 2, *Protestant Denominations* (San Francisco: Harper and Row, 1978), 447–48; the Articles of Faith are posted online at http://www.natlprimbaptconv.org.

112. Howard Dorgan, *Giving Glory to God in Appalachia: Worship Practices of Six Baptist Subdenominations* (Knoxville: University of Tennessee Press, 1987), 88–89; cf. 10, for a sampling of the predestinarian language in statements of faith published by Primitive associations.

113. J. J. Lambeth (Browns Summit, N.C.) to Sylvester Hassell, 8 March 1898, Sylvester S. Hassell Papers, collection no. 321, series 1, folder 1, Southern Historical Collection, Wilson Library, University of North Carolina, Chapel Hill. On Two-Seed theology, see W. L. Allen, "Two-Seed-in-the-Spirit Predestinarian Baptists," in *Dictionary of Baptists in America*, ed. Bill J. Leonard (Downers Grove, Ill.: InterVarsity, 1994), 270–71; Crowley, *Primitive Baptists*, 118–33; and Piepkorn, *Profiles in Belief*, 2:445–46. Variants of the two-seed theory have surfaced in modern racist ideologies; see Michael Barkun, *Religion and the Racist Right: The Origins of the Christian Identity Movement*, rev. ed. (Chapel Hill: University of North Carolina Press, 1997), 159–62.

114. James Petigru Boyce, *Abstract of Systematic Theology* (Philadelphia: American Baptist Publication Society, 1887), 339. On the influence of the Philadelphia tradition in the South, see Holifield, *Theology in America: Christian Thought from the Age of the Puritans to the Civil War* (New Haven, Conn.: Yale University Press, 2003), 284–86.

115. J. L. Dagg, *A Manual of Theology* (Charleston, S.C.: Southern Baptist Publication Society, 1857), 306–7, 320.

116. Ibid., 312. Regarding divine foreknowledge, the Philadelphia Confession stated: "Although God knoweth whatsoever may, or can come to pass upon all supposed Conditions; yet hath he not decreed any thing, because he foresaw it as future, or as that which would come to pass upon such conditions." *A Confession of Faith…Adopted by the Baptist Association Met at Philadelphia, Sept. 25. 1742*, 6th ed. (Philadelphia, 1743), 21.

117. Boyce, *Abstract*, 116–17.

118. Ibid., 356–67.

119. Benjamin B. Warfield, "Revision of the Confession of Faith. I," *Herald and Presbyter*, 21 August 1889, CR, no. 31.

120. Hodge, *Systematic Theology*, 1:11, 15. On Boyce's theology and his study with Hodge, see the overview by Timothy George, "James Petigru Boyce," in *Theologians of the Baptist Tradition*, ed. Timothy George and David S. Dockery (Nashville: Broadman and Holman, 2001), 73–89.

121. John A. Broadus, *Memoir of James Petigru Boyce, D.D., LL.D.* (New York: Armstrong and Son, 1893), 265.

122. William Newton Clarke, *An Outline of Christian Theology* (1898; reprint, Edinburgh: Clark, 1908), 47–49, 147; Hutchison, *Modernist Impulse*, 117–21.

123. George M. Marsden, *Fundamentalism and American Culture*, 2nd ed. (New York: Oxford University Press, 2006), 216 (Mullins quotation from same page). On the similar intellectual quandaries faced by Mullins and his northern Baptist counterpart, Augustus Hopkins Strong, see Grant Wacker, *Augustus H. Strong and the Dilemma of Historical Consciousness* (Macon, Ga.: Mercer University Press, 1985), 166–68.

124. "Termites" quote from James Robison, "Satan's Subtle Attacks," sermon at the SBC Pastors' Conference, 10 June 1979, in *Going for the Jugular: A Documentary History of the SBC Holy War*, ed. Walter B. Shurden and Randy Shepley (Macon, Ga.: Mercer University Press, 1996), 33.

125. Two good overviews are by the sociologist Nancy Tatom Ammerman, *Baptist Battles: Social Change and Religious Conflict in the Southern Baptist Convention* (New Brunswick, N.J.: Rutgers University Press, 1990); and the

historian Bill J. Leonard, *God's Last and Only Hope: The Fragmentation of the Southern Baptist Convention* (Grand Rapids, Mich.: Eerdmans, 1990). Regarding the exodus of moderates from the SBC's seminaries, the figure of 80 percent is from Bill Leonard, cited in Laurie Goodstein, "Adrian P. Rogers, 74, Conservative Baptist Leader, Dies," *New York Times*, 16 November 2005, A21.

126. Charles Stanley, a television evangelist and pastor of Atlanta's megachurch First Baptist, has written that the doctrine of eternal security persuaded him to leave his familial Pentecostalism and become a Southern Baptist. See Stanley, *Eternal Security: Can You Be Sure?* (Nashville: Oliver-Nelson, 1990), 1–5.

127. See the comments on the Sandy Creek tradition in Leonard, *God's Last and Only Hope,* 33–34.

128. W. A. Criswell, "Doctrine of Predestination" (sermon on Isa. 46:9–11), 20 November 1955, and "God Hath Chosen You" (sermon on 2 Thess. 2:13–14), 18 May 1958, both online at Criswell Sermon Library, http://www.wacriswell.org. For an overview of Criswell's career and theology, see Paige Patterson, "W. A. Criswell," in George and Dockery, eds., *Theologians of the Baptist Tradition,* 233–56.

129. John R. Rice, *Predestined for Hell? No!* (Murfreesboro, Tenn.: Sword of the Lord, 1958), 81.

130. Ibid., 17–18, 27–29.

131. Ibid., 80.

132. Ibid., 19. On Graham's ARP background, as well as his later split with Rice, see William Martin, *A Prophet with Honor: The Billy Graham Story* (New York: William Morrow, 1991), 59, 219–24, 239; Billy Graham, *Just as I Am: The Autobiography of Billy Graham* (San Francisco: HarperCollins, 1997), 302–4. Another product of the ARP Church, the North Carolina novelist Doris Betts, has written compellingly of this tradition; see her "Resting on the Bedrock of Original Sin," in *The Christ-Haunted Landscape: Faith and Doubt in Southern Fiction*, ed. Susan Ketchin (Jackson: University Press of Mississippi, 1994), 230–59.

133. Ernest C. Reisinger and D. Matthew Allen, *A Quiet Revolution: A Chronicle of Beginnings of Reformation in the Southern Baptist Convention* (Cape Coral, Fla.: Founders, 2000), 40, 45; Geoffrey Thomas, *Ernest C. Reisinger: A Biography* (Edinburgh: Banner of Truth Trust, 2002), 198–216.

134. R. Albert Mohler, Jr., "Baptist Theology at the Crossroads: The Legacy of E. Y. Mullins," *Southern Baptist Journal of Theology* 3, no. 4 (Winter 1999): 13 (Mullins quoted on same page); Reisinger and Allen, *Quiet Revolution,* 28–35. For the Baptist Faith and Message of 1925, see Pelikan and Hotchkiss, eds., *Creeds and Confessions,* 3:437–44.

135. Reisinger and Allen, *Quiet Revolution,* 49; Russell H. Dilday, *Columns: Glimpses of a Seminary under Assault* (Macon, Ga.: Smyth and Helwys, 2004), 64.

136. Reisinger-Patterson correspondence quoted in Reisinger and Allen, *Quiet Revolution,* 51–52.

137. Robert B. Selph, *Southern Baptists and the Doctrine of Election* (1988; reprint, Harrisonburg, Va.: Sprinkle, 1996), 7, 90, 120.

138. Reisinger and Allen, *Quiet Revolution,* 53.

139. Thomas J. Nettles, *By His Grace and for His Glory: A Historical, Theological, and Practical Study of the Doctrines of Grace in Baptist Life* (1986; reprint, Lake Charles, La.: Cor Meum Tibi, 2002), 254 (on Mullins), and 73–107, 388 (on Gill).

140. Adrian Rogers, *Predestined for Hell? Absolutely Not!* (Memphis: Love Worth Finding Ministries, n.d.), 5, 9, 16–17.

141. Collin Hansen, *Young, Restless, Reformed: A Journalist's Journey with the New Calvinists* (Wheaton, Ill.: Crossway, 2008), 69; on Mohler's purge of

Southern, 72–74. For the text of the 1858 Abstract of Principles, see Pelikan and Hotchkiss, eds., *Creeds and Confessions*, 3:316–20.

142. William R. Estep, "Doctrines Lead to 'Dunghill,' Prof Warns," *Baptist Standard*, 26 March 1997, available online at the Founders site, http://www .founders.org/journal/fj29/article1.html.

143. Keith Hinson, "Prof's Attack on Calvinism Renews Debate among Baptists," 18 April 1997, online at http://www.sbcbaptistpress.org/bpnews .asp?ID=3530.

144. Frank S. Page, *Trouble with the TULIP: A Closer Examination of the Five Points of Calvinism* (Canton, Ga.: Riverstone Group, 2000), 6, 28–37, 60, 63, 73–74.

145. Ken Camp, "Election Could Prove Troubling to Calvinists in SBC," *Baptist Standard*, 23 June 2006, online at http://www.baptiststandard.com/index .php?option=com_content&task=view&id=5188&Itemid=134; Tony Cartledge, "Seminary Presidents Mohler and Patterson Debate Calvinism," *Associated Baptist Press*, 13 June 2006, online at http://www.abpnews.com/index.php?option=com_ content&task=view&id=1199&Itemid=119; Michael Foust, "Patterson, Mohler: Calvinism Shouldn't Divide SBC," *Baptist Press News*, 13 June 2006, online at http://www.bpnews.net/bpnews.asp?id=23457; audio recording (CD) of SBC Pastors' Conference, sess. 1, 12 June 2006, available from SBC Tapes, Fort Worth, Texas.

146. Tammi Reed Ledbetter, "Baptists and Calvinism: Event Was Called Off, but Not the Debate," *Baptist Press*, 18 October 2006, online at http://www .bpnews.net/bpnews.asp?ID=24192.

147. Ergun Caner, "Questions on Neo-Calvinism, Part 1," posted on 11 October 2006 at http://www.erguncaner.com; Tom Ascol, "What Really Happened to the Debate, Pt. 3," posted on 10 October 2006 at http://www.founders.org/blog. On Ergun Caner, the prophet Muhammad, and pedophilia, see the "People" note in *Christian Century* 122 (8 March 2005): 21; cf. the related article on an earlier debate, Alan Cooperman, "Anti-Muslim Remarks Stir Tempest," *Washington Post*, 20 June 2002, A3.

148. Ed Setzer, "Calvinism, Evangelism, and SBC Leadership," in *Calvinism: A Southern Baptist Dialogue*, ed. E. Ray Clendenen and Brad J. Waggoner (Nashville: Broadman and Holman, 2008), 14.

149. Timothy George, "Is Jesus a Baptist?" plenary address at conference, "Baptist Identity: Convention, Cooperation, and Controversy," Union University, Jackson, Tenn., 20 February 2007, online at http://www.beesondivinity.com/ templates/System/details.asp?id=25215&PID=430520.

Epilogue

1. Caroline Overington, "Pastor Advises the President, Eyes the Globe," *Age* (Melbourne, Australia), 26 March 2005, 12; James Cowan, "A Purpose Driven Country," *National Post* (Toronto, Canada), 28 April 2008, A3; "The Top 20 over 15 Years," *USA Today*, 30 October 2008, 4D. On John Edwards, see Amy Sullivan, *The Party Faithful: How and Why Democrats Are Closing the God Gap* (New York: Scribner's, 2008), 126.

2. Rick Warren, *The Purpose-Driven Life: What on Earth Am I Here For?* (Grand Rapids, Mich.: Zondervan, 2002), 22–23, 98, 196.

3. Ibid., 196.

4. Rick Warren, "Making the Most of Your Time," sermon at Saddleback Church, 11 June 2005 (transcribed by the author); Jonathan Edwards, "The Preciousness of Time," in *The Works of Jonathan Edwards*, vol. 19, *Sermons and*

Discourses, 1734–1738, ed. M. X. Lesser (New Haven, Conn.: Yale University Press, 2001), 250, 259.

5. Rick Warren, "Class 101: Discovering Saddleback Membership," photocopied curriculum distributed at Saddleback Church, 12 June 2005.

6. Tom Holladay and Kay Warren, *Foundations: A Purpose-Driven Discipleship Resource: Teacher's Guide* (Grand Rapids, Mich.: Zondervan, 2003), 1:218–21.

7. A helpful overview of the hallmarks of megachurches is Scott Thumma, "Exploring the Megachurch Phenomena: Their Characteristics and Cultural Context," Hartford Institute for Religion Research, online at http://hirr.hartsem .edu/bookshelf/thumma_article2.html. See also Scott Thumma and Dave Travis, *Beyond Megachurch Myths: What We Can Learn from America's Largest Churches* (San Francisco: Jossey-Bass, 2007). On Saddleback in the wider context of American evangelicalism, see Randall Balmer, *Mine Eyes Have Seen the Glory: A Journey into the Evangelical Subculture in America*, 4th ed. (New York: Oxford University Press, 2006), 322–34.

8. Tom Holladay, interview with the author, 14 June 2005.

9. Ibid. The *Foundations* curriculum echoes Holladay's assertion that Calvinism and Arminianism are both biblical. "We believe that Scripture teaches both truths, and to exclude one set of verses over the other is unbalanced. God allows us the freedom to choose to love him or not. Our freedom to choose cannot supercede the sovereign election of God." Tom Holladay and Kay Warren, *Foundations: A Purpose-Driven Discipleship Resource: Participant's Guide* (Grand Rapids, Mich.: Zondervan, 2003), 116.

10. Increase Mather, *A Discourse Concerning the Uncertainty of the Times of Men, and the Necessity of Being Prepared for Sudden Changes & Death* (Boston, 1697), 17.

11. Jacob Weisberg, *The Bush Tragedy* (New York: Random House, 2008), 104.

12. Quoted in D. W. Bebbington, "Moody as Transatlantic Evangelical," in *Mr. Moody and the Evangelical Tradition*, ed. Timothy George (London: Clark, 2004), 83.

13. Quoted in George M. Marsden, *Fundamentalism and American Culture*, 2nd ed. (New York: Oxford University Press, 2006), 43.

14. Bob DeWaay, *Redefining Christianity: Understanding the Purpose Driven Movement* (Springfield, Mo.: 21st Century Press, 2006), 114, 104.

15. Marshall Davis, *More than a Purpose: An Evangelical Response to Rick Warren and the Megachurch Movement* (Enumclaw, Wash.: Pleasant Word, 2006), 57.

16. Rick Warren, *The Purpose Driven Church: Growth without Compromising Your Message and Mission* (Grand Rapids, Mich.: Zondervan, 1995), 25–26. On Criswell's Calvinism, see above, ch. 6.

17. The Laudians recognized that "the doctrine of predestination had often been a radical dissolvent of a churchly and sacramental outlook," observes Dewey D. Wallace, Jr., *Puritans and Predestination: Grace in English Protestant Theology, 1525–1695* (Chapel Hill: University of North Carolina Press, 1982), 99. So too Nicholas Tyacke, *Anti-Calvinists: The Rise of English Arminianism, c. 1590–1640*, rev. ed. (Oxford: Clarendon, Oxford University Press, 1990), 176: "It was no accident that during the Arminian ascendancy altars and fonts came to dominate church interiors, for the two were logically connected, sacramental grace replacing the grace of predestination." Similarly, Anthony Milton, *Catholic and Reformed: The Roman and Protestant Churches in English Protestant Thought, 1600–1640* (Cambridge: Cambridge University Press, 1995), 544, notes that from the Laudians' perspective, "Calvinist predestinarianism *could not fail* to undermine the sacraments."

18. Balmer, *Mine Eyes Have Seen the Glory*, 117.

19. Robert Lowell, *Collected Prose*, ed. Robert Giroux (New York: Farrar, Straus, and Giroux, 1987), 287.

20. Charles Hodge, *Systematic Theology*, 3 vols. (New York: Scribner's, 1871–1872), 1:10.

21. Rudolf Otto, *The Idea of the Holy: An Inquiry into the Non-rational Factor in the Idea of the Divine and Its Relation to the Rational*, 2nd ed., trans. John W. Harvey (London: Oxford University Press, 1950), 88–89.

22. Quoted in G. K. Chesterton, *Saint Thomas Aquinas* (Garden City, N.Y.: Image, Doubleday, 1956), 141.

23. *Tischreden*, no. 5070, quoted in Martin Luther, *Letters of Spiritual Counsel*, trans. Theodore Tappert (Philadelphia: Westminster, 1955), 131.

24. Jonathan Edwards, "Personal Narrative" (c. 1740), in *The Works of Jonathan Edwards*, vol. 16, *Letters and Personal Writings*, ed. George S. Claghorn (New Haven, Conn.: Yale University Press, 1998), 792–93.

25. Flannery O'Connor, "Parker's Back," in O'Connor, *Everything That Rises Must Converge* (New York: Farrar, Straus, and Giroux, 1965), 235, 244.

26. Ibid., 244.

Glossary

1. Richard A. Muller, *Dictionary of Latin and Greek Theological Terms Drawn Principally from Protestant Scholastic Theology* (Grand Rapids, Mich.: Baker, 1985), 88.

2. In defending double predestination, Calvin lamented that many people, "as if they wished to avert a reproach from God, accept election in such terms as to deny that anyone is condemned. But they do this very ignorantly and childishly, since election itself could not stand except as set over against reprobation." John Calvin, *Institutes of the Christian Religion*, ed. John T. McNeill and trans. Ford Lewis Battles (Philadelphia: Westminster, 1960), III.23.1, p. 947.

3. Muller, *Dictionary*, 235. Some advocates of the fully double position, such as Cornelius Van Til (1895–1987), a longtime professor at Westminster Seminary, call it "equal ultimacy." Cornelius Van Til, *The Defense of the Faith* (Philadelphia: Presbyterian and Reformed Publishing, 1955), 413–16, as discussed in G. C. Berkouwer, *Divine Election*, trans. Hugo Bekker (Grand Rapids, Mich.: Eerdmans, 1960), 177n8, 189n31.

4. A good survey by a group of evangelical scholars is James K. Beilby and Paul R. Eddy, eds., *Divine Foreknowledge: Four Views* (Downers Grove, Ill.: InterVarsity, 2001).

5. See, e.g., Samuel Willard, *A Compleat Body of Divinity in Two Hundred and Fifty Expository Lectures on the Assembly's Shorter Catechism* (Boston, 1726), 263.

6. See, e.g., Francis Turretin, *Institutes of Elenctic Theology*, trans. George Musgrave Giger and ed. James T. Dennison, Jr., 3 vols. (Phillipsburg, N.J.: P&R, 1992), 1:332–33, who points out that scripture uses "equivalent phrases" in speaking of the saved and the damned.

7. See, e.g., the explanation by the conservative Presbyterian Loraine Boettner, *The Reformed Doctrine of Predestination* (Grand Rapids, Mich.: Eerdmans, 1951), 150–53.

8. Muller, *Dictionary*, 129–30, 132.

9. Numbered as part of 2 Maccabees 12:45 in some translations.

10. See, e.g., Willard, *Compleat Body of Divinity*, 263.

11. See the explanation in Muller, *Dictionary*, 292, and the lengthier discussion of the infra-supra debate in Karl Barth, *Church Dogmatics*, vol. 2, pt. 2, *The Doctrine*

of God, trans. G. W. Bromiley et al. (Edinburgh: Clark, 1957), 127–45. Barth noted that supralapsarianism's advantage is that it puts the free grace of God "so consistently and definitely at the head of all Christian knowledge and understanding" (135). Various Reformed scholastic perspectives on infra-supra are also discussed and excerpted in Heinrich Heppe, *Reformed Dogmatics: Set Out and Illustrated from the Sources*, trans. G. T. Thomson and ed. Ernst Bizer (1950; reprint, Grand Rapids, Mich.: Baker, 1978), 150–89.

12. Roger E. Olson, *Arminian Theology: Myths and Realities* (Downers Grove, Ill.: InterVarsity, 2006), 17–18; see the opposing view in Muller, *Dictionary*, 294.

Index

Page numbers in italics refer to illustrations.

Abbott, Benjamin, 100, 112–13, 118, 127
Abraham and Sarah, 110
Absolute monarchism, 104, 105, 255n.7
Abstract of Systematic Theology (Boyce),
   199, 203, 204
Act of Uniformity (1662), 76
Actes and Monuments (Foxe), 34
Acts, Book of, 17, 65, 87, 119
Adam. *See* Fall of Adam and Eve
Adams, John, 106
Adams, John Quincy, 106
Adopting Act (1729), 176–77
Adventists
   anti-predestinarianism of, 103
   and the Bible, 122–24
   and the Christian Connection, 262n.95
   on free will, 262n.102
   and republicanism, 10
African Americans
   Baptists, 194, 197–98
   and Calvinism, 261n.78
   Lutherans, 164, 274n.113
   Methodists, 117–18
   and New Divinity, 119
   and race, racism, and slavery, 117–18,
      180–81
African Methodist Episcopal (AME) Church,
   117–18
Age of Reason. *See* Enlightenment
The Age of Reason (Paine), 100–101, 103,
   109, 110
Agony of predestination, 57–72, 125
Alarme to Unconverted Sinners (Alleine), 66

ALC. *See* American Lutheran Church (ALC)
All for Jesus (Faber), 144
Alleine, Joseph, 66, 253n.79
Allen, Richard, 117–18
Alliance of Reformed Churches throughout
   the World Holding the Presbyterian
   System, 184
Altes und Neues (Old and New), 158,
   165–66
Althaus, Paul, 270n.57
AME. *See* African Methodist Episcopal
   (AME) Church
American Civil War, 180–83
American Lutheran Church (ALC), 160,
   168, 274n.113
American Revolution, 10, 100, 102–3, 152
Ames, William, 44, 47, 60
Amyraut, Moïse, 51
Andover Review, 162
Andover Seminary, 114
Andrewes, Lancelot, 42, 43
Andrews, Jedediah, 106
Angels, 17, 19
Anglicanism
   anti-predestinarianism of, 75–80, 104
   and Cambridge events of 1590s, 239n.114
   definition of, 219–20
   and first American bishop, 80
   high-church wing of, 75, 78, 145–46
   and Jefferson, 105
   and latitudinarianism, 75, 81–85
   in nineteenth century, 239n.113
   and obedience to God, 80

Anglicanism (*continued*)
  and sacramentalism, 9, 43, 80, 266n.153
  and *via media* (middle way), 239
  See also Church of England
Anti-Calvinismus (Pfeiffer), 160
Anti-Missourian Brotherhood, 166
Anti-predestinarianism. *See* specific churches
  and theologians
Antichrist, 33, 43, 147
Antinomians, 34, 51, 57, 70–71
Anxiety of predestination, 57–69, 125
Apocrypha, 24, 225
*An Appeal to the People in Behalf of Their
  Rights as Authorized Interpreters of the
  Bible* (C. Beecher), 132
Aquinas, Thomas. *See* Thomas Aquinas
Aristotle, 25, 154
Armilla aurea (golden chain), 34–35, 66,
  222–23
Arminian Magazine, 97
Arminianism
  and Breck, 71–72
  Burnet on, 82
  and Charles I, 240n.119
  and conditional predestination, 8, 38–39,
    49, 51, 93–94, 192, 214, 243n.35
  and Cutler, 250n.17
  definition of, 220
  and Edwards, 16, 71–72, 76
  English version of, 42–43
  "five-point" Calvinism versus, 37–43
  and James I, 239n.116
  Samuel Johnson on, 78–79
  Mayhew on, 96–97
  and Methodists, 116
  in New England, 71–72
  and Pelagianism, 53
  and sacramentalism, 286n.17
  and Wesley, 9, 74, 92
Arminius, Jacob, 37–39, 92, 141, 220,
  239n.110
Ascol, Tom, 205, 206, 207
Associate Reformed Presbyterian (ARP)
  Church, 284n.132
Astrology, 19, 86
Atonement
  and Christian Scientists, 124
  limited atonement, 39, 48, 109, 158, 179,
    223
  and Mormons, 128
  Remonstrants on, 39
Augsburg Confession (1530), 150, 153
Augustine of Hippo
  and Anglican sacramental piety, 266n.153
  on baptism, 134, 155
  Beecher family on, 130–35, 178–79
  and the Bible, 217

  compared with Luther, 28
  contemporary secular philosophers on, 5
  conversion and ordination of, 266n.151
  on equality of Christians, 232n.24
  and Eucharist, 149
  on free will and God's foreknowledge, 19,
    20, 39, 140, 231n.13
  on grace, 19, 22, 28, 187
  Hodge on, 181
  illustration of, 21
  on infant baptism and unbaptized infants,
    20, 178, 188
  mother of, 24, 135, 144
  Neoplatonism of, 28
  on original sin, 5, 20, 22, 61, 132, 177,
    255n.7
  on perseverance, 1, 20
  on predestination, 4, 7, 12, 19–22, 25,
    28–31, 53, 60, 63, 82, 162, 265n.144
  on prevenient grace, 238n.107
  on purgatory, 24, 143
  on reprobation, 30
  women's exclusion from theology of, 133
  youth of, 34
Augustinus (Jansen), 141
Autobiography (Franklin), 106

Bach, Johann Sebastian, 160
Bacon, Francis, 120, 123, 124, 181
Bailyn, Bernard, 104
Ballou, Hosea, 109–10
Ballou, Hosea, II, 108–10
Balmer, Randall, 216
Báñez, Domingo, 140, 141
Bangs, Nathan, 113–14
Baptism
  and Anglicanism, 80
  Augustine on, 134, 155
  and Baptists, 148
  Calvinists on, 188
  and Catholicism, 145, 146
  Donatists on, 24
  and the elect, 23–24
  by immersion at Saddleback Church, 212
  infant baptism, 20, 70, 148, 279n.72
  Jenson on, 171
  of Jesus, 126
  Krauth on, 155
  and original sin, 145
  Spirit baptism, 118
Baptist Faith and Message (1925), 204, 215
Baptists
  and African Americans, 194, 197–98
  and baptism, 148
  and the Bible's inerrancy, 168, 175,
    200–201, 205, 207

and eternal security, 201, 206, 284n.126
General and Particular factions of, 193
historical background on predestination
   controversy of, 193–200
Kehukee Primitive Baptist Association, 197
and London Confessions (1644, 1689),
   193, 198, 203, 281n.95
New Hampshire Confession (1833) of,
   193–94, 204
no-offers theology of, 196–98, 206
and Philadelphia Confession, 283n.116
and predestination controversy, 11, 175,
   193–208
Primitive Baptists, 194–98
and slavery, 198
Two-Seed-in-the-Spirit Predestinarian
   Baptists, 198
and Westminster Confession, 193
See also Southern Baptist Convention
Barnes, Albert, 179, 180
Barry, A. L., 169
Barth, Karl, 170, 242n.25, 288n.11
Bartlett, Bernard, 16
Baxter, Richard, 66
Beauty of holiness, 42
Beecher, Catharine, 130–32, *133*, 266n.153
Beecher, Charles, 132–33, *133*
Beecher, Edward, 132–33, *133*, 277n.21
Beecher, Henry Ward, 132, *133*, 183
Beecher, Lyman, 130–31, *133*, 135, 177–79,
   183, 276nn.19–20
Beecher family, 10, 103, 130–35, *133*, 162,
   177–79
Beeson Divinity School, 208
Belgic Confession (1561), 39
Bellamy, Joseph, 112, 114, 258n.46
Bellarmine, Cardinal Robert, 60
Benedict, Philip, 39
Benedict XIV, Pope, 141
Berkouwer, Gerrit Cornelis, 270n.57
Bernard of Clairvaux, 68
Betts, Doris, 284n.132
Beza, Theodore, 33, 35, 37, 48, 182
Bible
  and Abbott, 113
  and Adventists, 122–24
  and Augustine, 217
  and Christian Scientists, 124–26
  Clarke on, 200
  as composite of multiple authorial agen-
   das, 193
  Franklin on, 107
  on free choice, 261n.87
  Geneva Bible, 33
  Hodge on, 180, 217
  inerrancy of, 150, 168, 175, 193,
   200–201, 205, 207

  interpretation of, by the elect, 252n.48
  Jefferson's Bible, 105–6
  Luther versus Zwingli on authority of,
   28–29
  and Methodists, 116
  and Mormons, 126–29
  Paine on, 100–103, 110
  on predestination and election in New
   Testament, 17–19
  and Presbyterians, 176, 179–80
  and proof texting, 199–200
  Revised Standard Version (1952) of, 198
  Revised Version (1881–1885) of, 186,
   187
  on slavery, 180
  and Southern Baptists, 168, 201, 205, 207
  Sproul on, 192
  and Stone-Campbell Christians, 120–22
  as storehouse of facts, 199, 217
  Thomson's new translation of, 104
  Turretin on, 287n.6
  and Universalism, 110
  Walther on, 164
  See also specific books of the Bible, such
   as Romans, Letter to
Biel, Gabriel, 28, 234n.56
Blackburn, George A., 191
Black Americans. *See* African Americans
Body of Divinity (Ridgley), 178
Boer, Harry, 270n.49
Boettner, Loraine, 192–93, 281n.91
Bolsec, Jérôme-Hermès, 31
Book of Common Prayer, 33, 40, 76, 105
Book of Concord, 155, 164
Book of Mormon, 127–30
Boothe, Charles Octavius, 194
Boston Evening-Post, 88, 95
Boston Gazette, 89
Boyce, James Petigru, 199, 200, 203, 204,
   205
Boylston, Zabdiel, 87
Bozeman, T. Dwight, 59, 66, 69, 236n.90
Braaten, Carl, 166–67
Bradstreet, Anne, 67
Bradwardine, Thomas, 28
Breck, Robert, 71–72
Bridges, James R., 191
Briggs, Charles Augustus, 187, 193
Broadus, John, 199
Brown, Anne, 70
Brown, Peter, 22, 232n.22
Brownson, Orestes, 147
Bucer, Martin, 32
Bullinger, Heinrich, 65–66, 228, 247n.74
Burnet, Gilbert, 81–83, 175
Bush, George W., 209, 214
Bushman, Richard, 127, 129

Caldwell, Patricia, 245n.56
Calling, 220
Calvin, John
  on astrology, 86
  compared with Perkins, 36
  critics of, 14–15, 31
  death of, 31
  on double predestination, 147, 148,
    287n.2
  on election and reprobation, 30–31,
    235n.69
  and Eucharist, 14, 29
  on Fall of Adam and Eve, 235n.71
  Fisk on, 117, 260n.68
  on God's providence, 85–86, 251n.48
  on grace, 187
  illustration of, 15
  on infant baptism, 148, 279n.72
  Jefferson on, 106
  on original sin, 5
  on predestination, 14, 15, 16, 29–31,
    235n.79
  and Reformation, 234n.64
  on reprobation, 30–31, 235n.69
  See also Calvinism
Calvin, Twisse and Edwards on the
    Universal Salvation of Those Dying in
    Infancy (Stagg), 190–91
Calvinism
  Arminianism versus "five-point"
    Calvinism, 37–43
  and baptism, 188
  Baptists on, 202, 206–8
  Burnet on, 82
  Catholic polemic against, 145–48
  compared with Islam, 4, 45, 80, 95, 98,
    99, 202, 206, 207, 254–55n.102
  definition of, 220
  and divine providence, 85–86
  Dominicans accused of, 141
  Lowell on, 216–17
  Mayhew on, 96–97
  Methodists versus New England
    Calvinists, 112–19
  and original sin, 255n.7
  and TULIP, 39–40, 47–49, 67–68, 115,
    202, 206–7, 228
  and unconditional predestination, 8,
    39–40, 47–49, 53–54, 72, 79, 94, 138
  Walther on, 164
  Weber on, 58–59, 69, 149
  and women, 260n.74
  See also Calvin, John
Calvinism Improved (Huntington), 109,
  112
Cambridge theologians, 34–37, 40, 236n.90,
  239n.114

Campbell, Alexander, 120–21, 126, 130,
  194, 261n.87
Campbellites, 10, 120–22
Caner, Emir, 207
Caner, Ergun, 207
Canons of Dort (1618–1619), 39–42, 47–49,
  53, 58, 71, 185, 228
Canticles, Book of, 68
Cape Ann earthquake, 88–89
Carroll, John, 143
Cases of conscience, 66–67
Caskey, Marie, 178
Cassian, John, 22, 226–27, 232n.25
Cassidy, Cardinal Edward, 169
Casuistry, 66–67
Catherine of Aragon, 32
Catholic Answers, 144
Catholic World, 146–47
Catholicism
  in colonial Maryland, 8
  and communion of saints, 143–44
  compared with Lutheranism, 138–39
  compared with Puritanism, 59–62, 68
  and compatibilism, 7
  and Council of Trent, 34, 139, 143, 169
  and indulgences, 26–27, 138, 169,
    233n.46
  and Joint Declaration on the Doctrine of
    Justification with Lutherans, 168–71
  and justification, 139, 145
  Lowell on, 216–17
  and Mass, 25–26, 27, 32, 153, 169
  Mather on, 45
  predestination and anti-Protestant polemic
    of, 145–48
  and sacramentalism, 7, 9, 10, 24–27, 70,
    142, 145, 146
  and salvation, 147
  and scholastic controversies over predesti-
    nation, 139–42
  Stowe on, 134–35
  and Vatican II, 142, 143, 168–69
  Weber on, 58, 147
  "works righteousness" of, 59, 139
  See also Molinism; Purgatory; and specific
    popes and theologians
Challoner, Richard, 143
Chandler, Thomas Bradbury, 80
Charity for the Suffering Souls (Nageleisen),
  144
Charles I, King, 42–43, 48, 104, 240n.119
Charles V, Emperor, 32
Charnock, Stephen, 54
Chauncy, Charles, 90
Checkley, John, 77–78
Chosen by God (Sproul), 192
Chosen by God Conference, 281n.89

Christ
  apostles of, 17
  baptism of, 126
  and call to repentance and conversion,
    54–55
  compassionate promises of, 66–67, 92,
    152
  and covenant of grace, 55
  Edwards on, 68
  as elect and reprobate, 170
  ethical teachings of, 105, 106
  Jefferson on, 105–6
  and last judgment, 62–64
  love of, 68
  miracles of, 105
  Paine on, 101
  parables of, 30–31, 106
  Resurrection of, 105
  and salvation, 38, 45, 55, 150, 151, 158,
    190
  as second Adam, 55, 110
  Second Coming of, 62–64, 71, 123
  and Sermon on the Mount, 17, 182, 188
  Shepard on, 68
  Turretin on, 54
  virgin birth of, 101
  Willard on, 52
Christendom College, 142
A Christian and Plaine Treatise of the
    Manner and Order of Predestination
    (Perkins), 36, 38
Christian Church (Disciples of Christ),
    261n.82
Christian Churches/Churches of Christ,
    261n.82
Christian Connection, 122
Christian Examiner, 178, 179–80
Christian Reformed Church (CRC), 149,
    270n.49
Christian Scientists, 103, 124–26
Christianity at the Cross Roads (Mullins),
    200
Christianity Not Mysterious (Toland), 105
Chrysostom, John, 19, 82, 143
Church of England
  and Act of Uniformity (1662), 76
  Arminianism versus "five-point"
    Calvinism, 37–43
  and Elizabeth I, 69
  English Reformation and rise of Puritanism,
    32–37
  history of, 9, 32–43, 45–48
  Cotton Mather on, 83
  Thirty-nine Articles of, 33, 40, 48, 81–83,
    92–93, 98, 175
  Tractarian movement of, 144
  and Wesley, 91

  and Whitefield, 91
  See also Anglicanism
The Church of England Vindicated from the
    Charge of Arminianism (Toplady), 98
Churches of Christ, 261n.82
City of God (Augustine), 24
Civic humanism, 104
Civil War. See American Civil War; English
    Civil Wars (1641–1651)
Clap, David, 88
Clark, Elizabeth, 188
Clarke, William Newton, 200
Clement VIII, Pope, 141
Cleveland, Grover, 173
Colgate Theological Seminary, 200
College of New Jersey. See Princeton
    University
Colman, Benjamin, 62
Colonial America, 8–9
  See also New England Puritanism
Columbia University, 78
Columbus Theological Magazine, 159
Common Sense (Paine), 100, 102–3
Common Sense Applied to Religion
    (C. Beecher), 131–32
Communion. See Eucharist
Communion of saints, 143–44
Como, David, 51
Compatibilism, 5, 6
The Compatibility of Free Choice (Molina),
    140
Compleat Body of Divinity (Willard), 52
Concordia (Molina), 140
Concordia Seminary, 155, 157, 167
Conditionality
  and Arminianism, 8, 38–39, 49, 51,
    243n.35
  in Bible, 54–55
  and Christ's call to repentance and conver-
    sion, 54–55
  and covenant of grace, 55–56
  definition of, 6
  Paul on, 55
  and Puritanism, 55–56, 243n.35
Confessional subscription, 175–80
Confessions (Augustine), 19–20, 24
Congregationalism
  and Andover Seminary, 114
  and Beecher family, 132, 134
  and Breck's Arminianism, 71–72
  and conversion, 125, 134
  and Cutler, 78
  and Eddy, 125
  and Edwards, 80, 177
  and Finney, 179
  Haskel's attack on Methodists, 113
  and Haynes, 119

Congregationalism (*continued*)
  and Hussey, 196–97
  and Moody, 260n.77
  revised creed (1883) of, 184, 186
  and Westminster Confession (1647), 184
Congregationalist newspaper, 132
Conkin, Paul K., 261n.81
Conversion
  Arminius on, 38
  of Augustine, 266n.151
  Christ's call to, 54–55
  and Congregationalists, 125, 134
  definition of, 220
  Jonathan Edwards on, 134
  and Lutheranism, 150–51
  of Paul, 18, 216
  of Shepard, 61
  of Wesley, 91, 92, 110
Cooke, Samuel, 79
Cooper, William, 87–88, 93–94
Corinthians, First Letter to, 17, 61, 123,
    128, 129, 257n.26
Cotterill, Thomas, 249n.5
Cotton, John, 50–51, 71
Council of Orange, Second, 22–23, 168
Council of Trent, 34, 139, 143, 169
Covenant of grace, 55–56
Covenant of works, 51, 55
  See also Good works
Covenant theology, 54–57, 59, 244n.49,
    245n.57
Crane Theological School, Tufts University,
    257n.27
Cranmer, Thomas, 32–33
CRC. *See* Christian Reformed Church
    (CRC)
Creabilis et labilis (creatable and fallible),
    220
Creatus et lapsus (created and fallen), 221,
    223
Criswell, W. A., 201–2, 215, 216
Cromwell, Oliver, 48, 54, 76
Crosby, Howard, 187
Crowther, Hal, 194
Cumberland Presbyterian Church, 190
Cutler, Timothy, 78, 250n.17
Cyril, 143

Dagg, John Leadley, 198–99
Dana, James, 80
Daniel, Book of, 123
Davies, Julian, 240n.119
Davis, Jefferson, 182
Davis, Marshall, 215
Day of Doom (Wigglesworth), 63, 88
De Auxiliis controversy, 141

De Doctrina Christiana (Milton), 56
De servo arbitrio (Luther), 156
Death, 62–64, 130–31, 133
Declaration of Independence, 104, 105, 109
Declaration of Sentiments, 38
Declaratory Act (1879), 183–84
Declaratory Statement (1903), 189–90
Decrees, eternal, 221
Decretum horribile (dreadful decree), 94,
    221
Definite Synodical Platform (1855), 153, 155
Deism, 90, 100–103, 105, 106, 122
Dent, Arthur, 60, 66–67, 68, 247n.80
Dering, Edward, 69
Determinism, 5
Deuteronomy, Book of, 45, 55
DeWaay, Bob, 215
Dickey, Charles, 173, 189
Dickinson, Jonathan, 79, 176
Dilday, Russell, 204
"Divine Decrees" (Haynes), 119
*The Doctrine of Predestination Stated and
    Asserted* (Toplady), 98
Dominicans, 8, 53, 140–42, 224, 228
Donovan, C. F., 147
Dort Canons (1618–1619), 39–42, 47–49,
    53, 58, 71, 185, 228
Double covenant federalism, 55
Double predestination
  Calvin on, 147, 148, 287n.2
  Catholics' opposition to, 147, 148
  definition of, 221, 287n.3
  Gottschalk on, 23
  rejection of, by Missouri Synod
    Lutherans, 274n.122
  Second Council of Orange on, 22–23, 168
Dow, Lorenzo, 116
Duffy, Eamon, 144–45
Dulles, Avery, 170
Dulles, John Foster, 170
Dutch Reformed Church, 8, 149, 270n.49
Dwight, Timothy, 114, 177–78

Earthquakes, 88–90, 210
Eaton, Nathaniel, 60
Ecstatic agony of predestination, 65–72
Eddy, Mary Baker, 124–26, 263n.111
Edward VI, King, 32, 33
Edwards, John (Anglican theologian)
  as Calvinist, 76–78, 98
  on probationary middle state, 76, 95–96
  and Whitefield, 93
Edwards, John (U.S. politician), 209
Edwards, Jonathan
  and Arminianism, 16, 71–72, 76
  Chandler on, 80

on Christ, 68
on conversion, 134
and Eucharist, 16, 62, 70
Freedom of the Will by, 80, 114, 128, 177
and Hawley's suicide, 65
as infralapsarian, 52
meditation and prayer by, 127
Miller on, 72
on natural ability versus moral ability, 114
New Divinity successors of, 112, 114
on original sin, 177
and predestination, 52, 214, 218
and presidency of College of New Jersey, 177
revival preaching of, 71, 84, 90, 119, 211
and scholasticism, 72, 226
on sin and hell, 84–85
Swing on, 183
writings by, 69, 80, 114, 177
The Efficacy of the Fear of Hell (Stoddard), 84
Egan, Cardinal Edward, 147
Eklegomai (to choose, to elect), 17
ELCA. *See* Evangelical Lutheran Church in America (ELCA)
Election
   Ames on, 47
   baptism of the elect, 23–24
   Beza on elect church, 48, 182
   and Bible interpretation, 252n.48
   Bullinger on, 65–66
   Burnet on, 82
   Calvin on, 30–31, 235n.69
   and Catholicism, 142, 146
   and chosen few, 45, 59–61, 234n.56
   definition of, 221
   evidence of, in New England, 46
   Gerhard on, 157, 166
   Hewit on, 146
   Hutchinson on unconditional election, 51
   of infants, 175–79, 184–85, 187–90, 193
   Jenson on, 170–71
   Luther and Lutherans on, 149–51, 157–61, 166–67, 170–71
   Mather on, 45, 67
   Molina on, 270n.56
   Murray on, 109
   New Testament on, 17–19
   Paul on, 46
   Perkins on, 37, 60
   Peter, Second Letter of, on, 192
   Presbyterians on, 184–92
   Remonstrants on, 39
   Selph on unconditional election, 204
   Shepard on, 56
   Thomas Aquinas on, 54, 241–42n.18

Toplady on, 74–75
Turretin on, 52, 54
Tyndale on, 252n.48
Universalism on, 107–10
Walther on, 157
Wesley on, 74, 92
Westminster Confession on, 48, 175–76
Willard on, 52, 60, 67, 242–43n.30
See also Predestination; Renate
Elements of Popular Theology (Schmucker), 153
Elizabeth I, Queen, 33, 40, 69
Emblemes (Quarles), 41
Emerson, Ralph Waldo, 179
Emmons, Nathanael, 115, 130
English Arminianism, 42–43
English Civil Wars (1641–1651), 48
English Reformation, 32–37
   See also Church of England
Enlightenment, 9, 10, 75, 81–90, 104, 176, 217
Ephesians, Letter to, 17, 108, 198, 210, 215
Episcopal Church, 81, 118, 134–35, 170, 182, 187, 266n.153
Epistles. *See* specific epistles, such as Romans, Letter to
Erasmus, 27, 150, 156, 234n.52
Erikson, Kai, 56–57
The Error of Modern Missouri, 162
The Errors of Hopkinsianism (Bangs), 114
Esau and Jacob, 18, 28, 30, 55, 60, 109, 140, 152, 176, 181, 202, 205
Estep, William, 205–6
Eternal decrees, 221
Eternal security, 201, 206, 221, 284n.126
   See also Perseverance
Ethnic and racial groups. *See* African Americans; Immigrants
Eucharist
   and Augustine, 149
   and Calvin, 14, 29
   and Catholicism, 25–26, 27, 142, 145
   and Christ's love, 64
   and Edwards, 16, 62, 70
   fear of unworthy partaking of, 61–62, 64
   Laud and Laudians on, 43, 286n.17
   Luther on, 28, 149, 154
   and Lutheranism, 149, 153, 216
   Preston on, 61
   Rubin on importance of, 27
   Stoddard on, 70
   and Thomas Aquinas, 24–26, 230n.9
   and transubstantiation, 25–26, 27
   Walther on, 273n.108
Evangelical Lutheran Church in America (ELCA), 166–67, 169–70
Evangelical Lutheran Synod, 167, 274n.113

Evangelicals, 9–10, 12, 90–99, 221–22
Eve. *See* Fall of Adam and Eve
Ewing, Finis, 190
The Examination of Tilenus before the Triers
    (Womock), 76
Exercisers, 114–15, 259n.58
Exodus, Book of, 18, 30, 54, 79
Experience and Gospel Labours (Abbott),
    112–13
Exposition of the Thirty-nine Articles
    (Burnet), 81–83, 175

Faber, Frederick William, 144
Faith
    Dagg on, 199
    Luther on, 149
    and Lutheranism, 151–52, 157–61,
        167–68
    merit versus, 151–52
    Protestant doctrine of faith alone, 139
    Wesley on, 253n.80
    Westminster Confession on, 55
A Faithful Narrative (Edwards), 65
Fall of Adam and Eve
    Lyman Beecher on, 179
    Calvin on, 235n.71
    Cotton on, 51
    and covenant of works, 51, 55
    and Pelagianism, 38
    Perkins on, 36, 56
    Joseph Smith on, 128
    and Westminster Confession, 56
    Womock on infant damnation and, 176
    See also Original sin
Falwell, Jerry, 11, 207
Fatalism, 4–5, 7, 19, 80, 98, 99, 181–82, 202
Fiering, Norman, 81, 83
Finney, Charles, 115–16, 179
Fisher, Alexander Metcalf, 130–31, *131*
Fisk, Wilbur, 111–12, 116–17, 260n.68
Fiske, John, 61
Five points. *See* TULIP
Fordham University, 170
Foreknowledge
    Augustine on, 19, 20, 39, 140, 231n.13
    definition of, 222
    Formula of Concord (1577) on, 151
    Holladay on, 213–14
    and *intuitu fidei*, 152, 167
    Molina on, 39, 140–41
Formula of Concord (1577), 150–51, 159,
    162, 163, 166, 168
Forty-two Articles, 33
Foster, John W., 173
Foundations curriculum, 212–14, 286n.9
Founders Ministries, 203–5, 208

Foxcroft, Thomas, 89
Foxe, John, 34
Francis de Sales, 68
Franklin, Benjamin, 88, 89, 105, 106–7, 177
"Free Grace" (Wesley), 94–95
Free will
    and Adventists, 123–24, 262n.102
    Augustine on, 19, 20
    Catholic view of, 151–52
    and compatibilism, 5, 6
    Jonathan Edwards on, 80, 114, 128
    and God's foreknowledge, 19, 20, 39,
        140–41, 151, 152, 167, 213–14,
        231n.13
    and God's sovereignty, 79
    and good works, 139, 142, 169
    and Jehovah's Witnesses, 124
    Justin Martyr on, 19
    Luther and Lutherans on, 27–28, 148,
        150–51
    and Mormons, 127–28
    New England theology on, 114–15
    and Paul's Letter to the Romans, 18–19
    predestination versus, 6
    and prevenient grace, 38
    and Stone-Campbell Christians, 120
    Thomas Aquinas on, 140
    Wesley on, 92
    See also Arminianism; Liberty; Molinism
Freedom of the Will (Edwards), 80, 114,
    128, 177
French Calvinists, 8
Friedrich Wilhelm III, King, 153–54
Fritschel, Gottfried, 156
Fritschel, Sigmund, 156
Fuller, Andrew, 205–6
Fundamentalism, 193, 222

Galatians, Letter to, 18, 110
Garrigou-Lagrange, Reginald, 142
Gatta, John, 134
Genesis, Book of, 18, 127, 181
Geneva, Switzerland, 14–16, 29–33, 46
Geneva Bible, 33
George III, King, 103, 104
George, Timothy, 208
Gerhard, Johann, 151, 156–57, 166,
    272n.74
Gifford, George, 34
Gill, John, 109, *195*, 196–98, 204, 206,
    282n.105
Gnadenwahlslehrstreit (election-of-grace
    doctrine controversy), 150, 153–68
Gnosticism, 19, 231n.14
God
    absolute monarchy of, 104, 163, 255n.7

anger of, 84–85, 185
antecedent and consequent wills of, 239n.110, 267n.14
benevolence of, 38, 90, 176, 199
Calvin on providential activity of, 251n.48
foreknowledge of, 19, 20, 39, 140–41, 151, 152, 167, 213–14, 231n.13
glorification of, 242n.30
humans as clay in hands of potter, 18, 19, 55, 205
of Islam, 206
justice of, 38, 198–99
latitudinarians on, as Supreme Architect, 81
love of, 202
mercy of, and salvation, 18, 36–37
miracles of, 85, 90
Molina on natural versus free knowledge of, 140
obedience to, 51, 55, 80
and open theism, 124
and preexistence doctrine, 129, 130, 132–33, 224–25
proofs of existence of, 66
providence of, 2, 12, 30, 85–90, 225
revealed and hidden wills of, 56
simplicity of, 37
sovereignty of, 54, 79, 178, 197, 202
Thomas Aquinas on God as primary cause, 25, 244n.44
as Trinity, 84, 144
See also Providence
Godly ministers, 34, 43, 66, 222
God's Operations of Grace but No Offers of His Grace (Hussey), 196
Golden chain, 34–37, 66, 222–23
Gomarus, Franciscus, 38
Good works, 59, 139, 142, 169, 199
See also Covenant of works
Goodwin, John, 51
Gospel Magazine, 97
Gospels. See specific Gospels, such as Matthew, Gospel of
Gottschalk (monk), 23, 28
Grace
Augustine on, 19, 22, 28, 187
Calvin on, 187
Catholic-Lutheran Joint Declaration on, 169–71
and Catholicism, 139, 142, 146
covenant of, 55–56
"Free Grace" by Charles Wesley, 94–95
Gill on, 204
Leslie on, 78
and Lutheranism, 150–51, 159–60
and Methodists, 117

Protestant theology of grace alone, 34, 38, 58, 117, 139, 169
Remonstrants on, 39
Shepard on, 69
Thomas Aquinas on, 169, 234n.55
Westminster Confession on, 48
William Ockham on, 28
See also Prevenient grace
Graham, Billy, 202–3, 203
Gratia praeveniens (prevenient grace), 38
Great Awakenings, 71, 84, 107, 115, 119, 201, 255n.7
The Great Christian Doctrine of Original Sin Defended (Edwards), 177
The Great Controversy (White), 123–24
Gregory of Rimini, 28
Gruet, Jacques, 14–15
Guelzo, Allen, 5, 116, 229–30n.6

Hagar, 110
Hahn, Scott, 147
Haines, M. L., 174
Half-Way Covenant, 70
Hall, David D., 60, 61, 70
Hamilton, Alastair, 59
Hanks, Nancy, and Thomas Lincoln, 197
Hansen, Collin, 205
Harlan, John, 173
Harms, Claus, 154
Harrison, Benjamin, 172–74, 174, 186, 189
Harry Potter novels, 209
Harvard College/University, 52, 60, 63, 89, 108
Harvard Divinity School, 114, 179, 257n.27
Haskel, Daniel, 113–14
Hassell, Cushing Biggs, 196, 197
Hassell, Sylvester, 197, 198
Hastings, Selina, 97
Hatch, Nathan O., 116, 261n.79
Haug, Hans Robert, 162, 270n.50
Hawley, Joseph, 65
Haynes, John, 60
Haynes, Lemuel, 119
Haynes, Roger, 60
Hebrews, Letter to, 143, 183
Hecker, Isaac, 146
Heimert, Alan, 255n.7
Hell
Chauncy on, 90
Jonathan Edwards on, 84–85
fear of, 61, 64, 118
Mormons on, 129
as punishment for sin, 83–85
Stoddard on, 84
unborn souls consigned to, 255n.102
and Universalism, 109–10, 112

Helvetic Confession, Second (1566), 65–66, 247n.80
Helwys, Thomas, 193
Hemphill, Samuel, 106–7, 176–77
Henry VIII, King, 32, 42
Herald of Gospel Liberty, 122
Hervey, James, 255n.102
Hett, Anne, 65, 246n.71
Hewit, Augustine Francis, 145–48, 217
Hickory, N.C., 161, 214
Hildegard of Bingen, 61
Himes, Joshua V., 262n.95
Hincmar, archbishop of Reims, 23
History of Cosmopolite (Dow), 116
History of the Church of God, from Creation to A.D. 1885 (Hassell), 197
Hochstetter, Christian, 272n.75
Hodge, Archibald Alexander, 186
Hodge, Charles, 155, 179–81, 187, 198–200, 217, 279n.70
Holifield, E. Brooks, 61, 109
Holiness movement, 103, 118
Holladay, Tom, 212–14, 286n.9
Holy Spirit
    and the Bible, 186, 192
    and elect, 71
    and good works, 169
    and interpretation of providential significance of events, 85
    and Joint Declaration on the Doctrine of Justification, 169
    and Pentecostalism, 10, 71
    and prevenient grace, 38
    salvation through, 167, 190
    Westminster Confession on, 55
    See also Grace
Hooker, Thomas, 55
Hopkins, Samuel, 106, 114, 134
"The Horrible Decree" (Wesley), 94
Howe, Daniel Walker, 276n.20
Huguenots, 8, 48, 181, 197
Hume, David, 120, 261n.84
Hunnius, Aegidius, 151, 223
Huntington, Joseph, 109, 112
Huntington, Samuel, 109
Hussey, Joseph, 196–97, 282n.104
Hutchinson, Anne, 51, 71
Hymns, 74, 75, 94–95, 168
Hymns on God's Everlasting Love (Wesley and Wesley), 94
Hyper-Calvinism, 195–96, 202, 203, 204, 282n.105
Hypothetical universalism, 51, 242n.23

Iconoclasts, 6
Immigrants, 10–11, 70, 144, 148–49, 155, 166

Indulgences, 26–27, 138, 169, 233n.46
Inerrancy of the Bible, 150, 168, 175, 193, 200–201, 205, 207
Infants
    Augustine on baptism of, and unbaptized infants, 20, 178, 188
    baptism of, 20, 70, 279n.72
    limbo for unbaptized infants, 144
    moral exercises in, 259n.58
    Mormons on sinlessness of, 280n.82
    mortality rate for, 177
    and original sin, 177
    salvation versus damnation of, 155, 175–79, 184–85, 187–91, 193, 279n.70
Infralapsarianism
    definition of, 36, 223
    distinction between supralapsarianism and, 36, 237n.97
    Edwards as infralapsarian, 52
    and New England Puritans, 49–54
    and Southern Baptist Convention, 199
    Turretin as infralapsarian, 52
    and Westminster Confession, 49–50
Inoculation controversy, 87–88
Institutes of the Christian Religion (Calvin), 14, 15, 29–31
Internet, 11–12, 205–7, 215–16
InterVarsity Press, 192
Intuitu fidei (in view of faith)
    Althaus on, 270n.57
    definition of, 223
    Gerhard on, 272n.74
    Kolb on, 274n.119
    Lutherans on, 151–52, 157–61, 166–68, 274n.119
    and synergism, 274n.119
Iowa Synod of Lutheran Church, 156, 160
Irenaeus, 231n.11
Isaiah, 60, 101
Islam, 4, 45, 80, 95, 98, 99, 202, 206, 207, 254–55n.102

Jacob and Esau, 18, 19, 28, 30, 55, 109, 140, 152, 176, 181, 202, 205
James I, King, 40–43, 239n.116
James II, King, 77
James, Letter of, 126, 143
Jansen, Cornelius Otto, 141
Jansenism, 141, 197
Jefferson, Thomas, 105–6, 122
Jehovah's Witnesses, 124
Jenks, Francis, 178
Jenson, Robert, 166–67, 170–71
Jerome, 20

Jesuits
  accused of Pelagianism, 141
  Hassell on, 197
  as missionaries in New World, 8, 34
  Molinism of, 39, 53, 60, 140–41, 224,
    228
  and twentieth-century ecumenical move-
    ment, 170
Jesus. *See* Christ
Joel, Book of, 119
John, Gospel of
  Augustine on, 20
  and conditionality, 55
  on eternal life, 137
  and eternal security, 206
  Fisk on, 117
  on humanity united with Christ, 108
  Jefferson on, 105–6
  and Mormons, 128, 264n.129
  predestinarian verses of, 17, 20, 56, 117
John Paul II, Pope, 143, 170
John the Baptist, 126
John XXIII, Pope, 169
Johnson, Herrick, 189
Johnson, Samuel, 78–80
Joint Declaration on the Doctrine of
    Justification, 168–71
Jones, Abner, 122
Jones, Bob, Sr. and Jr., 202
Judaism, 18–19
Judas (apostle), 149
Judas Maccabeus, 24
Jude, Epistle of, 17
Julian of Eclanum, 232n.22
Justification, 28, 139, 145, 146, 169–71,
    223
Justin Martyr, 19

Kaufman, Peter, 69
Keating, Karl, 144
Kehukee Primitive Baptist Association, 197
Keith, George, 176
Keller, Julia, 2
Kenrick, Francis Patrick, 145, 146
King, L. J., 138, 266n.2
King, Martin Luther, Jr., 194
King Follett Discourse, 264n.133
King's College, 78
The King's Highway (Hewit), 146
Knox, John, 27, 29, 46
Kolb, Robert, 274n.119
Krauth, Charles Porterfield, 155–56, 161

Lane Seminary, 177
Last judgment, 62–64

Latitudinarianism, 75, 81–85, 176, 199
Latter-day Saints. *See* Mormons
Laud, William, 43, 46–47, 48
Laudians, 216, 286n.17
Law, William, 95
LDS. *See* Mormons
Lee, Jarena, 118
Left Behind novels, 63
Lehre und Wehre (Doctrine and Defense),
    155, 156
Lenoir College (Lenoir-Rhyne University),
    161
Leo X, Pope, 32
Leo XIII, Pope, 144, 190
Leonard, Bill, 193–94, 284n.125
Leslie, Charles, 77–78
Lewis, C. S., 210
Liberal, 223
Liberty, 103, 104, 106, 115–16, 119
  See also Free will
Liberty Theological Seminary, 207
Life Experience and Gospel Labors (Allen),
    118
Lightning rods, 88, 89
Limbo, 144
Limited atonement
  Barnes on, 179
  definition of, 223
  and TULIP, 39
  Walther on, 158
  and Westminster Confession, 48
  Winchester on, 109
  See also Atonement
Lincoln, Abraham, 197
Locke, John, 104
Loma Linda University, 124
London Confessions (1644, 1689), 193, 198,
    203, 281n.95
Lord's Supper. *See* Eucharist
Lost Cause ideology, 181–82
Loughlin, James F., 148
Lowell, Robert, 65, 216–17
Loy, Matthias, 155, 159–61
Luke, Gospel of, 45, 55, 83, 108, 124
Luther, Martin
  Calvin on, 29
  compared with Augustine, 28
  compared with Zwingli, 28–29
  critics of, 32
  and Eucharist, 27, 28, 149, 154
  on human will, 27–28, 148, 150
  on indulgences, 26–27, 138, 169
  on intellectual hubris, 218
  on justification by grace through
    faith, 28
  Marius on, 234n.52
  Ninety-five Theses of, 26, 154, 166, 168

Luther, Martin (*continued*)
O'Hare's anti-Protestant biography of, 147
on predestination, 10, 28, 136, 149, 150, 156, 161, 216
and Reformation, 234n.64
on sacraments, 28
Schmucker on, 153
Small Catechism of, 166
Luther Seminary, 157, 166–67
Lutheran World Federation, 169
Der Lutheraner, 155, 158, 161
Lutheranism
and Augsburg Confession, 150, 153
Brief Statement of, 167–68
and Catholic-Lutheran Joint Declaration on the Doctrine of Justification, 11, 168–71
compared with Catholicism, 138–39
Definite Synodical Platform (1855) of, 153, 155
and election, 149–51, 157–61, 166–67, 170–71
and Eucharist, 149, 153
and faith, 151–52, 157–61, 167–68
and Formula of Concord (1577), 150–51, 159, 162, 163, 166, 168
in Germany, 153–54, 162–63
and *Gnadenwahlslehrstreit* (election-of-grace doctrine controversy), 150, 153–68
hymns of, 168
immigrant Lutherans in American Midwest, 10, 11, 148–49, 155, 166
and *intuitu fidei,* 151–52, 157–61, 166, 167
Iowa Synod of, 156, 160
and justification, 146, 169–71
and Madison Agreement, 166–67, 274n.117
Missouri Synod of Lutheran Church, 150, 153–64, 167–70, 216, 274n.113, 274n.119, 274n.122
Norwegian Synod of, 155, 157, 160, 164–67
Ohio Joint Synod, 153, 155, 159–63, 166
and Pietism, 152–53
predestination controversy in Missouri Synod, 11, 150, 153–64, 167–68, 216, 271n.71
and sacramentalism, 10, 149, 155, 170–71
scholastic disputes within, 156–60
and Synodical Conference, 156–64
Thirteen Theses of Missouri Synod, 158, 160, 168
and unionism, 168, 274n.113

Weber on, 147, 149
See also American Lutheran Church (ALC); Evangelical Lutheran Church in America (ELCA)
Lyford, C. P., 130

Maccabees, Books of, 24, 138, 143, 225
MacCulloch, Diarmaid, 32–33
Machen, J. Gresham, 191, 200
MacKellar, Thomas, 185
MacKinnon, Malcolm, 59
Madison Agreement, 166–67, 274n.117
Makemie, Francis, 175–76
Malachi, Book of, 18, 109
Manducatio impiorum (eating of Christ's body by the godless), 149
Manual of Theology (Dagg), 198–99
Marius, Richard, 234n.52
Mark, Gospel of, 17
Marsden, George, 200
Marshall, Andrew, 194, 197–98
Mary, Queen, 29, 33, 46
Maryland Colony, 8, 230n.11
Mass, 25–26, 27, 32, 153, 169
See also Catholicism
Massa perditionis (mass of perdition), 22
Massachusetts Bay Colony, 8, 9, 47, 57, 61–62, 65, 71, 230n.11
See also New England Puritanism
Mather, Cotton
on Burnet's *Exposition,* 83
on conditional predestination, 214
on Dort-Westminster consensus, 48
on John Edwards's works, 76
and father's death, 78
Franklin's satires of, 88
on predestination anxiety, 67, 68
on Puritans' move to New England, 46
and smallpox inoculation, 87
Mather, Increase
Andrews as protégé of, 106
on Connecticut apostasy, 78
death of, 78
on election, 45, 67
on predestinarian agony, 64–65
on predestination, 44–45, 60
on preparation for unexpected death, 63
Matthew, Gospel of
Calvin on, 30–31
on chosen few, 60
and conditionality, 55
Edwards on, 76
on everlasting punishment, 83
on God's will, 20
on Jesus' invitation to those who labor, 56, 92, 152

on last judgment, 62
on not tempting God, 87
Paine on, 101
on virgin birth, 101
and Wigglesworth's *Day of Doom*, 63
May, Henry F., 78
Mayhew, Experience, 96–97
McBeth, Leon, 281n.95
McCormick Seminary, 189
McGiffert, Michael, 69
McIntire, Carl, 202
McLoughlin, William G., 261n.77
Megachurches, 12, 204–5, 208–17, 284n.126
Melanchthon, Philipp, 11, 148, 150, 151, 153, 156, 227–28
Memento mori, 62–63
The Message (Peterson), 210
Methodism
    and African Americans, 117–18
    in antebellum period, 110–19
    and anti-predestinarian view of, 103, 112–19, 146–47
    and the Bible, 116
    churches constructed by Methodists, 261n.79
    and ecstatic experience, 112–13
    and grace, 117
    Hewit on, 146–47
    hymns of, 74, 75, 94–95
    New England Calvinism versus, 112–19
    and prevenient grace, 110–11, 117, 197, 228
    and republicanism, 10
    and "Rock of Ages," 74, 75
    and speaking in tongues, 119
    and Spirit baptism, 118
    Universalists versus, 110–12
    Wesley as founder of, 9, 74, 91
    and women, 117, 118, 260n.70
    See also Wesley, John; Wesley, Charles
Michaelius, Jonas, 8
Miller, Perry, 57, 59, 72, 244n.43, 244n.45
Miller, William, 122–23, 262n.95
Millerites. *See* Adventists
Milton, John, 56
The Minister's Wooing (Stowe), 133, 134
Miracles, 85, 90, 105
Missouri Synod of Lutheran Church
    and Catholic-Lutheran Joint Declaration on the Doctrine of Justification, 169–70
    and Eucharist, 153, 216
    predestination controversy in, 150, 153–64, 167–68, 216, 274n.119
    rejection of double predestination by, 274n.122
    Thirteen Theses of, 158, 160, 168

and unionism, 274n.113
Mitchell, Mr., 111
Modernist, 223–24
Mohler, R. Albert, Jr., 205, 206–7
Moldstad, John A., Jr., 167
Molina, Luis de, 39, 53, 82, 140–41, 151, 224, 270n.56
Molinism, 39, 53, 60, 116, 140–42, 224, 228
Monarchism. *See* Absolute monarchism
Monfort, James, 185
Monica, St., 24, 135, 144
Moody, Dwight L., 214–15, 260n.77
Moral ability, 114
Moralism, 236n.90
Moravian Church, 170
Mormons
    and the Bible, 126–29
    and Book of Mormon, 127–30
    critics of Mormonism, 130
    and doctrine of ongoing revelation, 128–29
    on free will, 127–28
    on infant sinlessness, 280n.82
    on original sin, 103, 126, 130
    and predestination generally, 103
    preexistence doctrine of, 129, 130, 224–25
    on remedial hell, 129
    and republicanism, 10
    and "Rock of Ages," 75
    See also Smith, Joseph, Jr.
Mors improvisa (unforeseen death), 62
Mors repentina (sudden death), 62
Moses, 18
Most, William G., 142
Muhlenberg, Henry Melchior, 152
Muller, Richard, 36, 221, 238n.102, 239n.110
Mullins, Edgar Young, 200, 203–4
Murray, John, 108, 109
Muslims. *See* Islam
Mysterium tremendum et fascinans (mystery before which one both trembles and is fascinated), 217–18

Nageleisen, John A., 136, 143–44
National Primitive Baptist Convention, 198
Natural ability, 114
Natural disasters, 2, *3*, 88–90, 210, 229n.1
Natural rights theories, 104
Nelson, Thomas A., 144
Neoplatonism, 28, 108
Nettles, Thomas J., 204, 205
New Divinity theology, 114, 119, 134, 178
New-England Courant, 88

New England Puritanism
and church members' evidence of election, 46
doctrines of, 9, 46–49
and ecstatic agony of predestination, 65–72
and Eucharist, 61–62
and Half-Way Covenant, 70
and last judgment, 62–64
logic of covenant of, 54–57
Increase Mather on predestination, 44–45
and *memento mori*, 62–63
overview of, 8–9, 236n.90
and predestinarian anxiety, 57–69
predestinarian experience converted from agony to ecstasy, 65–68
reactions to, in eighteenth century, 70–72
and sacramentalism, 9
and supralapsarians versus infralapsarians, 49–54
and Westminster Confession (1647), 48, 55, 71
New England theology, 114–19
See also Calvinism; New Divinity theology; New England Puritanism; and specific theologians
New Hampshire Confession (1833), 193–94, 204
New Netherland, 8
New York *Daily Tribune,* 190
New York Evangelist, 185
New York Times, 169, 174, 190
Newton, Sir Isaac, 86
Niccolls, Samuel J., 173–74, 186, 188, 189
Niebuhr, H. Richard, 72
No-offers theology, 196–98
Noah, 180–81
Noll, Mark, 102–3, 179, 180, 253n.80, 276n.20
Nonjuring clergy, 77–78
Norwegian Lutheran Church of America, 166–67, 168
Norwegian Society of America, 166
Norwegian Synod of Lutheran Church, 155, 157, 160, 164–67
Notes on the Epistle to the Romans (Barnes), 179

Obedience, 80
Oberlin College, 115
Oberman, Heiko A., 30, 139, 234n.64
Ockham. *See* William Ockham
O'Connor, Flannery, 209, 218
O'Hare, Patrick, 147, 148
Ohio Joint Synod of Lutheran Church, 153, 155, 159–63, 166

Oldtown Folks (Stowe), 133
On Free Choice of the Will (Augustine), 20
On the Gift of Perseverance (Augustine), 20
On the Predestination of the Saints (Augustine), 20
OPC. *See* Orthodox Presbyterian Church (OPC)
Open theism, 124
The Openness of God (Rice), 124
Orange, Second Council of, 22–23, 168
Ordo salutis (order of salvation), 35–36
Origen, 108, 129, 130, 132, 224, 228, 257n.26, 257n.35
Original sin
Augustine on, 5, 20, 22, 61, 132, 177, 255n.7
and baptism, 145
Calvin and Calvinism on, 5, 255n.7
definition of, 224
Jonathan Edwards on, 177
Mormons on, 103, 126, 130
Pagels on, 12
Taylor on, 177
Wesley on, 92
Westminster Confession on, 277n.31
Orthodox Presbyterian Church (OPC), 191–92
Otto, Rudolf, 217
Oxford movement, 134

Page, Frank, 206
Pagels, Elaine, 12, 265n.144
Paine, Thomas, 100–103, 109, 110, 116, 122
Palmer, Benjamin Morgan, 180–81
Palmer, Phoebe, 118, 260n.74, 260n.77
Park, Edwards A., 114, 115
Parker, Daniel, 198
Patterson, Paige, 204, 206–7
Patton, Francis, 183, 186
Paul
and conditionality, 55
conversion of, 18, 216
on election, 46
on fatalism, 5
on fatherhood of God, 66
jail escape by, 65
Jefferson on letters of, 105
on Lord's Supper, 61
Miller on, 123
on perseverance, 48
and predestination, 17–19, 35, 53, 101–3, 140, 217
on salvation, 22
on servants and masters, 180
See also specific epistles, such as Romans, Letter to

Paul V, Pope, 53, 141, 224, 228
Paulist Fathers, 146
PCA. *See* Presbyterian Church in America
(PCA)
PCUS. *See* Presbyterian Church in the United
States (PCUS)
PCUSA. *See* Presbyterian Church in the
United States of America (PCUSA)
Pelagianism
and Arminianism, 53
Augustine versus, 20, 238n.107
and Lyman Beecher, 178–79
definition of, 224
Gifford on, 34
Jesuits accused of, 141
and original sin, 22, 23
See also Pelagius; Semi-Pelagianism
Pelagius, 20, 130, 132, 133, 178, 224,
232n.22
See also Pelagianism
Penance, 26, 145, 153
Pentecostalism, 10, 71, 103, 112, 118,
284n.126
Perkins, William
compared with Calvin, 36
on election, 37, 60
on the Fall, 36, 56
A Golden Chaine by, 34–37, 66
on predestination, 34–38, 49, 53–54, 60,
140, 196, 225, 236n.90, 237n.97
and prisoners going to the gallows, 67
on sacraments, 61
on sin, 238n.99
Perseverance, 1, 47–48, 67–68
See also Eternal security
Peter, First Letter of, 17, 111
Peter, Second Letter of, 79, 83, 143, 184,
192
Peter Martyr, 32
Peterson, Eugene, 210
Peterson, Robert A., 192
Pfeiffer, August, 159–60
Philadelphia Confession, 283n.116
Philippi, Friedrich Adolph, 157
Pieper, Franz A. O., 157, 167, 168
Pietism, 59, 152–55, 166, 236n.90
Pigot, George, 78
Pilmore, Joseph, 118
Pius V, Pope, 27
Plain Theology for Plain People (Boothe),
194
Plaine Mans Path-way to Heaven (Dent), 60,
66–67
Plato, 129
Plea for the West (L. Beecher), 135
Plymouth colony, 8
Pontoppidan, Erik, 166

Pope, Alexander, 85
Popular religion, 25–26
Porterfield, Amanda, 247n.85
Post praevisa merita (after foresight of mer-
its), 151, 224, 270n.56
Practical syllogism (*syllogismus practicus*),
66–67
Praeteritio. See Preterition
Prayer, 38, 76, 115
See also Book of Common Prayer
Prayers for the dead. *See* Purgatory
The Precisianist Strain (Bozeman), 59
Predestinarian, 224
See also Predestination
Predestination
Anglicans against, 75–80
anxiety of, 57–69, 125
Arminian (conditional) predestination, 6,
8, 38–39, 49, 51, 93–94, 192, 243n.35
Arminianism versus "five-point"
Calvinism, 37–43
Calvinist (unconditional) predestination,
8, 39–40, 47–49, 53–54, 72, 79,
94, 138
consequences of controversies over,
216–18
controversies over generally, 3–4
and decline of mystery, 209–18
definition of, 2–3, 224
ecstatic agony of, 65–72
and English Reformation, 32–37
evangelicals against, 90–99
experience of, converted from agony to
ecstasy, 65–68
fatalism distinguished from, 4–5
goal of, 27
history of, in colonial America, 8–9
and identification of the elect, 70–71
latitudinarian attitude toward, 81–85
in literature and politics, 4, 229n.4
origins of, 17–23
overview of Puritan attitudes toward,
70–72
Protestantism and predestinarian piety,
27–32
questions concerning generally, 6, 12–13
and revivalism, 71, 84, 90–91
sacramental attitude toward, 70
sacramentalism versus, 6–7, 9, 23–27, 76,
216
See also Double predestination;
Election; Infralapsarianism; New
England Puritanism; Reprobation;
Supralapsarianism; and specific churches and specific theologians
"Predestination: Remarks on Romans
9:18–21" (Paine), 101–3

Predestined for Hell? Absolutely Not! (Rogers), 204–5
Predestined for Hell? No! (Rice), 202–3
Preexistence, 129, 130, 132–33, 224–25
Prelapsarian. *See* Supralapsarianism
Presbyterian Church in America (PCA), 191–92
Presbyterian Church in the United States of America (PCUSA), 170, 182–84, 187, 189, 190, 281n.87
Presbyterian Church in the United States (PCUS), 182, 190–91
Presbyterian Church (U.S.A.), 189–90, 192
Presbyterian Standard, 191
Presbyterians
  and Adopting Act (1729), 176–77
  in antebellum period, 119
  and the Bible, 176, 179–80
  Brownson on, 147
  and confessional subscription, 175–80
  and Declaratory Act (1879), 183–84
  and Declaratory Statement (1903), 189–90
  on election, 184–92
  and heresy trials/allegations, 106–7, 176–79, 187
  liberal and conservative divergence among, 188–93
  and Lord's Supper, 27
  merger between PCUSA and Cumberland Presbyterian Chuch, 190
  Old School–New School schism among, 179–83
  regional variations among, 180–83
  revision of Westminster Confession by, 11, 172–75, 183–91, 269n.40
  and slavery, 180–81
  and Stone, 121, 122
  Westminster Confession of, 11, 107, 121, 147, 175–80, 269n.40, 277n.31
Preston, John, 61, 242n.23
Preterition, 185, 186, 199, 225
Preus, Herman Amberg, 165, 167, 168
Preus, J. A. O., 168
Preus, Robert, 168
Prevenient grace
  Arminius on, 38–39
  Augustine on, 238n.107
  definition of, 225
  and Methodists, 110–11, 117, 197, 228
  Molina on, 141
Primitive Baptists, 194–98, 282n.104
Primitivism, 119, 236n.90
Prince, Thomas, 89
Princeton Seminary, 179–81, 186, 191, 199, 217, 281n.87

Princeton University, 79, 153, 176, 177, 186, 189
Proginōskō (to foreknow), 17
  See also Foreknowledge
Prognōsis (foreknowledge), 17
  See also Foreknowledge
Proorizō (to predestine, to decide beforehand), 17
  See also Foreknowledge
The Protestant Ethic and the Spirit of Capitalism (Weber), 44, 58, 147
Protestantism. *See* Megachurches; Reformation; and specific churches
Providence, 2, 12, 30, 85–90, 225
  See also God
Psalms, Book of, 234n.52, 238n.107
Purgatory
  in anti-Catholic literature, 136–37
  Augustine on, 24, 143
  Bible proof of, 24, 138, 143, 268n.22
  books on, 144
  consolation of, 10–11, 138, 144–45
  Cranmer on, 33
  definition of, 225
  and indulgences, 26–27, 138, 169, 233n.46
  Masses and other prayers for souls in, 10–11, 24, 26, 32, 135, 138, 143–45, 169
  Murray on, 109
  Nageleisen on, 143–44
Purgatory (Faber), 144
Purgatory (Schouppe), 144
Puritan Reformed Theological Seminary, 72
Puritanism
  Bozeman on interlinked agendas of, 236n.90
  and cases of conscience, 66–67
  compared with Catholicism, 59–62, 68
  and compatibilism, 7
  and conditionality, 243n.35
  conflicts between Arminians and Puritans in England, 42–43
  and covenant of works, 51, 55
  covenant theology of, 54–57, 59, 244n.49, 245n.57
  definition of, 225–26, 236n.90
  and English Civil Wars (1641–1651), 48
  English Reformation and rise of, 32–37
  history of, in America, 8–9
  overview of attitudes toward predestination, 70–72
  and Pietism, 59
  Shepard on predestination, 45–48
  Stowe on, 134
  usefulness of term *Puritan*, 72, 236n.90

Weber on, 58–59, 69
  See also New England Puritanism
The Purpose-Driven Life (Warren), 12,
  209–11, 215

Quarles, Francis, 41

Race, racism, 117–18, 180–81
Reconciliationism, 5
Reformation, 26, 32–37, 168, 217, 234n.64
  See also Calvin, John; Luther, Martin
Reformed, 226
Reformed Church in America, 170
Reformed Doctrine of Predestination
  (Boettner), 192–93
Rehearsal (Leslie), 77–78
Reid, Thomas, 120
Reine Lehre (pure doctrine), 164
Reis, Elizabeth, 245n.57
Reisinger, Ernest, 203–4
Relly, James, 108, 257n.29
Remonstrants, 39, 226
Renate, 226
  See also Election
Reprobation
  Augustine on, 30
  Calvin on, 30–31, 235n.69
  definition of, 226
  gender difference in, 245n.57
  Hewit on, 146
  Jenson on, 170–71
  Perkins on, 37
  Willard on, 52, 242–43n.30
  See also Predestination
Republicanism, 10, 100–104, 178
Revelation, Book of, 71, 124, 143
Revivals. *See* Great Awakening
Rian, Edwin H., 281n.87
Rice, John R., 172, 202–3, 203, 206
Rice, Richard, 124, 263n.105
Rich, Caleb, 110
Riches of Gods Love (Twisse), 51–52
Ridgley, Thomas, 178
Rigdon, Sidney, 264n.129
Roanoke "Lost" colony, 8
"Rock of Ages," 74–75
Rogers, Adrian, 204–5
Romans, Letter to
  Augustine on, 28
  Calvin on, 30
  in Geneva Bible, 33
  Gnostic text compared with, 231n.14
  and golden chain, 35, 66, 222
  on humans as clay in hands of potter, 18,
    19, 55, 205

and infant damnation, 176
on Jacob and Esau, 18, 19, 28, 30, 55,
  109, 140, 181, 202, 205
and Jefferson, 105
Lutherans on, 159
Increase Mather on, 45
Miller on, 123
Paine on, 101–3
predestinarian verses of, 17–19, 54–55,
  109, 159, 210
Rice on, 202
Rogers on, 204–5
Schaff on, 185–86
Stuart on, 265n.144
and Warren, 210
Susanna Wesley on, 91
Rowling, J. K., 209
Rubin, Miri, 27
Russell, Charles Taze, 124
Russo, Richard, 1

Sacramentalism
  and Anglicanism, 9, 43, 80, 266n.153
  and Arminianism, 286n.17
  and Catholicism, 7, 9, 10, 24–27, 70, 142,
    145, 146
  in England before Reformation, 32
  and English Arminianism, 42–43
  goal of, 27, 28
  Hahn on, 147
  Krauth on, 155–56
  and Luther, 28, 149
  and Lutheranism, 10, 149, 155, 170–71
  and New England Puritanism, 9, 70
  Perkins on, 61
  predestination versus, 6–7, 9, 23–27, 76,
    216
  rise of medieval sacramentalism, 23–27
  sacramental attitude toward predestina-
    tion, 70
  Stowe on, 134–35
  of Thomas Aquinas, 24–25
  See also specific sacraments, such as
    Baptism and Eucharist
Saddleback Church, 12, 209–16
Saints, 26, 62, 70–71
  See also Communion of saints
Saltonstall, Gurdon, 78
Salvation
  Arminius on, 38
  Catholic-Lutheran Joint Declaration on,
    169–71
  and Catholicism, 147
  and Christ, 38, 45, 55, 150, 151, 158,
    190
  and Christian Scientists, 124

Salvation (*continued*)
and covenant of works, 51, 55
Hodge on, 180
of infants, 155, 175–79, 184–85, 187–88,
193, 279n.70
Lutheran Formula of Concord (1577) on,
150–51, 159, 162, 166, 168
Samuel, First Book of, 103
Sancroft, William, 77, 81
Sandys, Edwin, 33
Sarah and Abraham, 110
SBC. *See* Southern Baptist Convention
(SBC)
Schaff, Philip, 177, 185–86, 188, 190,
276n.10
Schmidt, Friedrich August, 157–60, 162,
164–67, 272n.75
Schmucker, Samuel Simon, 152–53, 155
Scholasticism
Catholic scholastic controversies, 139–42
definition of, 226
Protestant scholasticism, 8, 37, 49
of Thomas Aquinas, 8, 24–25
Schouppe, François Xavier, 144
Science, 86, 200
*Science and Health with Key to the
Scriptures* (Eddy), 126
Scientia media (middle knowledge), 39,
140–41, 226
Scopes "Monkey Trial," 200
Scottish common sense philosophy, 120,
261n.84
Scripture. *See* Bible
Scripture-Doctrine of Original Sin (Taylor),
177
SDA. *See* Adventists
Seabury, Samuel, 73, 80
Second Coming, 62–64, 71, 123
Second Council of Orange, 22–23, 168
Second Great Awakening, 107, 115
Second Helvetic Confession (1566), 65–66
Second Treatise of Government (Locke), 104
Second Vatican Council, 142, 143, 168–69
Self-examination, 58–59, 244n.49
Selph, Robert, 215
Semi-Pelagianism, 22, 38, 226–27
See also Pelagianism
Seneca, 29
Seventh-day Adventists. *See* Adventists
Sewall, Betty, 60–61
Sewall, Samuel, 60–61
Shakespeare, William, 69
Sharon, Gerald, 212
Shepard, Thomas
childhood of, 247n.85
on Christ, 68
conversion of, 61

on election, 56
on grace, 69
Hutchinson on, 51
and Laud, 46–47
in New England, 47, 60
on predestination, 45–48
Sibbes, Richard, 62
The Signs and Causes of Melancholy
(Baxter), 66
Silas, 65
Simplicitas Dei (God's simplicity), 37
Simpson, James, 252n.48
Sin, 83–85, 114, 180, 238n.99
See also Original sin
The Sincere Convert (Shepard), 45–46
"Sinners in the Hands of an Angry God"
(Edwards), 84
Sladen, John, 93–94
Slavery, 180–81, 198
Smallpox inoculation, 87–88, 93
Smith, Elias, 122
Smith, Henry Boynton, 182–83, 185
Smith, Joseph, Jr., 100, 126–30, 132, 190,
263n.115, 264n.129, 264n.133
Smith, Joseph, Sr., 126
Smith, Timothy L., 260–61n.77
Snow, Lorenzo, 129
Snyder, Stephen, 131
Socinians, 84–85
South, Robert, 255n.102
Southern Baptist Convention (SBC)
and Baptist Faith and Message (1925),
204, 215
and Criswell, 201–2, 215
founding of, 198
and inerrancy of the Bible, 168, 200–201,
205, 207
and Internet, 205–7
and London Confession, 198, 203
and megachurches, 12, 204–5, 208–17,
284n.126
membership size of, 175
post-1979 conservative revolution in,
200–208
and predestination controversy, 11,
198–208
seminaries of, 199–201, 204, 205, 207,
284n.125
and slavery, 198
and Westminster Confession, 198
See also Baptists
Southern Baptist Founders Conference,
203–5, 208
*Southern Baptists and the Doctrine of
Election* (Selph), 204
Southern Baptist Theological Seminary,
199–200, 205

Southwestern Baptist Theological Seminary, 204, 206, 207
Sower, Christopher, 152
Sparrowhawk, Nathaniel, 60
Speaking in tongues, 119
Spira (Spiera), Francesco, 60–61
Spirit baptism, 118
Sprat, Thomas, 86
Sprecher, Samuel, 153
Sproul, R. C., 192, 281n.89
St. Olaf College, 166
Stacy, Nathaniel, 111
Stagg, John Weldon, 190–91
Stanley, Charles, 284n.126
Stebbins, Thomas, 65
Steffens, D. H., 161
Stellhorn, Friedrich W., 162, 163
Stephan, Martin, 154
Stewart, Dugald, 120
Stoddard, Solomon, 70, 84
Stoicism, 19, 29
Stone, Barton, 121, 122, 126
Stone, Irving, 57
Stone-Campbell Christians, 103, 120–22
Stoneites, 10, 121
Stowe, Harriet Beecher, 81, 133–35, 133, 266n.151
Stowe, Henry, 133
Stuart, Moses, 265n.144
Suárez, Francisco, 140
Sublapsarian. See Infralapsarianism
Suelflow, August, 164
Suicide, 64–65
Summa Theologiae (Thomas Aquinas), 24, 25, 49, 140, 169
Sündfluth (sin flood, the Deluge), 162
Supralapsarianism
    Arminius on, 38
    Barth on advantage of, 288n.11
    Cotton on, 50–51
    definition of, 36, 227
    distinction between infralapsarian and, 36, 237n.97
    Gomarus as supralapsarian, 38
    Hewit on, 148
    Huntington on, 109
    Hussey as supralapsarian, 196–97
    and New England Puritanism, 49–54
    Perkins as supralapsarian, 36, 49, 196
    Turretin on, 52
    Twisse as supralapsarian, 52, 57, 196
    Willard as supralapsarian, 52, 227
Swing, David, 183, 188, 189
Sword of the Lord, 202
Syllogismus practicus (practical syllogism), 66–67
Synergism, 150, 157, 227–28, 274n.119

Synodical Conference of Lutheran Church, 156–64
Systematic Theology (Jenson), 170–71

TAN Books, 144
Tasters, 114, 115
Taves, Ann, 143
Taylor, Edward, 68, 78
Taylor, John, 177
Taylor, John W., 190
Taylor, Nathaniel William, 116, 153
Tentatio praedestinationis (predestinarian temptation or trial), 65–66, 125, 228
Teresa of Ávila, St., 140
Testimony of a Dying Catholic Girl, 136–38
Tetzel, Johann, 26, 138
Texas Baptist Standard, 205–6
Theologische Monatshefte, 156
Thessalonians, Second Letter to, 167, 201
Thirty-nine Articles, 33, 40, 48, 81–83, 92–93, 98, 175
Thomas à Kempis, 68
Thomas Aquinas
    ecstatic visions of, 218
    on election, 54, 241–42n.18
    on free will, 140
    on God's antecedent and consequent wills, 267n.14
    on grace, 169, 234n.55
    "O Salutaris Hostia" (O Saving Victim) by, 24, 230n.9
    on predestination, 25, 49, 53, 60, 140
    on primary and secondary causes, 25, 244n.44
    Puritan uses of, 49, 53–54, 241n.18, 243n.32
    sacramentalism of, 24–25
    scholasticism of, 8, 24–25
    on superstition, 233n.45
    theology of generally, 228
    on transubstantiation, 25–26
Thomism, 140–42, 228
    See also Thomas Aquinas
Thompson, Ernest Trice, 191
Thomson, Charles, 104–5
Tillotson, John, 81, 83–84, 86, 95, 176
Timothy, First Letter of, 17, 22, 31, 113, 137, 141, 267nn.13–14
Timothy, Second Letter of, 127
Toland, John, 105
Toleration Act (1689), 76
Toplady, Augustus Montague, 73–74, 97–99
Tornadoes, 2, 3, 229n.1
Torrey, Reuben A., 215
Tractarian movement, 144
Transubstantiation, 25–26, 27

Trent, Council of, 34, 139, 143
Triers commission, 76
Trinity, 84, 144
   See also God
Trouble with the TULIP (Page), 206
True Religion Delineated (Bellamy), 112
Tufts University, 108, 257n.27
TULIP, 39–40, 47–49, 67–68, 115, 202,
   206–7, 228
   See also Calvinism
Turell, Ebenezer, 62
Turell, Jane Colman, 62
Turner, James, 177, 252n.60
Turretin, Francis, 52, 53, 54, 287n.6
Twain, Mark, 130, 190
Twisse, William, 49–52, 50, 54, 57, 196
Two-Seed-in-the-Spirit Predestinarian
   Baptists, 198
Tyacke, Nicholas, 239n.113, 240n.119
Tyndale, William, 252n.48

Unconditionality
   in Bible, 54
   Calvinist (unconditional) predestination,
     8, 39–40, 47–49, 53–54, 72, 79, 94,
     138
   Hutchinson on unconditional election, 51
   Selph on unconditional election, 204
Union Theological Seminary, 187
Unitarian Universalist Association, 108, 228
   See also Universalism
Unitarianism, 90, 108, 114, 178
   See also Unitarian Universalist
     Association
United Church of Christ, 170
United Norwegian Lutheran Church in
   America, 166
U.S. Constitution, 10
Universalism
   anti-predestinarianism of, 101, 103,
     107–10, 123
   and the Bible, 110
   in Book of Mormon, 128
   and Crane Theological School, Tufts
     University, 257n.27
   definition of, 228
   early Universalists, 108–10
   and hell, 109–10, 112
   merger of, with Unitarians, 108
   Relly on, 257n.29
   and Elias Smith, 122
   See also Unitarian Universalist Association
University of Pennsylvania, 109
Updike, John, 172, 191, 280n.86
Urban IV, Pope, 24
USA Today, 169

Valeri, Mark, 258n.46
Van Dyke, Henry J., Jr., 189
Van Dyke, Henry J., Sr., 186, 187
Van Til, Cornelius, 287n.3
Vance, James I., 182, 191
Vatican II, 142, 143, 168–69
Veritas Redux (Edwards), 95
Via media (middle way), 239
Via moderna (modern way), 28
Virgil, 104–5
Vocatio (calling), 220
Vogel, Dan, 264n.127
Vorstius, Conrad, 40, 239n.116

Wallace, Dewey D., Jr., 236n.86, 240n.119,
   286n.17
Walsham, Alexandra, 85–86
Walther, Carl Ferdinand Wilhelm, 154–64,
   165, 273n.108
Warfield, Benjamin Breckinridge, 186,
   187–89, 199
Warren, Kay, 212, 286n.9
Warren, Rick, 12, 203, 209–16
Wartburg Seminary, 156
Wawrykow, Joseph, 25
Web sites. See Internet
Weber, Max, 25, 44, 58–59, 69, 127, 147,
   149
Werly, Monsieur, 14
Wesley, Charles, 91, 92, 94–95
Wesley, John
   anti-predestinarian view of, 9, 75, 91–99,
     113, 124, 214
   and Arminian Magazine, 97
   and Arminianism, 9, 74, 92
   conversion of, 91, 92, 110
   death of, 99, 109
   on election, 74, 92
   on faith, 253n.80
   on free will, 92
   and hymns, 94–95
   on Mahometan Christians, 255n.102
   as Methodist founder, 9, 74, 91
   on original sin, 92
   parents of, 91
   portrait of, at mother's grave, 96
   and prevenient grace, 197
   Toplady's conflict with, 74–75, 97–99
   on unborn souls consigned to hell,
     255n.102
   Whitefield's conflict with, 91–95, 97,
     110–11
Wesley, Samuel, 91
Wesley, Susanna, 73, 91, 95, 96, 110–11
Wesleyan University, 111, 116
Westminster Confession (1647)

and Baptists, 193
and Declaratory Act (1879), 183–84
and Declaratory Statement (1903),
189–90
and double covenant federalism, 55
Franklin on, 107
Hodge on, 155, 179–80, 187
on infant salvation versus damnation, 155,
175–79, 184–85, 187–91
and New England Puritanism, 48, 55, 71
on original sin, 277n.31
on pope as Antichrist, 147
revision of, in late nineteenth and
early twentieth centuries, 11, 172–75,
183–91, 269n.40
and Stone, 121
theology of, 48–50, 53, 55–56, 58, 104,
175–80
Westminster Theological Seminary, 191
Wharton, Charles, 143
Whig theology, 276n.20
Whiston, William, 84–85, 86
Whitaker, William, 40, 236n.90
White, Father Andrew, 8, 230n.11
White, Ellen G., 123–24, 262n.95, 262n.102
White, James, 207, 262n.95
White, Peter, 239n.113
White, William, 82
Whitefield, George
and Great Awakening, 91, 107, 119
portrait of, 93
on predestinarian comfort, 92
on probationary state, 95–96
and Relly, 108
on Tillotson, 95
Wesley's conflict with, 91–95, 97, 110–11
Whitgift, John, 40
Why I Am Not a Calvinist, 192
Why I Am Not an Arminian, 192
Wigglesworth, Michael, 61–64, 64, 88, 226,
246n.68
Will. See Free will
Willard, Samuel
baptism of Benjamin Franklin by, 106

on election and reprobation, 52, 60, 67,
242–43n.30
on God's unconditional sovereignty, 54
portrait of, 53
and scholasticism, 226
as supralapsarian, 52, 227
William III, King, 77, 91
William Ockham, 28
Williams, Michael D., 192
Williams, Roger, 200
Wilson, Joshua Lacy, 178
Winchester, Elhanan, 108–10, 257n.35
Winiarski, Douglas, 71
Winship, Michael, 47, 86, 247n.75
Winthrop, John (Harvard professor), 89
Winthrop, John (Massachusetts Bay Colony
governor), 65, 230n.11
Wollaston, William, 258n.46
Women
of Beecher family, 10, 81, 130–35, 133,
266n.151, 266n.153
and Calvinism, 260n.74
exclusion of, from Augustine's theology,
133
and Methodism, 117, 118, 260n.70
ordination of, 118
and reprobation, 245n.57
Stowe on theology inclusive of, 133–34
Womock, Laurence, 76, 176
Woodmason, Charles, 194
Woolverton, John, 80
Works. See Good works

Yale College/University, 78, 113, 114,
115–16, 130, 177, 250n.17
Young, Brigham, 128, 129
Young, Restless, Reformed (Hansen), 205

Zanchius, Jerome, 98
Zaret, David, 244n.49
Zitatentheologe (quotation theologian), 163
Zwingli, Huldrych, 28–29, 226